D1521363

An Illustrated Guide
to Eastern Woodland
Wildflowers and Trees

350 Plants Observed
at Sugarloaf Mountain,
Maryland

MELANIE CHOUKAS-BRADLEY

ILLUSTRATED BY TINA THIEME BROWN

An Illustrated Guide to Eastern Woodland Wildflowers and Trees

350 Plants Observed at Sugarloaf Mountain, Maryland

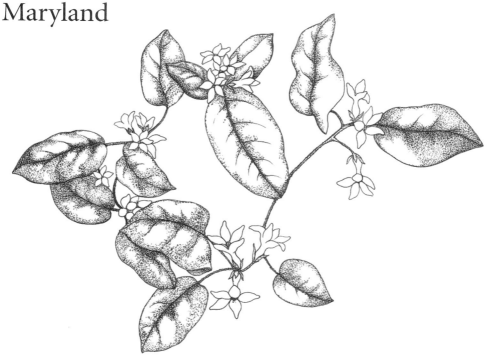

University of Virginia Press

CHARLOTTESVILLE AND LONDON

Melanie Choukas-Bradley is the author of *City of Trees: The Complete Field Guide to the Trees of Washington, D.C.* and a longtime contributor to the *Washington Post*. She teaches field botany for the USDA Graduate School. Tina Thieme Brown has worked as a landscape artist and environmentalist for twenty-five years. She teaches art at the U.S. Botanic Garden, is an artist on the Countryside Artisans Studio Tour, and creates art inspired by the Sugarloaf Mountain countryside in her 1790s log cabin studio. Choukas-Bradley and Brown lead Sugarloaf Mountain field trips for the Audubon Naturalist Society of the Central Atlantic States and other organizations.

University of Virginia Press
© 2004 by Melanie Choukas-Bradley
Illustrations © 2004 by Tina Thieme Brown
All rights reserved
Printed in the United States of America on acid-free paper

First published 2004

First paperback edition published 2007
ISBN 978-0-8139-2692-6 (paper)

9 8 7 6 5 4 3 2 1

The Library of Congress has cataloged the hardcover edition as follows:

Library of Congress Cataloging-in-Publication Data
Choukas-Bradley, Melanie.
   An illustrated guide to eastern woodland wildflowers and trees: 350 plants observed at Sugarloaf Mountain, Maryland / Melanie Choukas-Bradley; illustrated by Tina Thieme Brown.
      p.   cm.
   Includes bibliographical references and index.
   ISBN 0-8139-2251-8 (cloth: alk. paper)
   1. Wildflowers—Maryland—Sugar Loaf Mountain Region—Identification.
2. Trees—Maryland—Sugar Loaf Mountain Region—Identification. 3. Woody plants—Maryland—Sugar Loaf Mountain Region—Identification. 4. Wildflowers—Maryland—Sugar Loaf Mountain Region—Pictorial works. 5. Trees—Maryland—Sugar Loaf Mountain Region—Pictorial works. 6. Woody plants—Maryland—Sugar Loaf Mountain Region—Pictorial works. I. Brown, Tina Thieme, 1952– II. Title.
   QK165.C48 2004
   582.13'09752'87—dc21   2003011149

Preparation of this book was assisted by a grant from Sugarloaf Regional Trails.

This book is published in association with the Center for American Places, Santa Fe, New Mexico, and Staunton, Virginia (www.americanplaces.org).

For Mike and Nita Choukas and Bill and Paula Bradley
who love the natural world

For Jackie and Armand Thieme:
They sent me out to play, and I fell in love with the flowers
and the trees

Contents

Preface

It is early spring in an eastern North American woodland. Along a well-worn walking path, a small cluster of fragrant pink flowers unfolds. The five-lobed flowers hug the ground, clinging to a woody, trailing stalk that bears leathery evergreen leaves. The leaves and tiny pointed flower buds that have recently opened on this low-growing plant have survived winter in the temperate zone under layers of ice and snow.

The plant is called trailing arbutus, or—in New England—mayflower. Indigenous to rocky woods throughout most of eastern North America, trailing arbutus has long been beloved for its early flowers with their surprisingly tropical fragrance. Once a popular herbal medicine, trailing arbutus is the state flower of Massachusetts and the provincial flower of Nova Scotia. For American Indians, colonial settlers, and the generations that have followed, this plant has embodied the hope of spring.

Eastern North America, home of the trailing arbutus, is a land of interior lowlands, forested mountain chains, rolling piedmont, and flat, expansive coastal plain. With its four distinct seasons, ample rainfall, and diversity of natural habitat, the eastern half of the continent nourishes hundreds of native wildflowers: plants of woodland, field, meadow, rocky barren, and wetland. The trailing arbutus and the flowers of deceptively delicate-looking woodland plants such as bloodroot, spring beauty, round-lobed hepatica, rue-anemone, and trout-lily emerge just as the ground thaws, long before the trees leaf out above them.

Those early spring flowers are followed by the more bodacious blooms of summer field and forest: the black-eyed Susan, state flower of Maryland; the orange butterfly weed; and the dazzling cardinal flower. Autumn brings forth a profusion of goldenrods and asters to delight the eye and confound the botanist trying to sort them out by species. Then, just as the first snow flies in November, the golden-strand petals of the witch-hazel tree unfurl.

The eastern half of the continent has seen rampant development in recent decades, but in the wild places that have been preserved, the wildflowers go on blooming, each in its chosen season and habitat.

About midway down the eastern coast of North America, in the rural Maryland piedmont some thirty-five miles northwest of Washington, D.C., and fifty miles west of Baltimore, Sugarloaf Mountain stands alone. Rising above the surrounding farms and villages to the modest height of 1,282 feet and crowned with cliffs of pink quartzite that are accented with windswept table mountain pine boughs and mountain laurel leaves, the small monadnock called Sugarloaf is a magnet for those living in nearby cities and suburbs.

Each day, something rather remarkable happens on Sugarloaf, a privately owned park of more than 3,000 acres that is open to the public year-round. Families come to hike and picnic on the mountain, and when they do, they slow down. A young girl reaches down to pick up a fallen oak leaf from the forest floor, and her harried parents are soothed by the sound of the wind in the branches. As they slowly make their way down the nearest hiking trail, the family notices the tiny flared flowers of the trailing arbutus that are partially hidden beneath the plant's green leaves, a sign of spring in the still wintry woodland. Sunlight flashes on the blades of mountain laurel leaves, and a red-tailed hawk soars overhead. All along the path the branchlets of tulip-tree, chestnut oak, black birch, and tupelo are adorned with the buds that will give birth to halos of new leaves and flowers during the weeks ahead.

This family probably will visit again during the warmer days of May or

Sugarloaf Mountain summit, looking west over the Monocacy River valley

Woodland scene, Sugarloaf Mountain

June, to see the tulip-trees crowned with multihued flowers or to view the mountain laurel in bloom. And when the little girl grows up, chances are she will return to Sugarloaf with her own children, almost as reliably as the wood thrush or the ovenbird comes back again and again to nest.

Evolution of This Book

With this book Tina Brown and I wish to document and celebrate the plant life of one beloved place in eastern North America. Sugarloaf Mountain, like all such wild areas lying close to population centers, provides the opportunity for large numbers of people to experience a pristine landscape. Sugarloaf attracts some 200,000 visitors annually. The mountain and its adjacent farmland also serve as a "green lung" for the Washington metropolitan area, cooling and cleaning the air.

Sugarloaf Mountain, the only real mountain in the historic Maryland piedmont, began forming more than 500 million years ago and was once part of a high mountain chain. When the surrounding countryside eroded around it, Sugarloaf's quartzite held fast. The relatively pristine nature of today's Sugarloaf, with its nearly fifteen miles of hiking trails, is owed to the vision and persistence of Gordon Strong, a wealthy nineteenth- and twentieth-century midwesterner who fell in love with the mountain and spent his life-time purchasing it woodlot by woodlot. He then preserved it for posterity under the direction of the private nonprofit corporation called Stronghold, Inc. (To read more about the mountain itself, please consult our companion volume, *Sugarloaf: The Mountain's History, Geology, and Natural Lore.*)

The Sugarloaf Mountain setting serves as a preserve for hundreds of na-tive and naturalized herbaceous and woody plant species, some rare and threatened. From the mountain's rocky upland woods to the rich, moist streamsides of its lower slopes, Sugarloaf offers a number of critical habitats favored by the 350 plant species covered in this book. The patchwork of farms, woodlands, and wetlands adjacent to the mountain provides addi-tional critical habitat for plants and wildlife.

Native plants served as nourishment and medicine for generations of American Indians and colonial settlers. The trailing arbutus was valued as a remedy for bladder, kidney, and abdominal ailments. In fact, its popular-ity as an herbal remedy and fragrant spring flower led to its extirpation in many areas. The mountain slopes of Sugarloaf and all the other hills and vales stretching up and down eastern North America were a grocery store and pharmacy for generations of gatherers schooled in the ways of harvest-ing wild greens, roots, and fruit and employing plants as medicine. The heath family plants that thrive in the acidic soils of Sugarloaf's upland woods in-clude blueberries and huckleberries, prized by people and wildlife, and the trailing arbutus and mountain laurel, toxic plants that were once used as medicine.

Collecting plants is now strictly prohibited on Sugarloaf. Instead, Tina Brown and I view the mountain as a learning laboratory for the many visi-tors who come to the mountain each year and for readers of this book. Most of the plants of Sugarloaf are native to a wide swath of eastern North Amer-ica, and some have larger ranges. A number of plants were brought to this country from Europe and Asia to be used as medicines in the New World. In describing the plants of this one place, Tina and I hope to help increase the knowledge of plants not only for Sugarloaf visitors but for everyone inter-ested in wildflowers and herbal lore.

Tina's pen-and-ink illustrations and my botanical descriptions were drawn from life. We spent nearly a decade in the field on Sugarloaf Moun-tain, sitting next to the plants as we described and illustrated them, our botany books splayed out around us on the ground. We carefully studied the plants we found, and we scrutinized our reference books in order to create a useful and comprehensive wildflower guide. We have also included information about the herbal histories of Sugarloaf's plants and their importance to wildlife.

From the first wine-red skunk cabbage bloom of February to the last witch-hazel flower of December or January, there is something blooming on Sugarloaf nearly year-round. We hope that both the regular visitors to Sugarloaf Mountain and readers who live in New York or London will be enriched by an acquaintance with the flora of this one small but remarkable mountain in Maryland.

We also hope that we might inspire readers to begin a similar project with their own regional flora. Conducting a survey of what grows in your backyard, recording your observations year-round, and then compiling a simple illustrated description with your own botanical key can be a rewarding and educational exercise. If you really learn the plants that grow in a small radius, you will be acquiring a surprisingly global education. When you travel elsewhere, you will recognize family characteristics in plants you have never seen before, and your botanical knowledge will grow exponentially. And if development pressures threaten (as they do in Sugarloaf country and nearly everywhere else in the world), perhaps documentation of your trees and wildflowers will assist you in your efforts to preserve natural areas.

Acknowledgments

Tina and I wish to thank the many people who generously contributed time and energy to this book. Author and teacher Cris Fleming was a tireless fountain of botanical wisdom and a supportive friend. We thank director Penelope Kaiserlian, managing editor Ellen Satrom, and the rest of the talented staff at the University of Virginia Press and the designer, Julie Burris, for their dedication to this book. President George F. Thompson and editor Randall B. Jones of the Center for American Places believed in this project and brought it to fruition. Sugarloaf Regional Trails provided grants, moral support, historical information, and natural lore. Thank you to Minny Pohlmann, Rex Sturm, Anne Sturm, Tom Proctor, Chet Anderson, Peg Coleman, Ellen Gordon, and Bev Thoms. Thanks to David F. Webster and Susan Dunn of Stronghold, Inc., and former superintendent Ben Smart for sharing information about the history and natural history of Sugarloaf. Special thanks to botanist Richard Wiegand for his thorough knowledge of Sugarloaf plants. We are grateful to botanists Stanwyn G. Shetler of the Smithsonian Institution, Carole Bergmann, and Kerrie Kyde for answering our endless questions. We also thank botanist Alan Whittemore of the

National Arboretum and horticulturists Susan F. Martin of the National Arboretum and Philip M. Normandy of Brookside Gardens for helping with plant identification. We are grateful to Charles Fenyvesi, author and horticulturist, Neal Fitzpatrick, executive director of the Audubon Naturalist Society, and Peter Raven, director of the Missouri Botanical Garden, for believing in this project and giving it their support. Tina thanks Owen J. Sexton and Alwyn H. Gentry for encouraging her to combine art and science. Our thanks to butterfly conservationist Pat Durkin for sharing information about the relationship between the Baltimore checkerspot butterfly and the turtlehead plant. We appreciate the regional history and natural history shared by Fawn A. E. Foerster and Glenn Cumings of Black Hill Regional Park. A very special thanks to our dear friends the late Jeff Daniels and Terrie Daniels for computer support, moral support, and copyediting. Our deep gratitude to Jim, Jacob, and Josh Brown and Jim, Sophie, and Jesse Choukas-Bradley who provided boundless support over many years. Thanks also to our extended families and close friends, who inspired and cheered us on.

An Illustrated Guide to Eastern Woodland Wildflowers and Trees

350 Plants Observed at Sugarloaf Mountain, Maryland

Introduction

This illustrated guide to wildflowers should make it possible to identify almost any flowering plant a visitor is likely to see on Sugarloaf Mountain, Maryland, whether it is a tree, shrub, woody vine, or herbaceous plant. Most Sugarloaf plants are indigenous to a large part of the eastern United States, and often adjacent Canada too, so this guide will prove helpful in settings far from Sugarloaf and its surroundings. Naturally, the closer the plants to be identified are to Sugarloaf Mountain and the mid-Atlantic piedmont, the more comprehensive the guide will be. In addition to the hundreds of native North American species included here, many plants indigenous to Europe and Asia that have become naturalized on this continent are also covered. We have included every flowering plant we have seen during ten years of extensive hiking and exploration on Sugarloaf and mentioned others that could possibly be growing here.

The guide is organized according to a scientific classification system that recognizes similarities among plant families and genera within their larger divisions, classes, and orders. Classifying living organisms in a systematic manner, based on similar and dissimilar characteristics, is a branch of knowledge known as taxonomy. Modern plant classification is an evolving science, but it still embodies many of the elements introduced by Carl von Linnaeus, an eighteenth-century Swedish naturalist and botanist. We have followed the taxonomic arrangement presented in Henry A. Gleason and Arthur Cronquist's *Manual of Vascular Plants of Northeastern United States and Adjacent Canada,* second edition. In this system dicotyledons or "dicots" (plants sending up two seed leaves) precede monocotyledons or "monocots" (plants sending up one seed leaf).

We believe that the best way to fully appreciate plants is to learn about them in relation to the genus and family to which they belong. Anyone who learns the identifying characteristics of the mustard family, for instance, will begin to recognize mustard family members in the woods behind his or her house, in the garden, and also while traveling far from home.

Learning about plant habitats is another essential aspect of basic botany. If you know, for example, that skunk cabbage is usually found growing in or near seeps and springs, then you will learn to look for this plant when out in those wetland habitats. The pink lady's slipper prefers acidic soil (such as Sugarloaf's), while the yellow lady's slipper thrives in the alkaline soils of the mountains to the west. Much of plant learning is subliminal; as your knowledge and sensitivity grow, recognizing plant habitats will become as automatic as sensing where a gas station or a grocery store might be. Soon you will come to anticipate when your favorite wildflowers will bloom.

Anyone who has ever hiked a woodland trail or, for that matter, walked down the street to the corner market has probably found himself or herself wondering, "What is that plant over there?" Answering that simple question is the first priority of this guide to wildflowers. In the past every community had people who knew the answers to such questions, but with the increasing urbanization and suburbanization of our culture, we must now rely on books we carry into the field with us. But the portable, simply-worded guides and the more complex, scientifically worded botanical manuals both have their drawbacks. With this book we want to help readers discover a plant's name and also to provide enough information that identifying the species will then lead to a deeper knowledge and appreciation of each plant.

The Botanical Keys

Tina Brown and I find the complicated identification systems used by many botanical guides overly technical and often confusing. Getting through them usually involves several trips to the glossary and often ends in frustration. However, when we do manage to "key out" a plant successfully, it is an undeniably rewarding experience.

When we enrolled in wildflower identification courses taught by Cris Fleming through the USDA Graduate School and Audubon Naturalist Society, we discovered a book called *Newcomb's Wildflower Guide*. Lawrence Newcomb, the author, decided to develop a key to wildflowers that ordinary people could use. His key is not only user-friendly, but because the end result is so often success, his system is fun! However, in his effort to simplify plant identification, Newcomb organized his wildflower text and illustrations according to visible physical characteristics rather than family relationship. In this book we wanted to present wildflowers with their families. The Botanical Key to Flowering Plants borrows heavily on elements used by Newcomb. The key is organized according to flower structure and leaf arrangement in a manner similar to his. However, the key is cross referenced to text and illustrations presented within plant families.

Our goal in creating our botanical keys was simple: to help the reader identify a plant as quickly and as easily as possible. We encourage everyone to learn some simple botanical terminology such as "petiole" (leaf stalk), "sessile" (without a leaf stalk), "entire" (describing a leaf margin without teeth), etc. These botanical terms are used in the text describing plant families, genera, and species, and the illustrated glossary defines the botanical words in this guide. However, our keys contain no such botanical terminology. Using a key is enough of a challenge without having to struggle with vocabulary.

The Botanical Key to Flowering Plants is designed to get you from the key to the text and illustrations with minimal confusion. Therefore, we give the page number sometimes for an individual species, sometimes for a genus (group of species), and sometimes for a family (group of genera). Here is how it works.

Look at the flower, but please do not disturb the plant or its habitat in any way. Is it an herb (a plant with a nonwoody stalk or stalks) or woody plant (tree, shrub, or woody vine)? If it is an herb, look carefully at the flower. Is it regular or irregular? A regular flower has two to many similar petals or petal-like parts, which may be separate or fused (joined). An irregular flower has parts that are not uniform in size and/or structure.

Flowering herbs are separated into the following categories: Irregular Flowers, Flowers with Two Regular Parts, Flowers with Three Regular Parts, Flowers with Four Regular Parts, Flowers with Five Regular Parts, Flowers with Six Regular Parts, Flowers with Seven or More Regular Parts, and Flowers with Parts Too Numerous, Tiny, and/or Indistinct to Easily Count.

Within these categories, the next step is to determine the leaf arrangement of the plant. Leaf arrangements include: Basal Leaves Only (leaves growing from the base of the plant at or near the ground), No Leaves Visible at Flowering Time, Alternate Simple Leaves, Alternate Compound Leaves,

Regular
flowers

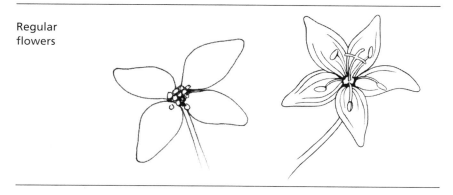

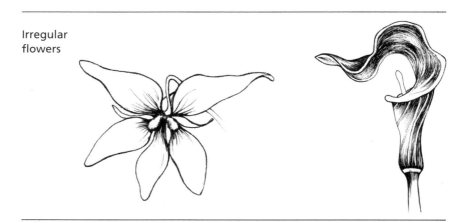

Irregular flowers

Opposite or Whorled Simple Leaves, and Opposite or Whorled Compound Leaves. A simple leaf is a leaf that may be untoothed, toothed, or lobed but has one continuous margin. A compound leaf is a leaf that is divided into separate leaflets. Opposite leaves grow in pairs along the plant stalk. Whorled leaves are three or more leaves arranged opposite one another along the plant stalk. Alternate leaves grow without another leaf immediately opposite on the stalk.

Next comes a series of choices. Read the first line of text to the far left (for example: "Yellow flowers"). If this applies to your plant, read the next indented line of text beneath it. If that line applies to the plant, keep reading each further indented line until you identify the plant or plant group. Skip any lines that do not apply to the plant. For example: The plant has a red flower, so "Yellow flowers" does not apply to it. Nor does the next line, "Blue flowers." Finally you come to "Red flowers." The first indented line beneath it reads, "Small flowers (¼" wide) in long clusters," but your flower is 1 inch wide and grows at the end of a single stalk. So scan down until a similarly indented line describes the flower you are looking at. Keep sorting through the levels of indentation until you come to a description that matches your plant and ultimately gives your plant name and its page number.

If your flower belongs to a woody plant, it is described in the section at the end of this key. Here you are presented with a set of similar choices. However, because fewer flowering trees, shrubs, and woody vines are included in this guide, there will be fewer choices to make in the botanical key.

When a plant is a tree, shrub, or woody vine that does not have showy flowers, it is included in the Botanical Key and Guide to Trees, Shrubs, and Woody Vines (see p. 333). This is a simplified key organized according to plant habit (tree, shrub, or vine) and leaf arrangement. It is less comprehensive than the key and guide to flowering plants and is organized according to physical characteristics rather than plant families.

If you fail to find your wildflower by using the botanical key, consider whether you can key out the plant in a different way. Sometimes it is hard to distinguish between simple and compound leaves if the leaves are deeply lobed. Plants vary greatly, and as more than one botany teacher has proclaimed, "The plants don't read the botany books."

If you are unable to key out a plant during your first attempt, go back to the beginning and start again. Some categories are arbitrary. The category Flower Parts Too Numerous, Tiny, and/or Indistinct to Easily Count is highly subjective and includes plants with many different types and numbers of parts. If you have assigned a plant to that category and it hasn't keyed out, look again. Maybe you can make out several or more small petals after all. Some plants bear both alternate and simple leaves or leaves that are both compound and simple. In most of those cases we have keyed in from both leaf arrangements, but we could not foresee every eventuality. If you come up empty-handed, make an educated guess or flip through the text and illustrations. A few hours in the field will clue you in to a basic truth about plant identification: it is a rewarding but humbling avocation!

If you are using these botanical keys in Connecticut or Kentucky (or even along the Potomac River), they will not be fully comprehensive for your area. Therefore you may want to carry another guide with you, either a popular field guide such as Newcomb's or Peterson's or a more technical botanical manual. See our Suggested Reading and Bibliography.

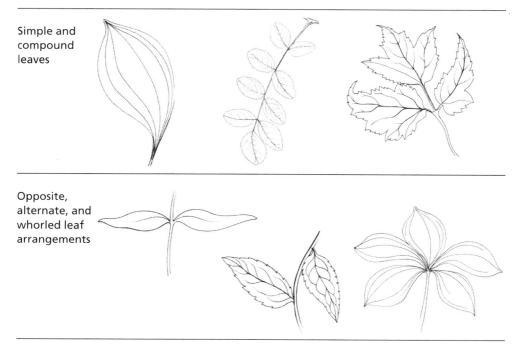

Simple and compound leaves

Opposite, alternate, and whorled leaf arrangements

Guide to Flowering Plants

Tina and I worked closely together to emphasize the plant features we felt were most essential to wildflower identification and appreciation. When the botanical key gives a page number for a wildflower, that page in the guide presents a description of the plant with a botanically accurate drawing. If the key sends you to a plant family or genus rather than an individual species, peruse the pages identified in the key to locate the individual plant.

The plant species is identified by one or more common names and one or more binomial scientific names, given in Latin, the universal language of botanists. Each individual species is identified by its Latin genus name (beginning with an uppercase letter) and a specific epithet (beginning with a lowercase letter). When plants are identified by more than one Latin name, we usually first give the name preferred in the *Annotated Checklist of the Vascular Plants of the Washington-Baltimore Area*, by Stanwyn G. Shetler and Sylvia Stone Orli for the Smithsonian Institution's National Museum of Natural History. Following the plant's common name and scientific name, its family name is given.

The written description of each plant contains information about the flowers and leaves (and sometimes the fruit), the height, and, often, the growth habit (overall shape), the plant's preferred habitat and indigenous range, herbal lore, and wildlife lore where applicable. Although we have consulted many books on the herbal histories of plants, we are most indebted to Steven Foster and James A. Duke for their Peterson Field Guide Series' *Field Guide to Medicinal Plants: Eastern and Central North America*, a work that we quote frequently.

At the end of the plant description is a section identified as "On Sugarloaf." In this closing section blooming dates and locations specific to Sugarloaf Mountain are presented, followed by "Similar species," listing plants that could be confused with your plant. For a place other than Sugarloaf Mountain, the blooming dates can be estimated by taking into account how far north or south of central Maryland you are located. You may also have to consider a greater number of similar species before being assured of a correct plant identification.

In the guide each family is described before its member species are presented, with both global family characteristics and specifics about the family on and around Sugarloaf. It is fascinating to learn, for instance, that the spicebush growing along Sugarloaf's Bear Branch is in the same family as the plants that produce avocados, cinnamon, and bay leaves.

You might want to take some time perusing the illustrated botanical glossary at the back of this book. Terms you may wish to acquaint yourself with include "glabrous" (hairless) and "pubescent" (hairy). Sometimes whether a plant is glabrous or pubescent will be diagnostic. A small hand lens is often helpful in the field for close observation of plant parts. Learning the names of common leaf shapes also will help your identification efforts. Terms such as "cordate" (heart-shaped), "ovate" (egg-shaped), and "lanceolate" (lance-shaped) are used in the guide.

The sources quoted in this book are botanical manuals and herbal reference works that are indexed according to common and/or scientific plant names. Cited works are preceded by asterisks in the bibliography. To locate a particular citation, consult the bibliography for information about the edition quoted and then search for the relevant plant species, genus, or family in the index of the cited book.

Some Sugarloaf Specifics

Sugarloaf Mountain's upland woods are dominated by oak and hickory species, with chestnut oak the most common tree. The rocky, acidic soils of the mountain's higher elevations also support other deciduous trees and some evergreen trees; shrubs such as mountain laurel, pinxter flower, and the low-growing trailing arbutus; and pink lady's slipper, violet wood-sorrel, and many other herbaceous wildflowers.

In the rich, moist soils of the lower slopes, and especially along the springs and streamsides of Bear Branch and Furnace Branch, many native wildflowers thrive. Species growing in those rich lower woods include spicebush, Indian cucumber root, large whorled pogonia, showy orchis, round-lobed hepatica, smooth Solomon's seal, and false Solomon's seal.

The color-coded trails mentioned throughout the flowering plants guide are described in detail in our companion volume, *Sugarloaf: The Mountain's History, Geology, and Natural Lore.* Information about the 2,100-acre Monocacy Natural Resources Management Area adjacent to Sugarloaf is included in that book. It also contains detailed descriptions of the mountain's setting and seasons. The two volumes are meant to complement each other in the home library and in the field.

Following pages: Sugarloaf Mountain and the Monocacy Natural Resources Management Area

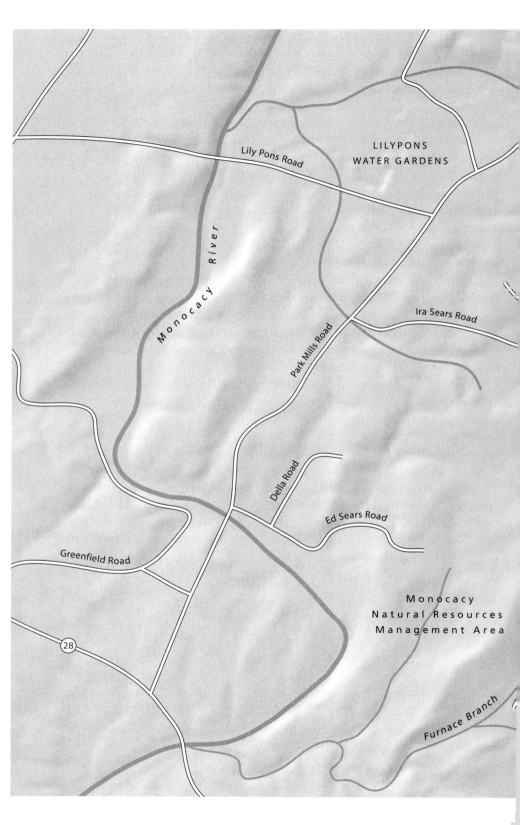

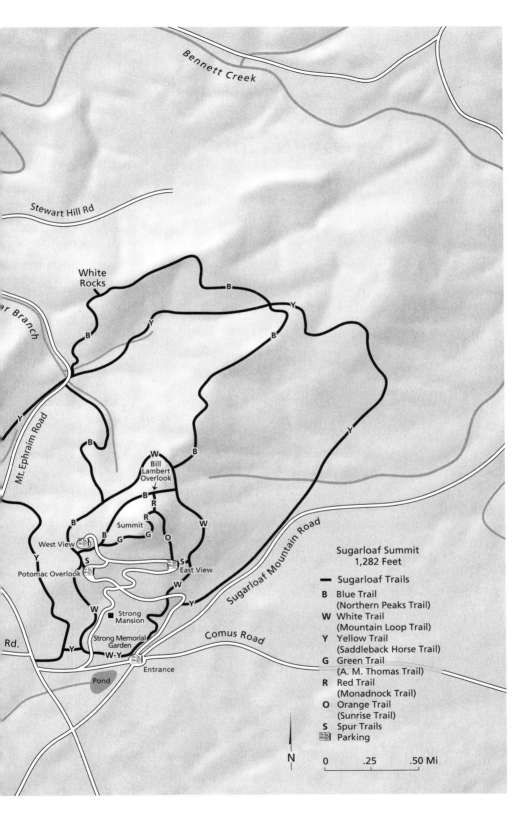

Bennett Creek

Stewart Hill Rd

White
Rocks

B

Y

B

B

Y

B

Y

ar Branch

Y

Mt. Ephraim Road

B

W
Bill
Lambert
Overlook

Y

B

R

R

W

B

Summit

G

G

O

West View

S

B

Potomac Overlook

S

S

East View

Y

W

W

Y

Rd.

W

Strong
Mansion

Strong Memorial
Garden

Y

W-Y

Entrance

Comus Road

Sugarloaf Mountain Road

Pond

**Sugarloaf Summit
1,282 Feet**

— Sugarloaf Trails

B Blue Trail
(Northern Peaks Trail)
W White Trail
(Mountain Loop Trail)
Y Yellow Trail
(Saddleback Horse Trail)
G Green Trail
(A. M. Thomas Trail)
R Red Trail
(Monadnock Trail)
O Orange Trail
(Sunrise Trail)
S Spur Trails
Parking

N

0   .25   .50 Mi

Botanical Key to Flowering Plants

See Introduction, pp. 2–5, to learn how to use the botanical key to flowering plants.

I. HERBS

A. Irregular Flowers

Basal Leaves Only

Simple Basal Leaves

Leaves toothed
  Flowers with 5 irregular petals. Flower color purple, lavender, or white.
  Leaves heart-shaped, egg-shaped, or lobed. Violets *(Viola)*. Pp. 80–83
Leaves untoothed
  Large, reddish, hooded early spring flowers. Large net-veined leaves
  (appearing with flowers or slightly later). Skunk cabbage *(Symplocarpus foetidus)*. P. 305
  Flowers not large and reddish (although may be pink or small and reddish). Leaves parallel-veined. Orchids *(Orchidaceae)*. Pp. 325–28, 332
  Dark green leaves with white markings. Small white flowers on a straight stalk. Downy rattlesnake-plantain *(Goodyera pubescens)*. P. 326

Compound Basal Leaves

Leafy green, brown, or green and brown striped hood over small club-shaped projection. Jack-in-the-pulpit *(Arisaema triphyllum)*. P. 306
Small white flowers in round heads. White clover *(Trifolium repens)*. P. 134
Purplish-pink flowers. Naked-flowered tick-trefoil *(Desmodium nudiflorum)*. P. 138

No Leaves Visible at Flowering Time

Thick, fleshy yellow-brown plant resembles an upright pine cone. Squawroot *(Conopholis americana)*. P. 226

Several flowers on thin, upright stalk that may or may not be fleshy. Orchids *(Orchidaceae)*. Pp. 330–32

Alternate Simple Leaves

Spring to early summer flowers

Very small 4-lobed blue and white flowers. Leaves may be opposite and alternate on same plant.

Leaves bluntly toothed. Flowers growing on long stalks from the leaf axils. Bird's-eye speedwell *(Veronica persica)*. P. 223

Leaves with untoothed or barely toothed margins. Flowers growing in terminal clusters. Thyme-leaved speedwell *(Veronica serpyllifolia)*. P. 224

Flowers with 5 irregular petals. Flower color lavender, yellow, or white. Violets *(Viola)*. Pp. 83–85

Summer to fall flowers

Leaves toothed

Flowers pale to deep blue or red with 2 upper and 3 lower flared lobes. Lobelias (including Indian tobacco and cardinal flower) *(Lobelia)*. Pp. 230–34

Flowers orange or yellow with a spurred pouch with 3 flared lobes in front.

Flowers orange. Spotted jewelweed *(Impatiens capensis)*. P. 162

Flowers yellow. Yellow or pale jewelweed *(Impatiens pallida)*. P. 162

Leaves untoothed

Several to many flowers on an upright stalk

A common summer wildflower. Yellow and orange flowers with spurs at the back in crowded upright cluster. Butter-and-eggs *(Linaria vulgaris)*. P. 220

Uncommon to rare and threatened orchids

Flowers uniformly tangerine. Yellow-fringed orchid *(Platanthera ciliaris)*. P. 329

Flowers purple. Large purple-fringed orchid *(Platanthera grandiflora)*. P. 330

Flowers greenish-white. Green wood orchid *(Platanthera clavellata)*. P. 330

Flowers borne singly or 2–4 per cluster. Two larger blue upper petals and 1 white lower petal. Asiatic dayflower *(Commelina communis)*. P. 309

Alternate Compound Leaves

Leaves not trifoliate (don't have 3 leaflets)

Early spring yellow flowers with delicate fernlike leaves. Yellow corydalis *(Corydalis flavula)*. P. 53

Small purplish-pink flowers in round heads. Leaves pinnately compound. Crown vetch *(Coronilla varia)*. P. 136

Leaves trifoliate (with 3 leaflets)

Many tiny flowers in dense round or cylindric heads. Clovers *(Trifolium)*. Pp. 134–35

Flowers not in dense round heads

Few leaves per plant. Purplish-pink flowers in loose, elongate clusters. Tick-trefoils *(Desmodium)*. Pp. 138–40

Leafy or bushy plants

Yellow flowers. Wild indigo *(Baptisia tinctoria)*. P. 137

Creamy white flowers with a purple blush. Borne singly or in clusters in upper leaf axils. Chinese bush clover *(Lespedeza cuneata)*. P. 138

Opposite or Whorled Simple Leaves

Stem Leaves Whorled

Large whorled pogonia *(Isotria verticillata)*. P. 328

Stem Leaves Merely Opposite

Bright red flowers. Bee-balm *(Monarda didyma)*. P. 193

Yellow flowers. Horse-balm *(Collinsonia canadensis)*. P. 191

Purplish-pink flowers with 6 slightly unequal petals: 2 larger upper and 4 smaller lower. Clammy cuphea *(Cuphea viscosissima)*. P. 144

Reddish-brown or greenish flowers. Maryland figwort *(Scrophularia marilandica)*. P. 222

Tiny white flowers with 4 slightly unequal lobes in round clusters in the leaf axils. Virginia Bugleweed *(Lycopus virginicus)*. P. 194

Small blue and white flowers with 4 unequal lobes. Leaves may be opposite, alternate, or both

Flowers in leaf axils; leaves bluntly toothed. Bird's-eye speedwell *(Veronica persica)*. P. 223

Flowers in terminal clusters; leaves barely toothed or untoothed. Thyme-leaved speedwell *(Veronica serpyllifolia)*. P. 224

Showy 2-lipped flowers about 1" long

Flowers with 2 upper and 3 lower flared or partially flared lobes

Flowers borne in terminal clusters. Foxglove beardtongue *(Penstemon digitalis)*. P. 216

Flowers borne singly or in pairs from the upper leaf axils. Monkey-flowers *(Mimulus)*. P. 221

Flowers with hooded upper lip

White or pale pink stalkless flowers in dense terminal clusters. Turtlehead *(Chelone glabra)*. P. 218

Blue flowers
    Leaves toothed. Showy skullcap *(Scutellaria serrata)*. P. 196
    Leaves untoothed (or with a few toothed lower leaves). Hyssop skullcap *(Scutellaria integrifolia)*. P. 197
Flowers 2-lipped and 5-lobed; less than or up to 1" long. Flowers pink, purple, lavender, blue, or white. Mint family members *(Lamiaceae)*. Pp. 200–211.
Irregular purple-pink flowers with prominent lower lip and upper lip apparently missing. American germander *(Teucrium canadense)*. P. 196
Flowers with hooded upper lip and flared lower lip; less than 1" long. Skullcaps *(Scutellaria)*. Pp. 198–99

B. Regular Flowers

Flowers with Two Regular Parts

Opposite Simple Leaves

Small white flowers with 2 deeply notched petals (so deeply notched they may appear to be 4 petals). Enchanter's nightshade *(Circaea lutetiana)*. P. 145

Flowers with Three Regular Parts

Basal Leaves Only

White 3-petaled flowers ½–1" across. Some leaves arrow-shaped (leaf shape varies). Growing in wet places. Broad-leaved arrowhead *(Sagittaria latifolia)*. P. 303

Flowers with Four Regular Parts

Alternate Simple Leaves

White flowers
    Leaves untoothed
        Spring flowers. Canada Mayflower *(Maianthemum canadense)*. P. 315
        Summer to fall flowers
            Flowers may not open all the way; leaves broadly arrow-shaped; stem prickly. Halberd-leaved tearthumb *(Polygonum arifolium)*. P. 72
            Flowers tiny, in long spike. Leaves ovate or elliptic; stem not prickly. Jumpseed *(Tovara virginiana)*. P. 72
    Leaves toothed (regularly or sparsely)
        Most leaves with stalks. Leaves have garlic odor when crushed. Lower leaves with long stalks. Upper leaves often short-stalked. Garlic-mustard *(Alliaria petiolata)*. P. 92

Most leaves without stalks or nearly stalkless (a few lower leaves may be petioled)

Some leaves usually clasping the plant stalk. Flowers small (less than ¼" across). Leaves sparsely toothed. Smooth rockcress *(Arabis laevigata)*. P. 91

Flowers about 1" across, white, pink, or purple. Dame's-rocket *(Hesperis matronalis)*. P. 93

Upper leaves stalkless, lower leaves petioled. Flowers ½" across. Leaves sparsely and bluntly toothed. Growing in springs, seeps, and near streams. Spring cress *(Cardamine bulbosa)*. P. 89

Deep purplish-pink or deep pink flowers

Leaves heart-shaped or triangular, alternate or opposite, coarsely toothed. Fruit a disklike seedpod. Honesty *(Lunaria annua)*. P. 94

Upper leaves usually narrow (lower leaves may be heart-shaped or triangular), shallowly toothed. Fruit a small, slender, linear seedpod. (Flowers may also be white.) Dame's-rocket *(Hesperis matronalis)*. P. 93

Yellow flowers

Spring flowers. Small flowers in roundish clusters with lobed or divided lower leaves and toothed to nearly entire upper leaves. Common winter-cress *(Barbarea vulgaris)*. P. 90

Late spring to summer flowers

Flowers 1–2" wide

Fruit an erect capsule, about 1" long, tapering toward the tip. Common evening-primrose *(Oenothera biennis)*. P. 146

Fruit capsule less than 1" long and broadening toward the tip. Sundrops *(Oenothera fruticosa)*. P. 148

Flowers ½–¾" wide

Fruit a small cubic capsule, rounded at base. Seedbox *(Ludwigia alternifolia)*. P. 148

Fruit not cubic. Petals notched at tips. Small sundrops *(Oenothera perennis)*. P. 148

Alternate Compound Leaves

White flowers, less than ¼" across

Plant 3–10" tall. Hairy bittercress *(Cardamine hirsuta)*. P. 88

Plant 8–24" tall, growing in or near springs and streams. Pennsylvania bittercress *(Cardamine pensylvanica)*. P. 89

Yellow flowers. Common winter-cress *(Barbarea vulgaris)*. P. 90

Opposite or Whorled Simple Leaves

Leaves Whorled

Leaves in whorls of 4. Wild licorice *(Galium circaezans)*. P. 237
Prickly-sticky plant with leaves usually in whorls of 6–8. Cleavers *(Galium aparine)*. P. 235

Stem Leaves Merely Opposite

Creeping or floating aquatic plants
    Leaves with a few blunt teeth. Golden saxifrage *(Chrysosplenium americanum)*. P. 113
    Leaves without teeth. Water purslane *(Ludwigia palustris)*. P. 149
Nonaquatic plants
    Yellow flowers. St. Andrew's-cross *(Hypericum hypericoides)*. P. 77
    Flowers not yellow
        Plant stalk fleshy. Flowers upright, funnel-shaped, white-lavender, growing in axils of purple-green leaves; lower leaves tiny and scalelike. Pennywort *(Obolaria virginica)*. P. 172
        Plant stalk not fleshy
            Trailing plants
                Flowers white to pale pink in terminal pairs. Leaves untoothed. Partridgeberry *(Mitchella repens)*. P. 237
                Flowers white to pale lavender in upright clusters. Common speedwell *(Veronica officinalis)*. P. 222
            Upright plants
                White or pale lilac, ¼"-long summer flowers in small terminal clusters. Common Sugarloaf woodland plant. Long-leaved houstonia *(Houstonia longifolia)*. P. 238
                Pale blue spring flowers, ⅓–½" wide. Uncommon on Sugarloaf. Bluets *(Houstonia caerulea)*. P. 239
                Flowers deep pink or purplish-pink. Leaves opposite or alternate. Honesty *(Lunaria annua)*. P. 94

Opposite Compound Leaves

White, pink, purplish-pink, or lavender flowers
    Leaves opposite or whorled, palmately divided into several lobes or leaflets. Cut-leaved toothwort *(Dentaria laciniata)*. P. 86
    Basal leaves with 3 leaflets; a smaller pair of stem leaves with 3 leaflets. Slender toothwort *(Dentaria heterophylla)*. P. 87

Flowers with Five Regular Parts

Basal Leaves Only

Simple Basal Leaves

Small white flowers in terminal clusters. Early saxifrage *(Saxifraga virginiensis)*. P. 113

Compound Basal Leaves

Purplish-pink flowers. Leaves with 3 leaflets. Violet wood-sorrel *(Oxalis violacea)*. P. 159
White flowers
> Tiny flowers in small round clusters. Wild sarsaparilla *(Aralia nudicaulis)*. P. 164
> Flowers ½–1" wide. Wild strawberry *(Fragaria virginiana)*. P. 114

No Leaves Visible at Flowering Time

Plants lacking chlorophyll (not green)
> Flower stalk thick; white waxy, nodding flower. Indian pipe *(Monotropa uniflora)*. P. 107
> Flower stalk slender; flower with flared lobes. One-flowered cancer-root *(Orobanche uniflora)*. P. 227

Alternate Simple Leaves

Tiny clustered flowers that often do not fully open. Swollen nodes (sometimes with hairs) where leaves attach to plant stalk. Polygonums (smartweeds, tearthumb, lady's-thumb) *(Polygonum)*.
> Leaves lance-shaped, ovate, or elliptic
>> Pink (rarely white) flowers
>>> Leaves with a dark splotch resembling a thumbprint. Shortish hairs at leaf nodes. Lady's-thumb *(P. persicaria)*. Pp. 69, 70
>>> Leaves without thumbprint; no hairs at leaf nodes. Pennsylvania smartweed *(P. pensylvanicum)*. P. 70
>>> Leaves without thumbprint; long hairs at leaf nodes. Long-bristled smartweed *(P. cespitosum)*. P. 71
>> Greenish-white flowers. Leaves often dotted; plant grows in wet places. Water smartweed *(P. punctatum)*. P. 71
> Leaves arrow-shaped or heart-shaped
>> Sprawling prickly plant of wet places. Leaves arrow-shaped. Arrow-leaved tearthumb *(P. sagittatum)*. P. 71
>> Twining vine with heart-shaped or arrow-shaped leaves. Climbing false buckwheat *(P. scandens)*. P. 72

Flowers fully open
Yellow flowers
Spring to early summer flowers with long-stalked basal leaves and variable stem leaves
Common Sugarloaf woodland plant with kidney-shaped basal leaves and variably lobed stem leaves. Kidneyleaf buttercup *(Ranunculus abortivus)*. P. 46
Uncommon Sugarloaf plant with variable, often 3-lobed leaves. Growing in seeps, springs, and near streams. Hooked crowfoot *(Ranunculus recurvatus)*. P. 48
Summer to fall flowers
Flowers tiny (¼" across). Ridged yellow flax *(Linum striatum)*. P. 156
Flowers ½–1½" across.
Flowers bell-shaped. Ground-cherries *(Physalis)*. P. 182
Flowers not bell-shaped
Flowers stalked and ⅔–1" across. Moth mullein *(Verbascum blattaria)*. P. 214
Flowers not stalked and ¾–1" across. Leaves flannel-textured. Common mullein *(Verbascum thapsus)*. P. 215
Orange flowers blooming in summer. Butterfly weed *(Asclepias tuberosa)*. P. 177
White, pink, lavender, violet, blue, or purple flowers
Spring to early summer flowers
Low-growing plant with early spring white to pale pink flowers and evergreen leaves. Trailing arbutus *(Epigaea repens)*. P. 95
Violet or pink star-shaped flowers. Plant with toothed, heart-shaped, clasping leaves. Venus's looking-glass *(Triodanis perfoliata)*. P. 229
Flowers blue, trumpet-shaped, nodding, clustered. Leaves untoothed. Virginia bluebells *(Mertensia virginica)*. P. 188
Summer to fall flowers with evergreen leaves. Low-growing plant with small white bell-shaped flowers. Wintergreen *(Gaultheria procumbens)*. P. 97
Summer to fall flowers with nonevergreen leaves
Small flowers (⅕–1" across) in clusters
Flower clusters elongated and one-sided. Uncommon woodland plant with tiny flowers (⅛" or less across). Virginia stickseed *(Hackelia virginiana)*. P. 188
Flower clusters elongated but not one-sided. Small flowers (¼" across). Common large plant with reddish stalk. Pokeweed *(Phytolacca americana)*. P. 60

Flower clusters rather flat-topped
  Tiny white flowers (about ¼" across) with leaf whorl just be-
  low flower cluster. Leaves entire. Flowering spurge *(Euphorbia corollata)*. P. 153
  White or pink flowers ½" across; leaves toothed or nearly
  entire. Toothed white-topped aster *(Seriocarpus asteroides)*.
  P. 261
  Deep purple late summer–early fall flowers in flat-topped
  or concave clusters. New York ironweed *(Vernonia novebora-censis)*. P. 276
Larger flowers (⅔–1" across) in elongated cluster. Moth mullein
(Verbascum blattaria). P. 214
Flowers borne singly or in small clusters that are not elongated or
flat-topped
  Funnel-shaped or trumpet-shaped flowers with fused petals
    Upright plant with white or lavender trumpet-shaped flowers
    3–5" long. Leaves sharply toothed and sometimes lobed.
    Jimsonweed *(Datura stramonium)*. P. 180
    Vines. Flowers white, pink, violet, or purple, funnel-shaped.
    Trailing or climbing vines. Morning glories, wild potato vine,
    bindweeds *(Ipomoea, Calystegia, Convolvulus)*. Pp. 183–85
  Flowers star-shaped
    Petals usually swept back
      Flowers ¼–½" across, white or pale violet. Black night-
      shade *(Solanum nigrum)*. Pp. 180, 181
      Flowers ½–1" across, violet or blue (rarely white). Leaves
      simple or compound. Bittersweet nightshade *(Solanum dulcamara)*. P. 179
    Petals not swept back
      Plant with white or lavender flowers; spiny leaves and stalk.
      Horse nettle *(Solanum carolinense)*. P. 178
      Plant with white flowers; without spiny leaves and stalk.
      White avens *(Geum canadense)*. P. 118

Alternate Compound Leaves

White flowers
  Tiny flowers in clusters
    Flowers in large flat-topped clusters
      Flower clusters 2–7" across, round; flat-topped or concave, often
      with tiny purple flower at center. Feathery compound leaves with
      sheathed leaf stalks. Queen Anne's lace *(Daucus carota)*. P. 167

Flower clusters 1–4" across, not uniformly round but slightly irregular in shape; flat-topped or convex. Feathery compound leaves without sheathed leaf stalks. Yarrow *(Achillea millefolium)*. P. 264

Flowers in small rounded or uneven clusters

Flower clusters rounded. Leaves with 3 or more toothed leaflets. Moist woodland plant blooming in spring. Sweet cicely *(Osmorhiza claytonii)*. P. 166

Flower clusters small and irregular. Tiny beaked fruit quickly appears. Leaves usually with 3 toothed—sometimes lobed—leaflets. Honewort *(Cryptotaenia canadensis)*. P. 169

Flowers in tall branched spikes. Goatsbeard *(Aruncus dioicus)*. P. 121

Flowers ⅓–1" or more wide

Flowers ⅓–¾" across, sometimes missing 1 or more petals. Leaves variable—simple or compound; lower leaves with 3 or more leaflets. White avens *(Geum canadense)*. P. 118

Flowers white (or pinkish), ½–1½" across with thin, pointed petals. Leaflets usually 3. Bowman's root *(Porteranthus trifoliatus)*. P. 120

Yellow flowers

Flowers ⅛–½" across, with pinnately compound (or mostly pinnately compound) leaves

Summer to fall flowers ¼–½" across in upright clusters. Leaves with 3 to 15 larger leaflets interspersed with smaller leaflets. Agrimonies *(Agrimonia)*. Pp. 121–22

Spring flowers about ¼" wide in loose clusters. Variable leaves pinnately compound, trifoliate, or deeply lobed. Spring avens *(Geum vernum)*. P. 120

Flowers ¼–1" across with palmately compound leaves.

Plants with evenly sized, regularly toothed leaflets

Plant with 3 leaflets. Indian strawberry *(Duchesnea indica)*. P. 115

Slender-stemmed plants with 5 leaflets

A creeping plant with leaflets wedge-shaped at the base and toothed only above the middle. Dwarf cinquefoil *(Potentilla canadensis)*. P. 116

An upright or partially upright plant with leaflets toothed for ¾ of their length. Common cinquefoil *(Potentilla simplex)*. P. 117

Erect, stout-stalked plant with 5–7 leaflets Flowers pale yellow. Rough-fruited cinquefoil *(Potentilla recta)*. P. 118

Plants with 3 evenly sized, untoothed leaflets. Leaflets indented at the tip and creased down the middle. Wood-sorrels *(Oxalis)*. P. 160

Plants with variously and irregularly toothed, lobed, and divided leaves. The buttercup and crowfoot genus *(Ranunculus)*. Pp. 46–48

Orange-red and yellow flowers
    Bell-shaped nodding flowers ¾–2" long with leaves once or twice
    divided into 3 bluntly toothed leaflets. Wild columbine *(Aquilegia
    canadensis)*. P. 43
Blue, purple, lavender, violet (or rarely white) flowers
    Mostly purple nodding, bell-shaped flowers ¾–2" long. European
    columbine *(Aquilegia vulgaris)*. P. 42
    Violet or blue star-shaped flowers with swept-back petals. Leaves com-
    pound or simple. Bittersweet nightshade *(Solanum dulcamara)*. P. 179
    Small lavender 5-parted flowers in thistlelike heads. Heads are ¾–1"
    across. Bracts below flower heads may be black-tipped. Spotted knap-
    weed *(Centaurea maculosa)*. P. 285

Opposite or Whorled Simple Leaves

Stem Leaves Usually Whorled

Yellow flowers. Leaves usually in whorls of 4. Whorled loosestrife *(Lysimachia quadrifolia)*. P. 108
White or pale pink flowers
    Petals fringed. Starry campion *(Silene stellata)*. P. 68
    Petals not fringed
        Dark green evergreen leaves with white markings. Waxy petals
        rounded at their tips. Striped wintergreen *(Chimaphila maculata)*.
        P. 105
        Middle leaves in whorls of four. Small flowers with reflexed petals and
        a 5-parted crown called a corona. Four-leaved milkweed *(Asclepias
        quadrifolia)*. P. 177
        Flowers ⅔–1' across, with 5–10 petal-like parts. Rue-anemone
        (Anemonella thalictroides). Page 40

Stem Leaves Merely Opposite

White flowers
    Leaves toothed
        Tiny flowers (¹⁄₁₆–¼" across) in long, thin spikes up to several inches
        tall. White vervain *(Verbena urticifolia)*. P. 189
        Small flowers (¼" across) in loose clusters. Quickweed *(Galinsoga
        quadriradiata)*. P. 264
    Leaves untoothed
        Petals deeply cleft
            Flowers ⅛–⅓" across
                Petals cleft ½ their length or less. Plant very pubescent. Mouse-
                eared chickweed *(Cerastium vulgatum)*. P. 65

Petals so deeply cleft they appear to number 10. Plant mostly hairless with some pubescence on leaf stalks. Common chickweed *(Stellaria media)*. P. 63

Flowers ½" across

Petals so deeply cleft they appear to number 10. Plant pubescent. Star chickweed *(Stellaria pubera)*. P. 64

Flowers ½–¾" across and swollen below the petals. Plant mostly hairless. Bladder campion *(Silene vulgaris)*. P. 67

Flowers white or very pale pink, 1" across. Swollen and pubescent below the petals. Evening lychnis *(Silene latifolia)*. P. 66

Petals not cleft. Small, 5-lobed, somewhat tubular or bell-shaped flowers. Indian hemp *(Apocynum cannabinum)*. P. 174

Pink flowers

Petals usually shallowly notched or toothed and broadest at the tip. Wild pink *(Silene caroliniana)*. P. 68

Flowers star-shaped

Flowers deep pink with white spots; petals shallowly toothed. Deptford pink *(Dianthus armeria)*. P. 66

Flowers pink with a greenish or yellow center. Rose pink *(Sabatia angularis)*. P. 172

Flowers white or pale pink with darker pink stripes. Spring beauty *(Claytonia virginica)*. P. 61

Pink, rose-purple, lavender, greenish, or white flowers

Small flowers in rounded clusters. Each flower has 5 reflexed petals beneath a 5-parted crownlike corona. Milkweeds *(Asclepias)*. Pp. 175–77

Red, orange, or coral flowers. Small flowers ¼–⅓" wide on long stalks, growing from the leaf axils. Scarlet pimpernel *(Anagallis arvensis)*. P. 110

Yellow flowers

At least some leaves toothed or lobed. Funnel-shaped flowers 1–2" long. Upper leaves often untoothed. Lower leaves bluntly toothed and lobed. Downy false-foxglove *(Aureolaria virginica)*. P. 217

Leaves untoothed

Petals fringed or toothed at the tip. Fringed loosestrife *(Lysimachia ciliata)*. P. 109

Petals not fringed or toothed at the tip.

All leaves opposite. The St. John's-worts *(Hypericum)*. Pp. 74–77

Lower leaves opposite, upper leaves alternate. Ridged yellow flax *(Linum striatum)*. P. 156

Violet or blue-violet flowers

Trailing plant with evergreen leaves. Periwinkle *(Vinca minor)*. P. 173

Upright plant with deciduous leaves. Wild blue phlox *(Phlox divaricata)*. P. 186

Opposite or Whorled Compound Leaves

Leaves Usually Whorled

White or pale pink flowers
> Flowers ⅔–1" across, with 5–10 petal-like parts. Rue-anemone *(Anemonella thalictroides)*. P. 40
> Tiny flowers in small round clusters. Leaves with 3–5 leaflets. Plant 3–8" tall. Dwarf ginseng *(Panax trifolius)*. P. 165

Leaves Whorled or Merely Opposite

Greenish-white flowers, ⅔–1⅓" across on long, upright stalks. Leaves whorled or simply opposite, usually with 3 toothed, lobed leaflets. Plant 2–3½' tall. Thimbleweed *(Anemone virginiana)*. P. 48
Lavender-pink flowers and palmately compound, opposite or whorled leaves. Geraniums and cranesbills *(Geranium)*. P. 161

Flowers with Six Regular Parts

Basal Leaves Only

Yellow flowers
> Flowers nodding; leaves mottled green and brown. Trout-lily *(Erythronium americanum)*. P. 310
> Flowers star-shaped; leaves shiny, narrow, and grasslike. Yellow stargrass *(Hypoxis hirsuta)*. P. 315

Blue-violet, lavender, purple, pink, or white flowers
> Flowers ½–¾" across, blue-violet with yellow center. Leaves long, narrow, and grasslike. Stout blue-eyed grass *(Sisyrinchium angustifolium)*. P. 323
> Flowers ½–1" across with 6–12 blue, pink, white, lavender, or purple petal-like parts. Leaves with 3 rounded lobes and a heart-shaped base. Round-lobed hepatica *(Hepatica americana)*. P. 41

Orange flowers
> Flowers large, 3–4" wide; leaves long (several inches to 1') and narrow. Day-lily *(Hemerocallis fulva)*. P. 318

Alternate Simple Leaves

Yellow flowers
> Pale yellow nodding, bell-shaped flowers about 1" long
>> Leaves pierced by the plant stalk. Perfoliate bellwort *(Uvularia perfoliata)*. P. 311
>> Leaves not pierced by the plant stalk. Sessile bellwort *(Uvularia sessilifolia)*. P. 312

Greenish or yellowish flowers in small clusters on drooping stalks. Heart-shaped or egg-shaped leaves are alternate, opposite, or whorled. Wild yam *(Dioscorea)*. P. 321
White or very pale yellow-green flowers
    Small dangling, bell-shaped flowers hanging beneath the leaves. Smooth Solomon's seal *(Polygonatum biflorum)*. P. 312
    Tiny creamy-white flowers in foamy-looking terminal clusters. False Solomon's seal *(Smilacina racemosa)*. P. 313

Opposite or Whorled Simple Leaves

White or pale pink flowers with 5–10 petals or petal-like parts
    Leaves large, deeply lobed, circular in outline. Solitary flower grows beneath them. Mayapple *(Podophyllum peltatum)*. P. 49
    Whorled stem leaves are simple or compound; long-stalked basal leaves compound. One to several flowers growing above the stem leaves. Rue-anemone *(Anemonella thalictroides)*. P. 40
Greenish-yellow flowers
    Leaves whorled. Flowers ⅓–¾" across with swept-back petals hanging beneath the top leaf whorl. Indian cucumber root *(Medeola virginiana)*. P. 316
    Leaves whorled, opposite, or alternate. Small clustered flowers on drooping stalks. Wild yam *(Dioscorea)*. P. 321

Flowers with Seven or More Regular Parts

Basal Leaves Only

Yellow flowers
    Leaves toothed and/or lobed
        Dandelion-like flower head on a thick, reddish, scaly stalk. Leaves appear after flowers, and leaf shape suggests a colt's foot. Coltsfoot *(Tussilago farfara)*. P. 291
        Familiar dandelion. Leaves toothed, lobed, and/or divided. Common dandelion *(Taraxacum officinale)*. P. 290
    Leaves untoothed or barely toothed
        Basal leaves purple-veined and with purplish lower surfaces (a few small stem leaves sometimes present). Rattlesnake weed *(Hieracium venosum)* P. 292
        Leaves not purple-veined. Field hawkweed *(Hieracium caespitosum)*. P. 293
Flowers not yellow
    Flowers white. Eight or more delicate petals; flower at first cup-shaped but later nearly flat, 1–2" wide. Leaf circular in outline but deeply lobed and bluntly toothed. Bloodroot *(Sanguinaria canadensis)*. P. 51

Flowers blue, pink, lavender, purple, or white, ½–1" across with 6–12 petal-like parts. Leaves with 3 rounded lobes and a heart-shaped base. Round-lobed hepatica *(Hepatica americana).* P. 41

Alternate Simple Leaves

Yellow flowers
  Spring to early summer flowers
    Basal leaves purple-veined and with purplish lower surfaces. A few small stem leaves sometimes present. Rattlesnake weed *(Hieracium venosum).* P. 292
    Flowers ½–1¼" wide. Stem leaves pinnately lobed. Basal leaves variable.
      Basal leaves heart-shaped or egg-shaped with heart-shaped base. Golden ragwort *(Senecio aureus).* P. 246
      Basal leaves egg-shaped with tapered base. Round-leaved ragwort *(Senecio obovatus),* mentioned under "Similar species," P. 246
      Basal leaves narrow and tapered at base. Balsam ragwort *(Senecio pauperculus).* P. 247
  Summer to fall flowers 1¼–4" wide
    Flowers golden-yellow with chocolate center, 1½–4" wide. Black-eyed Susan *(Rudbeckia hirta).* P. 249
    Flowers greenish-yellow with drooping petal-like rays. Plant stalk with vertical "wings." Wingstem *(Verbesina alternifolia).* P. 250
  Summer to fall flowers ¼–1¼" wide
    Leaves with untoothed or barely toothed margins. Flowers ½–1" wide in terminal clusters. Hawkweeds *(Hieracium).* Pp. 294–95
    Leaves lobed and toothed
      Flowers ½–1¼" wide. Leaves with spiny teeth and stalkless, clasping bases. Sow-thistles *(Sonchus).* P. 296
      Flowers about ¼" wide. Lettuce species *(Lactuca).* P. 298
White, pale pink, pale greenish, blue, purple, or lavender flowers
  Spring to early summer flowers
    Flowers ½–1" across; white or pale pink with yellow centers; in small clusters. Fleabanes *(Erigeron).* Pp. 252–54
    Flowers 1–2½" across. White with yellow center. One flower head per stalk. Ox-eye daisy *(Leucanthemum vulgare).* P. 248
  Summer to fall flowers
    Flowers bell-shaped. Creamy white, pinkish, or greenish rays in nodding, slightly flared, bell-shaped heads, ½–1½" long. Lion's-foot *(Prenanthes).* P. 298

Flowers not bell-shaped
>> Blue flowers
>>> Flowers stalkless, 1–1½" wide. Chicory *(Cichorium intybus).*
P. 295
>>> Flowers ½" or less across. In large, branched clusters. Tall blue
lettuce *(Lactuca biennis).* P. 297
>>> *See also* asters, *next.*
>> White, blue, lavender, violet, or purple flowers ¼–1½" across, with
lance-shaped, egg-shaped, or heart-shaped leaves, either toothed
or untoothed. Flower heads borne in clusters of various shapes.
Many species blooming on Sugarloaf. Asters *(Aster).* Pp. 255-60

Alternate Compound Leaves

Flowers bell-shaped; leaves simple and/or compound. Lion's-foot *(Prenanthes).* P. 298

Flowers not bell-shaped. Flowers with greenish-yellow centers and drooping lemon-yellow petal-like rays. Green-headed coneflower *(Rudbeckia laciniata).* P. 250

Opposite or Whorled Simple Leaves

Leaves Usually Whorled

White flowers. Stem leaves usually whorled. Flowers ⅔–1" across with 5–10 petal-like parts. Whorled leaves simple or compound; leaves or leaflets with 3 blunt lobes. Compound basal leaves. Rue-anemone *(Anemonella thalictroides).* P. 40

Leaves Usually Merely Opposite

White flowers 1–2" across with 6–9 petals. Deeply lobed leaves are circular in outline. Mayapple *(Podophyllum peltatum).* P. 49

Yellow flowers. Yellow sunflowers *(Helianthus).* Pp. 251–52

Opposite or Whorled Compound Leaves

Leaves Usually Whorled

White flowers. Flowers ⅔–1" across with 5–10 petal-like parts. Whorled leaves compound or simple; leaves or leaflets with 3 blunt lobes. Compound basal leaves. Rue-anemone *(Anemonella thalictroides).* P. 40

Leaves Usually Merely Opposite

Golden-yellow flowers, 1½–2½" across. Leaves pinnately compound. Tickseed sunflower *(Bidens polylepis).* P. 251

Flower Parts Too Numerous, Tiny, and/or Indistinct to Easily Count

Basal Leaves Only

White to pale pink flowers, in several small terminal clusters resembling pussy toes. Plantain-leaved pussytoes *(Antennaria plantaginifolia)*. P. 275

Alternate Simple Leaves

Greenish flowers
    Bristly plant stalk with stinging hairs. Wood nettle *(Laportea canadensis)*. P. 59
    Plant stalk without stinging hairs
        Tiny flowers in tall branched clusters. Bitter dock *(Rumex obtusifolius)*. P. 73
        Small flower clusters surrounded by leafy bracts, growing from the leaf axils and terminally. Three-seeded mercury *(Acalypha rhomboidea)*. P. 152
        See also horseweed, *next.*
White flowers
    Upper leaves often untoothed; lower leaves usually toothed
        Flowers in large, branched clusters. Each tiny flower head greenish with many upright whitish rays that do not spread. Plant 1–7'. Horseweed *(Conyza canadensis)*. P. 266
        Creamy white and yellow flowers in narrow, upright, usually unbranched clusters. Plant 6–30". Silverrod *(Solidago bicolor)*. P. 271
    Leaves with untoothed or wavy margins. Tiny bell-shaped flowers with overlapping bracts, in branched clusters. Lower leaf surfaces and plant stalk densely white-woolly. Sweet everlasting *(Gnaphalium obtusifolium)*. P. 289
    Leaves toothed and sometimes lobed
        Small flowers in flat clusters. Main stem leaves fan-shaped with triangular teeth or shallow lobes. Pale Indian plantain *(Arnoglossum atriplicifolium)*. P. 284
        Small white flowers protrude from tubular green envelope. Flower heads borne in loose terminal and upper axillary clusters. Leaves more or less lance-shaped; plant stalk ribbed or grooved. Pilewort *(Erechtites hieracifolia)*. P. 288
Yellow flowers. Small golden-yellow flowers borne in variously arranged clusters. Common summer-to-fall wildflowers of Sugarloaf. Goldenrods *(Solidago)*. Pp. 266–74

Purple or purplish-pink flowers
    Flowers in roundish, egg-shaped, or cylindric bristly heads
        Leaves spiny-toothed and often lobed. Thistles *(Cirsium, Carduus).*
        Pp. 286–87
        Leaves egg-shaped or heart-shaped with smooth, wavy, or shallowly
        toothed margins. Common burdock *(Arctium minus).* P. 283
Flowers borne in yellowish, brownish, or greenish prickly burs. Leaves
coarsely toothed and often shallowly lobed (like a maple leaf). Common
cocklebur *(Xanthium strumarium).* P. 284

Alternate Compound Leaves

White flowers
    Small flowers in tall, narrow clusters. Many stamens give the flowers a
    "fuzzy" look. Toothed leaflets often lobed and/or grouped in patterns of
    threes. Black cohosh *(Cimicifuga racemosa).* P. 44
    Small flowers in loose, branched clusters
        Minute white or greenish-white flowers in tight, bristly clusters.
        Lower leaves usually long-stalked and divided into 3 toothed leaflets,
        the outer 2 leaflets often so deeply cleft that the leaf appears to have 5
        leaflets. Snakeroots *(Sanicula).* Pp. 170–71
        Creamy white "starburst" flower clusters. Leaves twice divided with
        bluntly lobed and/or toothed leaflets. Tall meadow-rue *(Thalictrum
        pubescens).* P. 45
Small greenish flowers in erect or slightly nodding clusters
    Leaves fernlike, aromatic, densely white-woolly beneath. Not common
    on Sugarloaf. Mugwort *(Artemisia vulgaris).* P. 302
    Leaves may be slightly white-woolly beneath but not densely so. Upper
    leaves often alternate, lower leaves opposite. Common on and around
    Sugarloaf. Common ragweed *(Ambrosia artemisiifolia).* P. 300

Opposite or Whorled Simple Leaves

Greenish flowers
    At least some leaves usually 3-lobed (2-lobed and unlobed leaves also
    often present). Tiny flowers in erect or arching clusters. Great ragweed
    (Ambrosia trifida). P. 301
    Leaves not lobed
        Plant with stinging hairs. Minute flowers in spreading or drooping
        clusters. Stinging nettle *(Urtica dioica).* P. 56
        Plants without stinging hairs
            Leaves shiny, plant stalk translucent. Flowers minute in small
            branching clusters from the leaf axils. Clearweed *(Pilea pumila).*
            P. 58

Leaves not shiny. Minute flowers in stiff, compact, continuous or interrupted clusters, growing from the leaf axils. False nettle *(Boehmeria cylindrica)*. P. 57
White flowers
Leaves egg-shaped or heart-shaped. Small flowers in clusters
Leaves with stalks ¾" or longer. White snakeroot *(Eupatorium rugosum)*. P. 282
Leaves without stalks or with very short stalks. Round-leaved thoroughwort *(Eupatorium rotundifolium)*. P. 279
Leaves lance-shaped, stalkless, with leaf bases often fused around the plant stalk. Boneset *(Eupatorium perfoliatum)*. P. 280
Purple, violet, or blue-violet flowers
Flowers dusky purplish-pink. Leaves whorled. Plant tall (3–10'). Joe-Pye-weeds *(Eupatorium)*. P. 278
Flowers violet or blue-violet. Leaves merely opposite. Plant 6"-3'. Mistflower *(Eupatorium coelestinum)*. P. 277

Opposite Compound Leaves

Greenish flowers in erect or slightly nodding clusters. Leaves fernlike. Opposite and alternate leaves often on the same plant. Common ragweed *(Ambrosia artemisiifolia)*. P. 300
Yellow flowers
Orange-yellow central disk with or without a few surrounding yellow petal-like rays. Flower heads surrounded by narrow leafy bracts. Leaves with 3–5 sharply toothed leaflets. Beggar-ticks *(Bidens frondosa)*. P. 261
Small central disk with or without a few surrounding paler yellow petal-like rays. Needlelike barbed fruit soon appears. Leaves fernlike with lobed, toothed leaflets. Spanish needles *(Bidens bipinnata)*. P. 262

II. WOODY PLANTS

Trees

A. *Irregular Flowers*

Alternate Simple Leaves

Purplish-pink flowers. Redbud *(Cercis canadensis)*. P. 141

Alternate Compound Leaves

White flowers. Black locust *(Robinia pseudoacacia)*. P. 142

Opposite Simple Leaves

Lavender flowers. Paulownia *(Paulownia tomentosa).* P. 224

B. Regular Flowers

Flowers with Four Regular Parts

Alternate Simple Leaves

Yellow flowers. Common witch-hazel *(Hamamelis virginiana).* P. 54

Opposite Simple Leaves

White flowers, ½–1¼" long, with slender, delicate petals. Borne in drooping, airy clusters. Fringe-tree *(Chionanthus virginicus).* P. 212
Showy white or pale pink flowers 2–4" across, with wide petal-like parts
that are notched at the tip. Flowering dogwood *(Cornus florida).* P. 150

Flowers with Five Regular Parts

Alternate Simple Leaves

White or pale pink flowers, ¾–1½" across
  Flowers slightly asymmetrically star-shaped with narrow petals. Com-
  mon shadbush *(Amelanchier arborea).* P. 130
  Flowers with full (not narrow) petals. Sweet cherry *(Prunus avium).*
  P. 131

Opposite Simple Leaves

Small red flowers borne in clusters in early spring. Red maple *(Acer
rubrum).* P. 157

Flowers with Six Regular Parts

Alternate Simple Leaves

Leaves always lobed. Large, showy tulip-shaped flowers that are green, orange, and yellow. Tulip-tree *(Liriodendron tulipifera).* P. 34
Leaves lobed and unlobed, often on the same tree. Small yellow-green
flowers in showy round clusters. Leaves unlobed, lobed in a mittenlike pattern, and 3-lobed. Sassafras *(Sassafras albidum).* P. 39
Leaves not lobed. Purple, maroon, or brownish flowers that are somewhat
bell-shaped. Large tropical-looking leaves. A small tree or large shrub.
Pawpaw *(Asimina triloba).* P. 36

Shrubs

Flowers with Four Regular Parts. *See key entries under* Trees

Flowers with Five Regular Parts

Alternate Simple Leaves

Leaves evergreen

Flowers ¾–1" across, white or pale pink with a deep pink ring at the center. Borne in snowball-shaped clusters. Abundant on Sugarloaf. Mountain laurel *(Kalmia latifolia)*. P. 98

Flowers white or pale pink, 1–2½" across, in large clusters. Uppermost petal spotted greenish-yellow. Not common on Sugarloaf. Great rhododendron *(Rhododendron maximum)*. P. 102

Leaves not evergreen

White, pink, or purplish flowers

Leaves untoothed or minutely toothed. Flowers bell-shaped or funnel-shaped

Large, pink, showy, funnel-shaped, fragrant flowers with flared lobes and protruding stamens and pistil. Flowers 1–1¾" across. Pinxter flower *(Rhododendron periclymenoides)*. P. 99

Small, variously hued, bell-shaped flowers

Flowers flared. Deerberry *(Vaccinium stamineum)*. P. 104

Flowers tubular (not flared)

Leaves with tiny, shiny, resinous dots. Black huckleberry *(Gaylussacia baccata)*. P. 104

Leaves without resinous dots. Lowbush blueberry *(Vaccinium pallidum)*. P. 103

Leaves always toothed. Flowers not bell-shaped or funnel-shaped

Small pink flowers, ¼" across, in flat-topped clusters. Japanese spiraea *(Spiraea japonica)*. P. 125

White flowers (sometimes pink-tinged or purple-tinged), ⅓–⅔" across, in flat or rounded, usually branched clusters. Red chokeberry *(Aronia arbutifolia)*. P. 129

Orange flowers. Flame azalea *(Rhododendron calendulaceum)*. P. 101

Alternate Compound Leaves

Prickly and/or bristly shrubs

Pink fragrant flowers, usually borne singly. Plant upright. Flowers 1–2" across with yellow stamens. Pasture rose *(Rosa carolina)*. P. 123

White or pale pink flowers in clusters

Plants with long, arching stalks
Fragrant flowers in large clusters. Leaves with 7–9 leaflets. An abundant plant of Sugarloaf fields, thickets, and roadsides. Multiflora rose *(Rosa multiflora)*. P. 124
Leaflets usually 3, with the middle leaflet largest. Plant bears reddish hairs on stalks and leaf stems. Wineberry *(Rubus phoenicolasius)*. P. 126
Flowers in small clusters. Leaflets usually 3–5 (sometimes 7). Plant lacks reddish hairs. Common blackberry *(Rubus allegheniensis)*. P. 127
Low trailing plants
Leaflets in 3s and 5s. Plant with curved prickles. Common dewberry *(Rubus flagellaris)*. P. 128
Shining, sometimes evergreen leaflets in 3s (sometimes 5s). Plant with thin, weak bristles. Swamp dewberry *(Rubus hispidus)*. P. 128

Opposite Simple Leaves

Leaves lobed. Tiny flowers in flat-topped clusters. Leaves maplelike. Maple-leaved viburnum *(Viburnum acerifolium)*. P. 242
Leaves not lobed
Leaves toothed. Small flowers in flat-topped clusters
Leaf stalks 1–3" long. Each flower has 8–10 stamens. Wild hydrangea *(Hydrangea arborescens)*. P. 111
Leaf stalks usually short (in one species may be up to 1¼" long). Each flower has 5 stamens. Black-haw and other viburnums *(Viburnum)* Pp. 243–44
Leaves untoothed. Yellow flowers. Bushy St. John's-wort *(Hypericum densiflorum)* and shrubby St. John's-wort *(H. prolificum)*. P. 77

Opposite Compound Leaves

Tiny white or pale yellow flowers in flat-topped clusters. Leaves pinnately compound. Common elderberry *(Sambucus canadensis)*. P. 241

Flowers with Six Regular Parts

Alternate Simple Leaves

Tiny yellow early spring flowers in dense clusters. Spicebush *(Lindera benzoin)*. P. 37

Woody Vines

A. *Irregular Flowers*

Opposite Simple Leaves

White or pale yellow extremely fragrant flowers of late spring and early summer. Japanese honeysuckle *(Lonicera japonica)*. P. 240

B. *Regular Flowers*

Flowers with Five Regular Parts

Alternate Compound Leaves

Small, greenish, star-shaped flowers. Palmately compound leaves. Virginia creeper *(Parthenocissus quinquefolia)*. P. 154

Opposite Compound Leaves

Showy red or orange-red trumpet-shaped flowers with spreading lobes. Leaves pinnately compound. Trumpet creeper *(Campsis radicans)*. P. 228

Flowers with Six Regular Parts

Alternate Simple Leaves

Small greenish flowers in clusters. A climbing prickly vine. Common greenbrier *(Smilax rotundifolia)*. P. 319

Guide to Flowering Plants

DICOTYLEDONS

Magnolia Family
Magnoliaceae

The magnolia family produces some of the world's most beautiful flowering trees and shrubs. **Family characteristics:** 13 genera and 225 species worldwide. Very interesting distribution with all species in either temperate and tropical southeast Asia or temperate southeastern North America through Central America and in parts of South America. The two genera found in the eastern United States—*Magnolia* and *Liriodendron*—also are found in Asia. According to V. H. Heywood's *Flowering Plants of the World,* "Fossil records indicate that the family was formerly much more widely distributed in the Northern Hemisphere." **Economic importance:** Very important ornamental trees and shrubs, especially of the *Magnolia* genus. New cultivars are continually being developed for the nursery trade. Some Asian magnolias used as medicines. Our native tulip-tree *(Liriodendron tulipifera)* is an important timber tree. **Flowers:** Perfect, regular, often very showy with 3 sepals and 6 or more petals. Often the sepals and petals are alike and are called tepals. Many conspicuous spirally arranged stamens. **Fruit:** A conelike aggregate of follicles, samaras, or (rarely) berries. **Leaves:** Alternate, simple, entire or lobed; deciduous or evergreen. **Growth habits:** Trees and shrubs. **Occurrence on Sugarloaf:** The tulip-tree is one of Sugarloaf's most common large woodland trees. A few southern magnolias *(Magnolia grandiflora)* are planted near the base of the mountain. No native magnolias occur naturally on Sugarloaf, but four species are indigenous to Maryland or the nearby mountains of Virginia and West Virginia: the cucumber tree *(M. acuminata)* grows on Catoctin Mountain, the umbrella magnolia *(M. tripetala)* and Fraser or mountain magnolia *(M. fraseri)* grow in the mountains farther west, and the sweetbay magnolia *(M. virginiana)* is a coastal plain species. Both native and exotic magnolias are cultivated in the Baltimore-Washington area, and native magnolias occasionally escape from cultivation. This probably explains the occasional occurrence of umbrella magnolias east of the mountains.

Tree

Tulip-Tree (Tulip Poplar or Yellow Poplar)
Liriodendron tulipifera L.
Magnolia Family (Magnoliaceae)

The tulip-tree is the first tree to glimmer with the yellow-green hue of spring in the mid-Atlantic piedmont. The tree offers another spectacle in autumn when its distinctively shaped leaves turn yellow. Tulip-tree flowers, appearing in May, are large and multicolored, but because the tree is so tall and the flowers are borne high off the ground, many people miss them. Sugarloaf visitors are more apt to notice the remains of the upright woody fruit clusters on the tree's naked winter branchlets. Tulip-tree has long been an important timber tree. American Indians used it to make dugout canoes. Tulip-tree (or tulip poplar) is the official state tree of Indiana, Kentucky, and Tennessee. **Flowers:** Broadly tulip-shaped, 6-petaled, 1½–2½" tall. Petals are greenish at the top with a broad orange band near the base; 3 large sepals are usually down-curved. Many yellow stamens arranged around a yellowish

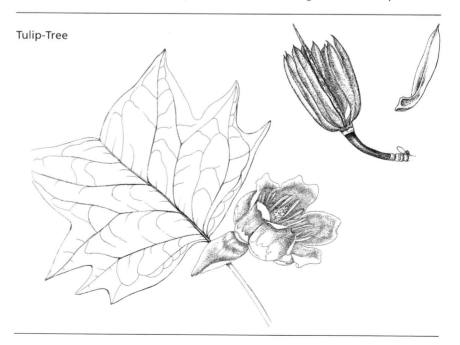

Tulip-Tree

conelike structure in the center of the flower. Flowers borne singly toward the ends of the branchlets after the leaves emerge in spring. **Fruit:** A brown, erect conelike aggregate of samaras, 1½–3" high. In the fall the winged samaras break free and fall to the ground, but the conelike central axis often remains on the tree through the winter. **Leaves:** Simple, alternate, deciduous; 4-lobed or sometimes with an extra pair of lobes at the base; 3–6" high and 3–6½" wide. Margin smooth. Leaf nearly flat across the bottom; top 2 lobes are separated by a wide and shallow V-shaped sinus. Usually glabrous. Petioles slender, 2–6" long. Large stipules often fall after leaves have matured. **Growth habits:** A tall, handsome tree with a long, straight trunk and oblong crown. Its profile is striking in winter because of its stature and the many candlelike remains of fall fruit. **Bark and twigs:** Bark becoming evenly and shallowly furrowed with age; light brown or gray. Twigs reddish-brown with rounded or oval leaf scars. Stipular scars encircling the twig. Winter buds flattened, shaped like ducks' bills. **Habitat and range:** Rich woods, coves, abandoned fields; southern New England to Michigan and Illinois, south to Florida and Louisiana. Often cultivated. **Herbal lore:** According to Steven Foster and James A. Duke (Peterson Field Guides' *Field Guide to Medicinal Plants: Eastern and Central North America*), "American Indians used bark tea for indigestion, dysentery, rheumatism, pinworms, fevers, and in cough syrups; externally, as a wash on fractured limbs, wounds, boils, snakebites. Green bark chewed as an aphrodisiac, stimulant. Bark tea a folk remedy for malaria, toothaches; ointment from buds used for burns, inflammation. Crushed leaves poulticed for headaches." **Wildlife lore:** Bees use the flowers for nectar, and many bird and mammal species feed on the samaras. Whitetail deer browse the seedling trees. **On Sugarloaf—Blooming time:** Late April–early June. **Locations:** Very common mountainwide; large stands become evident in early spring when the tree is the mountain's first to leaf out. **Similar species:** Leaves could possibly be confused with maple (*Acer* spp.) leaves.

Custard-Apple Family

Annonaceae

The custard-apple family is a largely tropical family of mainly trees and shrubs. One temperate zone species, the pawpaw *(Asimina triloba)*, grows in the Sugarloaf area, along Bear Branch. **Family characteristics:** 130 genera and 2,300 species worldwide. **Economic importance:** Members of the custard-apple family produce food for humans and wildlife and are the source of aromatic oils. **Flowers:** Perfect, regular, with 6 petals arranged in 2 whorls and 3 sepals. **Leaves:** Entire.

Tree or Shrub

Pawpaw

Asimina triloba (L.) Dunal
Custard-Apple Family (Annonaceae)

The pawpaw is the only member of the largely tropical custard-apple family that is indigenous to northeastern North America. **Flowers:** Purple, maroon, or brownish, just before the leaves in spring. Slightly drooping and somewhat bell-like with two layers of 3 petals (6 in all). The outer 3 petals curve backwards. Petals are ovate or nearly round; flowers 1–2" across, borne along the twigs. **Fruit:** Greenish-yellow banana-like berry, 2–6" long. Edible, delicious. Favored by humans, bears, raccoons, opossums, and wild turkeys. **Leaves:** Simple, alternate, deciduous, 6–12" long with an entire margin, abruptly pointed apex, and wedge-shaped base. Large leaves are tropical-looking. **Growth habits:** Small tree or tall shrub. **Twigs:** Slender, brown, pubescent when young, with dark brown woolly winter buds. **Habitat and range:** Moist woods, streamsides, riversides; scattered distribution in southern Ontario and eastern United States from New York to Florida, west to Nebraska and Texas. **Herbal lore:** Foster and Duke describe a contradictory herbal profile in Peterson Field Guides' *Field Guide to Medicinal Plants: Eastern and Central North America:* "Fruit edible, delicious; also a laxative. Leaves

Pawpaw

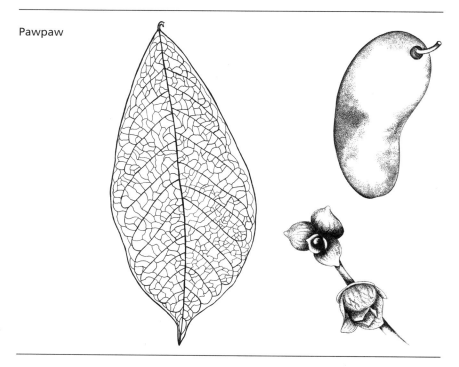

insecticidal, diuretic; applied to abscesses. Seeds emetic, narcotic (produce stupor). The powdered seeds, formerly applied to the heads of children to control lice, have insecticidal properties. Warning: Seeds toxic. Leaves may cause rash." **On Sugarloaf—Blooming time:** April–May. **Fruiting time:** Fruit matures in autumn. **Locations:** Quite common along lower stretches of Bear Branch and Bennett Creek. **Similar species:** None on Sugarloaf but could be confused with the umbrella magnolia *(Magnolia tripetala)* in the mountains to the west.

Laurel Family

Lauraceae

Fruit, leaves, and bark of laurel family plants provide avocados, bay leaves, cinnamon, and, closer to home, sassafras oil. In Greek mythology, when Daphne wanted to escape from Apollo, she became a laurel tree. The family does not include Sugarloaf's mountain laurel, which is in the heath family. **Family characteristics:** 30–50 genera and 2,000 plus species worldwide. Mainly tropical and subtropical with a few genera in temperate climates. **Economic importance:** Spices, herbs, and oils; fruit; ornamentals; timber; medicines. **Flowers:** Regular, perfect or unisexual, usually with 6 (sometimes 4) tepals. **Fruit:** A berry or drupe. **Leaves:** Alternate, simple, entire or lobed. **Growth habits:** Mostly trees and shrubs; often aromatic. **Occurrence on Sugarloaf:** Spicebush *(Lindera benzoin)* grows in the rich woods of Sugarloaf's lower slopes, especially along streams and near springs. Sassafras *(Sassafras albidum)* is common on the mountain, especially at forest edges along roads and some stretches of trail.

Shrub

Spicebush

Lindera benzoin (L.) Blume
Laurel Family (Lauraceae)

One of the earliest spring signs in eastern North America is the golden glow created by spicebush flowers. Spicebush shares its streamside habitat on Sugarloaf Mountain with skunk cabbage and cinnamon fern. As the spicebush blooms, brilliant green skunk cabbage leaves and fern fiddleheads simultaneously appear from the wet forest floor, creating a charming spring tableau. Spicebush twigs, leaves, and fruit exude a pleasant spicy fragrance when crushed and have been used to make tea and spice. **Flowers:** Yellow, before the leaves in early spring. Individual flowers ⅛–¼" across, with 6 petal-

Spicebush

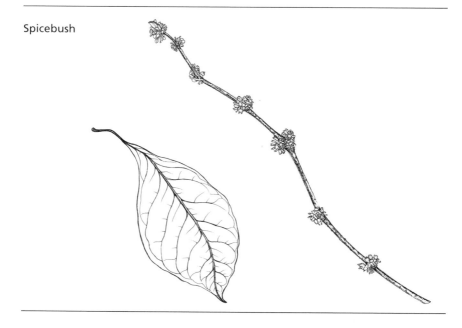

like sepals (or tepals). Flowers borne in dense lateral clusters. **Fruit:** Small, red, berrylike drupe (green when immature). **Leaves:** Simple, alternate, deciduous. Obovate, oblong-obovate, elliptic, or ovate, 2–6" long. Apex abruptly or gradually pointed, base wedge-shaped, narrowed to short petiole. Margins entire. Glabrous or barely pubescent below. **Height and growth habits:** Much-branched shrub up to 16' tall. **Twigs:** Slender, glabrous, brown, with spicy odor when scratched. Flower buds small, paired, round; leaf buds tiny, oblong, and obtuse. **Habitat and range:** Rich, moist woods, streamsides, and springs; southwestern Maine to southern Ontario, Iowa, and southeastern Kansas; south to Florida and Texas. **Wildlife lore:** Birds, deer, rabbits, and other small mammals favor the twigs and fruit of the aromatic spicebush. Spicebush swallowtail butterflies use this shrub as a larval host plant. **Herbal lore:** Spicebush leaves, bark, fruit, and twigs have all been used medicinally for a wide range of conditions from colds to rheumatism. Early American settlers used the fruit as an allspice substitute. **On Sugarloaf—Blooming time:** March–early May. **Fruiting time:** Late summer–fall. **Locations:** Rich woods, springs, and streamsides mountainwide; very common along Bear Branch. **Similar species:** Sassafras *(Sassafras albidum)* also has spicy leaves and twigs, but its leaves are often 2- or 3-lobed, its fruit is dark blue, and its twigs are greenish and glaucous. Dogwood *(Cornus* spp.) twigs and leaves have no spicy odor when crushed.

Tree

Sassafras

Sassafras albidum (Nutt.) Nees
Laurel Family (Lauraceae)

Sassafras produces three types of leaves, some unlobed, some 3-lobed, and some 2-lobed. This tree serves as a food source for wildlife and has long been used medicinally and as a tea, flavoring, and soup thickener. The flowering of the sassafras tree is an early sign of spring in Sugarloaf country. **Flowers:** Dioecious (male and female flowers on separate trees), yellow-green, in showy round clusters in early to mid spring. Small individual flowers star-shaped with 6 tepals. **Fruit:** A dark blue berrylike drupe, about ⅓" long and ellipsoid in shape, on a red or orange 1½–4" stalk. **Leaves:** Simple, alternate, 3–7½" long. Three major leaf shapes, often all on the same tree: (1) ovate; (2) mittenlike, with one large lobe and one smaller "thumb"; and (3) 3-lobed. Margin smooth. Base wedge-shaped. Velvety-pubescent or glabrous beneath. Petiole ⅔–3½" long. Young leaves emerge with the spring flowers. Autumn color: orange, yellow, and red. **Growth habits:** Small to medium-sized tree. **Bark and twigs:** Bark brown or reddish-brown and furrowed. Twigs greenish, glaucous, with spicy odor when broken. Terminal bud present. **Habitat and range:** Woods, thickets, roadsides, fields; southern Maine to Michigan, south to Florida and eastern Texas. **Wildlife lore:** According to Melvin L. Brown and Russell G. Brown's *Woody Plants of Maryland*, "Upland gamebirds, squirrels, and numerous songbirds eat the fruits; rabbits eat the bark in winter and deer browse the twigs and leaves." **Herbal lore:** Long a cherished herbal, sassafras has fallen into disfavor during recent years since the discovery that a component of oil of sassafras may be carcinogenic. This has not dissuaded many of those who swear by sassafras root-bark tea as a spring tonic and blood purifier. Sassafras roots, twigs, and leaves have been employed to treat wide-ranging medical conditions, including arthritis and liver, bowel, and kidney ailments. **On Sugarloaf—Blooming time:** March–May. **Fruiting time:** Late summer–fall. **Locations:** Common on the mountain and throughout Sugarloaf country, especially along roadsides and in hedgerows. **Similar species:** Spicebush *(Lindera benzoin)* is a shrub with early yellow flowers and spicy twigs. Spicebush leaves are always unlobed, and its fruit is red. Spicebush is found in wet woodlands, often along streams (including Bear Branch).

Buttercup Family

Ranunculaceae

A large family of plants containing many familiar garden ornamentals belonging to the genera *Clematis, Aconitum, Helleborus, Anemone,* and *Delphinium.* Several Sugarloaf wildflowers, native and naturalized, belong to the buttercup family, including—of course—the buttercups! Many plants of this family have been used as herbal medicines. A number are toxic. According to Heywood's *Flowering Plants of the World,* "Victorian medical books give lurid details of the symptoms and deaths of gardeners who have inadvertently eaten *Aconitum* tubers, having confused them with Jerusalem artichokes." **Family characteristics:** 50 genera and 2,000 species worldwide. **Flowers:** Usually regular; petals present or absent. Often the sepals are petaloid. Stamens usually numerous. Flower parts are often borne on a receptacle that resembles a thimble. **Fruit:** A follicle, achene, berry, or capsule. **Leaves:** Usually alternate, sometimes opposite, whorled, or basal only. Often deeply toothed, lobed, or divided. **Growth habits:** Mostly herbs, some shrubs and woody vines. **Occurrence on Sugarloaf:** Several species in varied habitats. In addition to the herbaceous plants described and illustrated in the next entries, a woody vine called virgin's bower *(Clematis virginiana)* is briefly described in the Botanical Key and Guide to Trees, Shrubs, and Woody Vines.

Rue-Anemone (Windflower)

Anemonella thalictroides (L.) Spach
Buttercup Family (Ranunculaceae)

The genus name of this plant, *Anemonella,* comes from the Greek word for wind. Rue-anemone (or windflower) trembles in the slightest breeze. This delicate spring wildflower grows in masses along a few stretches of Sugarloaf's trails. **Flowers:** White or pale pink, ⅔–1" across, with 5–10 petal-like sepals. One to several flowers on a single slender plant stalk. **Leaves:** Stem leaves whorled, compound or simple, each leaf or leaflet with (usually) 3 blunt teeth or lobes. Stem leaves grow just below the flower stalks; compound basal leaves on long petioles. **Height:** 3–8". **Habitat and range:** Woodlands; New England to Minnesota and Kansas; south to Florida and Arkansas. **Herbal lore:** American Indians used the root tea to treat abdominal upsets. (Plant may have toxic properties.) **On Sugarloaf—Blooming time:** Late March–May. **Locations:** White Trail, Yellow Trail, Bear Branch, Mount Ephraim Road. **Similar species:** Bloodroot *(Sanguinaria canadensis)* and round-lobed hepatica *(Hepatica americana)* have somewhat similar flowers, but both have basal leaves only. Bloodroot and round-lobed hepat-

Rue-Anemone

ica are less common on Sugarloaf than rue-anemone, but all three species can be found in close proximity to one another along Bear Branch. The locally rarer wood anemone *(Anemone quinquefolia)* grows in a few places in the Monocacy Natural Resources Management Area but not on the mountain proper. Wood anemone has (mostly) 5 petal-like sepals (may have 4–9) per flower, and its deeply 3- or 5-lobed leaves are also whorled. Consult *Newcomb's Wildflower Guide* by Lawrence Newcomb or *A Field Guide to Wildflowers of Northeastern and North-Central North America* by Roger Tory Peterson and Margaret McKenny for illustration.

Round-Lobed Hepatica

Hepatica americana (DC.) Ker Gawl.
Buttercup Family (Ranunculaceae)

A charming spring wildflower, variously colored blue, pink, lavender, or white. Common in many northeastern woodlands but rare on Sugarloaf. **Flowers:** ½–1" wide, with 6–12 blue, pink, white, lavender, or purple petal-like sepals. Slightly cup-shaped to nearly flat with 3 sepal-like bracts beneath the petal-like sepals and a reddish pubescent stem. One flower per stem. **Leaves:** Very distinctive basal leaves only, each with 3 rounded lobes and heart-shaped base. Petiole pubescent. **Height and growth habits:** 3–7" high; flowers upright or slightly nodding, leaves recumbent or partially upright. **Habitat and range:** Upland woods; eastern Canada south to Georgia and Missouri. **Herbal lore:** American Indians used leaf tea of this and a similar species, sharp-lobed hepatica or liverleaf *(H. acutiloba),* for a variety of ail-

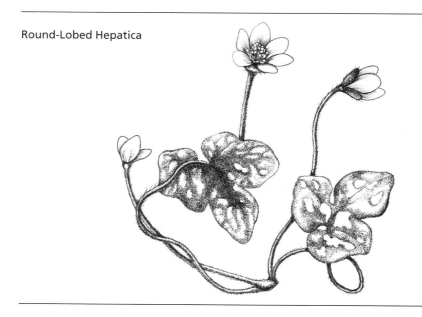

Round-Lobed Hepatica

ments, including coughs, fevers, and liver complaints. **On Sugarloaf—Blooming time:** Late March–April. **Location:** Bear Branch. **Similar species:** Rue-anemone *(Anemonella thalictroides)* is far more common on Sugarloaf and has stem leaves as well as basal ones. Bloodroot *(Sanguinaria canadensis)* has larger flowers and variously lobed (not strictly 3-lobed) basal leaves. All three species grow along Bear Branch and bloom simultaneously. Sharp-lobed hepatica *(H. acutiloba)* has leaves with pointed, rather than rounded, lobes. It grows in the mountains of far western Maryland, according to Melvin L. Brown and Russell G. Brown's *Herbaceous Plants of Maryland*.

Columbine

Aquilegia L.
Buttercup Family (Ranunculaceae)

Two species of columbine, one native and one introduced, grow in northeastern North America, and both are found on Sugarloaf. The more common is a Eurasian species which has become naturalized. Our native columbine was reported in a 1987 Stronghold plant survey. I have yet to see it growing on the mountain but have seen it blooming on rocky ledges in the area.

European Columbine *(Aquilegia vulgaris* L.). **Flowers:** Purple, blue, white, or pink (ours mostly purple), nodding, ¾–2" long and wide; 5-parted, somewhat bell-shaped. The 5 petals bear erect but incurved hollow spurs that give the flower a horned look. (Stamens do not protrude beyond the rest

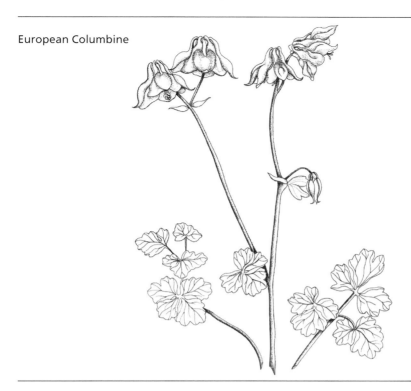

of the flower, or if they do, only barely protrude. In the following species the stamens dramatically protrude.) **Leaves:** Alternate, compound, once or twice divided into 3 bluntly toothed and/or lobed leaflets. Lower leaves long-petioled; uppers may be sessile or nearly so. Size variable. **Height:** 1–3'. **On Sugarloaf—Blooming time:** May–June. **Locations:** Mountain roadsides, parking and picnic areas. **Similar species:** Leaves and flowers unique to genus. Flower color distinguishes this species from the native one.

Wild Columbine (Canadian Columbine) (*Aquilegia canadensis* L.). **Leaves** and **flower** shape similar to European columbine, but flowers are orange-red and yellow, and the spurs on the petals are longer and less incurved (but may be slightly so). Stamens protrude beyond the petals. **Habitat and range:** Rocky woods, moist rock ledges, cliffs, rocky clearings, some peat bogs; eastern United States and Canada west to Saskatchewan and Texas. **Herbal lore:** American Indians used the seeds and roots medicinally. Minute amounts of the crushed seed were used as a "love charm," according to Foster and Duke. In their book, Peterson Field Guides' *Field Guide to Medicinal Plants: Eastern and Central North America,* they note that this plant is potentially poisonous. **In Sugarloaf area—Blooming time:** April–June. **Locations:** Look for wild columbine in rocky areas.

Black Cohosh (Black Snakeroot)

Cimicifuga racemosa (L.) Nutt.
Buttercup Family (Ranunculaceae)

A tall plant that is quite dramatic in bloom. **Flowers:** Small, creamy white, in long, narrow terminal clusters (racemes). Buds are round. When they open, the petals and sepals soon fall off, leaving many white stamens that give the flowers a fuzzy look. Stamens are less than ½" long. Each plant stalk bears one to several flower clusters 3–20" long. **Leaves:** Alternate, compound, and very large. Often growing in a pattern of 3s. The 3 large leaflets are divided into smaller subleaflets that are toothed and ovate, or sometimes lobed. Leaflets and subleaflets vary in size. **Height and growth habits:** 3–8'; tall, narrow flower clusters extend upwards from the leaves. **Habitat and range:** Woodlands, roadsides; Massachusetts to Indiana, south to South Carolina and Missouri. **Herbal lore:** Black cohosh root has been used to treat many conditions, including bronchitis, rheumatism, snakebite, menstrual problems, and childbirth. Foster and Duke report in Peterson Field Guides' *Field Guide to Medicinal Plants: Eastern and Central North America:* "Research has confirmed estrogenic, hypoglycemic, sedative, and anti-inflammatory activ-

Black
Cohosh

ity. Root extract strengthens female reproductive organs in rats." **On Sugarloaf—Blooming time:** June–August. **Locations:** Blue Trail, Yellow Trail, Red Trail, Mount Ephraim Road. **Similar species:** None on Sugarloaf.

Tall Meadow-Rue

Thalictrum pubescens Pursh
(Thalictrum polygamum)
Buttercup Family (Ranunculaceae)

A tall early summer wildflower with fuzzy white apetalous flowers and delicate fernlike leaves. **Flowers:** Cream or white flower clusters at the apex of the plant. The flowers are showy because of their stamens (Peterson and McKenny call them "starry bursts of white threadlike stamens" in *A Field Guide to Wildflowers of Northeastern and North-Central North America*). Each flower is about ¼–½" across, borne in roundish clusters of few to many. **Leaves:** Alternate, compound, twice pinnately divided (easily misconstrued to be whorled). The subleaflets usually have 3 or more rounded or blunt lobes and/or teeth (some are unlobed or 2-lobed and mittenlike). Overall leaf several inches long; subleaflets variable in size. **Height:** 3–8'. **Habitat and**

Tall Meadow-Rue

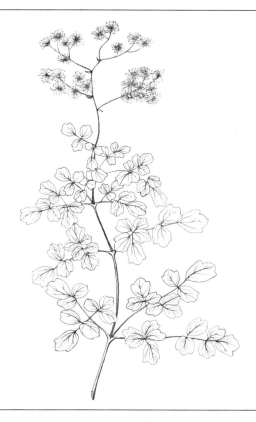

range: Rich woods, moist meadows, and stream banks; eastern Canada to North Carolina, Tennessee, and Indiana. **On Sugarloaf—Blooming time:** June–July. **Locations:** Mount Ephraim Road, Yellow Trail. Also may be found along other mountain roadsides and moist sections of trail. **Similar species:** None likely on Sugarloaf. Early meadow-rue *(T. dioicum)* is a local wildflower which might possibly be found on the mountain. Its leaves are similar, but its earlier spring flowers are drooping, and it's a shorter, more delicate plant. Several other meadow-rues (*Thalictrum* spp.) are native to Maryland, with a few more species in other parts of eastern North America.

Kidneyleaf Buttercup (Aborted Buttercup, Small-Flowered Crowfoot)

Ranunculus abortivus L.
Buttercup Family (Ranunculaceae)

This plant (Sugarloaf's most common buttercup) has inconspicuous flowers with tiny yellow petals and basal leaves that are vaguely kidney-shaped. **Flowers:** Small, with 5 short, thin yellow petals and more conspicuous green centers; ¼–⅓" across. **Leaves:** Basal leaves roughly kidney-shaped with rounded teeth, on long petioles. Basal leaf blades ¾–2½" across. (Some basal leaves may be lobed or divided.) Stem leaves alternate and divided into several narrow lobes, sessile or nearly so. **Height:** 6"–2'. **Habitat and range:** Woodlands; much of United States and Canada. **On Sugarloaf—Blooming**

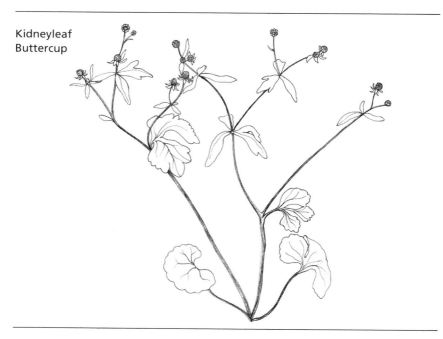

Kidneyleaf
Buttercup

time: March–June. **Locations:** Mountainwide. **Similar species:** The basal leaves separate it from other buttercup and crowfoot species.

Bulbous Buttercup

Ranunculus bulbosus L.
Buttercup Family (Ranunculaceae)

This and the common (or tall) buttercup *(R. acris)* are familiar field and roadside wildflowers of spring and early summer. **Flowers:** Brilliant shiny yellow with 5 roundish petals and usually reflexed sepals, on long stalks. Flowers roughly an inch across when fully open. **Leaves:** Alternate, compound, variable. The principal basal leaves have 3 divided, toothed leaflets,

Bulbous Buttercup

the middle leaflet long-stalked. Leaf stalks pubescent, leaflets downy. Smaller stem leaves are less divided. Plant stalk thickens toward the base, and the root is bulbous. **Height:** 6–18". **Habitat and range:** Fields, meadows, lawns, roadsides; European native, widely naturalized. **On Sugarloaf— Blooming time:** Spring–early summer. **Locations:** Fields, roadsides, open trailsides mountainwide. **Similar species:** Common or tall buttercup *(R. acris)* is not treated individually here. Its sepals are not reflexed, and its basal leaves are divided into unstalked segments. Common buttercup does not have a bulbous root. It blooms slightly later than bulbous buttercup, but blooming times overlap, and locations are similar.

Hispid Buttercup

Ranunculus hispidus Michx.
Buttercup Family (Ranunculaceae)

Hispid buttercup is uncommon on Sugarloaf. Its **leaves** are alternate and usually divided into 3 deeply toothed leaflets. The plant is pubescent, as least when young. The basal leaves are about as long as wide and sometimes are merely deeply 3-lobed rather than divided.

Other Sugarloaf *Ranunculus* species

Hooked Crowfoot

Ranunculus recurvatus Poir.
Buttercup Family (Ranunculaceae)

Hooked crowfoot has pale yellow 5-petaled **flowers** about ⅓" across with sepals that are about the same length or slightly longer than the small petals. **Leaves** are alternate (but may appear opposite), 3-lobed, and irregularly toothed (quite variable in size); lower leaves on long petioles, upper leaves short-stalked to nearly sessile. Plant stalk is pubescent. Plant 6"–2' tall with few leaves and flowers. **Habitat and range:** Moist woods, stream banks; Quebec and Maine to Minnesota, south to Georgia and Mississippi. **On Sugarloaf—Blooming time:** April–July. **Locations:** Bear Branch, Mount Ephraim Road; possible in other moist mountain locations.

Cursed Crowfoot

Ranunculus sceleratus L.
Buttercup Family (Ranunculaceae)

Cursed crowfoot has a glabrous plant stalk and pale yellow **flowers** slightly smaller than those of the preceding species (¼–⅜" across). Cursed crowfoot is a plant of shallow freshwater and wet meadows. Uncommon on Sugarloaf.

Thimbleweed (Tall Anemone)

Anemone virginiana L.
Buttercup Family (Ranunculaceae)

A summer wildflower with a colorful herbal history (*see* "Herbal lore" *below*). Named for the fruit, which resembles a sewing thimble. **Flowers:** 5 petal-like sepals are green, greenish-white, or white. Flower ⅔–1⅓" across on long, upright stalk. **Leaves:** Opposite or whorled, compound. Each leaf (usually) has 3 leaflets, which are toothed and lobed, sometimes deeply so. Leaves softly or roughly hairy to the touch, variable in size, on pubescent petioles.

Basal leaves long-stalked with leaflets deeply cleft. **Height and growth habits:** 2–3½'; upright with flowers on long terminal stalks (1 flower per stalk; 1 to few per plant). **Habitat and range:** Open woods, thickets; eastern Canada to North Dakota, south to Georgia, Alabama, and Arkansas. **Herbal lore:** In Peterson Field Guides' *Field Guide to Medicinal Plants: Eastern and Central North America,* Foster and Duke report that thimbleweed is: "Expectorant, astringent, emetic. American Indians used root decoction . . . for whooping cough, tuberculosis, diarrhea. Root poulticed for boils. In order to revive an unconscious patient, the smoke of the seeds was blown into the nostrils. To divine the truth about acts of a 'crooked wife,' the roots were placed under her pillow, to induce dreams." **On Sugarloaf—Blooming time:** June–August. **Locations:** Sugarloaf Mountain Road, Mount Ephraim Road; possible along other mountain roadsides and trailsides. **Similar species:** Resembles yellow flowering members of the buttercup family (Ranunculaceae). Wood anemone *(A. quinquefolia)* is a locally uncommon spring-flowering plant that blooms in the Monocacy Natural Resources Management Area along Furnace Branch. Wood anemone is less than 1' in height, with white or pale pink petal-like sepals. It blooms from April to June.

Barberry Family
Berberidaceae

This family of herbaceous plants and shrubs is represented by a single native wildflower species on Sugarloaf—the mayapple or mandrake *(Podophyllum peltatum)*—and a cultivated Asian shrub briefly described in the Botanical Key and Guide to Trees, Shrubs, and Woody Vines. **Family characteristics:** 13 genera and 650 species worldwide. **Flowers** usually have 4 or 6 sepals and as many or more petals (but there are variations). **Fruit:** a berry or capsule. **Leaves** alternate or basal, simple or compound. **Occurrence near Sugarloaf:** Although not found on Sugarloaf, two notable spring wildflowers of this family grow in the Maryland piedmont and mountains, often in calcareous soils, according to Cristol Fleming, Marion Blois Lobstein, and Barbara Tufty *(Finding Wildflowers in the Washington-Baltimore Area)*: the uncommon twinleaf *(Jeffersonia diphylla)* and blue cohosh *(Caulophyllum thalictroides)*.

Mayapple (Mandrake)
Podophyllum peltatum L.
Barberry Family (Berberidaceae)

The umbrella-like leaves of the mayapple form springtime carpets in moist open woodlands of eastern North America. Mayapple blooms near the sum-

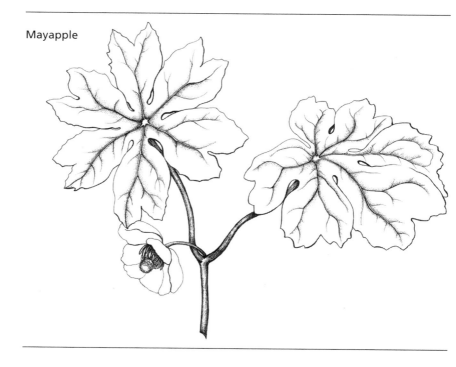

Mayapple

mit of Sugarloaf. **Flowers:** A single creamy white cup-shaped flower, with 6–9 waxy petals and showy pistil and stamens, nods from the axil of the plant's 2 large long-stemmed leaves. Flower 1–2" across. **Fruit:** The ovoid or ellipsoid berry is yellowish and 2 or more inches long when ripe later in the summer. The ripe pulp is edible. However, the unripe fruit, seeds, and all other parts of the plant are poisonous. **Leaves:** Extremely showy pair of umbrella-like leaves on flowering plants (single leaves on nonflowering plants). Oppositely arranged, on long petioles, leaf blades are 5–12" across, toothed and deeply lobed almost to the center, where the petiole attaches from below the blade. Overall leaf outline nearly circular. **Height:** 10"–2'. **Habitat and range:** Moist, rich open woods and shady areas; Quebec to Florida, west to Minnesota and Texas. **Herbal lore:** The poisonous mayapple has strong medicinal properties that American Indians and early European settlers utilized. The plant served as a treatment for jaundice, hepatitis, and syphilis, among other conditions. Foster and Duke report in Peterson Field Guides' *Field Guide to Medicinal Plants: Eastern and Central North America:* "Etoposide, a semisynthetic derivative of this plant, is FDA-approved for testicular and small-cell lung cancers." **On Sugarloaf—Blooming time:** April–May. **Locations:** Red Trail, Orange Trail, and most other mountain trails and roadsides; Bear Branch. **Similar species:** No other wildflower on or near Sugarloaf is apt to be confused with mayapple.

Poppy Family

Papaveraceae

This family is best known for the opium poppy and many brightly colored garden ornamentals. The family has a brash reputation, but it is represented on Sugarloaf by one of our most delicate and ephemeral spring wildflowers. **Family characteristics:** 25 genera and 200 species worldwide. **Economic importance:** The opium poppy *(Papaver somniferum)* is far and away the most important plant economically. It is also the source of the culinary poppy seed. According to Heywood's *Flowering Plants of the World,* seeds from other family members yield oils used in soap-making. Many family members are garden plants. **Flowers:** Perfect, regular, often showy, usually with 2 or 3 sepals that soon fall off and 4 to 12 petals. **Fruit:** A capsule. **Leaves:** Alternate, varied in shape; many plants yield a milky or colored juice. **Growth habits:** Herbs, some shrubs. **Occurrence on Sugarloaf:** Bloodroot *(Sanguinaria canadensis)* blooms in early spring along Bear Branch and Mount Ephraim Road. Celandine *(Chelidonium majus)* grows along rural roads in the area and might be found growing close to the mountain.

Bloodroot

Sanguinaria canadensis L.
Poppy Family (Papaveraceae)

One of eastern North America's most beautiful spring wildflowers, bloodroot is among the first to bloom and the most ephemeral. The plant gets its name from the orange-red juice exuded by the root, juice which has been used as everything from a wart remedy to a love charm! **Flowers:** White flowers, each with 8 or more thinnish petals. One flower per stem; at first cupshaped but later opening flat or nearly so, 1–2" wide. Flowers spring as if by magic from Sugarloaf's winter carpet of fallen leaves. **Leaves:** A large single basal leaf, 3–8" across, often partially wrapped around the flower stalk. Leaf is circular in outline but deeply lobed and bluntly toothed. **Height and growth habits:** 3–12"; upright or slightly leaning. **Habitat and range:** Rich woods; eastern Canada south to Florida and Oklahoma. **Herbal lore:** Although toxic, the root enjoyed widespread use among American Indians for a variety of illnesses, including asthma, bronchitis, and rheumatism. The root juice was popular as a dye, and Foster and Duke report in Peterson Field Guides' *Field Guide to Medicinal Plants: Eastern and Central North America:* "A bachelor of the Ponca tribe would rub a piece of the root as a love charm on the palm of his hand, then scheme to shake hands with the woman he desired to marry. After shaking hands, the girl would be found willing to marry him in 5–6 days." Foster and Duke note that in the modern world "the alka-

Bloodroot

loid sanguinarine" found in bloodroot "has shown antiseptic, anesthetic, and anticancer activity. It is used commercially as a plaque-inhibiting agent in toothpaste, mouthwashes, and rinses." However, their book contains the warning: "*Do not ingest.* Jim Duke has experienced tunnel vision from nibbling the root." Please do not attempt to examine the root of this or any other native wildflower. Help preserve this increasingly scarce woodland plant. **On Sugarloaf—Blooming time:** March–April. **Locations:** Bear Branch, Mount Ephraim Road, Monocacy Natural Resources Management Area. **Similar species:** Rue-anemone *(Anemonella thalictroides)* has smaller flowers, often more than one per stem, and stem leaves. The round-lobed hepatica *(Hepatica americana),* rare on Sugarloaf, has a smaller flower and distinctly 3-lobed basal leaves.

Bleeding-Heart or Fumitory Family

Fumariaceae

Plants of this family are sometimes included in the poppy family (Papaveraceae). A single wildflower of the bleeding-heart family grows on Sugarloaf, although two other species are common along the Potomac and other nearby rivers; *see* "Similar species" *under* yellow corydalis *(Corydalis flavula),* next entry. **Family characteristics:** 19 genera and 400 species worldwide. Mainly indigenous to northern temperate zone; only a few species found in the Southern Hemisphere. **Economic importance:** Of little economic importance; a few members of the family such as Dutchman's breeches and bleeding-heart (*Dicentra* spp.) are grown as garden ornamentals. **Flowers** usually perfect, irregular, and unusually shaped (*see* drawing of yellow corydalis, next entry). Many members, including bleeding-heart, are "bilaterally symmetrical," a phrase used by Gleason and Cronquist *(Manual of Vascular Plants of Northeastern United States and Adjacent Canada)* and other botanists. **Fruit** is usually a capsule (sometimes a one-seeded nut). **Leaves** are usually alternate compound, often with deeply dissected leaflets (somewhat fernlike in our several native species). **Growth habits:** Plants are herbaceous. **Occurrence on Sugarloaf:** Yellow corydalis *(Corydalis flavula)* grows along the Blue and Red Trails.

Yellow Corydalis

Corydalis flavula (Raf.) DC
Bleeding-Heart or Fumitory Family (Fumariaceae)

A delicate spring wildflower with intricately divided leaves. Yellow corydalis is uncommon on Sugarloaf. **Flowers:** Yellow, irregular, ¼–½" long in small, loose clusters (racemes). Upper lip of somewhat tubular flower bears a fringed crest (lower lip also usually fringed). Flower has a small spur at the back. **Leaves:** Alternate, compound, deeply dissected in feathery pattern, green or gray-green in color. Petiole and plant stalk may be pinkish. **Height and growth habits:** 4–15"; erect or slightly sprawling, usually branching. **Habitat and range:** Open woods, disturbed sites; New York and southern Ontario to South Dakota, south to North Carolina, Louisiana, and Okla-

Yellow Corydalis

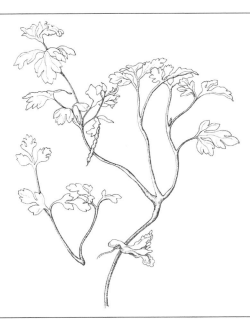

homa. **On Sugarloaf—Blooming time:** April–May. **Locations:** Red Trail, Blue Trail; uncommon along other trails and roadsides. **Similar species:** None on Sugarloaf. The leaves resemble those of other bleeding-heart family members found near Sugarloaf: Dutchman's breeches *(Dicentra cucullaria)* and squirrel-corn *(Dicentra canadensis)* are both common along the Potomac and other nearby rivers and streams and on local moist, rocky slopes. Those species bear white flowers, the first in the shape of a small pair of britches, the second heart-shaped. Eastern wild bleeding-heart *(Dicentra eximia)* bears pink heart-shaped flowers and is found in rocky woods and outcrops in the mountains. Another *Corydalis* species is native to Maryland and grows in the nearby Catoctin Mountains. Pale or pink corydalis *(C. sempervirens)* has pink flowers that are yellow at the tip.

Witch-Hazel Family

Hamamelidaceae

A medium-sized family of 26 genera and 100 or more species of trees and shrubs. The fall-blooming common witch-hazel *(Hamamelis virginiana)* is the only family member growing on Sugarloaf, but sweetgum *(Liquidambar styraciflua)*, also in the witch-hazel family, is a bottomland tree which is very common on Maryland and Virginia's coastal plain. **Family characteristics— Economic importance:** Ornamental trees and shrubs; wood from some species used in furniture making; medicinals and cosmetics (*see* common witch-hazel, next entry). **Flowers:** Usually 4 or 5-parted, often with separate petals and partially fused sepals. **Fruit:** A woody capsule. **Leaves:** Alternate (rarely opposite), simple, deciduous or evergreen. **Occurrence on Sugarloaf:** Common witch-hazel is quite common along Sugarloaf trails and roads.

Tree or Shrub

Common Witch-Hazel

Hamamelis virginiana L.
Witch-Hazel Family (Hamamelidaceae)

Common witch-hazel is a well-known herbal, and its branchlets are favored by water diviners. The only fall-blooming tree in our native flora, common witch-hazel contributes golden flowers and golden leaves to Sugarloaf's autumn landscape. **Flowers:** Yellow, with 4 small, spreading, ribbonlike petals. Each petal ½–1" long. Flowers borne in small axillary clusters as the leaves turn gold in autumn. They remain for a time after the leaves have dropped. **Fruit:** A short, thick 2-beaked capsule which becomes woody and splits at

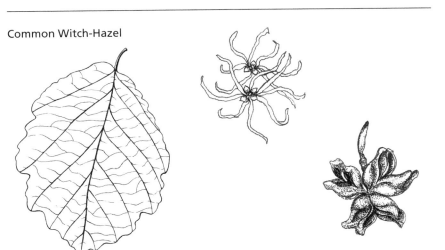

the top to release seeds. Capsules take about a year to mature and may remain on the tree for years. **Leaves:** Alternate, simple, deciduous, 2–6" long. Leaf blade is broadly obovate, oblong, or ovate with a scallop-toothed margin and unequal base. **Growth habits:** Small tree or shrub. **Bark and twigs:** Bark light brown, smooth or slightly scaly. Twigs with slightly flattened, curved end buds that are covered with dense yellow-brown hairs. **Habitat and range:** Woods, streamsides; eastern United States and extreme southeastern Canada. **Herbal lore:** Witch-hazel has astringent properties and is the source of witch-hazel liniment and many other topical preparations. Witch-hazel also was used internally by American Indians as a tea for sore throats, colds, and a number of other medical conditions. **Wildlife lore:** Squirrels, ruffed grouse, and other birds eat the fruits, and whitetail deer browse the leaves and young branchlets. **On Sugarloaf—Blooming time:** September–January. **Locations:** Common mountainwide; look for common witch-hazel as you ascend the stone steps of the Green Trail and along the Orange Trail. **Similar species:** The scalloped leaves with unequal bases and yellow autumn flowers distinguish this tree or large shrub from all others in our local native flora.

Nettle Family

Urticaceae

The infamous stinging nettle *(Urtica dioica)* is an Old World plant with a rich medicinal and culinary history. This plant and a handful of other nettle family members grow around the base of Sugarloaf. **Family characteristics:**

45 genera and 700 species worldwide. **Economic importance:** Some family members are used in the textile industry. Ramie *(Boehmeria nivea)* is an Asian plant that yields one of the world's strongest fibers. Stinging nettle is used as a cooked green and herbal medicine. **Flowers:** Unisexual, with 3–5 sepals and no petals. Often small, in branched or unbranched clusters. **Fruit:** Usually an achene. **Leaves:** Alternate or opposite, simple. Some plants have stinging hairs. **Growth habits:** Mostly herbs or small shrubs, rarely trees. **Occurrence on Sugarloaf:** False nettle *(Boehmeria cylindrica)* and clearweed *(Pilea pumila)* are very common in moist habitats of Sugarloaf's lower trails; stinging nettle and wood nettle *(Laportea canadensis)* grow along Mount Ephraim Road. Stinging nettle grows abundantly along some stretches of the Potomac and in abandoned farm fields near the mountain.

Stinging Nettle

Urtica dioica L.
Nettle Family (Urticaceae)

A scourge of unwary hikers, stinging nettle is a plant with a surprising medicinal and culinary herbal history. The potent sting resulting from a close encounter with its stinging hairs often can be instantly relieved by squeezing the leaf or stem of jewelweed (touch-me-not) on the affected skin. Rich in iron, protein, and vitamins A and C, the young leaves of stinging nettle make a nutritious cooked green. (Needless to say, foragers must wear gloves, and, as a reminder, no plants may be harvested on Sugarloaf.) **Flowers:** Minute, greenish-white or greenish-yellow, in elongated spreading or drooping clusters growing from the uppermost leaf axils. Staminate and pistillate flowers on separate plants or separate parts of the same plant. **Leaves:** Opposite, simple, cordate or ovate, with large teeth; 2–10" long (sometimes with separate smaller leaf pairs springing from the axils). Leaves with some stinging hairs, although stinging hairs are more numerous on the longish petioles and the central plant stalk. **Height:** 1½–5'. **Habitat and range:** Roadsides, disturbed sites, river and creek banks; nearly cosmopolitan as a native or naturalized species. **Herbal lore:** In the Old World stinging nettle has been valued for centuries as an edible and medicinal plant. According to Alma R. Hutchens's *Indian Herbalogy of North America,* "Since the seventeenth century Russian Herbalists have given credit to Nettle as antiseptic, astringent, blood purifier, which are only a few of its properties." She goes on to say: "From some of the first books on herbs and their uses Nettle ranks high." Foster and Duke note that Russians still value the plant as a palliative for cholecystitis (inflammation of the gall bladder) and hepatitis. In their Peterson Field Guides' *Field Guide to Medicinal Plants: Eastern and Central North America,* Foster and Duke report that Germans use the root as a prostate

cancer treatment. It seems that French chefs who value nettle may really be onto something, for the plant has been used for just about every conceivable medical condition. Close to home, illustrator Tina Brown always reserves a spot for stinging nettle in her herb garden. She swears by the restorative power of fresh-brewed nettle tea. **On Sugarloaf—Blooming time:** June–September. **Locations:** Mount Ephraim Road; also probable along other roadsides and trailsides. (Common nearby along some stretches of the C&O Canal.) **Similar species:** False nettle *(Boehmeria cylindrica)* and clearweed *(Pilea pumila),* both abundant on Sugarloaf, lack the stinging hairs of *Urtica dioica.* Wood nettle *(Laportea canadensis)* is less common here and has alternate leaves.

False Nettle

Boehmeria cylindrica (L.) Sw.
Nettle Family (Urticaceae)

It's not what it's got, but what it's not got, that distinguishes this plant from other nettle family members! It doesn't have stinging hairs like stinging nettle *(Urtica dioica)* or wood nettle *(Laportea canadensis),* and it doesn't have shiny leaves like clearweed *(Pilea pumila).* **Flowers:** Minute, greenish, in stiff, compact, continuous or interrupted spikes, growing from the leaf axils. Spikes are bristly looking but not sharp to the touch. Spike may have a leafy tip. **Leaves:** Opposite, simple; toothed, mostly ovate, with long petioles. From 1" to several inches long. **Height:** 1–4'. **Habitat and range:** Moist soil;

False Nettle

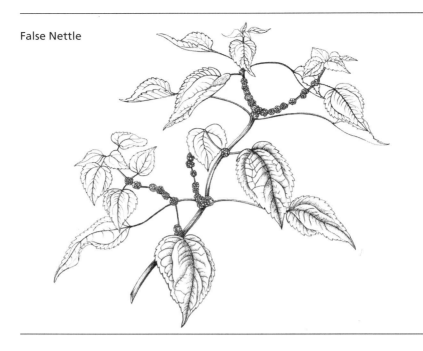

Quebec to Minnesota; south to Florida and New Mexico. **On Sugarloaf—Blooming time:** July–October. **Locations:** Damp soils and springs, primarily of the Yellow and White Trails; Mount Ephraim Road and Sugarloaf Mountain Road. **Similar species:** *see* introduction to plant *above.* Compare flowers to those of mint family members.

Clearweed (Richweed)

Pilea pumila (L.) A. Gray
Nettle Family (Urticaceae)

This plant is distinguished from other nettle family members of Sugarloaf by its shiny leaves and translucent, succulent stalk. **Flowers:** Minute, greenish or whitish, in branching clusters from the leaf axils. **Leaves:** Opposite, simple; ovate, toothed, clear glossy green; 3 prominent veins emerge from the wedge-shaped (cuneate) or rounded base. Petioles long, shiny, may be slightly pinkish. Leaf blades ¾–5" long. Plant stalk smooth and shiny, more or less angled. Whole plant glabrous or nearly so. **Height and growth habits:** 4"–3'; branched or unbranched. **Habitat and range:** Moist, rich soil, shaded or partially so; Quebec to Minnesota; south to Florida, Louisiana, and Oklahoma. **On Sugarloaf—Blooming time:** August–October. **Locations:** Yellow Trail and other trails; roadsides. Quite common mountainwide. **Similar species:** False nettle *(Boehmeria cylindrica)* often grows alongside clearweed, but its leaves are a dull green. Stinging nettle *(Urtica dioica)* and wood nettle

Clearweed

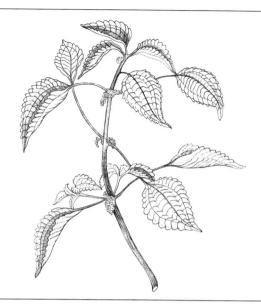

(Laportea canadensis) bear stinging hairs. Clearweed could be confused with mint family members. Use tiny flowers in branching clusters and shiny leaves to distinguish clearweed from mints. Another species of clearweed *(P. fontana)* has been reported elsewhere in Maryland, including in Baltimore County.

Wood Nettle

Laportea canadensis (L.) Wedd.
Nettle Family (Urticaceae)

A fourth nettle species, not common on Sugarloaf, grows in rich woods near the mountain. It is easily told from our common species. Wood nettle has a bristly stem with stinging hairs and large ovate, alternate **leaves.** Tiny greenish **flowers** are in loose clusters, staminate and pistillate separate. Pistillate clusters are larger and branched. **On Sugarloaf—Blooming time:** July and August. **Location:** Mount Ephraim Road (not as common as the previous three species).

Pokeweed Family

Phytolaccaceae

A family that includes medicinal and dye plants and some ornamentals. One species grows on and around Sugarloaf: pokeweed or pokeberry *(Phytolacca americana)*. Traditionally prized as a spring green, the mature plant and its berries are toxic to humans. However, the berries serve as food for wildlife. **Family characteristics:** 18 genera and 125 species worldwide. **Economic importance:** Commercial ornamentals and dye plants. Among medicinal family members are plants used to treat rabies, tumors, and syphilis, according to Heywood's *Flowering Plants of the World.* **Flowers:** Perfect or sometimes unisexual, regular, with 4 or 5 sepals and usually no petals. **Fruit:** A berry, drupe, samara, or achene. **Leaves:** Alternate, simple, entire. **Growth habits:** Trees, shrubs, woody vines, and herbs. **Occurrence on Sugarloaf:** Pokeweed grows along the Yellow Trail and area roadsides and in disturbed sites.

Pokeweed (Pokeberry)

Phytolacca americana L.
Pokeweed Family (Phytolaccaceae)

A tall plant with a branched reddish stalk and showy purple-black berries in late summer and autumn. **Flowers:** Small, creamy white, greenish-white, or pinkish-white, with 5 petal-like sepals that are rounded at the tips. Each flower ¼" or so across in elongated clusters (racemes) up to several inches long. **Fruit:** Round but slightly flattened shiny purple-black berries (green when unripe) in terminal clusters; berries much showier than flowers. **Leaves:** Alternate, simple, ovate to oblong-lanceolate, with entire (sometimes slightly wavy) margins and green or reddish petioles. Glabrous, 3–12" long. **Height and growth habits:** 3–10'; branched. **Habitat and range:** Fields, fence-rows,

Pokeweed

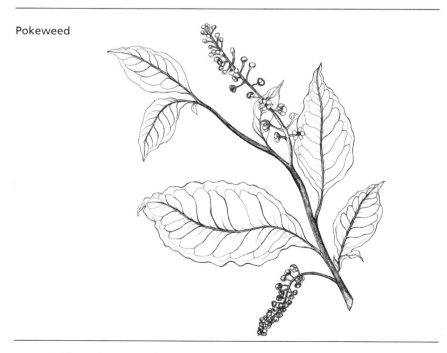

woodland clearings; Maine to Minnesota, south to the Gulf of Mexico. **Herbal lore:** The young shoots are a popular spring green (must be boiled in two changes of water), but mature plant and berries are poisonous. Native Americans did use berries, roots, and leaves for a number of medical conditions, however, both internally and externally (as a poultice). **Wildlife lore:** Although toxic to humans, pokeberries are an important food for mourning doves and many songbirds. They are also eaten by raccoons, foxes, and opossums. **On Sugarloaf—Blooming and fruiting time:** Summer–fall. **Locations:** Yellow Trail; roadsides, parking areas, and open sections of trail. **Similar species:** Mature plant not likely to be confused with any other species on Sugarloaf, but in the spring the plant has been confused with the extremely toxic false hellebore or Indian poke *(Veratrum viride).* Not included in this guide, false hellebore grows in neighboring seepage swamps and might be found on or near the mountain. Its leaves are heavily ribbed, and its flowers are star-shaped and 6-parted.

Purslane Family
Portulacaceae

A single species of the purslane family grows on Sugarloaf—the delicate spring beauty *(Claytonia virginica).* Another family member, common purslane *(Portulaca oleracea),* an Old World fleshy plant that has long been cultivated for its nutritious leaves, shows up as a weed in gardens throughout the mid-Atlantic region, where it is valued and harvested by some gardeners. Fameflower *(Talinum teretifolium)* is a rare plant of the piedmont and mountains that has not been observed on Sugarloaf. **Family characteristics:** 20 genera and 500 species worldwide. Cosmopolitan. **Flowers:** Mostly perfect and mostly regular (seldom slightly irregular). Sepals: 2; petals 4–6 (rarely 2–3). **Fruit:** Usually a capsule. **Leaves:** Alternate or opposite, usually at least somewhat fleshy. **Growth habits:** Mostly herbs or low shrubs. **Occurrence on Sugarloaf:** Spring beauty is common in the Monocacy Natural Resources Management Area and along the lower part of Bear Branch near the confluence with Bennett Creek; an abundant spring wildflower in rich soils of the region, especially near streams and rivers.

Spring Beauty
Claytonia virginica L.
Purslane Family (Portulacaceae)

One of eastern North America's earliest and most delicate spring wildflowers, spring beauty carpets the ground in many areas. Uncommon on Sugar-

loaf, it is confined to rich woods near streams. **Flowers:** White or pale pink with darker pink candy stripes; 5-petaled, star-shaped, ½–1" across, growing in loose, small clusters. (Flowers bloom consecutively, so plant may bear only one mature flower at a time.) **Leaves:** Opposite, simple, entire; one pair of narrowly lanceolate or linear leaves per plant stalk. Leaves tapered at apex and base, 2½–7" long. **Height:** 4–12". **Habitat and range:** Rich woods, bottomland woods, fields; southeastern Canada and eastern United States. **On Sugarloaf—Blooming time:** March–early May. **Locations:** Bear Branch (lower sections), Bennett Creek, Monocacy Natural Resources Management Area. **Similar species:** The single pair of opposite, simple, entire, narrow leaves separates spring beauty from other early spring wildflowers of Sugarloaf and surrounding woodlands. Carolina spring beauty *(C. caroliniana)*— not found on Sugarloaf—has wider ovate-lanceolate leaves; it grows in far western Maryland, in the southern Appalachians as far south as Georgia, and as far north as Nova Scotia to Minnesota.

Pink Family

Caryophyllaceae

Many pink family flowers have notched petals (as if cut with pinking shears). The family includes the florist's familiar staple, the carnation *(Dianthus caryophyllus)*. Several members of this family are found on Sugarloaf, including common chickweed *(Stellaria media),* an important seed source for birds. In addition to the species described and illustrated in this book, at least two other pink family members might be encountered here: bouncing bet *(Saponaria officinalis)*, an introduced summer–fall wildflower of fields, roadsides, and other disturbed sites, and long-leaved stitchwort *(Stellaria longifolia)*, a weak-stemmed plant of moist soils blooming in spring and early summer. **Family characteristics:** 75 genera and 2,000 species world-wide; family members widespread throughout temperate zones; also grow on tropical mountains. **Economic importance:** Garden ornamentals, cut flowers. **Flowers:** Mostly perfect and regular, usually with 5 sepals and 5 petals (sometimes 4-parted; rarely lacking petals). Petals are often notched or fringed. **Fruit:** Usually a capsule. **Leaves:** Opposite (rarely alternate), simple, and entire. Stems often swollen at the leaf nodes. **Growth habits:** Herbaceous plants. **Occurrence on Sugarloaf:** Several species common or occasional on Sugarloaf, in woodlands, along roadsides, and in grassy areas and other disturbed sites.

Common Chickweed
Stellaria media (L.) Vill.
Pink Family (Caryophyllaceae)

This common lawn and garden weed has a noble herbal history tracing back to its Eurasian roots. Chickweed has been used internally and externally in the Old and New World for a variety of medical conditions. Even domesticated animals seem to enjoy its benefits. In *A Modern Herbal*, first published in 1931, Maude Grieve reported: "Both wild and caged birds eat the seeds as well as the young tops and leaves. Pigs like Chickweed, and also rabbits; cows and horses will eat it; sheep are indifferent to it, but goats refuse to touch it." **Flowers:** Small, white, ¼" or less across; 5 petals are so deeply divided they

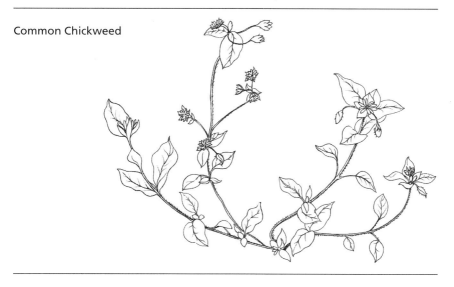

Common Chickweed

appear to number 10; 5 green sepals are slightly longer than the petals. Styles (*see* Glossary): 3. Flower stalk as long or longer than flower is across. Flowers spring from axils of highest leaves, singly or in small clusters. **Leaves:** Opposite, simple, with entire margins. Ovate, ⅓–1½" long. Upper leaves usually sessile; lower leaves on short, often pubescent petioles. Leaves otherwise mainly glabrous. **Growth habits:** Sprawling, partially sprawling, or upright; 4–15". **Habitat and range:** Gardens, lawns, meadows, waste places, and woodlands; a widely naturalized Eurasian native. **Herbal lore:** Widely used as an external remedy for many skin conditions and internally for coughs, rheumatism, and bowel, kidney, and stomach complaints. **On Sugarloaf—Blooming time:** Earliest spring through fall (nearly year-round). **Locations:** In mowed areas of mountain base, mountain roadsides, and most trails. **Similar species:** Star chickweed *(S. pubera)* has larger, showier flowers with petals slightly longer than sepals. Mouse-eared chickweed *(Cerastium vulgatum)* has petals that are less deeply cleft and 5 styles per flower.

Star Chickweed (Great Chickweed)

Stellaria pubera Michx.
Pink Family (Caryophyllaceae)

Star or great chickweed blooms in spring with a larger, showier flower than common chickweed's *(S. media)*. **Flowers:** White, about ½" across; 5 petals are so deeply cleft they appear to be 10; petals are slightly longer than sepals. Styles (*see* Glossary): 3. Flowers grow singly or in small, mostly terminal clusters. **Leaves:** Opposite, simple, with entire margins. Elliptic or ovate, sessile or with a tapered base, ½–3" long. Plant stalk and leaves with fine hairs (pubescence along plant stalk often in a pattern of 1 or 2 lines). **Height and**

Star Chickweed

growth habit: Several inches tall, sometimes with spreading stalk; erect or sprawling. Habitat and range: Woodlands; eastern United States. On Sugarloaf—Blooming time: April–May. Location: Bear Branch. Similar species: Common chickweed has smaller flowers with sepals slightly longer than petals. Mouse-eared chickweed *(Cerastium vulgatum)* petals are smaller and less deeply cleft, and its flowers have 5 styles.

Mouse-Eared Chickweed

Cerastium vulgatum L.
Pink Family (Caryophyllaceae)

Mouse-eared chickweed is common on the mountain, especially along roadsides. **Flowers:** Small, white, with 5 petals that are cleft about halfway (or a little less) in small terminal clusters (sometimes with only one in bloom at a time). Flowers ¼–⅓" wide with sepals about as long as petals. *Cerastium* chickweed species have 5 styles (*see* Glossary), visible with a hand lens, while *Stellaria* species (including common chickweed and star chickweed) have only 3. **Leaves:** Opposite, simple, entire, sessile, very pubescent (so is plant stalk). Mostly ovate or lance-ovate, ⅓–1½" long. **Height:** 4–18". **Habitat and range:** Lawns, roadsides, a common garden weed; Eurasian native, now widely established in North America. **On Sugarloaf—Blooming time:** May–June. **Locations:** Grassy areas along roadsides and trails mountainwide. **Similar species:** Common chickweed *(Stellaria media)* and star chickweed *(Stellaria pubera)* have petals that are so deeply cleft they appear to be 10, rather than 5.

Mouse-Eared Chickweed

Deptford Pink

Dianthus armeria L.
Pink Family (Caryophyllaceae)

A fairly common late spring and summer flower, Deptford pink grows in Sugarloaf's grassy areas. **Flowers:** Deep brilliant pink, with 5 toothed, white-spotted petals forming a ½" star; 2 to several thin, pointed bracts radiate upward from the lower calyx tube. Flowers in small terminal clusters (but may bloom singly). **Leaves:** Opposite, simple, linear; untoothed, with hairy margins, ½–2" long. Entire plant more or less pubescent. **Height:** 6–20". **Habitat and range:** Fields, grassy areas, roadsides; a European native widely naturalized in eastern United States and southern Canada. **On Sugarloaf— Blooming time:** May–September. **Locations:** Grassy areas and roadsides mountainwide. **Similar species:** None on the mountain.

Deptford Pink

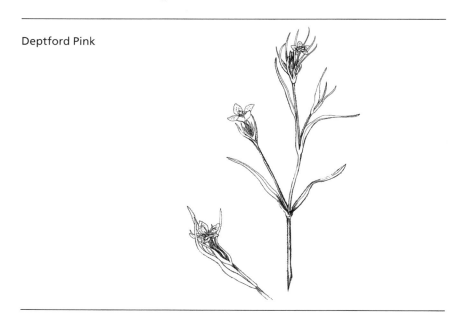

Evening Lychnis (White Campion, White-Cockle)

Silene latifolia Poir.
(Lychnis alba)
Pink Family (Caryophyllaceae)

A European native which has become widely naturalized throughout North America (including the Washington-Baltimore area), evening lychnis pops up here and there on Sugarloaf but is not common on the mountain. **Flowers:** Dioecious (male and female flowers on separate plants). White (sometimes pinkish), with 5 deeply cleft petals and female flowers with usually 5

Evening Lychnis

styles (*see* Glossary). Flowers about an inch across. Female flower has swollen, tubular, veiny, hairy calyx. Flowers open in the evening but may remain fully open during the day. **Leaves:** Opposite, simple, lanceolate or elliptic, sessile, softly pubescent (sometimes sticky-hairy), entire, 1–4" long. **Height:** 1–3'. **Habitat:** Fields, roadsides, disturbed sites. **On Sugarloaf—Blooming time:** May–September. **Locations:** Mountain roadsides and trails (can show up anywhere). **Similar species:** Bladder campion *(Silene vulgaris)* has a very inflated calyx, but it is glabrous or nearly so. Starry campion *(S. stellata)* has fringed petals.

Bladder Campion

Silene vulgaris (Moench) Garcke
(Silene cucubalus)
Pink Family (Caryophyllaceae)

Flowers: White (rarely pink), with 5 deeply cleft petals and 3 styles (*see* Glossary). Flowers ½–¾" across, with swollen, veined, glabrous (rarely pubescent) calyx. **Leaves:** Opposite, simple, ovate-lanceolate, ¾–3" long; entire, usually glabrous, sessile, and sometimes clasping. Plant stalk often glaucous. **Height:** 8"–2'. **Habitat and range:** Fields, roadsides, woodland borders; European native, widely naturalized in the United States. **On Sugarloaf— Blooming time:** May–August. **Locations:** We have seen this plant, which is naturalized throughout the Washington-Baltimore area, in fields surrounding Sugarloaf. **Similar species:** Evening lychnis or white campion *(S. latifolia)* has slightly larger flowers and is a softly pubescent plant. Starry campion *(S. stellata)* has fringed petals.

Starry Campion

Silene stellata (L.) Aiton
Pink Family (Caryophyllaceae)

Flowers: White, with 5 deeply fringed petals. About ¾" across, with a bell-shaped, softly pubescent calyx. **Leaves:** Opposite, simple, with middle leaves often in whorls of 4. Leaf blades lance-linear to lance-ovate, entire, pubescent, sessile, 1–4" long. **Height:** 1–3½'. **Habitat and range:** Open woods and clearings; eastern United States. **On Sugarloaf—Blooming time:** July–October. **Locations:** Roadsides, including the road up the mountain; possible along any trail. **Similar species:** ringed petals separate starry campion from similar species with merely cleft petals.

Wild Pink

Silene caroliniana Walter
Pink Family (Caryophyllaceae)

A low-growing plant of dry, rocky areas. I have never seen this plant on Sugarloaf Mountain but have encountered it on rock outcrops nearby. **Flowers** are about an inch across with 5 pink (rarely white), shallowly notched, shallowly toothed, or nearly entire petals. Petals are widest at the tip. Calyx narrowly tubular, sticky-hairy. **Leaves** are opposite, simple, linear-oblong to oblanceolate, the stem leaves sessile and the basal leaves with petioles; 1–4" long, pubescent. **Height:** 4–10". **Habitat and range:** Dry woods, rock outcrops; eastern United States. **On and near Sugarloaf—Blooming time:** April–June. **Locations:** Look for wild pink during the spring on rock outcrops on and near Sugarloaf. **Similar species:** Deptford pink *(Dianthus armeria)* has smaller white spotted flowers. A local wildflower that closely resembles wild pink is moss phlox or moss-pink *(Phlox subulata)*. I have yet to see it on Sugarloaf Mountain but have found it nearby. Like wild pink, moss phlox grows in open rocky woods. It has notched petal-like lobes joining at the base to form a tube, and many narrow, almost needlelike leaves.

Smartweed or Buckwheat Family

Polygonaceae

The smartweed or buckwheat family produces plants valued as garden ornamentals and food sources, including buckwheat, rhubarb, and common sorrel. **Family characteristics:** 30 genera and 1,000 species worldwide. **Flowers:** Perfect or unisexual, usually small, and often not opening all the way. There are 3–6 (usually 5) sepals, which are often petaloid, and no true petals. **Fruit:** An achene. **Leaves:** Usually alternate (rarely opposite), often with a sheath encircling the swollen leaf node, described in greater detail in the next entry, the Smartweed *(Polygonum)* genus. **Growth habits:** Mostly herbs, some shrubs, a few tropical trees. **Occurrence on Sugarloaf:** Several species of smartweed and members of two other genera grow on Sugarloaf in a number of different habitats. In addition to the smartweed family members described and illustrated in the following entries, sheep sorrel *(Rumex acetosella)* is common in local fields, disturbed sites, and along roadsides. It resembles the cultivated garden sorrel *(R. acetosa),* to which it is closely related. Its sour-tasting leaves are alternate, simple, with arrow-shaped bases, and its tiny reddish or greenish flowers are borne in branched clusters.

Smartweeds, Lady's-Thumb, Tearthumbs, and Climbing False Buckwheat

Polygonum L.
Smartweed or Buckwheat Family (Polygonaceae)

These humble flowering plants are notorious for their resistance to identification. They are abundant on Sugarloaf, and the most common are among the trickiest to identify. Several species are found here, with flower color ranging from pink to white to greenish-white. General characteristics of the *Polygonum* genus follow, with brief individual species definitions. Should you

Lady's-Thumb

undertake to sort out them out, good luck! **Flowers:** No petals are present. What you see are several petaloid sepals (often 5), which usually don't open all the way, so the flowers appear to be in bud. Flowers are tiny, in spikes or heads. Our species: pink, white, or greenish-white. **Leaves:** Alternate, simple, usually with entire margins (but some species could be considered lobed). Arising from each swollen leaf node, there is a collarlike sheath encircling the plant stalk. This sheath is called an ocrea. In some species slender hairs protrude from the top of the ocrea. **Growth habits:** A trailing or upright herbaceous plant. One species here, climbing false buckwheat *(P. scandens),* is a twining vine. **Herbal lore:** Many species have been used here and abroad for a number of medical conditions. **Blooming time:** Summer–fall.

Leaves Lanceolate, Ovate, or Elliptic

Flowers Pink (or Sometimes White)

Lady's-Thumb (*P. persicaria* L.). Toward the base or in the middle of many (but not all) of the lanceolate **leaves,** there is a black or dark green splotch resembling a thumbprint. Shortish slender hairs arise from the top of the ocrea (*see above*). A widely naturalized European native with dense flower clusters. **On Sugarloaf:** Common on and around uplands and disturbed sites.

Pennsylvania Smartweed (Pinkweed or Pink Knotweed) (*P. pensylvanicum* L.). Very similar to lady's-thumb *(P. persicaria)* but without the hairs arising from the top of the ocrea. (However, the upper margin of the ocrea may have a jagged appearance.) Tiny reddish hairlike glands may be visible (with a hand lens) on the upper plant stalk. **Flowers:** Usually pink, some-

Pennsylvania
Smartweed

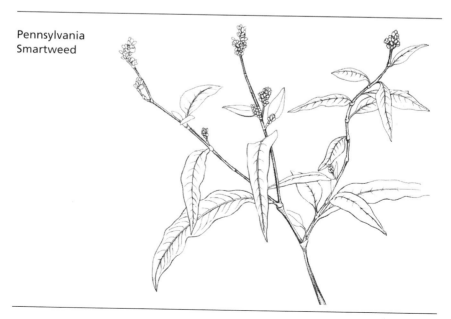

times white. Flower clusters thicker and showier than previous species with at least some petaloid sepals more often open. **Range:** Much of eastern United States and Canada. **On Sugarloaf:** Common on and around the mountain, especially in moist habitats.

Long-Bristled Smartweed (Asiatic Water-Pepper) (*P. cespitosum* Blume). Similar to lady's-thumb *(P. persicaria)* but with slenderer flower clusters and much longer bristles arising from the ocrea. **Range:** East Asian native, widely naturalized. **On Sugarloaf:** Common mountainwide.

Flowers Greenish-White

Water Smartweed (Dotted Smartweed) (*P. punctatum* Elliott). This species has greenish-white flowers with small glandular dots and lanceolate or elliptic leaves that are often dotted. Wet meadows, clearings, freshwater marshes and swamps throughout the United States, Canada, and in tropical America. **On Sugarloaf:** Look for it in wet areas along Mount Ephraim Road and the Yellow Trail.

Leaves Arrow-Shaped

Flowers White (or Sometimes Pink)

Arrow-Leaved Tearthumb (*P. sagittatum* L.). **Leaves:** Narrowly arrow-shaped with lobes pointing straight back or inward (*see* following species); plant stalk sprawling and prickly. **Flowers:** White, greenish-white, or pinkish. Freshwater marshes, wet meadows, and ditches; eastern United States and Canada. **On Sugarloaf:** Seeps and springs along Mount Ephraim Road, Sugarloaf Mountain Road, and the Yellow Trail.

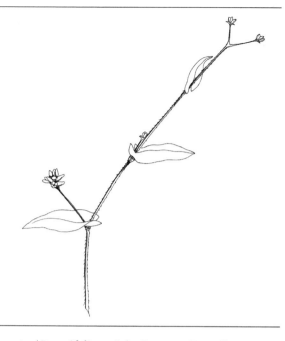

Halberd-Leaved Tearthumb (*P. arifolium* L.). **Leaves:** Broadly arrow-shaped with lobes pointed outward; plant stalk sprawling and prickly. **Flowers:** White (or pink). Wet places; eastern United States and Canada. **On Sugarloaf:** Seeps and wet areas along Mount Ephraim Road and the Yellow Trail.

Vine with Heart-Shaped or Arrow-Shaped Leaves

Flowers Greenish-Yellow or White

Climbing False Buckwheat (*P. scandens* L.). This twining vine is more conspicuous in fruit than in flower as its small greenish fruit is winged. **Habitat and range:** Woods, thickets, roadsides, bottomland woods, and freshwater marshes; eastern United States and Canada. **On Sugarloaf:** Thickets and roadsides edging the mountain.

Jumpseed (Virginia Knotweed)

Tovara virginiana (L.) Raf.
(*Polygonum virginianum* L.)
Smartweed or Buckwheat Family (Polygonaceae)

This species is sometimes included in the *Polygonum* genus, and *Polygonum virginianum* is the name preferred by Stanwyn G. Shetler and Sylvia Stone Orli in the Smithsonian Institution's *Annotated Checklist of the Vascular Plants of the Washington-Baltimore Area.* The plant bears a long, slender, sparsely flowered raceme of small greenish-white **flowers** with 4 petal-like sepals. The mature **fruit** "jumps" when lightly touched, thus the common name. The **leaves** of this species are ovate or elliptic and broader than the *Polygonum* spp. previously described. **Habitat and range:** Moist woods, roadsides, thickets; eastern United States. **On Sugarloaf:** Flowering and fruiting summer– fall. Mount Ephraim Road and the Blue Trail; likely elsewhere.

Bitter Dock (Broad or Broad-Leaved Dock)

Rumex obtusifolius L.
Smartweed or Buckwheat Family (Polygonaceae)

A tall European import with large leaves. **Flowers and fruit:** Tiny greenish flowers and green to brown fruit borne in tall branched racemes from the upper part of the plant. On close inspection individual flower clusters are in dense whorls, with each flower and (later) fruit drooping on a long, thin stalk. Small winged fruit has a spiny margin. **Leaves:** Alternate, simple, ovate or oblong with a heart-shaped (cordate) or rounded base. Lower leaves large (up to or exceeding a foot in length); upper leaves sometimes barely more than an inch long. Margins entire or shallowly wavy-toothed, petioles (except on uppermost nearly sessile leaves) long and stout. Petioles and plant stalks vertically grooved and angled. **Height:** 1–6'. **Habitat and range:** Disturbed sites, roadsides; European native, widely naturalized in the United

Bitter Dock

States and Canada. **On Sugarloaf—Blooming time:** Late spring and summer (both bitter dock and curly dock, mentioned below). **Locations:** Roadsides mountainwide and some trailsides (both bitter dock and curly dock). **Similar species:** Curly, curled, or yellow dock *(Rumex crispus)* is an important herbal medicinal which is also found on Sugarloaf. The wings of its fruit are not spiny but smooth or obscurely toothed. Curly dock has leaves narrower than those of bitter dock and very curled at the margins (bitter dock's may be somewhat curled).

St. John's-Wort Family

Hypericaceae
(Guttiferae, Clusiaceae)

This family includes common St. John's-wort *(Hypericum perforatum),* a traditional herbal remedy that has become popular in recent years as a treatment for mild depression. Common St. John's-wort grows on Sugarloaf and is described and illustrated here along with several other native St. John's-wort species. **Family characteristics:** 50 genera and 1,200 species worldwide. A cosmopolitan family but with most genera concentrated in the Tropics. **Economic importance:** The family produces ornamental plants and edible fruits, including mangosteen *(Garcinia),* timber, medicines, and essential oils for cosmetics. **Flowers:** 4 or 5 (usually) separate sepals and the same number of (usually) separate petals. **Fruit:** A capsule, berry, or drupe. **Leaves:** Opposite, simple, entire. **Growth habits:** Trees, shrubs, and herbs. Temperate zone species mostly shrubs and herbs. **Occurrence on Sugarloaf:** Wildflowers of the *Hypericum* genus bloom in summer and early fall in a number of Sugarloaf habitats: springs, fields, roadsides, trails (especially the Yellow Trail), and dry upland woods.

St. John's-Wort

Hypericum L.
St. John's-Wort Family (Hypericaceae)
(Guttiferae, Clusiaceae)

Several species of St. John's-wort grow on Sugarloaf. All have golden-yellow or coppery star-shaped flowers with 5 petals and simple, opposite, entire leaves. (St. Andrew's-cross, which follows and is now grouped in the same genus—*Hypericum*—has only 4 petals, as do some other genus members not found here). Most of Sugarloaf's St. John's-worts are herbaceous wildflowers; one is a shrub, and a second shrubby species common in the region might be found here.

Spotted St. John's-Wort
Hypericum punctatum Lam.

Flowers: Yellow, 5-petaled, starlike, ⅓–⅔" across, in terminal clusters. Petals are dotted with black, especially on the underside (obvious with hand lens, may be subtle to the naked eye). Twenty or more stamens per flower. **Leaves:** Opposite, simple, sessile, ovate-oblong, with entire margins and blunt tips. Dotted with black (most obvious on lower leaf surface). **Height and growth habits:** 10"–3'; erect and not much branching below the flower clusters. **Habitat and range:** Moist fields, open woods, grassy areas, and roadsides. Southeastern Canada to Florida and Oklahoma. **On Sugarloaf—Blooming time:** June–September. **Locations:** Quite common on mountain along roadsides; East View, Yellow Trail; may be found in open woods along other trails. **Similar species:** Common St. John's-wort *(H. perforatum),* which is not as common here, has a branched growth habit and flower petals dotted black only along the margins. Dwarf St. John's-wort *(H. mutilum),* a smaller and more delicate plant, has a yellow or coppery yellow flower that is ¼" or less across.

Dwarf St. John's-Wort (Small-Flowered St. John's-Wort)
Hypericum mutilum L.

This St. John's-wort resembles the previous species but has tiny yellow or coppery **flowers** ¼" or less 9 fewer (5–12) stamens—and its petals and leaves are not dotted with black. Unlike the previous species, this plant often branches. **Leaves:** Opposite, simple, sessile, ovate or elliptic, ½–1" long. **Height:** 10"–3'. **Habitat and range:** Wet soil; southeastern Canada to Florida and Texas. **On Sugarloaf—Blooming time:** July–September. **Locations:** Yellow Trail, Sugarloaf Mountain Road, Mount Ephraim Road. **Similar species:** Tiny flowers and ovate or elliptic leaves separate it from other St. John's-worts.

Common St. John's-Wort

Hypericum perforatum L.

This European native was once a popular herbal remedy, used for many medical conditions, internal and external. During the 1990s it staged an herbal comeback as a treatment for depression, serving as a natural alternative to antidepressant drugs. **Flowers:** Star-shaped, 5 petaled sun-yellow flowers in small, branching terminal clusters; ¾–1" wide, usually with black dots along the petal margins (more easily observed with a hand lens). Stamens 20 or more. **Leaves:** Simple, opposite, sessile, linear-oblong, with translucent dots; ¼–1½" long. **Height and growth habits:** 1–3'; branched. **Habitat and range:** Fields, roadsides; European native now widely naturalized in the United States and southern Canada. **Herbal lore:** The fresh flowers were traditionally tinctured (in alcohol) or infused in olive oil for use as a remedy for wounds, ulcers, and bruises. St. John's-wort tea was used to treat "bladder ailments, depression, dysentery, diarrhea, worms," according to Peterson Field Guides' *Field Guide to Medicinal Plants: Eastern and Central*

Common St. John's-Wort

North America by Foster and Duke. In addition to its widespread contemporary use as an antidepressant, Foster and Duke note that experimentally this plant has shown anti-inflammatory, antibacterial, and antiretroviral properties. Common St. John's-wort can cause photodermatitis in sensitive individuals. **On Sugarloaf—Blooming time:** Summer. **Locations:** Yellow Trail; mountain roadsides (not as common on the mountain as in surrounding fields). **Similar species:** The combination of relatively large flowers, small leaves, and branched growth habit distinguish this plant from other herbaceous species found on the mountain.

Other St. John's-Wort Species

Hypericum

Three other St. John's-wort species were identified on Sugarloaf (in addition to St. Andrew's-cross, which follows) during a 1987 Stronghold plant survey conducted by botanist Richard Wiegand. Canadian St. John's-Wort (*H. canadense* L.) grows in wet soil and has tiny yellow flowers (¼" or less across) and narrow leaves (linear to oblanceolate) ⅓–1⅔" long. Orange-Grass or Pineweed [*H. gentianoides* (L.) B.S.P.] grows in dry fields, rocky outcrops, and disturbed sites. It has small yellow flowers and tiny scalelike paired leaves. Bushy St. John's-Wort or Glade St. John's-Wort (*H. densiflorum* Pursh) is a much-branched shrub with very dense flower clusters of 7 to many golden-yellow flowers per cluster. Flowers are ½" across with showy stamens. Bushy St. John's-wort favors moist meadows and bottomlands. Another shrubby species is more common in the region and might be found on Sugarloaf, although Tina and I have not seen it here and it is not on Wiegand's survey list. Shrubby St. John's-Wort (*H. prolificum* L.) is a branched shrub, usually growing in dry open woods (may also grow in moist soil) and rocky outcrops. The golden-yellow flowers are a little larger than the preceding species (about ¾" across), but they are in smaller, less dense terminal clusters of 3–7, with a few flowers also growing in the upper leaf axils.

St. Andrew's-Cross

Hypericum hypericoides (L.) Crantz
(Ascyrum hypericoides)
St. John's-Wort Family (Hypericaceae)
(Guttiferae, Clusiaceae)

This small woody plant has curious 4-petaled flowers. The petals are unevenly spaced, suggesting an off-kilter cross or a butterfly. **Flowers:** Yellow, with 4 rather narrow petals, diverging in pairs (*see* illustration). There are 2 large sepals per flower (as long as the petals or nearly so) and 2 tiny (or non-

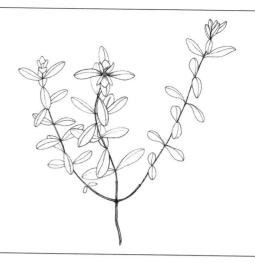

existent) ones. Flowers ½–1" across, borne on short stalks in the upper leaf axils. **Leaves:** Opposite, simple, sessile, variable in shape. Usually linear-oblong or elliptic with blunt apex and tapered or somewhat rounded base; ½–1½" long. **Height and growth habits:** 5"–1'; Usually much branched and somewhat sprawling. Older stems woody. **Habitat and range:** Dry or moist, rocky or sandy soil in open woods or fields; New Jersey to Kentucky, south to Florida and Texas. Also West Indies and Central America. **Herbal lore:** According to Foster and Duke in Peterson Field Guides' *Field Guide to Medicinal Plants: Eastern and Central North America,* "American Indians chewed the root for snakebites; root tea used for colic, fevers, pain, toothaches, diarrhea, dysentery; externally, as a wash for ulcerated breasts. Leaf tea used for bladder and kidney ailments, skin problems, and children's diarrhea." Despite this versatile range of applications, the authors warn that the plant may cause photodermatitis. **On Sugarloaf—Blooming time:** July–September. **Locations:** White Trail, Yellow Trail, Blue Trail, Mount Ephraim Road, Sugarloaf Mountain Road, and other mountain roadsides. **Similar species:** Most other 4-petaled, summer-blooming, yellow-blossomed wildflowers here are taller plants. Small sundrops *(Oenothera perennis)* has broad petals, which are notched at the apex and alternate leaves. Our St. John's-worts (other *Hypericum* species) have 5 petals per flower.

Violet Family

Violaceae

This family is best known for violets and pansies. **Family characteristics:** 16 genera and 800 species worldwide. Cosmopolitan but mainly temperate zone. **Economic importance:** Many of the several hundred members of the *Viola* genus are cultivated garden plants, including pansies and violets. Some family members used as medicinals. **Flowers:** Perfect, irregular or regular; 5 sepals and 5 petals. According to Heywood (*Flowering Plants of the World*), "All species of *Viola* have unequal petals with the lowermost pair, often the largest, forming a prominent spur. Their colored petals and scent attract pollinating insects which are said to be guided into the spur by linear markings, or honey guides, on the petals." When I first met Tina Brown, she had been studying ways flowers attract pollinators, and her description of these small lines on violets (and other flowers) as "runways for pollinators" made a lasting impression on me. **Fruit:** A capsule or berry. **Leaves:** Alternate or basal only; simple, usually with stipules. **Growth habits:** Herbs and shrubs. **Occurrence on Sugarloaf:** Violets grow in all habitats on Sugarloaf. Species are often difficult to sort out (*see* next entry).

Violets

Viola L.
Violet Family (Violaceae)

Violets are among Sugarloaf's most delightful wildflowers, blooming for several weeks during the spring. Species of purple, lavender, yellow, and white violets are found on the mountain. Some species grow near, or even in, the water; others are adapted to moist, rich woods or dry uplands. As pleasing as violets are to the eye, attempting to classify them by species can drive the mind crazy. Minute differences in leaf shape and pubescence divide one species from another, and violets confuse us even further by hybridizing. What follows is a list of species you are likely to encounter during your springtime rambles on the mountain. The list is organized by flower color, with brief descriptions. For more information on violets, consult a popular wildflower field guide such as Peterson's or Newcomb's or—for the truly intrepid—a more technical manual (Brown and Brown's *Herbaceous Plants of Maryland* or P. D. Strausbaugh and Earl L. Core's *Flora of West Virginia*). Approached with the right mix of adventurousness and humility, sorting out violets can be fun. However, should your efforts end in exasperation, just keep in mind that the violets never read the botany books.

Violet **flowers** are irregular, with 5 petals, the lowest petal ending in a spur at the back of the flower. In most species found on Sugarloaf, the **leaves** are on separate stalks (petioles). In a few, the flowers and leaves are on the same stalk. Separating violets into those with basal leaves (or leaves on separate stalks) and those with stem leaves is a helpful identification tool which we have employed here. One Sugarloaf species, the dog violet (*V. conspersa*), bears both stem and basal leaves. Although we have adopted much of the new botanical nomenclature published in Gleason and Cronquist's *Manual of Vascular Plants of Northeastern United States and Adjacent Canada (Second Edition)*, where violets are concerned we have stayed with most of the traditional nomenclature and classification, noting the Gleason and Cronquist changes following the older scientific name. In all but one case, our nomenclature choices are supported by Stanwyn G. Shetler and Sylvia Stone Orli in the Smithsonian Institution's *Annotated Checklist of the Vascular Plants of the Washington-Baltimore Area.*

Flower Color Lavender to Purple

Violets with Basal Leaves Only

Common Blue Violet (*Viola papilionacea* Pursh). (Included in *V. sororia* by Gleason and Cronquist and Stanwyn G. Shetler and Sylvia Stone Orli's *Annotated Checklist of the Vascular Plants of the Washington-Baltimore Area.*) **Flowers:** For starters, the common blue violet isn't blue but dark or light purple

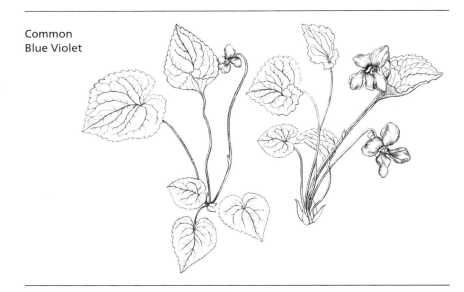

Common
Blue Violet

(and in at least one colony on Mount Ephraim Road, white). This is the common dooryard violet. Like most purple violets, the 5 petals are white or yellowish toward the center of the flower, and in this species the 2 side petals are bearded near the base. Flower stalks glabrous. **Leaves:** Heart-shaped, usually glabrous, although the petiole may be slightly pubescent. Leaves are slightly shorter, about the same height, or taller than the flowers. **On Sugarloaf—Blooming time:** March–June. **Locations:** Common mountainwide.

Woolly Blue Violet (*Viola sororia* Willd.). Similar to common blue violet but leaves, petioles, and flower stalks pubescent. **On Sugarloaf—Blooming**

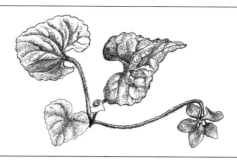

time: March–June. **Locations:** Mount Ephraim Road; may be found else-where but is less common than the preceding species.

Leconte's Violet (*Viola affinis* Leconte). (Included in *V. sororia* by Gleason and Cronquist but not by Shetler and Orli.) Very similar to the common blue violet, but the leaves are narrower, and all 3 lower flower petals are bearded toward the base (although bearding may be faint on lowest petal). **On Sugar-loaf—Blooming time:** April–June. **Locations:** Yellow Trail, White Trail. Fairly uncommon.

Ovate-Leaved Violet (Northern Downy Violet) (*Viola fimbriatula* Sm.). (Included in *V. sagittata* by Gleason and Cronquist but not by Shetler and Orli.) This violet is distinctively different from the first three. It is smaller, the whole plant is downy, and the leaves are usually ovate rather than heart-shaped. **Flowers:** Violet, white toward the center, the 3 lower petals usually bearded toward the base. (Specimens with little or no bearding on the low-est petal are found on Sugarloaf. Whether this is the result of hybridization or stubbornness, we do not know.) **Leaves:** Narrowly ovate, with varying shapes and petiole lengths; some leaves are slightly lobed near the base. Densely pubescent and forming rosettes at the base of the flower stalk that may lie rather flat to the ground. **On Sugarloaf—Blooming time:** April–May. **Locations:** White Trail, Yellow Trail, Blue Trail, Mount Ephraim Road.

Ovate-Leaved Violet

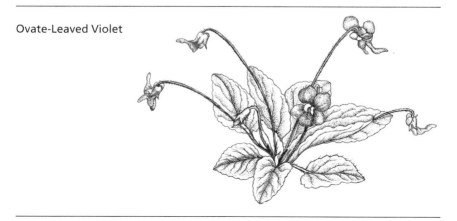

Southern Wood Violet

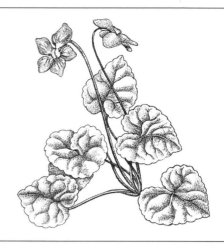

Southern Wood Violet (Southern Woolly Violet) (*Viola hirsutula* Brainerd). (Included in *V. villosa* by Gleason and Cronquist but not by Shetler and Orli.) Flower color and leaf shape distinguish this small violet from other species. **Flowers:** Reddish-purple; side petals bearded at the base. **Leaves:** Heart-shaped or kidney-shaped, usually rounded or bluntly pointed at the apex. Often lying horizontal to the ground. Slightly silvery with a hint of downiness above, often purplish below, at least along the veins. **On Sugarloaf—Blooming time:** April–May. **Locations:** Blue Trail, Yellow Trail; not common on Sugarloaf.

Marsh Blue Violet (Blue Marsh Violet) (*Viola cucullata* Aiton). This violet favors moist or wet habitats; it is often found growing near, or sometimes in,

Marsh Blue Violet

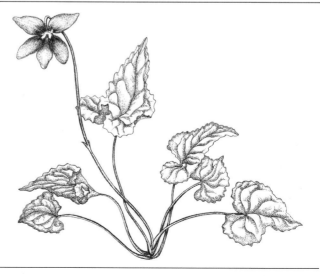

water. **Flowers:** Lavender, often with a darker purple blush toward the center. Side petals bearded with club-shaped hairs (club shape visible with a hand lens). Flowers usually quite a bit taller than the leaves, a characteristic that separates it from common blue violet *(V. papilionacea).* **Leaves:** Heart-shaped, ovate, or kidney-shaped, usually glabrous. **On Sugarloaf—Blooming time:** April–June. **Locations:** Bear Branch; springs, seeps, and small creeks along Mount Ephraim Road.

Three-Lobed Violet (*Viola triloba* Schwein.). (Included in *V. palmata* by Gleason and Cronquist but not by Shetler and Orli.) The leaves of this violet are usually, but not always, strikingly different from the typical heart shape that one associates with violets. **Flowers:** Purple, with 3 lower petals bearded toward the center (although bearding may be minimal or even nonexistent on lowest petal. **Leaves:** Usually 3-lobed, with widest lobe in the middle, but may be 5-lobed or unlobed and heart-shaped. Often a variety of leaf shapes on the same plant. **On Sugarloaf—Blooming time:** April–May. **Locations:** Blue Trail, Orange Trail, Yellow Trail.

Three-Lobed Violet

Wood Violet (Early Blue or Palmate-Leaved Violet) (*Viola palmata* L.). Similar to three-lobed violet *(V. triloba)* but leaves more evenly lobed and usually 5-lobed. Less common on Sugarloaf than three-lobed violet. **On Sugarloaf—Blooming time:** April–May. **Location:** Monocacy Natural Resources Management Area near Furnace Branch.

Violets with Stem and Basal Leaves

Dog Violet (American Dog Violet) (*Viola conspersa* Rchb.). **Flowers:** Lavender with darker veins; side petals bearded at base. Spur at the back of the flower up to ¼" long. **Leaves:** Stem and basal leaves present; stem leaves broadly heart-shaped with sharply toothed stipules; basal leaves broadly

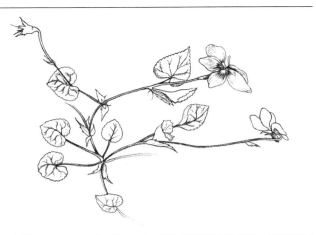

kidney-shaped. **Similar species:** Due to shared habitat, dog violet may be confused with marsh blue violet. Look for dog violet's long spur at the back of the flower and stem leaves with stipules. **On Sugarloaf—Blooming time:** April–May. **Locations:** Springs and seeps, Mount Ephraim Road; Bear Branch.

Flower Color White

Violets with Basal Leaves Only

See Common Blue Violet (*V. papilionacea*)

Primrose-Leaved Violet (Primrose Violet) (*Viola primulifolia* L.). **Flowers:** Small, white, the 3 lower petals with dark veins, on reddish stalks. **Leaves:** Ovate or oblong. Long petioles may be slightly reddish and appear winged at the top. **On Sugarloaf—Locations:** Damp open places on Yellow Trail.

Sweet White Violet (*Viola blanda* Willd.) is uncommon on Sugarloaf, and we have never encountered it here. It can be distinguished from the preceding species by its heart-shaped leaves. A plant of moist woods.

Violets with Stem Leaves

Field Pansy [*Viola kitaibeliana* R. & S. var. *rafinesquii* (Greene) Fern.]. (Classified as *Viola rafinesquii* Greene by Gleason and Cronquist.) **Flowers:** Small, creamy white to slightly bluish. **Leaves:** Small lower ones roundish, upper rather wedge-shaped with large, leafy, deeply lobed stipules. **On Sugarloaf—Blooming time:** April–May. **Location:** Mountain road.

Violets with Stem Leaves (Basal Leaves May or May Not Be Present)

Pale Violet (Cream or Creamy Violet) (*Viola striata* Aiton). A rather tall violet with creamy white flowers and heart-shaped stem leaves with sharply toothed stipules. (Basal leaves present early; soon die back.) **On Sugarloaf—Blooming time:** April–May. **Locations:** Furnace Branch, Monocacy Natural Resources Management Area; uncommon here.

Flower Color Yellow

Violets with Stem Leaves

Smooth Yellow Violet (Downy Yellow Violet) *(Viola pubescens* Aiton) *(Viola pensylvanica* Michx.). The only yellow violet commonly encountered on Sugarloaf. **Flowers:** Yellow, with purplish veins toward center. **Leaves:** Stem leaves present, ovate to heart-shaped, with small stipules. **On Sugarloaf—Blooming time:** April–May. **Locations:** White Trail, Monocacy Natural Resources Management Area.

Smooth Yellow Violet

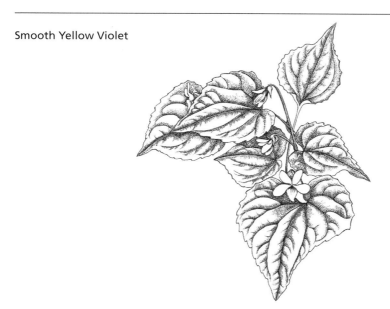

Mustard Family

Brassicaceae
(Cruciferae)

An extremely important food-producing family, yielding many vegetables including broccoli, cauliflower, cabbages, and the familiar condiment mustard. Many other plants in the family are grown for ornament, and a number have become troublesome weeds. Sugarloaf's mustard family members include native wildflowers, garden escapes, and one very damaging invasive: garlic-mustard *(Alliara petiolata)*. **Family characteristics:** 340 genera and 3,350 species worldwide. Widely distributed throughout the temperate regions of the Northern Hemisphere. Many species favor cool and cold climates. (Whenever I think of the mustard family, I picture my brother and sister-in-law's Alaska garden brimming with 25-pound cabbages and oversized broccoli and kohlrabi.) **Economic importance:** Food crops, garden ornamentals. **Flowers:** 4-petaled flowers are cross-shaped, giving rise to the former scientific name for the family, Cruciferae. **Fruit:** A long and slender podlike silique or shorter and wider silicle, dry fruits characteristic of the family. Two separate halves are often separated by a slender paperlike partition. Fruit usually splits open (dehiscent) to release seeds. **Leaves:** Usually alternate, less often opposite (although some Sugarloaf species are opposite or whorled); simple or so deeply lobed that they may appear compound; compound. **Growth habits:** Herbs, rarely shrubs. **Occurrence on Sugarloaf:** Family members found in every habitat from upland woods to springs, streams, stream banks, and disturbed sites. In addition to the species described and illustrated in this guide, you may also find other family members in grassy areas and other disturbed sites including a plant called cow cress, field cress, or field peppergrass *(Lepidium campestre);* a plant named wild peppergrass or poor-man's pepper *(Lepidium virginicum);* and the common garden weed known as shepherd's purse *(Capsella bursa-pastoris).* Field mustard *(Brassica rapa)*—a plant with bright yellow flowers and clasping leaves—often grows near the mountain base. Only wild peppergrass or poor-man's pepper is native; the other three plant species just mentioned are introduced species.

Cut-Leaved Toothwort (Cut-Leaved Pepperroot)

Dentaria laciniata Muhl. ex Willd.
(Cardamine concatenata)
Mustard Family (Brassicaceae)

A spring-blooming eastern woodland wildflower that grows in abundance on rich soil in a few Sugarloaf locations. **Flowers:** Small, 4-petaled, ½–1" across; white, pink, or lavender, in small upright terminal cluster. **Leaves:** Opposite or whorled, simple or compound; usually there is a whorl of 3 leaves beneath the flower cluster. Leaves are deeply, palmately cut into several long, thin lobes or leaflets, with toothed or untoothed margins. Overall leaf 2–5" across, petioled. **Fruit:** Thin beaked silique, 1–2" long (including beak), present with or after the flowers. **Height and growth habits:** 6–15"; upright. **Habitat and range:** Moist, rich woods; Maine, Quebec, and Minnesota south to Florida, Louisiana, and Oklahoma. **On Sugarloaf—Blooming time:** Late March–May. **Locations:** Yellow Trail, Blue Trail along northern ridge and near White Rocks, Bear Branch, Monocacy Natural Resources Management Area. **Similar species:** The leaves distinguish it from the less

common slender toothwort *(D. heterophylla)*, which follows. Note the large basal leaves of slender toothwort.

Slender Toothwort (Appalachian Toothwort)

Dentaria heterophylla Nutt.
(Cardamine angustata)
Mustard Family (Brassicaceae)

Slender toothwort grows in rich soil, often alongside the more common cut-leaved toothwort *(D. laciniata)*. Slender toothwort comes into bloom in April, several days behind the cut-leaved toothwort. Thereafter they are often found in simultaneous bloom. **Flowers:** Smallish, 4-petaled, ½–1" across; a deeper purplish-pink than the preceding species, in upright terminal clusters. **Fruit:** A narrow silique, about 1" long, tapered at both ends. **Leaves:** Two types: (1) a 3-leafleted, toothed basal leaf, rather like a large strawberry leaf, 2–4" across; (2) a smaller pair of opposite or subopposite stem leaves, each deeply cut with 3 narrow toothed or untoothed lobes. **Height:** 4–15". **Habitat and range:** Rich woods; New Jersey to Indiana, south to Georgia and Mississippi. **On Sugarloaf—Blooming time:** April–May. **Locations:** Yellow Trail and other trails, Bear Branch, Monocacy Natural

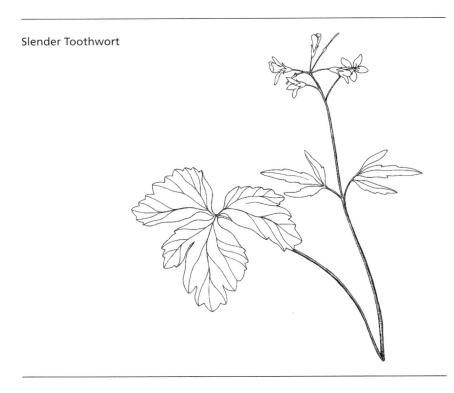

Resources Management Area. **Similar species:** *See* cut-leaved toothwort *(D. laciniata)*, which has paler flowers and stem leaves only.

Hairy Bittercress

Cardamine hirsuta L.
Mustard Family (Brassicaceae)

Hairy bittercress is a small, rather inconspicuous naturalized plant that isn't found in the Peterson or Newcomb wildflower guides. It is common on Sugarloaf. **Flowers:** Tiny (less than ¼" across), white, 4-petaled, in upright terminal clusters. **Fruit:** Small, thin, erect siliques often present with the flowers. **Leaves:** Alternate, pinnately compound. Stem leaves few, each with 5–9 leaflets bearing sparse long hairs (visible with a hand lens). Basal leaves in a rosette. **Height and growth habits:** 3–10"; upright or slightly leaning. **Habitat and range:** A wide-ranging Old World plant now naturalized in a variety of habitats from New York to Illinois and Alabama. **On Sugarloaf— Blooming time:** March–May. **Locations:** Yellow Trail; near parking lot at mountain base; East View; common mountainwide. **Similar species:** Pennsylvania bittercress *(C. pensylvanica)* is a larger plant, less common on Sugarloaf, and confined to springs and streams.

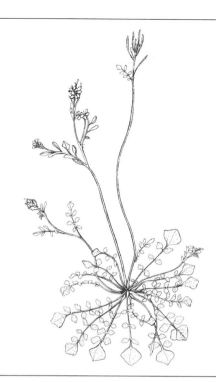

Pennsylvania Bittercress

Cardamine pensylvanica Muhl. ex Willd.
Mustard Family (Brassicaceae)

Similar to hairy bittercress but a larger, lusher plant (8–24" tall), Pennsylvania bittercress is best distinguished by habitat. It grows in Sugarloaf's springs, seeps, and streams. **Range:** Most of the United States and southern Canada. **On Sugarloaf**—Blooming **time:** Spring through early summer. **Locations:** Springs, seeps, and streams near Mount Ephraim Road and along Yellow Trail; Furnace Branch; Monocacy Natural Resources Management Area.

Spring Cress (Bulbous Cress)

Cardamine bulbosa (Schreb. ex Muhl.) B.S.P.
(Cardamine rhomboidea)
Mustard Family (Brassicaceae)

A spring-flowering plant of moist eastern woodlands that grows along Sugarloaf's streamsides and in seeps and springs. **Flowers:** White, 4-petaled, about ½" across in loose, upright clusters. **Leaves:** Alternate, simple; basal leaves ovate, heart-shaped, or nearly round on long petioles. Petioles grow shorter going up the plant stalk, and upper leaves are sessile or nearly so. Stem leaves more narrowly ovate (compared to basal leaves), oblong, or lanceolate. Margins bluntly, rather sparsely and irregularly toothed (or nearly smooth). **Height:** 8–24". **Habitat and range:** Moist or wet woods and fields or shallow water; eastern United States and Canada. **On Sugarloaf—Blooming time:** April–June. **Locations:** Bear Branch and other wet locations along mountain roads and trailsides. **Similar species:** Leaves separate spring cress from native toothworts (*Dentaria* spp.). Garlic-mustard *(Alliaria petiolata)* is far more common than spring cress and has regularly heart-shaped or triangular leaves with a garlic odor when crushed.

Common Winter-Cress (Yellow-Rocket)

Barbarea vulgaris R. Br.
Mustard Family (Brassicaceae)

Common winter-cress bears showy clusters of brilliant yellow flowers in spring. A common mustard family plant on and around Sugarloaf. **Flowers:** Small (less than ½" across), yellow, 4-petaled, usually in several upright clusters. **Fruit:** Slender silique, erect or spreading, about 1" long. **Leaves:** Alternate and variable. Basal leaves are long (up to several inches) and lobed, with an ovate or roundish terminal lobe and 2–8 smaller side lobes. Leaves often follow this pattern partway up the plant stalk, but upper leaves are small (1" or less) and not as regularly lobed. Upper leaves may have rounded or

Common
Winter-Cress

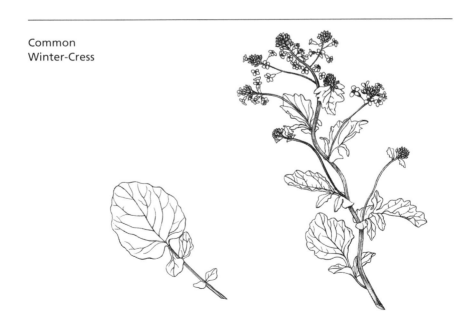

pointed teeth or small lobes; sometimes their margins are entire. Leaves clasp the stem. **Height:** 1–2'. **Habitat and range:** Meadows, streamsides, roadsides; a European native, widely naturalized in eastern Canada and the United States. **Herbal lore:** Used in Europe as a poultice for wounds. In Peterson Field Guides' *Field Guide to Medicinal Plants: Eastern and Central North America,* Foster and Duke report that the Cherokees ate the greens as a blood purifier, but they warn that studies show the plant may cause kidney malfunction. **On Sugarloaf—Blooming time:** April–June. **Locations:** Meadows and streamsides on and around Sugarloaf, roadsides, most trails. **Similar species:** Early winter-cress *(B. verna)* is far less common on and around Sugarloaf. Very similar to common winter-cress, early winter-cress basal leaves have more lobes per leaf (8–20), and most early winter-cress upper leaves are also lobed. Early winter-cress siliques are 1½–3" in length, longer than those of common winter-cress.

Smooth Rockcress
Arabis laevigata (Muhl.) Poir.
Mustard Family (Brassicaceae)

A spring wildflower with small, rather inconspicuous flowers. Smooth rockcress is fairly common on Sugarloaf. **Flowers:** Small, bell-shaped, white or greenish-white, 4-petaled (each petal ¼" or less in length); flowers borne in a loose, elongated terminal raceme. **Fruit:** Thin horizontal or drooping

Smooth Rockcress

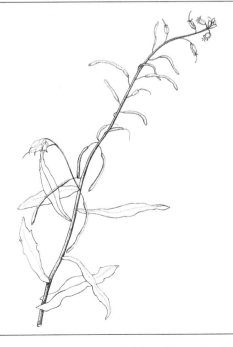

silique, 1–4" long. **Leaves:** Alternate, simple, sessile or with clasping base. Lanceolate or linear, with smooth or sparsely toothed margins, 2–5" long. Plant stalk may have a whitish bloom. **Height and growth habits:** 1–3'; may lean or nod. **Habitat and range:** Woods, rocky hillsides; southwestern Canada to South Dakota, south to Georgia and Oklahoma. **On Sugarloaf—Blooming time:** April–June. **Locations:** Blue Trail, Orange Trail, mountain road (below Strong Mansion), Monocacy Natural Resources Management Area; quite common mountainwide. **Similar species:** Simple, lanceolate or linear, clasping or sessile leaves and long, thin siliques separate this plant from similar mustard family members of Sugarloaf. However, several other rockcress *(Arabis)* species are indigenous to Maryland and the mid-Atlantic region.

Garlic-Mustard

Alliaria petiolata (M. Bieb.) Cavara & Grande
(Alliaria officinalis)
Mustard Family (Brassicacea)

Garlic-mustard, so named for its garlic-scented leaves, is a European native which has spread throughout the eastern United States. The plant has become an ecological problem, as it grows in dense stands, crowding out na-

Garlic-Mustard

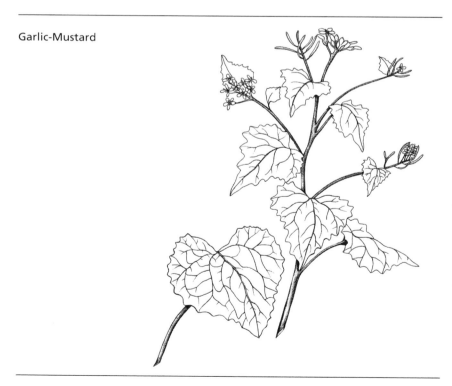

tive wildflowers. Kerrie Kyde, a Sugarloaf-area plant ecologist, is studying means to control garlic-mustard effectively where and when it threatens native plant populations. **Flowers:** Small, white, 4-petaled, in clusters. Flowers ¼–½" across. **Fruit:** 1–3" silique. **Leaves:** Alternate, simple, heart-shaped (cordate) or triangular, with coarse, blunt teeth. The lower leaves on long petioles, upper leaves often short-stalked or nearly sessile; 1–5" long. Leaves have garlic odor when crushed. **Height:** 6"–3'. **Habitat and range:** Grows in a number of habitats, including moist open woods, floodplains, and roadsides, and other disturbed sites; widely naturalized from Europe. **On Sugarloaf—Blooming time:** April–June. **Locations:** Mountainwide. There is a large patch of garlic-mustard along the Red Trail near the summit. **Similar species:** The combination of large heart-shaped or triangular leaves and white flowers separates garlic-mustard from other mustard family members found on Sugarloaf.

Dame's-Rocket (Dame's-Violet)

Hesperis matronalis L.
Mustard Family (Brassicaceae)

Although its showy flowers brighten the spring landscape throughout the Washington area and eastern North America, dame's-rocket is a nonnative

Dame's-Rocket

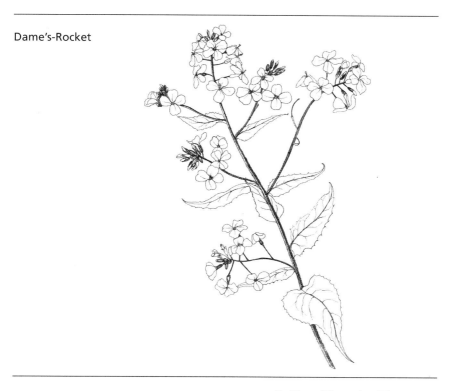

garden escape that could prove harmfully invasive should it follow in the footsteps of its fellow family member, garlic-mustard *(Alliaria petiolata)*. Dame's-rocket has been planted to ornament area roadsides when, in my opinion, native wildflowers should prove ornament enough. **Flowers:** Purple, pink, or white, 4-petaled, in showy terminal clusters. Each flower ¾–1¼" across. **Fruit:** A narrow silique. **Leaves:** Alternate or subopposite, simple, lanceolate, ovate-lanceolate, or deltoid-lanceolate, sessile or short-petioled (although a few lower leaves may have long petioles), shallowly toothed, pubescent; 2–6" long. **Height:** 1–3½'. **Habitat and range:** Roadsides, thickets, open woods, bottomlands; a Eurasian native that has escaped from cultivation in the eastern United States and Canada. **On Sugarloaf—Blooming time:** May–July. **Locations:** Mount Ephraim Road; common along area roadsides. **Similar species:** Honesty *(Lunaria annua)* has similar flowers, but its leaves are heart-shaped or broadly triangular, and its showy silicles are elliptic. Phlox *(Phlox)* species have 5 petals.

Honesty (Moneywort)

Lunaria annua L.

Mustard Family (Brassicaceae)

Honesty has showy flowers and large roundish, flattened fruit, which is used in dried arrangements. This is a European native that has escaped from cultivation. **Flowers:** Brilliant purplish-pink, 4-petaled, ¾–1¼" across, in terminal clusters. **Fruit:** An elliptic silicle, which is thin, flat, and ¾–1¾" across at maturity. **Leaves:** Alternate, opposite or subopposite, simple, heart-

Honesty

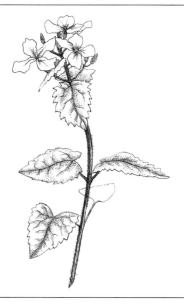

shaped or triangular, with coarse teeth. With petioles or sessile; 1–3½" long.
On Sugarloaf—Blooming time: April–June. **Location:** Mountain road near intersections of White and Yellow Trails. **Similar species:** Dame's-Rocket *(Hesperis matronalis)* has narrower leaves and flowers ranging from white to purple.

Heath Family

Ericaceae

As is the case with the carrot or parsley family (Apiaceae), the heath family produces both highly edible and highly toxic plant species (mountain laurel is toxic). Members of the heath family thrive in the acidic soils of Sugarloaf's upland woods and rocky outcrops. The evergreen shrub called mountain laurel *(Kalmia latifolia)* is Sugarloaf's most dominant flowering plant. Several other family members produce showy flowers and, in the case of blueberries and huckleberries *(Vaccinium, Gaylussacia),* edible fruit. According to Alexander C. Martin, Herbert S. Zim, and Arnold L. Nelson's *American Wildlife and Plants: A Guide to Wildlife Food Habits,* blueberries "are important to the scarlet tanager, bluebird, thrushes, and other songbirds as well as to the black bear, chipmunk, white-footed mouse, and other mammals. Deer and rabbits browse freely on the plants." **Family characteristics:** 125 genera and 3,500 species worldwide. Cosmopolitan. **Economic importance:** Important ornamentals including many species of rhododendron and azalea *(Rhododendron);* significant food plants: blueberries, cranberries, bilberries *(Vaccinium).* **Flowers:** Regular or somewhat irregular, usually perfect, with 4 or 5 sepals that are frequently fused at the base and 4 to 5 petals often fused to form a bell-shaped or bowl-shaped tube. **Fruit:** Capsule, drupe, or berry. **Leaves:** Mostly alternate, simple, often evergreen and leathery. **Growth habits:** Mainly shrubs. **Occurrence on Sugarloaf:** Family members found in all habitats. In addition to the species described and illustrated in the next entries, *see also* Botanical Key and Guide to Trees, Shrubs, and Woody Vines.

Shrub (appearing herbaceous)

Trailing Arbutus (Mayflower)

Epigaea repens L.
Heath Family (Ericaceae)

Trailing arbutus has an unforgettable fragrance that is well worth getting down on your hands and knees (or even lower!) to experience. Because it re-

Trailing Arbutus

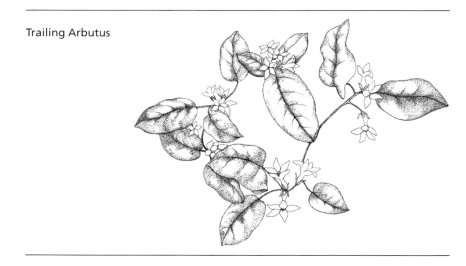

quires some gymnastics to appreciate this low-growing plant fully, Smithsonian botanist Stan Shetler calls the trailing arbutus a "belly plant." When you find this plant in bloom, inhale deeply but please do not disturb the plant or its habitat. Trailing arbutus is in the heath family, along with mountain laurel, azalea, rhododendron, and blueberry. These plants are happily suited to Sugarloaf's acidic soil. Trailing arbutus has a persistent woody stem, and although it is diminutive in size, botanical manuals group it with shrubs. It is one of Sugarloaf's earliest and most delightful wildflowers. As mentioned in the preface, the trailing arbutus (or mayflower) is the state flower of Massachusetts and the provincial flower of Nova Scotia. **Flowers:** Pale pink or white, perfumed, each flower a small tube ending in 5 flared lobes. About ½" long, growing in small terminal and upper axillary clusters. **Leaves:** Alternate, evergreen, leathery. Ovate or oblong, with entire margin and a rounded or heart-shaped base. Leaves ¾–3½" long, often pubescent, especially on upper surface and along the margin and petiole. **Growth habits:** A trailing plant with a woody stem, growing close to the ground. **Habitat and range:** Rocky or sandy acid soil; Newfoundland to Saskatchewan, south to Florida, Mississippi, and Iowa. **Herbal lore:** American Indians used the leaf tea for urinary tract disorders and as a blood purifier. A folk remedy for kidney stones, it was sold by Shakers as "gravel plant." Although apparently effective, it does have toxic properties. This plant was extirpated in many areas where it was harvested as an herbal and for its fragrant spring flowers. **On Sugarloaf—Blooming time:** Late March–early May. **Locations:** Blue Trail, White Trail, Yellow Trail, Mount Ephraim Road. **Similar species:** None on Sugarloaf.

Shrub (appearing herbaceous)

Wintergreen (Checkerberry, Teaberry)
Gaultheria procumbens L.
Heath Family (Ericaceae)

A delicate plant that is common in woodlands of the northern United States and Canada, wintergreen grows south to Georgia and Alabama in the mountains. It is the state herb of Maine. Tina and I have found wintergreen next to the Red Trail on Sugarloaf and near the banks of Furnace Branch in the Monocacy Natural Resources Management Area. **Flowers:** White, waxy, bell-shaped, and drooping, ending in 5 tiny lobes. Flowers ¼–½" long, dangling singly or in small clusters. **Fruit:** A showy bright red "berry" (technically a capsule surrounded by a fleshy calyx). Edible and tasting of wintergreen. **Leaves:** Alternate, simple, shiny evergreen, leathery and glabrous, with a strong wintergreen flavor. Elliptic or obovate, shallowly toothed or entire, ¾–2" long. **Height and growth habits:** 2–6"; in the words of Brown and Brown (*Woody Plants of Maryland*), "Aromatic, soft-woody shrub(s), the short, upright, leafy branches from horizontal, running stems just under the soil surface." **Habitat and range:** Dry or moist acidic woods; Newfoundland to Manitoba, south to Georgia and Alabama (in the mountains) and Kentucky. **Herbal lore:** Once the source of oil of wintergreen, this plant has been used in liniments and other medicines. In Peterson Field Guides' *Field Guide to Medicinal Plants: Eastern and Central North America,* Foster and Duke warn that the pure essential oil has highly toxic properties. They write: "Traditionally, leaf tea used for colds, headaches, stomachaches, fevers, kidney ailments. . . . Experimentally [wintergreen is] analgesic, carminative, anti-inflammatory, antiseptic. In experiments, small amounts have delayed the

Wintergreen

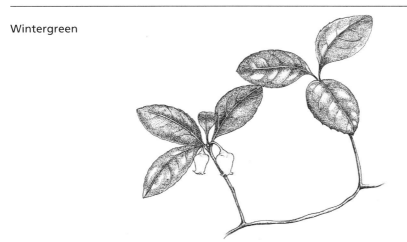

onset of tumors." **Wildlife lore:** According to Brown and Brown: "The fruits are eaten by ruffed grouse, wild turkey and other birds. Deer and black bear eat the twigs, leaves and fruits." **On Sugarloaf—Blooming time:** June–August. **Fruiting time:** Maturing in late summer or early fall; remaining on the plant through winter. **Locations:** Red Trail; Monocacy Natural Resources Management Area; possible elsewhere in cool woods of Sugarloaf. **Similar species:** In the absence of flowers or fruit, use the glabrous leaves to separate from trailing arbutus *(Epigaea repens)*. Could also be confused with very young mountain laurel *(Kalmia latifolia)* plants, which are toxic. The wintergreen leaf and fruit flavor is diagnostic, but this plant is too scarce in the Sugarloaf area to nibble, and plant gathering is prohibited in local parks.

Shrub

Mountain Laurel
Kalmia latifolia L.
Heath Family (Ericaceae)

Mountain laurel is the state flower of Connecticut and Pennsylvania. At Sugarloaf the flowering of the mountain laurel is the botanical event of the year and spring's dramatic farewell! During good blooming years mountain laurel adorns the entire mountain with clustered white and pink flowers against shiny evergreen leaves. The laurel is particularly beautiful in the places where it spills over Sugarloaf's quartzite rocks. **Flowers:** White or pink, 5-lobed, ¾–1" across, with a deep pink ring at the center. Ten stamens are at first arched and inserted into the corolla, and there are purple dots at the spots where they join. Later they spring free of the corolla. Flowers borne on long viscid, pubescent flower stalks in roundish snowball-sized clusters. The flower buds resemble Christmas mints. **Leaves:** Alternate (or nearly opposite), simple, evergreen; 2–6" long, elliptic or lanceolate, tapered to both ends, on (sometimes reddish) petiole. **Height:** 3–20'. **Habitat and range:** Usually acidic (and often rocky) woods; eastern United States west to Indiana and Louisiana. **Herbal lore:** Mountain laurel is a toxic plant, which once was used medicinally. According to Foster and Duke (Peterson Field Guides' *Field Guide to Medicinal Plants: Eastern and Central North America*): "American Indians used leaf tea as an external wash for pain, rheumatism, in liniments for vermin. Historically, herbalists used minute doses to treat syphilis, fever, jaundice, heart conditions, neuralgia, and inflammation. Warning: Plant is highly toxic; even honey from flowers is reportedly toxic. Avoid use." **On Sugarloaf—Blooming time:** Late May–early June. Often blooming on Memorial Day. **Locations:** Abundant mountainwide. **Similar species:** Great rhododendron *(Rhododendron maximum)* and other evergreen rhododendrons have

Mountain Laurel

been planted on the mountain and may appear to be growing wild. They have larger flowers. The mountain's cultivated azaleas (*Rhododendron* spp.) growing along the roadside have smaller leaves and, except for the white specimens, are more brilliantly colored. Not likely to be confused with our native deciduous pinxter flower or pink azalea (*Rhododendron periclymenoides*), which blooms in April and early May.

Shrub

Pinxter Flower (Pink Azalea)

Rhododendron periclymenoides (Michx.) Shinners
(Rhododendron nudiflorum)
Heath Family (Ericaceae)

An eastern North American shrub of delicate beauty and fragrance. Sugarloaf visitors drawn to the display of cultivated azaleas planted along the mountain road often leave unaware that this flowering native azalea can be found on a short walk down any of the mountain's scenic trails. Even without leaving your car, you may catch a glimpse of the wild pinxter flower (or pink azalea) in the spring woodlands near the road. The pinxter flower blooms just as the leaves are emerging on Sugarloaf's trees and shrubs, co-

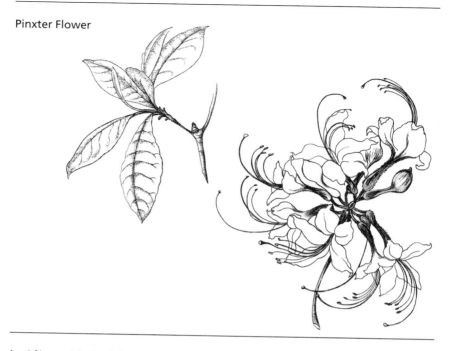

Pinxter Flower

inciding with the blooming time of the cultivated azaleas. **Flowers:** Round-ish clusters of several pale to deep pink flowers that are deliciously and subtly fragrant (degree of fragrance varies). Dark pink more or less pubescent corolla tube flares into 5 paler pink lobes. Pink stamens and pistil are long, protruding, and upswept. Flowers 1–1¾" across, emerging just before or with the new leaves. (Note: Some botanical guides describe this plant as lacking or nearly lacking in fragrance, which seems to be true for only a few Sugarloaf specimens.) **Leaves:** Alternate (but may appear whorled in terminal clusters), simple, with finely hairy entire margins. Oblong, obovate, or elliptic, with wedge-shaped base and short petiole (to nearly sessile); 1¾–4" long. A pale spring green as they emerge with flowers. **Height and growth habits:** 2–8'; branching toward the top. **Habitat and range:** Woods, stream banks; New England to South Carolina and Tennessee. **On Sugarloaf—Blooming time:** April–May. **Locations:** Most trails and wooded roadsides. **Similar species:** Mountain laurel *(Kalmia latifolia)* has evergreen leaves and smaller, later flowers. Great rhododendron *(R. maximum)* has evergreen leaves and later blooms. Several other native *Rhododendron* species grow elsewhere in Maryland *(see* Brown and Brown's *Woody Plants of Maryland).* The rare orange-flowered flame azalea *(R. calendulaceum)* of Garrett County is planted near the pond at the mountain's base. Two small clusters of an unidentified nonindigenous *Rhododendron* bloom near the White Trail at the same time the pinxter flower blooms. They have pale rose flowers (1 of 5—or sometimes 6—lobes is gold-spotted) and evergreen leaves. The paler lower leaf surface of this mystery *Rhododendron* is rusty-spotted.

Shrub

Flame Azalea

Rhododendron calendulaceum (Michx.) Torr.
Heath Family (Ericaceae)

The flame azalea is so rare in Maryland that the Department of Natural Resources gives it an S1 ranking on its list of *Rare, Threatened, and Endangered Plants of Maryland*. S1 is the level of highest concern. These plants are considered "critically imperiled" and are actively tracked by the Wildlife and Heritage Division of DNR. Only a few flame azaleas are known to naturally occur in Maryland, in a small number of sites in Garrett County. Several flame azaleas are planted on Stronghold property near the pond at the mountain base. Spring **flowers** are orange, funnel-shaped with 5 flared lobes, and fragrant. **Leaves** are oblong, obovate, or oblanceolate; entire; not fully grown when flowers appear in May. **Habitat and range:** Mountain woods; Pennsylvania and southern Ohio to Georgia and Alabama.

Flame Azalea

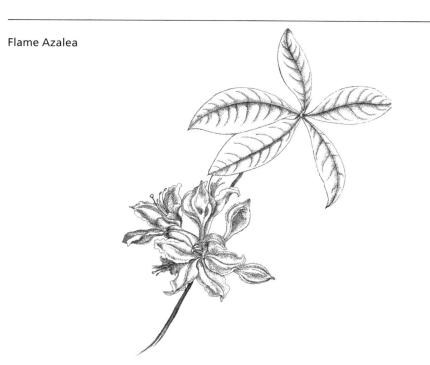

Shrub

Great Rhododendron (Rosebay, Great Laurel)

Rhododendron maximum L.
Heath Family (Ericaceae)

A larger-bloomed, larger-leafed relative of mountain laurel, great rhododendron is an evergreen flowering shrub of moist woods and streamsides. It creates scenic thickets in the hills and mountains of Virginia, Pennsylvania, and western Maryland, often growing beneath hemlock trees. The few specimens of great rhododendron flanking the roadside below the Strong Mansion were undoubtedly planted there. **Flowers:** White to pale pink, 1–2½ inches across, in large, round terminal clusters. Flowers are 5 petaled, and the uppermost petal is spotted greenish-yellow. **Leaves:** Mostly alternate (some may be opposite), simple, leathery, evergreen. Oblong-obovate, with entire margins; 3–10" long. **Height and growth habits:** Large shrub or small tree, rarely up to 30' tall. **Habitat and range:** Often forms dense thickets in moist, acidic woods; common along streams and in swamps; southeastern Canada, eastern United States, in the mountains south to Georgia and Alabama. **On Sugarloaf—Blooming time:** June–July. Often blooming on the summer solstice. **Locations:** Mountain roadside near the Strong Mansion and at the mountain base. **Similar species:** Mountain laurel *(Kalmia lati-*

folia) has smaller flowers and is abundant on Sugarloaf. Pinxter flower or pink azalea *(R. periclymenoides)* is an earlier-blooming deciduous species.

Shrubs

Blueberry, Deerberry, Huckleberry
(Vaccinium, Gaylussacia)
Heath Family (Ericaceae)

Sugarloaf's blueberries, deerberries, and huckleberries bloom in spring and early summer, fruiting soon thereafter. Blueberries and huckleberries are highly prized edibles; deerberries are inedible raw but may be used in pies and marmalade, according to Brown and Brown's *Woody Plants of Maryland.* All species are important food sources for wildlife.

Lowbush Blueberry (Late Lowbush Blueberry)
Vaccinium pallidum Aiton
(Vaccinium vacillans)

Lowbush blueberry is Sugarloaf's most common blueberry, growing along hillsides flanking large stretches of most trails. Lowbush blueberrry often grows alongside deerberry and huckleberry. **Flowers:** Small, bell-shaped or tubular, greenish-white, pinkish, or purplish, with 5 very shallow lobes at the tip. Each flower about ¼" long, in small, loose clusters. **Fruit:** A dark blue, often glaucous berry. **Leaves:** Simple, alternate, entire or minutely toothed. Leaves paler below. Ovate, elliptic, or obovate, ⅔–2" long; short-petioled to sessile or nearly so. Young twigs usually bright green or sometimes reddish-green. **Height and growth habits:** 6"–3½' tall; a low shrub often growing in large colonies. **Habitat and range:** Dry upland woods, old

Lowbush Blueberry

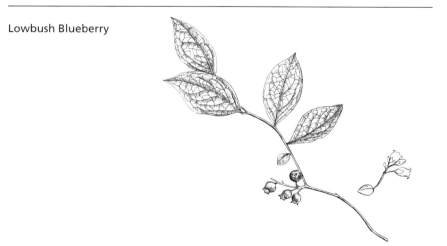

fields, thickets, clearings; eastern United States and Canada. **On Sugarloaf—Blooming time:** April–June. **Fruiting time:** June into summer. **Locations:** Very common in open dry woods mountainwide. **Similar species:** Highbush blueberry *(V. corymbosum)* is a 3–15' shrub of Sugarloaf's wetland areas. Its flowers are pinkish or whitish, its berries blue. Deerberry *(V. stamineum)* has mature flowers that are flared at the tip (not tubular). Common lowbush or early low blueberry *(V. angustifolium)* might possibly be found on or around Sugarloaf. It has leaves that are usually not much paler below. Sugarloaf's common huckleberry species—black huckleberry *(Gaylussacia baccata)*—has leaves that are covered with shiny yellowish resinous dots (visible with hand lens or sharp naked eye).

Deerberry

Vaccinium stamineum L.

Deerberry often grows alongside lowbush blueberry on Sugarloaf. Distinguish it by its flared (not tubular) white, greenish-white, or purplish **flowers** and its larger berry, which is green, bluish, or purplish. Deerberry has entire **leaves.**

Deerberry

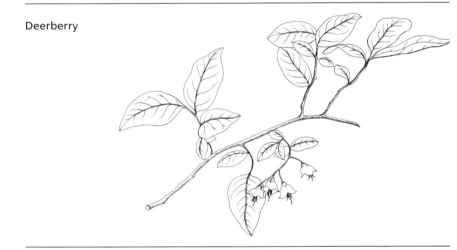

Black Huckleberry

Gaylussacia baccata (Wangenh.) K. Koch

Distinguish black huckleberry from blueberries and deerberry by the tiny, shiny resinous dots on its **leaves** (use a hand lens if necessary). Its **flowers** are pink or reddish, and its leaves entire. Huckleberry **fruit,** while edible and very similar to blueberry's, is a black or dark blue fleshy drupe containing 10 seeds. **Locations:** Trails and roadsides mountainwide.

Black
Huckleberry

Pyrola, Wintergreen, or Shinleaf Family

Pyrolaceae

A single member of this family is common on Sugarloaf, striped or spotted wintergreen *(Chimaphila maculata),* one of the mountain's most delightful early summer wildflowers. **Family characteristics:** 4 genera and 46 species worldwide. Mainly in the northern temperate and Arctic zones, as far south as Mexico and the West Indies. **Economic importance:** A few ornamentals and medicinals. **Flowers:** Perfect, regular, with 4 or 5 sepals and 4 or 5 petals. **Fruit:** A capsule. **Leaves:** Alternate or (as in our species) whorled or rarely opposite. Leaves usually evergreen; many species with basal or nearly basal leaves. **Growth habits:** Perennial herbs (some semiwoody). **Occurrence on Sugarloaf:** Most trails are graced by striped wintergreen with its waxy, nodding early summer flowers.

Striped Wintergreen (Spotted Wintergreen)

Chimaphila maculata (L.) Pursh
Pyrola, Wintergreen, or Shinleaf Family (Pyrolaceae)

A charming early summer wildflower with evergreen leaves and nodding, often paired flowers. A botanist acquaintance of mine says the flowers remind him of old-fashioned street lamps. The plant stalk is often somewhat woody, especially near the base. **Flowers:** Frequently in pairs but may grow singly or several per stalk; 5 waxy white or pale pink petals are rounded at tips. Pistil is showy, short, wide, and usually green. Flowers ½–1" across. **Fruit:** Small, round woody capsules stay on the plant through winter. My daughter calls them little pumpkins. (This plant obviously inspires the imagination.) **Leaves:** Opposite or (more often) whorled, simple, lanceolate, dark green or blue-green with white stripes along the veins. Thick, leathery, evergreen, ¾–3" long, with sparse sharp, shallow teeth. **Height:** 2–10". **Habitat and range:** Dry, acidic woods; New England to Michigan, south to Georgia and Alabama. **On Sugarloaf—Blooming time:** June–early July. **Locations:**

Striped Wintergreen

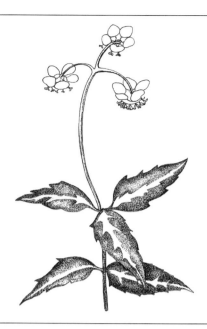

Trails mountainwide. **Similar species:** None on Sugarloaf although pipsis-sewa or prince's-pine *(C. umbellata)*, a widely distributed North American/Eurasian plant, grows in the mid-Atlantic region. Its leaves lack white stripes.

Indian Pipe Family

Monotropaceae

A family of saprophytic and parasitic plants without chlorophyll and conse-quently lacking any green (plants are white, purple, red, yellow, or brown). Saprophytes live on decayed organic matter or receive their nutrients in a symbiotic fungal association. The one common Sugarloaf species—Indian pipe *(Monotropa uniflora)*—is an all-white saprophyte. **Family characteris-tics:** 10 genera and 12 species worldwide. (Plants of this small family are sometimes included in the pyrola family.) **Flowers:** Perfect, regular, with 2–6 often bractlike sepals and 3–8 (usually 4 or 5) petals. Petals either distinct or joined in a lobed tube. **Fruit:** A capsule or berry. **Leaves:** Alternate, scale-like (not green). **Growth habits:** Fleshy herbs without chlorophyll. **Occur-rence on Sugarloaf:** Indian pipe is quite common along Sugarloaf trails but is nowhere abundant. A second species—pinesap *(M. hypopithys)*—has been reported on Sugarloaf, but we haven't seen it on the mountain. Its flow-ers are smaller, with several per stalk (Indian pipe flowers are solitary). Pine-sap is dull yellow or red (while Indian pipe is white).

Indian Pipe

Monotropa uniflora L.
Indian Pipe Family (Monotropaceae)

An all-white plant (rarely pink) that lacks chlorophyll and gets its nutrients from decaying organic matter or in symbiotic association with fungi. Such plants are called saprophytes. The thick stem and nodding flower resemble a small white pipe. The plant blackens with age, and when in fruit, it turns upright. **Flower:** White, waxy, nodding bell-like flower, ½–1½" long with stiff petals that are broadest at the apex. One flower per stalk. Individual stalks often clustered. **Leaves:** Small, white, scalelike, alternately arranged, and inconspicuous, on a thick white stalk. **Height:** 2–10". **Habitat and range:** Rich woods; much of North America, south to Colombia; eastern Asia. **Herbal lore:** American Indians used the plant externally for warts and sore eyes and internally for colds and convulsions. Physicians later used tea as a sedative and antispasmodic. The plant may have toxic properties. **On Sugarloaf—Blooming time:** June–September. **Locations:** Most trails; quite common on Sugarloaf. **Similar species:** Could possibly be confused with one-flowered cancer-root *(Orobanche uniflora),* a white or pale lavender parasitic plant that blooms earlier in the spring. Indian pipe has a thicker, waxier stem and a more nodding flower. *See* Indian pipe family description for a second *Monotropa* species possible here.

Indian Pipe

Primrose Family

Primulaceae

This family is best known and loved for the many ornamental primroses (*Primula* spp.) that are grown as garden and potted plants and gave us the saying "down the primrose path." Several Sugarloaf wildflowers belong to the primrose family. **Family characteristics:** 30 genera and 1,000 species worldwide. Cosmopolitan but with most family members in the northern temperate zone. **Economic importance:** Many ornamental plant genera (including *Cyclamen* and *Primula*); some medicinals and dye plants. **Flowers:** Regular, perfect, usually with 5 separate sepals and 5 separate or fused petals. Petals in some genera, such as shooting star *(Dodecatheon),* are swept back. **Fruit:** A capsule. **Leaves:** Basal and/or opposite or whorled, simple, and usually entire. **Growth habits:** Mostly herbs. **Occurrence on Sugarloaf:** The most noteworthy family members on and near the mountain are two species of loosestrife *(Lysimachia).* Whorled loosestrife *(L. quadrifolia)* and fringed loosestrife *(L. ciliata)* bloom in early summer along Mount Ephraim Road and nearby trails. A third member of the loosestrife genus, moneywort *(L. nummularia),* has been reported here, but Tina and I have yet to see it. It is a naturalized European native that grows in shallow streams and pools and in damp ground. Moneywort is a creeping plant with roundish opposite leaves and yellow flowers. (It is not included in this guide.) Scarlet pimpernel *(Anagallis arvensis)* is a low, sprawling plant that is quite common along roads and in grassy areas.

Whorled Loosestrife

Lysimachia quadrifolia L.
Primrose Family (Primulaceae)

A late spring–early summer wildflower of the eastern United States that is fairly common at Sugarloaf along Mount Ephraim Road and the Yellow Trail. **Flowers:** 5-petaled, starlike, yellow with red or orange streaks or dots toward the center, ⅓–⅔" across, on long, thin stalks, growing from the leaf axils. **Leaves:** Whorled, usually in several tiered whorls of 4 but may be in whorls of 3–6. Lanceolate or ovate, sessile or short-stalked, 1–5" long. **Height:** 1–3'. **Habitat and range:** Dry to moist open woods, thickets; Maine to South Carolina, west to eastern Minnesota, Kentucky, and Alabama. **Herbal lore:** According to Peterson Field Guides' *Field Guide to Medicinal Plants: Eastern and Central North America* by Foster and Duke: "American Indians used plant tea for 'female ailments,' kidney trouble, bowel complaints; root tea emetic." **On Sugarloaf—Blooming time:** June. **Locations:** Yellow Trail, Bear Branch, and Mount Ephraim Road. **Similar species:**

Fringed loosestrife *(L. ciliata)* has nodding flowers with slightly fringed or toothed petals and leaves with fringed petioles.

Fringed Loosestrife

Lysimachia ciliata L.
Primrose Family (Primulaceae)

Similar to the preceding species, fringed loosestrife also grows along Mount Ephraim Road. It comes into bloom slightly later in June, but its blooming time overlaps with whorled loosestrife *(L. quadrifolia)*. Fringed loosestrife's flowers are slightly larger and nodding, and its leaves are usually paired rather than whorled. **Flowers:** Yellow, with 5 petals that are slightly fringed or toothed around the apex; ½–1" across, not dramatically marked with red (as whorled loosestrife) but may have a pinkish blush at the center. On long, slender stalks from the upper leaf axils. **Leaves:** Opposite, simple, ovate, lanceolate, or cordate, 1½–6" long with entire or nearly entire margins and fringed petioles. **Height:** 1–3'. **Habitat and range:** Woods, moist meadows, springs, marshes, and stream banks; Canada and Alaska to Georgia, Louisiana, and New Mexico. **On Sugarloaf—Blooming time:** June–July. **Locations:** Mount Ephraim Road; also may be found along trails (particularly Yellow Trail) and other roadsides. **Similar species:** Whorled loosestrife, preceding. The fringed petioles of fringed loosestrife are the most reliable dis-

Fringed Loosestrife

tinguishing feature. Look at mid to lower leaves as the upper ones may be nearly sessile.

Scarlet Pimpernel (Poor Man's Weatherglass)

Anagallis arvensis L.
Primrose Family (Primulaceae)

A delicate Old World plant with small coral to scarlet flowers that open only in sunny weather (hence the second common name of the plant: poor man's

Scarlet Pimpernel

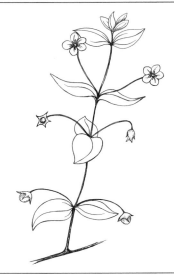

weatherglass). **Flowers:** Scarlet, orange, or coral, often with deeper color at the center; 5-lobed, ¼–⅓" across, on long, thin stalks from the leaf axils. **Leaves:** Opposite, simple, often with leaf pairs borne at right angles to the pairs above and below them (decussate). Sessile, ovate-elliptic, with smooth margins; ⅓–1" long, with dark spots on the lower surface. **Height and growth habits:** 4–12"; a low, sprawling plant. **Habitat and range:** Sandy fields, grassy areas, roadsides, and waste places; Eurasia, now widely naturalized. **On Sugarloaf—Blooming time:** June–August. **Locations:** Mountain roadsides and grassy areas. **Similar species:** The leaves could be confused with those of common chickweed *(Stellaria media)*. Look for the dark dots on lower leaf surfaces to identify scarlet pimpernel.

Hydrangea Family

Hydrangeaceae

A family of shrubs, small trees, and woody vines. Some family members are grown as ornamentals. **Family characteristics:** 17 genera and 170 species worldwide. (Plants of this family are sometimes included in the saxifrage family.) **Flowers:** 4–5 (rarely up to 12) petals; 4–5 (rarely up to 12) sepals. Flowers clustered in cymes, corymbs, or heads. **Fruit:** A capsule or, rarely, a berry. **Leaves:** Opposite or alternate, simple. **Occurrence on Sugarloaf:** Wild hydrangea *(Hydrangea arborescens)* is the only indigenous family member on Sugarloaf. Garden mock orange *(Philadelphus coronarius)* may be found in cultivation or escaped from cultivation.

Shrub

Wild Hydrangea (American Hydrangea)

Hydrangea arborescens L.
Hydrangea Family (Hydrangeaceae)

[Sometimes included in the Saxifrage Family (Saxifragaceae)]
A native flowering shrub of the eastern United States, wild hydrangea is moderately common along Sugarloaf's Mount Ephraim Road. **Flowers:** Creamy white, fragrant, small, star-shaped, with 5 petals and 8–10 stamens; flowers borne in broad flat-topped or convex clusters (cymes). **Leaves:** Opposite, simple, ovate or ovate-oblong with toothed margins, rounded to cordate base, and pointed apex. Several inches long on 1–3" petioles, with the exception of the uppermost leaf pair, which is usually sessile or short-stalked. **Height and growth habits:** 3–12' shrub. **Habitat and range:** Moist or dry (often rocky) woods, stream banks; New York to Ohio, south to Okla-

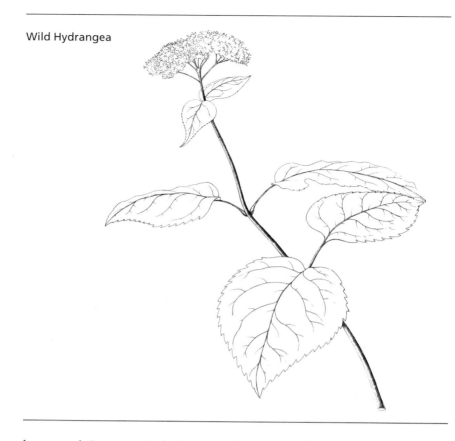

Wild Hydrangea

homa and Georgia. **Herbal lore:** In Peterson Field Guides' *Field Guide to Medicinal Plants: Eastern and Central North America,* Foster and Duke report: "American Indians used root tea as diuretic, cathartic, emetic; scraped bark poulticed on wounds, burns, sore muscles, sprains, tumors; bark chewed for stomach problems, heart trouble. Root traditionally used for kidney stones, mucous irritation of bladder, bronchial afflictions. Warning: Experimentally, causes bloody diarrhea, painful gastroenteritis, cyanide-like poisoning." **On Sugarloaf—Blooming time:** May–July. **Locations:** Mount Ephraim Road; other roadsides and trailsides. **Similar species:** Native viburnums (*Viburnum* spp.) have 5 stamens per flower and petioles usually less than 1".

Saxifrage Family

Saxifragaceae

Many eastern woodland wildflowers belong to the saxifrage family. Two wildflowers represent this family on Sugarloaf. Both are uncommon here, although one of the two, early saxifrage *(Saxifraga virginiensis)*, is common in rocky woods of the surrounding region. The family name means "rock-breaker." The second Sugarloaf species, golden saxifrage or water-carpet *(Chrysosplenium americanum)*, is a wetland plant. **Family characteristics:** 40 genera and 700 species worldwide. Many species in cool climates. **Flowers** are usually perfect, usually regular (or slightly irregular), often small, with 4–5 (usually 5) sepals and usually 5 petals. **Leaves** are variable.

Early Saxifrage

Saxifraga virginiensis Michx.
Saxifrage Family (Saxifragaceae)

Early saxifrage, indigenous to much of eastern North America, is well suited to Sugarloaf's open rocky woods. However, although it is a common local wildflower, early saxifrage is not common on Sugarloaf. I have encountered a few specimens along the Blue Trail over the years. It blooms in early spring. **Flowers:** White, 5-petaled, with 10 yellow stamens. Flowers are small (¼–½" across) and borne in a (usually branched) terminal cluster. A curious aspect of this plant is that it begins blooming when the viscid, pubescent plant stalk is very short. The stalk continues to grow to a height of 1' or more during blooming time. **Leaves:** A basal rosette of simple leaves that are ovate, obovate, or oblong, 1–3" long, usually toothed but sometimes entire. **Height:** 4–16". **Habitat and range:** Moist or dry, usually rocky, open woods and rock outcrops; New Brunswick to Manitoba, south to Georgia, Louisiana, and Oklahoma. **On Sugarloaf—Blooming time:** March–May. **Location:** Blue Trail. **Similar species:** Not likely to be confused with other Sugarloaf spring wildflowers. The basal rosette and white flowers clustered toward the apex of a branched viscid, pubescent stalk are diagnostic. A similar but much larger plant, swamp saxifrage *(S. pensylvanica)*, grows in seeps and springs in the hills and mountains to the west. It blooms later in the spring.

Golden Saxifrage (Water-Carpet, Water-Mat)

Chrysosplenium americanum Schwein. ex Hook.
Saxifrage Family (Saxifragaceae)

A diminutive creeping plant of northeastern North American springs, seeps, and moist soils, which only the most observant visitor is apt to notice at Sugarloaf. Here is a brief description of golden saxifrage for that curious and intrepid amateur botanist. **Flowers:** Small flowers have 4 greenish-yellow, greenish-red, or greenish-purple sepals (no petals) surrounding a shallowly 8-lobed central disk that is red, purple, brown, or green. Flowers ¼–⅓" across, borne toward the apex of the branching plant stalk. **Leaves:** Simple, opposite toward bottom of plant stalk, often alternate toward the top. Succulent, ovate or round, with a few blunt teeth. Leaves under 1" long, on short petioles. **Height and growth habits:** 2–8"; a sprawling plant which is prostrate at the base but may have an ascending apex; this growth habit is defined as decumbent. **Habitat and range:** Springs, seeps, seepage swamps, and wet soil; Quebec to Saskatchewan, south to Virginia, Kentucky, and Indiana. **On Sugarloaf—Blooming time:** April–June. **Locations:** Seeps and springs of Mount Ephraim Road and the Yellow Trail. **Similar species:** The flowers are distinctive and not likely to be confused with other Sugarloaf plants.

Rose Family

Rosaceae

The rose family not only produces the flowers that inspire romance, poetry, and song but also some of humanity's most important fruit crops: apples, plums, peaches, cherries, strawberries, raspberries, and blackberries. The rose family is also of critical importance to wildlife. Many birds, mammals, and reptiles find the fruits as delectable as we do, and prickly shrub species provide cover for small mammals and nesting sites for birds. **Family characteristics:** 100 genera and 3,000 species worldwide. Cosmopolitan but especially common in Europe, Asia, and North America. **Economic importance:** Immeasurable; extremely important economically for apples alone. Between the fruit and nursery trades, this family is responsible for major world commerce. **Flowers:** Usually perfect and regular; usually with 5 sepals and 5 petals (petals sometimes lacking; parts sometimes 4 to numerous). Many variations have been developed in cultivation. **Fruit:** Variable: a pome (apple), drupe (peach), aggregate (raspberry fruit is an "aggregate of drupelets"), achene, or follicle. **Leaves:** Alternate, simple or compound, usually stipulate. Stipules are sometimes modified to form spines. **Growth habits:** Trees, shrubs, and herbs. **Occurrence on Sugarloaf:** The rose family is represented on Sugarloaf by trees, shrubs, and herbs. Plants of this family grow everywhere on the mountain. In addition to the species described and illustrated in the next few entries, *see also* Botanical Key and Guide to Trees, Shrubs, and Woody Vines.

Wild Strawberry

Fragaria virginiana Duchesne
Rose Family (Rosaceae)

One of our most delectable native fruits, the wild strawberry is smaller but more intensely flavorful than cultivated varieties. The wild strawberry plant bears white flowers in spring. **Flowers:** White, 5-petaled, with yellow center,

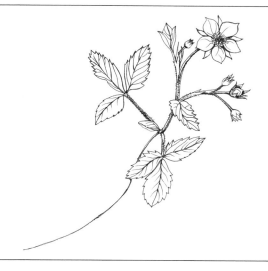

½–1" wide, growing singly or (more often) in small clusters on stalk separate from leaves. **Fruit:** Small (less than 1" long), red, round or egg-shaped. Delicious. **Leaves:** Basal leaves only, divided into 3 toothed leaflets, each ¾–2" long. **Height and growth habits:** A low, sprawling plant spread by runners. **Habitat and range:** Fields; United States and southern Canada. **On Sugarloaf—Blooming time:** April–May. **Fruit:** May–June. **Locations:** Roadsides, open trailsides, fields around mountain base. **Similar species:** Indian strawberry *(Duchesnea indica)* bears yellow flowers with five 3-toothed leafy bracts beneath the sepals; bracts are longer than the petals and sepals and remain when the plant is fruiting. Indian strawberry fruit resembles wild strawberry but is tasteless.

Indian Strawberry (False Strawberry)

Duchesnea indica (Andrews) Focke
Rose Family (Rosaceae)

Indian strawberry is an Asian native that has become naturalized in disturbed sites, lawns, and along roadsides in many parts of the eastern United States. Its trailing habit, leaves, and fruit resemble those of the wild strawberry *(Fragaria virginia)*, but its fruit is insipid and inedible. The flowers and leaves suggest those of dwarf cinquefoil *(Potentilla canadensis)* and common cinquefoil *(P. simplex)*. However, these cinquefoils (common on the mountain) have 5 leaflets per palmately compound leaf whereas Indian strawberry has only 3. **Flowers:** Yellow, 5-petaled, ½–1" wide. Below the petals and sepals are 5 triple-toothed leafy bracts that are slightly longer than the petals. **Herbal lore:** According to Foster and Duke (Peterson Field Guides' *Field Guide to Medicinal Plants: Eastern and Central North America*), "In Asia,

Indian
Strawberry

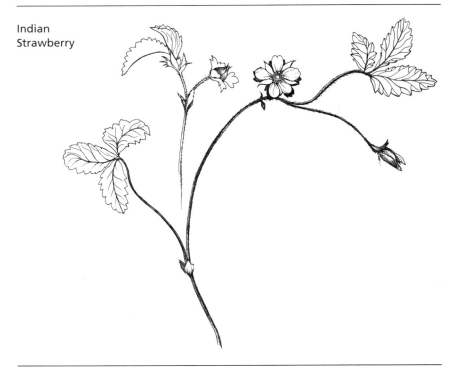

whole plant poultice or wash (astringent) used for abscesses, boils, burns, insect stings, eczema, ringworm, rheumatism, traumatic injuries. Whole-plant tea used for laryngitis, coughs, lung ailments. Flower tea traditionally used to stimulate blood circulation." **On Sugarloaf—Blooming time:** Spring–fall. **Locations:** Mowed areas, roadsides, and open trailsides mountainwide; along Furnace Branch in the Monocacy Natural Resources Management Area.

Dwarf Cinquefoil

Potentilla canadensis L.
Rose Family (Rosaceae)

A common spring wildflower of eastern North America, dwarf cinquefoil has 5-parted yellow flowers and 5-parted leaves. Easily confused with common cinquefoil *(P. simplex),* dwarf cinquefoil comes into bloom slightly earlier and has wedge-shaped leaflets. **Flowers:** Yellow, with 5 roundish or square-tipped petals, on long, pubescent stalk. Flowers ¼–¾" across. **Leaves:** Alternate (although may appear to bear basal leaves only), palmately compound; 5 leaflets are wedge-shaped at the sessile base and toothed only above the middle. Petiole often pinkish, pubescent. Entire leaf 1–3½" long and wide. **Height and growth habits:** A low, sprawling plant spread by runners.

Dwarf Cinquefoil

Habitat and range: Dry woods, fields; eastern Canada, eastern United States to Georgia and Tennessee. **Herbal lore:** Native Americans drank root tea for diarrhea. **On Sugarloaf—Blooming time:** March–June. **Locations:** Mountainwide. **Similar species:** Common cinquefoil has leaflets that are less wedge-shaped at the base and toothed for about ¾ of their length.

Common Cinquefoil (Old Field Five-Fingers)

Potentilla simplex Michx.
Rose Family (Rosaceae)

Very similar to the previous species, common cinquefoil comes into bloom slightly later (although the two may be found in simultaneous bloom). This wildflower is less common on Sugarloaf. It is a taller plant, with a greater number of stem **leaves**. The leaflets are less widely wedge-shaped at the base and are toothed for about ¾ of their length. The yellow 5-petaled **flowers** are

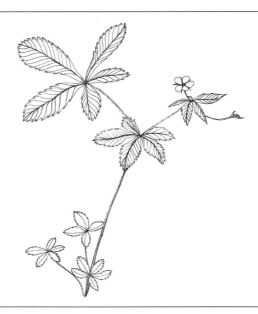

¼–½" across, on long, slender stalks. **On Sugarloaf—Blooming time:** Late April–July. **Locations:** Yellow Trail, Mount Ephraim Road.

Rough-Fruited Cinquefoil (Sulphur Cinquefoil)

Potentilla recta L.
Rose Family (Rosaceae)

A European native, this plant is a common naturalized wildflower of fields, roadsides, and disturbed sites throughout the eastern United States. A few specimens of rough-fruited cinquefoil are found along Mount Ephraim and Sugarloaf Mountain Roads and at East View. The following characteristics separate it from dwarf and common cinquefoils *(P. canadensis* and *P. simplex):* The plant is taller with a stiff, stout, erect central stalk (the other two species are slender-stalked). Rough-fruited cinquefoil's flower is larger (½–1" across) and pale yellow. A fourth species is possible here. Rough cinquefoil *(P. norvegica)* has a stout stalk, but its leaflets are in 3s, and its flowers are ¼–½" across. A circumboreal species which is locally common, I have not seen it on the mountain. **On Sugarloaf—Blooming time:** May–August.

White Avens

Geum canadense Jacq.
Rose Family (Rosaceae)

A late spring–early summer woodland wildflower native to eastern North America. White avens grows along many Sugarloaf trails and roadsides.

White Avens

Flowers: White, 5-petaled, ⅓–¾" across; often missing one or more petals. Petals are oblong-obovate. Sepals (about as long as petals) are pointed at tips. Flowers borne from upper leaf axils and terminally on stalks of varying lengths. **Fruit:** A greenish, round, bristly receptacle, ¼–⅔" across. **Leaves:** Alternate; basal and lower leaves compound, upper stem leaves usually simple. Lowest leaves may be pinnately compound, with 5 or more leaflets, but most have 3 leaflets (resembling a strawberry leaf). Lowest leaves on long stalks, upper leaves usually sessile. Leaf length varies from larger lower leaves (up to several inches long) to shorter upper leaves (1½" or less). Upper leaves lanceolate or elliptic. All leaves toothed, often pubescent and slightly rough to the touch on upper surface. Stipules at leaf axils. **Height and growth habits:** 1–3½' tall; plant stalk slender, often with an irregular zigzag. **Habitat and range:** Woods, thickets; Nova Scotia to Minnesota; south to Georgia and Texas. **On Sugarloaf—Blooming time:** June–August. **Locations:** Most trails and roadsides; West View. **Similar species:** In fruit may be confused with short-styled snakeroot *(Sanicula canadensis)*. Compare illustrations. Leaves (but not flowers) similar to honewort *(Cryptotaenia canadensis)*.

Spring Avens

Geum vernum (Raf.) T. & G.
Rose Family (Rosaceae)

Flowers: Small, yellow, 5-petaled, ¼" or less across, in sparse loose terminal clusters. **Fruit:** Burlike fruiting head (⅓–⅔" across) is stalked and raised above the calyx. **Leaves:** Alternate, compound, variable. Basal leaves may be long-stalked or not and compound or merely deeply lobed. Stem leaves pinnately compound or trifoliate; petioles vary. All leaves sharply toothed; some leaflets shallowly or deeply lobed. Stipules toothed or lobed. **Height:** 6–24". **Habitat and range:** Rich woods; southeastern Canada to Maryland, Tennessee, and Oklahoma. **On Sugarloaf—Blooming time:** April–June. **Location:** Mount Ephraim Road. **Similar species:** Flowers may be confused with those of kidneyleaf buttercup *(Ranunculus abortivus).* Compare leaves. Cinquefoils *(Potentilla* spp.) have larger flowers.

Bowman's Root (Indian Physic, False Ipecac)

Porteranthus trifoliatus (L.) Britton
(Gillenia trifoliata)
Rose Family (Rosaceae)

Bowman's root is a mountain plant with strong medicinal properties. It is rare on Sugarloaf. **Flowers:** In loose terminal clusters, white or pinkish, with 5 thin, pointed petals; each petal ½–1" long. Individual petals of a single

Bowman's
Root

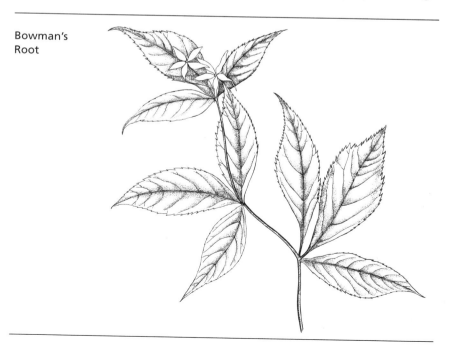

flower may vary in length, and the flower often has a slightly asymmetrical look. **Leaves:** Alternate, compound, with 3-toothed leaflets that are short-stalked or sessile. Stipules may be present. Each leaflet is 1–5" long, thinly textured, and glabrous or nearly so. **Height and growth habits:** 2–4', with spreading branches. **Habitat and range:** Upland woods, mostly in the mountains; southern Canada to Georgia and Alabama; west, irregularly, to southern Michigan and Missouri. **Herbal lore:** All parts of bowman's root have been used in minute quantities, as teas for colds, asthma, hepatitis, and other conditions. Plant is strongly laxative and emetic. Bowman's root also has served as a poultice for bee stings and rheumatism. **On Sugarloaf—Blooming time:** May–July. **Locations:** Mount Ephraim Road, White Trail. **Similar species:** None on Sugarloaf.

Goatsbeard

Aruncus dioicus (Walter) Fernald

Rose Family (Rosaceae)

You have to use your imagination to picture this plant's flower clusters as "goats' beards." Rare on Sugarloaf. **Flowers:** Tiny, white, 5-petaled, in tall, densely flowered, panicled spikes. Dioecious (male and female flowers on separate plants). **Leaves:** Alternate, compound, two or three times pinnately divided, long-petioled. Individual leaflets ovate-lanceolate, sharply, often doubly toothed, simple or sometimes slightly lobed. Leaflets 1–5½" long. **Height:** 3–7'. **Habitat and range:** Rich woods, streamsides, clearings; Pennsylvania and Ohio to Iowa, south to North Carolina, Alabama, and Arkansas. **On Sugarloaf—Blooming time:** May–July. **Location:** Mount Ephraim Road near Bear Branch. **Similar species:** Could be confused with black cohosh or black snakeroot *(Cimicifuga racemosa)*, which is far more common on Sugarloaf than goatsbeard. Small individual flowers of black cohosh are stalked while tiny individual goatsbeard flowers are stalkless.

Tall Agrimony

Agrimonia gryposepala Wallr.

Rose Family (Rosaceae)

This species and small-flowered agrimony *(A. parviflora)* have distinctive pinnately compound leaves with alternately smaller and larger paired leaflets. Tall agrimony is a fairly common Sugarloaf summer wildflower. In addition to the two agrimony species growing on Sugarloaf, several other genus members are indigenous to the northeastern United States. **Flowers:** Small (¼–½" across), yellow, 5-petaled flowers borne in spikelike racemes. **Fruit:** Small, cone-shaped, with hooked bristles that stick to clothing. **Leaves:** Alternate, pinnately compound, but upper leaves may be trifoliate; 3–11

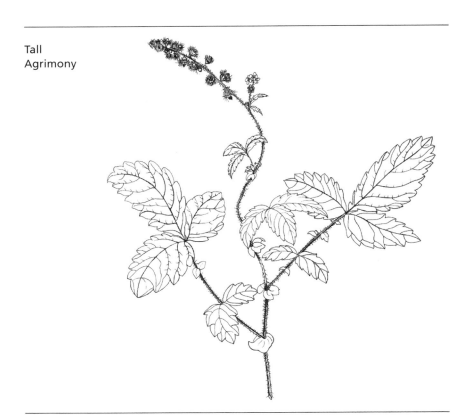

Tall
Agrimony

toothed larger leaflets are sessile or nearly so, ovate-lanceolate to obovate, with small leaflets borne in pairs between the larger ones. Overall leaf up to several inches long. Stipules present. **Height:** 1–4'. **Habitat and range:** Moist woods and meadows; clearings; Maine to Ontario and Montana, south in the mountains to Tennessee and North Carolina; also in California and New Mexico. **On Sugarloaf—Blooming time:** June–August. **Locations:** Mount Ephraim Road and other mountain roadsides; probable along trails. **Similar species:** *See* next entry, small-flowered agrimony *(A. parviflora)*.

Small-Flowered Agrimony (Small-Fruited Agrimony)

Agrimonia parviflora Aiton
Rose Family (Rosaceae)

Very similar to the preceding species, small-flowered agrimony has longer, narrower, and more numerous leaflets (11–15 large leaflets per leaf, interspersed with smaller ones). This species blooms slightly later (August–September) and is native to the eastern United States, Hispaniola, and Mexico. **On Sugarloaf—Locations:** Yellow Trail, Sugarloaf Mountain Road, Mount Ephraim Road, other area roadsides and trailsides.

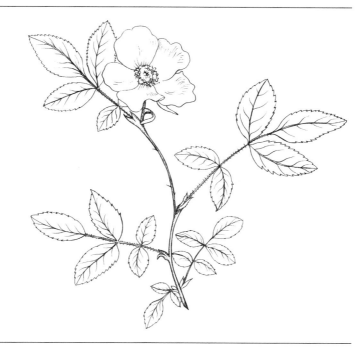

Shrub

Pasture Rose (Low Pasture Rose, Carolina Rose)

Rosa carolina L.
Rose Family (Rosaceae)

A delicately fragranced native rose that graces some of Sugarloaf's trails and roadsides in late spring. **Flowers:** Large, pink, usually borne singly, 1–2" across, 5-petaled, with yellow stamens. Rosebuds deeper pink. **Leaves:** Alternate, compound, each with several toothed, pinnately arranged leaflets. Leaf size varies. Prickles are slender, straight. **Height:** 1–3'. **Habitat and range:** Open woods, fields, roadsides; eastern United States. **On Sugarloaf— Blooming time:** May–June. **Locations:** White Trail and other trailsides, mountain roadsides. **Similar species:** Multiflora rose *(Rosa multiflora)* is an invasive Asian species that has proliferated throughout Sugarloaf's surrounding farmland and along mountain roadsides. It has smaller, paler flowers that grow in large clusters, and it is a larger shrub. Swamp rose *(R. palustris)* is a native rose that favors wetlands and might be found on or near the mountain. Distinguish swamp rose from pasture rose by its curved prickles.

Shrub

Multiflora Rose

Rosa multiflora Thunb.
Rose Family (Rosaceae)

"Vigorously colonial" is how one botanical manual describes this invasive Asian shrub. Colloquial invectives against it are usually a bit more blunt. The multiflora rose has tenaciously overtaken many a Sugarloaf-area field and hedgerow, to the disgruntlement of local farmers, homeowners, and also botanists (who worry about the native flora that multiflora rose and other pernicious invasives displace). However, in the May moonlight, when cascades of white flowers perfume the countryside, curses against the multiflora rose temporarily cease. This romance is short-lived and soon forgotten; the morning after lasts the rest of the year. **Flowers:** White and/or pale pink, 5-petaled, deliciously and subtly fragrant. Flowers ¾–1½" across in multi-flowered clusters. **Leaves:** Alternate, pinnately compound, usually with 7 to 9 leaflets. Leaflets toothed, ovate, elliptic, or obovate, ¾–3" long. Full leaf up to several inches long with fringed stipules. Plant stalk armed with serious prickles. **Height and growth habits:** 3–12'; a full shrub, often with arching or cascading flowering and fruiting branches; freely spreading and often dominating the shrubs and herbs around it. **Habitat and range:** Fields, thickets,

Multiflora
Rose

disturbed sites; east Asian native, now widely escaped from cultivation. According to Brown and Brown's *Woody Plants of Maryland,* "Used as root stock for grafting cultivated roses; these often sprout below the graft, replacing the cultivated variety. Recently much planted as a hedge fence and now escaping to fields, thickets and woodlands where it is becoming a pest." **Wildlife lore:** Provides food and shelter for many species of bird and mammal. **On Sugarloaf—Blooming time:** May–June. **Locations:** Some open stretches of trail and roadway on the mountain; far more common in the surrounding countryside. **Similar species:** Common blackberry *(Rubus allegheniensis)* blooms simultaneously and has somewhat similar 5-petaled white flowers. However, its leaves usually have only 3 or 5 leaflets. Not apt to be confused with pasture rose *(Rosa carolina)*, a shrub with larger, usually singly borne, deeper pink flowers.

Shrub

Japanese Spiraea

Spiraea japonica L.f.
Rose Family (Rosaceae)

Japanese spiraea is a low shrub with slender reddish-brown twigs. Several specimens of this Japanese garden plant have escaped from cultivation and

Japanese
Spiraea

are growing near West View. **Flowers:** Small (¼" across), pink, 5-petaled flowers in flat-topped clusters. **Leaves:** Alternate, simple, deciduous, lanceolate or ovate-lanceolate, sharply toothed, with pointed apex and tapered base; 2–6" long on short petiole or nearly sessile. **On Sugarloaf—Blooming time:** June–August. **Location:** Near West View. **Similar species:** None on Sugarloaf.

Shrubs

Blackberries, Dewberries, and Raspberries (including Wineberry)
Rubus
Rose Family (Rosaceae)

Raspberries have fruit that easily separates from its receptacle. Blackberries have fruit that adheres to the receptacle.

Raspberries (including wineberry)

Wineberry
Rubus phoenicolasius Maxim.

An Asian native which has escaped from cultivation in the Atlantic Coast states, wineberry thrives along Sugarloaf area roadsides and is showy in late June and July with its scarlet edible fruit. **Flowers:** 5 petals, white or pale pink, small; sepals much showier: pointed at apex and covered with reddish gland-tipped hairs (glands visible with naked eye but very striking with hand lens). **Fruit:** A scarlet "aggregate of drupelets" closely resembling the

Wineberry

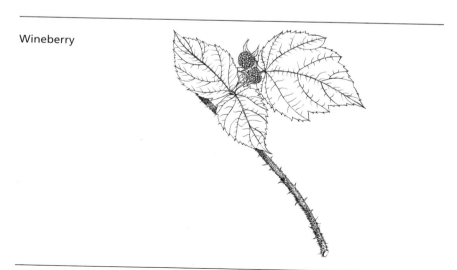

cultivated raspberry. Flavor and texture are sweetly or tartly succulent. Once the fruit is plucked, a prominent receptacle (often orange-tinged) remains on the plant. **Leaves:** Alternate, compound; 3 leaflets, ovate, heart-shaped (cordate), rounded, or shallowly lobed (like a maple leaf), with pointed or blunt teeth. The terminal leaflet is usually larger than the side ones. Leaflets densely white-tomentose beneath. Petioles and plant stalks bear reddish glandular hairs like those covering the sepals, as well as numerous sharp prickles. Overall leaf size roughly 3–10" long. **Height and growth habits:** A low shrub (may be several feet high) with long, arching stems. **On Sugarloaf—Blooming time:** May–July. **Fruiting time:** June–July. **Locations:** Roadsides and some trailsides mountainwide; common. **Similar species:** The other members of the *Rubus* genus common on Sugarloaf, blackberries and dewberries, have ripe black fruit adhering to its receptacle. The wild black raspberry *(R. occidentalis)* also has ripe black fruit, but its fruit separates from the receptacle. Growing near the mountain, wild black raspberry has not been identified on Sugarloaf so is not included in this guide. Note that blackberries, dewberries, and black raspberries bear unripe red fruit.

Common Blackberry

Rubus allegheniensis Porter

Sugarloaf's most common blackberry, this species is a shrub with characteristically arching or erect, usually thick, ridged or angled canes with stout prickles. **Flowers:** Large, white, 5-petaled, in clusters. Flowers ¾–2" across.

Common
Blackberry

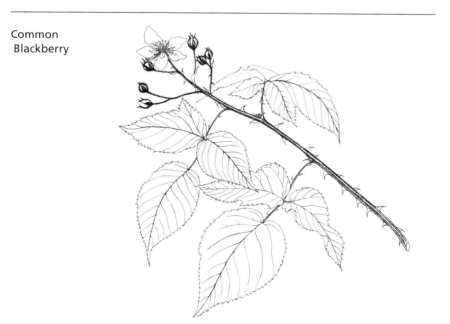

Fruit: Black, sweet, and juicy when ripe (red when unripe); fruit not easily separating from receptacle. **Leaves:** Alternate, compound, with 3–5 (or sometimes 7) toothed leaflets per leaf. **On Sugarloaf—Blooming time:** May–July. **Fruiting time:** June–September. **Locations:** Trails and roadsides mountainwide. **Similar species:** The dewberry species that follow are less common on Sugarloaf. They have mostly trailing, rather than arching, stalks. The *Rubus* genus is extremely complex and confusing, even for botanists. Consult Brown and Brown's *Woody Plants of Maryland* for additional species likely to be encountered in the Sugarloaf area.

Common Dewberry (Northern Dewberry)
Rubus flagellaris Willd.

The common dewberry is a low, trailing shrub (which may be slightly arched, especially when canes are young). It bears small, curved, broad-based prickles and leaflets in 3s and 5s. Common dewberry grows along Sugarloaf's trails and roadsides, producing white flowers and succulent fruit. It blooms in May and June, fruiting soon after.

Common Dewberry

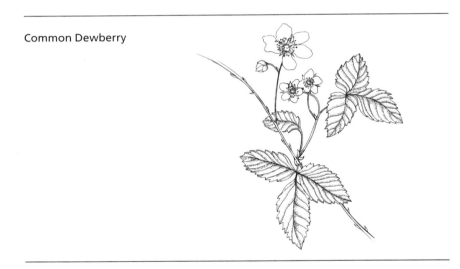

Swamp Dewberry
Rubus hispidus L.

A trailing shrub with straight or barely curved, thin, weak prickles and/or bristles (rather than broad-based curved prickles), swamp dewberry also differs from the preceding species by bearing shining and often partially evergreen leaflets, mostly in 3s (although some leaves bear 5 leaflets). Swamp dewberry blooms slightly later than common dewberry, and its fruit is not as sweet. It grows in Sugarloaf's moist woods and wetlands, including along the Blue Trail near Mount Ephraim Road.

Shrub or Small Tree

Red Chokeberry

Aronia arbutifolia (L.) Pers.
(Pyrus arbutifolia)
Rose Family (Rosaceae)

A shrub or small tree indigenous to eastern North America, red chokeberry is uncommon on Sugarloaf, growing along roads and around springs near the mountain base. **Flowers:** White (sometimes pink or purple-tinged), with 5 roundish or broadly obovate petals; flowers ⅓–⅔" across. Borne in flat or rounded, terminal, usually branched clusters. **Fruit:** A bright red pome, nearly round, ¼–½" in diameter. **Leaves:** Alternate, simple, toothed, oblong-lanceolate or obovate, 1–4" long on short petioles. Usually woolly below and glandular along the upper middle vein and the toothed margin. **Height:** 3–12'. **Habitat and range:** Swamps, bogs, woods; Newfoundland to Florida and Texas. **On Sugarloaf—Blooming time:** March–May. **Locations:** Yellow Trail, Mount Ephraim Road. **Similar species:** Could be confused with other woody plants in the rose family. Shadbush *(Amelanchier aborea),* the most common woody rose family member on the mountain, has narrow petals. Two other chokeberries are native to Maryland but are unlikely at Sugarloaf.

Red Chokeberry

Tree or Shrub

Common or Downy Shadbush (Serviceberry, Juneberry, Shadblow)

Amelanchier arborea (F. Michx.) Fernald
Rose Family (Rosaceae)

Spring's first arboreal blush on Sugarloaf and in many eastern North American woodlands is the creamy white blooming of the shadbush (or serviceberry). Shadbush flowers, which may also be pale pink, appear with the new leaves, which are often copper-tinted. Against the backdrop of Sugarloaf's pink-gray quartzite and a still wintry woodland, the unfurling of the shadbush is a subtly beautiful spring welcome. The blooming time of this tree and other members of the genus have traditionally coincided with the running of the shad (thus the names "shadbush" and "shadblow"). Another common name for the tree, serviceberry, sprang from the colonial tradition of holding memorial services in the spring for those who died during the winter. **Flowers:** Creamy white or pale pink, ¾–1½" across, slightly asymmetrically star-shaped with 5 thin petals. Some petals are gently reflexed toward or away from the flower center. Flowers borne in loose clusters (racemes) toward the ends of the branches with the emerging leaves. **Fruit:** A small, round, edible red or purple pome. **Leaves:** Simple, alternate, often coppery and folded when young during flowering time. Ovate, oblong, or obovate, 1–4" long with small, sharply pointed teeth. Gradually or abruptly pointed apex and cordate or rounded base. Densely pubescent on lower sur-

Common or Downy Shadbush

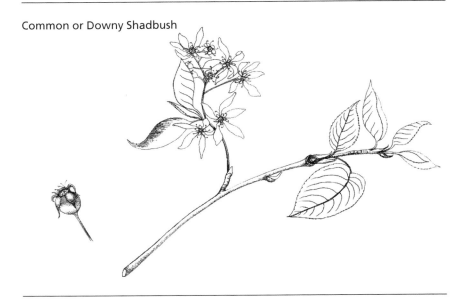

face when young but may become glabrous. **Growth habits:** A shrub or small to medium-sized tree. **Bark and twigs:** Bark smooth, gray on young trunks and branches, becoming darker and fissured with age. Twigs with lanceoloid buds, slightly curved at the tip, pinkish, greenish-yellow, or brown, ¼–⅔" long. **Habitat and range:** Woodlands; eastern Canada and the United States. **Wildlife lore:** *Amelanchier* species provide fruit for songbirds and mammals, including bear. They also serve as deer-browse. The fruit of this species is not as tasty and juicy as some other native American members of the *Amelanchier* genus. **On Sugarloaf—Blooming time:** March–April; Sugarloaf's first blooming native tree. **Locations:** Mountainwide; easily seen from Mount Ephraim Road and trails near White Rocks; Blue Trail (abundant along stretches of the northern mountain ridge). **Similar species:** Several other *Amelanchier* species grow in Maryland. Smooth shadbush or serviceberry *(A. laevis)* might be encountered on Sugarloaf or nearby. Its leaves are glabrous or only slightly pubescent beneath, and its fruit is sweet and juicy. Other early flowering trees of the rose family, such as cherries, peaches, and pears, have wider petals.

Tree

Sweet Cherry

Prunus avium L.
Rose Family (Rosaceae)

Years ago, while researching my book *City of Trees,* I discovered the frustrating world of cherry identification. In Washington, D.C., which is famous for its variety of introduced flowering cherry trees, the task is staggering. On Sugarloaf the job of sorting out early blooming *Prunus* species is decidedly less daunting, but that is not to say that it's easy. I have puzzled over many a stray Eurasian native, dropped down in the woods by a passing bird or planted by a settler years ago, and the results of my investigations have been mixed at best. I offer a description of one introduced early-blooming cherry that has made Sugarloaf woodlands home in some numbers. As for the rest, as far as I'm concerned, they will retain an aura of taxonomic mystery. Should you wish to investigate further, consult a woody plant guide such as Brown and Brown's *Woody Plants of Maryland.* The native black cherry *(P. serotina)*, a later-blooming species that is less common on Sugarloaf, is described in the Botanical Key and Guide to Trees, Shrubs, and Woody Vines. **Flowers:** White or pale pink, 5-petaled, ¾–1½" across; sepals untoothed. Each flower on a ¾–2" stalk. Before and with the young leaves. **Leaves:** Alternate, simple, ovate-oblong or obovate; singly or doubly toothed, usually with a small gland at the tip of the tooth (visible with hand lens); 10–14 pairs

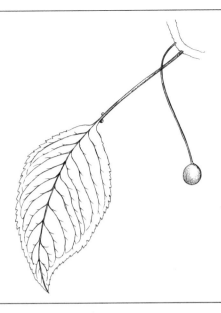

of main veins, which are pubescent below; tapered or rounded at the base, curved to a short point at the apex (acuminate); 2½–6" long. **Fruit:** Red or reddish-black, sweet and edible; heart-shaped or round, ⅓–1" in diameter. **Height and growth habits:** A medium-sized to tall tree, often with a straight trunk and cylindrical or pyramidal crown. **Bark:** Red-brown or gray, smooth on young trees but later becoming scaly or peeling, prominently marked with large horizontal lenticels. **Habitat and range:** Woods, edges of woods and fields, roadsides; a Eurasian native, escaped from cultivation. **On Sugarloaf—Blooming time:** March–May. **Fruiting time:** June–July. **Locations:** Sugarloaf woods and roadsides; common along edges of fields throughout the area. **Similar species:** The most common early-blooming tree apt to be confused with sweet cherry is the native shadbush or service-berry *(Amelanchier arborea)*. Shadbush has narrow petals. Sweet cherry is probably the most common tree-sized early blooming cherry on and around Sugarloaf. Probably.

Pea Family

Fabaceae
(Leguminosae)

An extremely important plant family for humanity, the pea family yields nutrient-rich peas, beans, soybeans, alfalfa, and many other farm crops fed to people or livestock or plowed into the soil to increase its nitrogen content.

As if such unparalleled usefulness was not enough for one plant family, this one claims beauty too—in the form of numerous species of flowering trees, shrubs, and herbaceous plants. **Family characteristics:** 700 genera and 17,000 species worldwide. Cosmopolitan. (This large family is sometimes subdivided.) **Economic importance:** Extremely significant sources of food, timber, and ornamental and dye plants. Many family members contain nitrogen-fixing bacteria in their roots, invaluable for improving soil quality. **Flowers:** Variable but typically (and in all common Sugarloaf species) like the flower of the familiar garden pea or bean: irregular, with 1 upstanding petal (called the banner or standard), 2 side petals (the "wings"), and 2 lower fused or partially fused petals forming a "keel." **Fruit:** A legume, usually dry and splitting along both sides but sometimes not splitting (indehiscent) and, rarely, fleshy. **Leaves:** Usually alternate, pinnately or palmately compound or (rarely) simple. Often stipulate with stipules sometimes modified to spines. **Growth habits:** Herbs, shrubs, and trees. **Occurrence on Sugarloaf:** Widespread and in most habitats. Two of the mountain's most beautiful spring flowering trees are in this family: redbud *(Cercis canadensis)* and black locust

White Sweet Clover

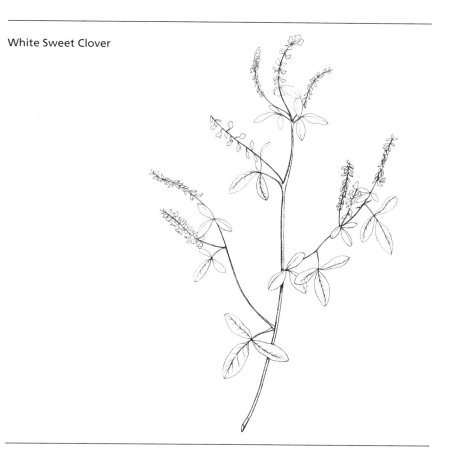

(Robinia pseudoacacia). Wildflowers include several common and uncommon species. In addition to the pea family members described and illustrated here, you may also find one or more of the following growing on or around the mountain: the vines hog peanut *(Amphicarpaea bracteata)* and groundnut *(Apios americana)*; black medick *(Medicago lupulina)*; yellow sweet clover *(Melilotus officinalis)* and white sweet clover *(Melilotus alba)*; two *Chamaecrista* species: partridge-pea *(C. fasciculata)* and wild sensitive plant or sensitive pea *(C. nictitans)*; or wild senna *(Senna marilandica)*.

Clovers

Trifolium L.
Pea Family (Fabaceae)

The tiny **flowers** of the clover genus (quite typically pea-shaped upon close examination) are borne in roundish or egg-shaped heads, and the very finely toothed **leaves** (which may appear entire without a hand lens) are trifoliate (or 3-leafleted). Several members of the clover genus grow on and around Sugarloaf.

White Clover

Trifolium repens L.

White clover is an introduced Eurasian species that is a good honey plant and has been used medicinally for rheumatism, gout, coughs, and fevers. **Flowers:** White and/or pale pink in round heads ⅓–1" across. **Leaves:** Basal leaves only. The 3 roundish or obovate leaflets are borne on a long, semi-prostrate petiole and are often marked with white or paler green. **Height and growth habits:** 2–10"; a creeping plant, common in lawns and mowed areas. **On Sugarloaf—Blooming time:** May–October. **Locations:** Very common in mowed areas on the mountain, especially near the mountain base.

Red Clover

Trifolium pratense L.

Red clover is an introduced European native, now widely naturalized throughout temperate North America. This clover has been used for a number of medical conditions (although Foster and Duke warn in Peterson Field Guides' *Field Guide to Medicinal Plants: Eastern and Central North America* that diseased red clover can be toxic). It is the state flower of Vermont. **Flowers:** Purplish-pink, in dense round heads ½–1½" across. **Leaves:** Alternate, trifoliate, usually softly pubescent below and along the petiole. Lower leaves long-petioled; upper leaves may be sessile or nearly so. Leaflets ovate, elliptic, or obovate and usually marked with a white inverted V. **Height:** 6–20".

Habitat: Fields, roadsides, disturbed sites. On Sugarloaf—Blooming time: May–November. Locations: Sugarloaf area roadsides, fields, and open trailsides.

Low Hop Clover

Trifolium campestre Schreb.

(T. procumbens)

This common yellow-flowered clover is a native of Eurasia and northern Africa. It has become naturalized along roadsides and in disturbed sites throughout North America. **Flowers:** Tiny, yellow, in small roundish heads ¼–½" long. **Leaves:** Alternate, trifoliate, with the middle leaflet stalked. This characteristic distinguishes low hop clover from hop or yellow hop clover *(T. aureum)*, which has all leaflets stalkless or nearly so. Introduced from Eurasia and common throughout the area, this second species might be found on Sugarloaf. **Height and growth habits:** 4–16"; usually prostrate or semiprostrate. **On Sugarloaf—Blooming time:** May–October. **Locations:** Common along Sugarloaf's roadsides and trails.

Rabbit-Foot Clover

Trifolium arvense L.

This clover, native to Eurasia and northern Africa, is uncommon on Sugarloaf. **Flowers:** Small, grayish-rose or grayish-white, in fuzzy oblong or cylindric heads ½–1½" high (suggesting a rabbit's foot). **Leaves:** Alternate, trifoliate, leaflets narrow, oblanceolate or linear, silky pubescent. **Height:** 4–16". **Habitat:** Fields, lawns, roadsides, disturbed sites. **On Sugarloaf—Blooming time:** May–October. **Locations:** Yellow Trail, mountain roadsides.

Crown Vetch

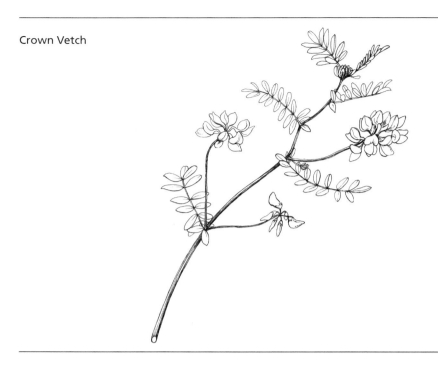

Crown Vetch (Axseed)

Coronilla varia L.
Pea Family (Fabaceae)

Frequently planted along highways for erosion control, crown vetch has escaped cultivation and become widely naturalized. **Flowers:** Purplish-pink (and sometimes white), often with pale to deepening color on the same flower; irregular (typically pea-shaped), ¼–½" long, in round heads about an inch (more or less) across. **Leaves:** Alternate, pinnately compound, with 11–25 small oblong-obovate leaflets. Overall leaf 1½–6" long. **Height and growth habits:** 1–3½' tall; branched and sprawling. **Habitat and range:** Roadsides, disturbed sites throughout the eastern United States and other regions where it has been planted; native to the Mediterranean. **On Sugarloaf—Blooming time:** June–October. **Locations:** Roadsides and trailsides, including Mount Ephraim Road and the Yellow Trail. **Similar species:** The combination of purplish-pink flowers in round clusters and pinnately compound (rather than trifoliate) leaves separate crown vetch from other members of the pea family growing on Sugarloaf.

Wild Indigo

Baptisia tinctoria (L.) R. Br. ex W. T. Aiton
Pea Family (Fabaceae)

A branching plant with gray-green or bluish leaves and bright yellow flowers. The plant yields a blue dye. **Flowers:** Yellow, about ½" long, irregular (typical pea family shape), in loose racemes or sometimes growing singly. **Leaves:** Alternate, trifoliately compound. Each leaflet ⅓–1½" long, entire; rounded or slightly indented at the apex, tapering to a sessile or short-stalked base. Each trifoliate leaf short-stalked or nearly sessile. Blue-green or gray-green foliage turns black when dead. **Height and growth habits:** 1–3'; branched and bushy. **Habitat and range:** Dry open woods, fields, clearings; Maine to Georgia and Tennessee, west to Ontario and Wisconsin. **Herbal lore:** Wild indigo has been widely used as an herbal remedy for internal and external medical conditions. American Indians used the root tea as an emetic and purgative, according to Foster and Duke (Peterson Field Guides' *Field Guide to Medicinal Plants: Eastern and Central North America*). The root also was used to assist healing of wounds, sprains, and bruises. In large amounts

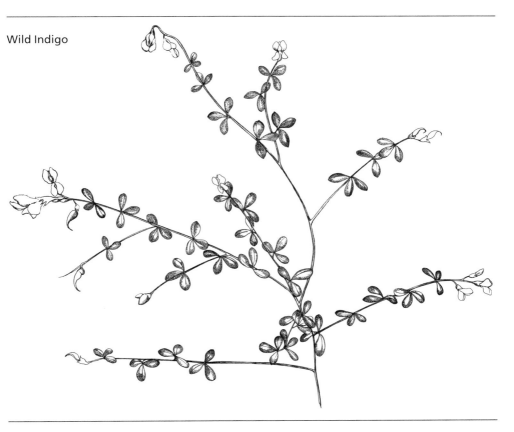

Wild Indigo

wild indigo can be toxic. **On Sugarloaf—Blooming time:** June–July. **Locations:** White Trail; probable along other trails and roadsides in dry open woods or clearings. **Similar species:** Large, bushy habit and showy yellow flowers distinguish this species from local clovers.

Chinese Bush Clover (Chinese Lespedeza)

Lespedeza cuneata (Dum. Cours) G. Don
Pea Family (Fabaceae)

A tallish, very leafy plant with a somewhat woody grooved stalk. **Flowers:** Irregular, creamy white, typical pea family flowers with a purple blush on the banner (*see* Glossary). Flowers borne (singly or clustered) in the upper leaf axils. **Leaves:** Trifoliate, with narrow (linear to wedge-shaped) leaflets that are truncate at the apex and mucronate. Lower leaves with leaflets an inch or more long; upper leaves may be tiny. Leaflets silky-pubescent below. **Height and growth habits:** 1–3½', usually branched, with ascending branchlets. **Habitat and range:** Native of eastern Asia; now cultivated and naturalized in the eastern United States; very invasive in some areas. In *Herbaceous Plants of Maryland,* Brown and Brown note, "Recently introduced and planted for erosion control, especially along roadsides; now escaping to roadsides and fields in numerous places." **On Sugarloaf—Blooming time:** August–October. **Locations:** Yellow Trail, Mount Ephraim Road; other trails and roadsides possible. **Similar species:** Several other bush clovers *(Lespedeza* species) are found on Sugarloaf, although none are common. All others have pink, violet, or purple flowers.

Naked-Flowered Tick-Trefoil

Desmodium nudiflorum (L.) DC.
Pea Family (Fabaceae)

A summer-blooming plant with flowers on a long, leafless central stalk; basal leaves are borne separately. **Flowers:** Purplish-pink, typically pea-shaped irregular flowers (¼–½" long) in loose, elongate cluster toward the apex of a long (up to 3½') stalk. Individual flowers stalked. **Fruit:** A segmented legume (called a loment) which bears prickly hairs that stick to animal fur and clothing (these fruits are often called "hitchhikers"). **Leaves:** A separate leaf-bearing stalk arises from near the base of the flowering stalk. Leaves compound, each with 3 (1–4") ovate, entire leaflets. Leaves up to several inches long, arranged in single or multiple whorls of (usually) 3–4 leaves. **Height:** Flowering stalk 1½–3½'. Leaf stalk 6–14". **Habitat and range:** Woods; Maine to Minnesota, south to Florida and Texas. **Herbal lore:** According to Foster and Duke (Peterson Field Guides' *Field Guide to Medicinal Plants: Eastern and Central North America*): "Cherokees chewed the root for

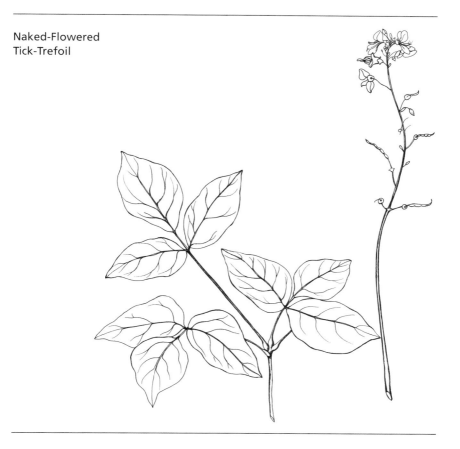

inflammation of mouth, sore bleeding gums, periodontal diseases with pus discharge. Root tea was used as a wash for cramps." **Wildlife lore:** According to Brown and Brown's *Herbaceous Plants of Maryland,* deer eat tick-trefoil species, and the seeds are an important food source for quail, grouse, pheasant, and wild turkey. **On Sugarloaf—Blooming time:** July–September. **Locations:** Mount Ephraim Road, other mountain roadsides and trailsides. **Similar species:** Other tick-trefoils bear flowers and leaves on the same stalk.

Other Tick-Trefoils

Desmodium species

There are nearly two dozen species of tick-trefoil indigenous to the eastern United States and 300 worldwide. Brown and Brown include more than 20 species of tick-trefoil *(Desmodium)* in *Herbaceous Plants of Maryland,* and Fleming, Lobstein, and Tufty list 9 species in *Finding Wildflowers in the Washington-Baltimore Area.* At least 3 species in addition to naked-flowered tick-trefoil *(D. nudiflorum)* are found on Sugarloaf. Unlike naked-flowered tick-trefoil, these 3 have flower clusters and leaves borne on the same stalk. All bloom from midsummer to early fall.

Panicled Tick-Trefoil [*D. paniculatum* (L.) DC.] has a stem which is usually branched and often glabrous. Its leaflets are narrow (lanceolate, ovate, or oblong), and the terminal leaflet is more than three times as long as wide. Leaflets glabrous or slightly pubescent. Stipules small, awl-like, ⅛–¼" long, and soon falling. **On Sugarloaf—Locations:** Mount Ephraim Road, other roadsides and trailsides.

Panicled
Tick-Trefoil

Hoary Tick-Trefoil [*D. canescens* (L.) DC.] is a branched, densely pubescent species. Its leaflets are ovate, and it has persistent ovate stipules (¼–½" long). **On Sugarloaf—Locations:** White Trail, other trails and roadsides.

Dillen's Tick-Trefoil [*D. glabellum* (Michx.) DC.] is listed in a 1987 Stronghold plant survey conducted by botanist Richard Wiegand, but we have not been able to identify this species here. Other tick-trefoils are likely on the mountain, their distinguishing characteristics so subtle as to make amateur identification difficult.

Tree

Redbud (Judas-Tree)

Cercis canadensis L.
Pea Family (Fabaceae)

Indigenous to much of the eastern United States and northern Mexico, red-bud is one of Sugarloaf's showiest spring-flowering trees. It is the state tree of Oklahoma. **Flowers:** Irregular, typically pea-shaped flowers are deep purplish-pink and clustered along the twigs, branches, and sometimes even down the trunk of the tree. Each flower about ⅓" long. Flowers appear before the leaves in spring. **Fruit:** 2–3½" long, light reddish-brown legume pointed at both ends, on thin stalk about ½" long. **Leaves:** Alternate, simple, deciduous, heart-shaped (cordate) with entire margin. The first leaves unfold at the tips of the branchlets when the tree is in full bloom in the spring. Mature leaf 2–5" long and 3–5" wide; 5–7 prominent palmately arranged veins arise from the base of the leaf blade. Petiole slender; small stipules soon fall. **Growth habits:** Small, widely branched tree. **Bark and twigs:** Bark gray, may be smooth, finely grooved, and/or scaly. Twigs reddish-brown, heavily lenticeled, with small lateral buds and no terminal buds. **Habitat and range:** Moist woods; southwestern Connecticut to northern Florida; west to Michigan, Iowa, eastern Nebraska, Texas, and northern Mexico. **On Sugarloaf—Blooming time:** March–May. **Locations:** Quite common mountainwide. **Similar species:** None on Sugarloaf. The similar Chinese redbud *(C. chinen-*

Redbud

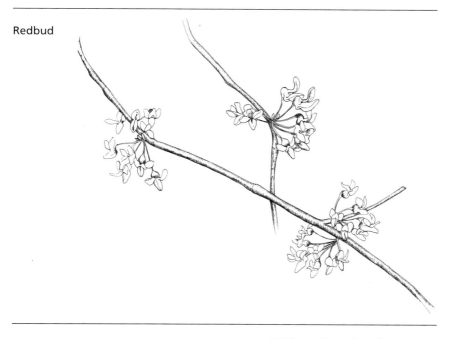

Guide to Flowering Plants 141

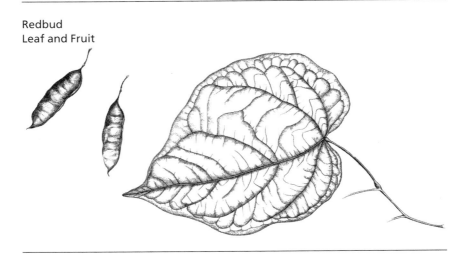

Redbud
Leaf and Fruit

sis), a shrubby species with darker flowers, is cultivated in home gardens throughout the Washington-Baltimore area. Our native redbud also is often cultivated.

Tree

Black Locust (False Acacia)
Robinia pseudoacia L.
Pea Family (Fabaceae)

As flowering dogwoods fall victim to a prevalent fungal blight, residents of the mid-Atlantic states increasingly rely on native black locusts to provide a white springtime display. The black locust blooms slightly later than the flowering dogwood, just before or with the leaves. During favorable years the black locust's springtime flower show is breath-taking. **Flowers:** Fragrant, creamy white, pendulous clusters of irregular, typically pealike flowers. Individual flowers 1" or less in length. **Fruit:** Flat reddish-brown legume, tapered to a point at both ends; 2–4" long, containing several flat brown seeds. **Leaves:** Alternate, pinnately compound, deciduous; 7–21 elliptic-ovate leaflets, including a terminal one. Each leaflet ¾–2¼" long, with a smooth or slightly wavy margin. Apex rounded or indented, often with a tiny bristle barely visible. Base rounded, wedge-shaped, or almost straight across. Total leaf length: 6–13". **Height and growth habits:** A medium-sized tree with an open, scraggly crown. **Bark and twigs:** Bark thick, brown, reddish-brown, or gray, deeply furrowed and ridged. Twigs usually have paired stipular spines. Winter buds small; end bud false. **Habitat and range:** Fields, woods, roadsides; Pennsylvania west to Indiana and Oklahoma, south to Georgia and

Alabama. Widely cultivated around the world for timber and ornament. **Herbal and wildlife lore:** This tree has a complex herbal history as a medicinal plant, both here and in Asia (where it has long been in cultivation). However, Foster and Duke (in Peterson Field Guides' *Field Guide to Medicinal Plants: Eastern and Central North America*) warn that all parts of the tree are toxic, even, perhaps, the honey derived from its flowers. In *Woody Plants of Maryland,* Brown and Brown tell a different story: "Excellent honey plant, but flowers are poisonous if eaten by livestock. Seeds used by quail and grouse; herbage bro[w]sed by deer and twigs much eaten by rabbits in winter." **On Sugarloaf—Blooming time:** May–June. **Locations:** Common on and around the mountain. **Similar species:** None on Sugarloaf.

Loosestrife Family

Lythraceae

This family is responsible for many dye plants, including *Lawsonia inermis,* which yields henna. Woody ornamentals of the loosestrife family include the

Asian crape-myrtle *(Lagerstroemia indica)*, a summer-blooming shrub or small tree that is popular in the Washington area. Many loosestrife family plants are indigenous to the eastern United States. The nonnative purple loosestrife *(Lythrum salicaria)* has become a problematic invasive in wetlands across the country. A single wildflower of this family grows on Sugarloaf: clammy cuphea *(Cuphea viscosissima)*, a summer to fall-blooming plant with uniquely shaped flowers. **Family characteristics:** 25 genera and nearly 500 species worldwide. **Flowers:** Perfect, regular or irregular, 4–8-parted. **Fruit:** Usually a capsule. **Leaves:** Simple, entire, usually opposite, sometimes whorled or alternate. **Growth habits:** Herbs, shrubs, and trees. **Occurrence on Sugarloaf:** One species found mountainwide but not very common.

Clammy Cuphea (Blue Waxweed)

Cuphea viscosissima Jacq.
(Cuphea petiolata)
Loosestrife Family (Lythraceae)

A summer to fall wildflower with small, uniquely shaped flowers. **Flowers:** Purplish-pink, irregular, with 6 unequal petals: the 2 upper petals larger than the 4 lower ones. Calyx tube ½" or less, ribbed, slightly swollen, viscid, pubescent. Flower ¼–½" wide; borne singly or in pairs in upper leaf axils. **Leaves:** Simple, opposite, entire; ovate-lanceolate, small, ½–2" long, on petioles. Plant stalk viscid-pubescent or "clammy." **Height and growth habits:**

Clammy Cuphea

6–20"; usually somewhat branched, sometimes slightly sprawling. **Habitat and range:** Fields, meadows, roadsides; New Hampshire to Illinois and Kansas; south to Georgia and Louisiana. **On Sugarloaf—Blooming time:** July–October. **Locations:** East View, mountain roadsides, some trailsides and open areas. **Similar species:** None on Sugarloaf.

Evening-Primrose Family

Onagraceae

The evening-primrose family contains many popular ornamentals. Several summer-blooming plants of the evening-primrose family grow on Sugarloaf. **Family characteristics:** 17 genera and 675 species worldwide. Cosmopolitan with a high concentration of plants in the western United States and Mexico. **Economic importance:** Among the family members grown as ornamentals are some greenhouse aquatics. Oil from the native common evening-primrose *(Oenothera biennis)* is used as an herbal medicinal. **Flowers:** Mostly perfect, regular or somewhat irregular. Usually 4-parted but this varies, with sepals as few as 2 or as many as 5; petals match sepals in number or, rarely, are absent. **Fruit:** Usually a capsule; less often nutlike or a berry. **Leaves:** Alternate or opposite, simple; entire, toothed or lobed. **Growth habits:** Herbs; less often shrubs or trees. **Occurrence on Sugarloaf:** Enchanter's nightshade *(Circaea lutetiana)* is a common Sugarloaf trailside plant, blooming from June through summer. Several other summer-blooming species included in this guide grow near the mountain base, along the Yellow Trail and the dirt roads circling the mountain. Water purslane *(Ludwigia palustris)* is, as the name implies, an aquatic plant, which grows in Sugarloaf springs, seeps, and streams. Two other native family members, not included in this guide, might be found here: purple-leaved willow-herb *(Epilobium coloratum)*, with opposite or alternate narrow leaves and small pink or white flowers, and biennial gaura *(Gaura biennis)*, with alternate narrow leaves and white flowers changing to pink or red.

Enchanter's Nightshade

Circaea lutetiana L.
(Circaea quadrisulcata)
Evening-Primrose Family (Onagraceae)

This plant with the bewitching common and Latin names graces eastern North American woodlands (including Sugarloaf's) in early summer, just when the profusion of springtime flowers is winding down. **Flowers:** Tiny, white, in (mostly terminal) racemes. Each flower has 2 petals, which are so

deeply notched they appear as 4; sepals: 2. Flowers ¼" or less across. **Fruit:** Small, fuzzy green, and egg-shaped; indehiscent (not splitting open), ⅛–¼" long. **Leaves:** Opposite, simple, ovate, with shallow, irregular teeth, 1–5" long. Lower petioles long; upper leaves with short petioles to almost sessile. Leaf blades glabrous or nearly so, petioles pubescent or glabrous. **Height and growth habits:** 10"–2'; upright plant with one to several flowering racemes. **Habitat and range:** Moist woods; circumboreal but not continuously so; in North America from southeastern Canada to Georgia and Oklahoma. **On Sugarloaf—Blooming time:** June–August. **Locations:** All trails, including Green Trail to the summit; West View, East View; roadsides. **Similar species:** None on Sugarloaf, although dwarf or Alpine enchanter's nightshade *(C. alpina)* grows in the mountains to the west.

Common Evening-Primrose

Oenothera biennis L.
Evening-Primrose Family (Onagraceae)

A tall, striking summer–fall wildflower with yellow blooms. Flowers supposedly open in the evening and close up during the day, but they have been known to stay bodaciously open all day long! **Flowers:** Yellow, with 4 petals that are shallowly incurved at the apex. Flowers 1–2" wide when open, ½–1"

long. Stigma cross-shaped. Sepals long, narrow, and reflexed when flowers are open. Flowers borne in upper leaf axils and/or terminal spike. **Fruit:** ¾–1¾" erect capsule tapering toward the tip. **Leaves:** Alternate, simple, lanceolate-oblong, sessile or short-petioled, with shallowly toothed to nearly entire margins. Often slightly pubescent, 1½–6" long. **Height and growth habits:** 1–6'; single-stalked or branched. Main stalk often reddish. **Habitat and range:** Open woods, fields, roadsides; most of the United States and southern Canada. **Herbal lore:** The seeds, roots, and leaves of this plant all have been used medicinally. American Indians used the root tea for bowel pains and poulticed the root for bruises. According to Foster and Duke (Peterson Field Guides' *Field Guide to Medicinal Plants: Eastern and Central North America*), "Recent research suggests seed oil may be useful for atopic eczema, allergy-induced eczema, asthma, migraines, inflammations, premenstrual syndrome, breast problems, metabolic disorders, diabetes, arthritis, and alcoholism"! **On Sugarloaf—Blooming time:** Midsummer–fall. **Locations:** Yellow Trail; Mount Ephraim Road, Sugarloaf Mountain Road, and other roadsides. **Similar species:** Sundrops and small sundrops *(O. fruticosa* and *O. perennis)* are day-blooming, late spring–late summer wildflowers that are found in a few places near the mountain base. Sundrops *(O. fruticosa)* has smaller fruit capsules (less than ½" long) that broaden toward their tips. Small sundrops *(O. perennis)* has smaller flowers with petals that are clearly notched, rather than just incurved, at the apex. Seedbox *(Ludwigia alternifolia)* and St. Andrew's-cross *(Hypericum hypericoides)* have smaller flowers.

Sundrops and Small (or Little) Sundrops

Oenothera fruticosa L. and *O. perennis* L.
Evening-Primrose Family (Onagraceae)

Two species of sundrops are found on and around Sugarloaf, but they are not as common as the similar, closely related common evening-primrose *(O. biennis)*. Sundrops bloom from late spring through late summer. Their **flowers** are similar to those of evening-primrose, but they are wide open during the day (however, evening-primrose also may remain in bloom in daylight hours). Sundrops *(O. fruticosa)* has a shorter **fruit** capsule than common evening-primrose (less than ½" long), and the capsule broadens toward the tip (while common evening-primrose capsules are tapered at the tip). Small sundrops *(O. perennis)* has smaller flowers, ½–¾" wide, that are clearly notched, rather than just incurved, at the tip. **On Sugarloaf—Locations:** Mount Ephraim Road; possible in other locations around the mountain.

Seedbox (Square-Pod Water-Primrose)

Ludwigia alternifolia L.
Evening-Primrose Family (Onagraceae)

As the common names imply, the most distinctive aspect of this plant is its fruit: a decorative woody, box-shaped capsule. Seedbox is a summer wildflower of Sugarloaf's springs, seeps, and moist soils. The fruit forms in late summer and fall. **Flowers:** A sunny yellow, 4-petaled, ½–¾" across, on short stalks growing from the leaf axils. Sepals about as long or slightly longer than the petals. **Fruit:** A small cubic capsule, which is rounded at the base. Its angles are slightly "winged." Capsule about ¼–½" across. **Leaves:** Alternate, simple, lanceolate, with entire or wavy margin, pointed apex, and tapered base; 2–4½" long, sessile or short-petioled, glabrous or finely pubescent. **Height and growth habits:** 2–3'; erect, often branched. **Habitat and range:** Swamps, marshes, wet meadows, and other moist habitats; Massachusetts, southern Ontario, and Iowa, south to Florida and Texas. **On Sugarloaf—Blooming time:** June–September. **Locations:** Yellow Trail, Mount Ephraim Road; may be found in other moist places along mountain trails and roads. **Similar species:** Other 4-petaled summer wildflowers: common evening-primrose *(Oenothera biennis)* and sundrops *(O. fruticosa)* have larger flowers (1–2" wide). Small sundrops *(O. perennis)* has petals that are notched at

the apex. St. Andrew's-cross *(Hypericum hypericoides)* is a smaller plant, and its leaves are bluntly pointed at the apex.

Water Purslane (Marsh Purslane)

Ludwigia palustris (L.) Elliott
Evening-Primrose Family (Onagraceae)

Water purslane is a wetland plant, often found floating on shallow water or prostrate in mud. Indigenous to a large part of the Northern Hemisphere, water purslane is a common plant in Washington-Baltimore area ponds, freshwater marshes, and shallow streams, according to Fleming, Lobstein, and Tufty *(Finding Wildflowers in the Washington-Baltimore Area)*. Water purslane has very small 4-parted, stalkless, green and/or reddish **flowers** growing in the leaf axils (June–September) and opposite, ovate, petioled **leaves. On Sugarloaf—Locations:** Bear Branch and springs and seeps in its vicinity; likely in other wet areas around the mountain base.

Dogwood Family

Cornaceae

This small family of mainly trees and shrubs is best known for the dogwood genus *(Cornus)*, a favorite of gardeners. Several dogwoods are indigenous to Maryland, but the only one common on Sugarloaf is the flowering dogwood *(Cornus florida)*. Sadly, a fungal blight has put the future of this beautiful native tree in jeopardy (*see* next entry). The other native Maryland dogwood species are small trees or shrubs with the exception of bunchberry (*C. canadensis*), a semiwoody, low-growing northern wildflower reaching south into the mountains of Garrett County. **Family characteristics:** 13–15 genera and more than 100 species worldwide. **Flowers** are regular and 4- or 5-parted. In some species, such as flowering dogwood, the tiny true flowers are clustered at the center of 4 large, showy petal-like bracts. **Fruit** is usually a drupe, sometimes a berry. **Leaves** are opposite or alternate, simple.

Tree

Flowering Dogwood

Cornus florida L.
Dogwood Family (Cornaceae)

Unsurpassed in beauty among our native flowering trees, the flowering dogwood is the state tree of Missouri, the state flower of North Carolina, and the state tree and flower of Virginia. However, we who cherish this tree may find ourselves wistfully describing its beauty to our grandchildren, much like our ancestors told us about the former glory of the American chestnut. The sad reality is that flowering dogwoods throughout the area are slipping away, victims of a fungus called *Discula anthracnose*. Sugarloaf's trees have been hard hit. Botanists and horticulturists worry about the survival of these cherished trees. The loss of our dogwoods extends beyond their aesthetic value to us, for their berrylike drupes are an important food source for songbirds and native mammals. **Flowers:** Just before or with the unfurling spring leaves, 2–4" across. Usually white but may be pink (some cultivated forms of flowering dogwood are deep pink to red). The 4- notched white "petals" are actually large bracts that surround the tiny yellowish or greenish true flowers clustered at the center. **Fruit:** Scarlet berrylike drupes, each ½" long or less, in small clusters. **Leaves:** Simple, opposite, deciduous, 2–6" long. Elliptic or ovate, abruptly pointed with broadly wedge-shaped or rounded base. Veins, characteristic of all dogwoods, curve along the leaf margin, which is entire. Autumn color: brilliant scarlet, crimson, wine. **Growth habits:** A small tree with a flat, bushy crown. **Bark and twigs:** Bark is broken into many

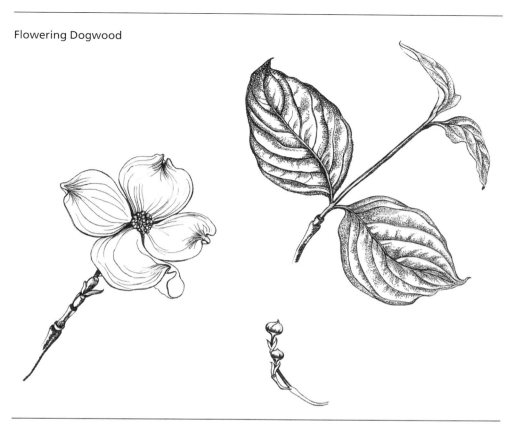

small squarish plates. Twigs greenish or purple, with separate leaf and flower buds. The flower buds are very distinctive: gray and onion-shaped, borne at the ends of the twigs, especially showy in winter. They have always reminded me of Eastern Orthodox church spires. **Habitat and range:** Woods; southern New England to Florida, west to Ontario, Michigan, eastern Texas, and northeastern Mexico. **Herbal lore:** Flowering dogwood has enjoyed a rich herbal history. Its twigs were used as chewing sticks (primitive toothbrushes) by American Indians, settlers, and slaves, and a tincture or tea made from dogwood root bark was used to treat malaria during the Civil War. **On Sugarloaf—Blooming time:** April–May. **Locations:** Once abundant mountain-wide, flowering dogwood is disappearing because of fungal disease. **Similar species:** Other native Maryland dogwood trees and shrubs (*Cornus* spp.) lack the large, showy white bracts of this species. Brown and Brown's *Woody Plants of Maryland* contains illustrated descriptions of indigenous dogwoods. Flowering dogwood is the only species common on Sugarloaf. *See* Botanical Key and Guide to Trees, Shrubs, and Woody Vines for brief discussion of other species.

Spurge Family

Euphorbiaceae

Two wildflowers of this cosmopolitan and economically important family grow on Sugarloaf, but neither is common on the mountain. Spurge family plants are significant sources of natural rubber, cassava or tapioca, castor oil, and tallow for soaps and candles. The poinsettia is in this family, in the *Euphorbia* genus, the same genus as Sugarloaf's flowering spurge. **Family characteristics:** 300 genera and 7,500 species of trees, shrubs, and herbs worldwide. **Flowers** are extremely variable, as are the **leaves,** which usually bear stipules (these may be modified into hairs, glands, or spines).

Common Three-Seeded Mercury

Acalypha rhomboidea Raf.
Spurge Family (Euphorbiaceae)

The most conspicuous aspect of this plant is the deeply lobed, leafy bract surrounding the flower cluster. **Flowers:** Tiny creamy and greenish flowers (staminate and pistillate separate). Staminate flowers in small spikes, pistillate flower clusters surrounded by a 5–9-lobed leafy bract. Flower clusters spring from the leaf axils and also grow terminally. **Leaves:** Alternate, simple, long-stalked (petioles often more than half as long as the leaf blade). Leaf blade ovate or rhombic, coarsely toothed, 1–3½" long. **Height:** 4–24". **Habi-**

Common
Three-Seeded Mercury

tat and range: Woods, roadsides, waste places, and gardens; eastern United States and Canada. On Sugarloaf—Blooming time: July–November. Locations: Yellow Trail, Mount Ephraim Road; likely along other trails and roadsides. Similar species: The leafy bract surrounding the flower clusters is distinctive. At least two other three-seeded mercury species grow in Maryland, but this is the only one that has been identified on Sugarloaf.

Flowering Spurge

Euphorbia corollata L.
Spurge Family (Euphorbiaceae)

This is a North American plant of eastern woods and fields and midwestern prairies. Several members of the *Euphorbia* genus that grow as weeds in lawns, gardens, and waste places of the Sugarloaf area are listed below under "Similar species." Flowering spurge is the local genus member with the showiest flowers, and it is the only one described and illustrated in this book. **Flowers:** White or greenish-white, with 5 roundish petal-like structures that are actually parts of an involucre. The tiny true flowers are inconspicuous, but the involucre simulates the familiar flower structure. Flowers ¼" or more across in terminal clusters. **Leaves:** Simple, alternate along stem, with a whorl of leaves just below the branched flower clusters. Elliptic-linear, entire, sessile or nearly so, 1–2½" long. **Height and growth habits:** 1–3½'; plant stalk simple from base to leaf whorl, then branched above. Plant stalk exudes a milky juice when broken (but please don't harm Sugarloaf plants!). **Habitat and range:** Open woods, fields in the east, prairies to the west; New Hampshire and Massachusetts to Minnesota, south to Florida and Texas. **Herbal lore:** According to Peterson Field Guides' *Field Guide to Medicinal Plants: Eastern and Central North America* by Foster and Duke, "American Indians used leaf tea for diabetes; root tea as a strong laxative, emetic, for

Flowering Spurge

pinworms, rheumatism; root poultice used for snakebites. Warning: Extremely strong laxative. Juice may cause blistering." **On Sugarloaf—Blooming time:** July–October. **Locations:** White Trail below Strong Mansion; uncommon on the mountain. **Similar species:** Not likely to be confused with other area wildflowers, but here is a list of additional genus members that grow locally: toothed spurge *(E. dentata);* spotted spurge, milk-purslane, eyebane, or wartweed *(E. maculata);* cypress spurge *(E. cyparissias),* a species with densely clustered linear leaves; and glade or purple spurge *(E. purpurea),* which is a Maryland endangered species that is found mostly in the Catoctin Mountains, according to botanist Cris Fleming. Consult Brown and Brown's *Herbaceous Plants of Maryland* for illustrated descriptions of these species and other spurges native to and naturalized in Maryland.

Grape Family

Vitaceae

This is a family that needs no introduction thanks to the *Vitis* genus and all it has provided humanity over the ages. Grapes are also important food for wildlife, and their tangled vines provide nesting sites and shelter. **Family characteristics:** 11 genera and 700 species worldwide, mainly in the Tropics and subtropics. **Economic importance:** The principal wine-making vine is *Vitis vinifera,* which originated in Asia. Other species are also used for wine making, including *V. aestivalis,* indigenous to Sugarloaf. Table grapes and raisins come from these and other species. **Flowers:** Regular, perfect or unisexual, with 4–5 sepals and 4–5 petals. Usually small and borne in clusters (cymes or racemes). **Fruit:** A berry. **Leaves:** Alternate, simple or compound. Often palmately veined, lobed or divided. **Growth habits:** Mostly climbing vines; some shrubs. **Occurrence on Sugarloaf:** Virginia creeper *(Parthenocissus quinquefolia)* is common mountainwide and is showy in autumn with its red leaves. It climbs trees, rocks, and fences or trails along the ground. Three grape species are treated in the Botanical Key and Guide to Trees, Shrubs, and Woody Vines.

Woody Vine

Virginia Creeper (Woodbine)

Parthenocissus quinquefolia (L.) Planch.
Grape Family (Vitaceae)

A trailing, climbing vine that attaches to tree trunks, rocks, fences, and thickets by means of adhesive disks at the ends of its tendrils. Virginia

Virginia Creeper

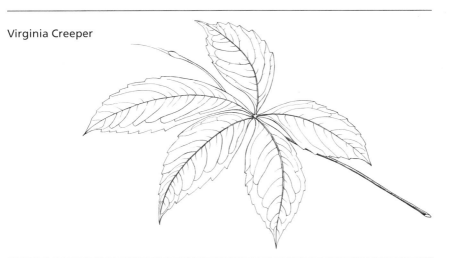

creeper flowers are not conspicuous; you are most apt to notice this plant in early to mid autumn when its leaves turn scarlet and wine-red and—along with scarlet and orange poison ivy vines—decorate the trees they climb. **Flowers and fruit:** Flowers small and not showy, greenish or green-brown, star-shaped and 5-parted, in clusters. Mature fruit a small blue-black or black berry (showier than the flowers). **Leaves:** Alternate, palmately compound, with 3–7 (usually 5) toothed, elliptic, oblong, or obovate leaflets. Overall leaf several inches across. **Growth habits:** A trailing or climbing vine. **Range:** Eastern and central United States and Canada. **Herbal lore:** American Indians used the leaves and roots medicinally for jaundice and other conditions. **Wildlife lore:** Berries are an important fall and winter food for songbirds. **On Sugarloaf—Blooming and fruiting time:** Flowers in summer; fruits mature in autumn and persist into winter (immature green fruit present from midsummer on). **Locations:** Common mountainwide and in the surrounding countryside. **Similar species:** Poison ivy *(Toxicodendron radicans)* leaves uniformly bear only 3 leaflets. Use the palmately compound leaves and trailing, climbing growth habit to distinguish from other native plants.

Flax Family

Linaceae

The flax plant *(Linum usitatissimum)*, one of humanity's most historically important crops, is in the flax family. The Egyptians began cultivating this plant in 5,000 B.C., and the plant may have been grown even earlier in the region that makes up present-day Turkey and Syria. Today the plant is still an important world crop. One variety of the species *L. usitatissimum* is grown as fiber flax, which is made into linen, rope, quality papers, and thread. Another variety is grown for flaxseeds, which yield linseed oil, used in making varnishes, paints, and printing ink. After the oil is pressed out, the remaining materials are made into cattle feed. In recent years flaxseed and flaxseed oil have been promoted by the health food industry as alternatives to saturated fats. Sugarloaf's native wildflowers of the flax family are members of the *Linum* genus. **Family characteristics:** 6 genera and 220 species worldwide. **Flowers** have 5 (sometimes 4) distinct sepals and petals. **Fruit:** A capsule or drupe. **Leaves:** Alternate, opposite, or both; simple, entire. **Growth habits:** Herbs, some shrubs, a few trees. **Occurrence on Sugarloaf:** Ridged yellow flax *(Linum striatum)* is an uncommon plant of Mount Ephraim Road wetlands. A second species is possible in drier habitats (*see* "Similar species," next entry).

Ridged Yellow Flax

Linum striatum Walter
Flax Family (Linaceae)

A yellow summer wildflower that seems bent on increasing the confusion in the already confusing yellow summer wildflower picture by bearing leaves that are opposite on the lower part of the plant and alternate on the upper part. **Flowers:** Tiny, about ¼" across, with 5 yellow petals. Borne in slender, loose, leafy, branched terminal clusters. The flower-bearing stalks are ridged or angled (visible with a hand lens). **Leaves:** Opposite on lower stalk, alternate above, simple. Sessile, entire, elliptic to oblanceolate or obovate, ½–2" long. **Height:** 6"–3'. **Habitat and range:** Damp or wet woods, swamps, bogs; eastern United States from Massachusetts to northern Florida, west to Michigan and eastern Texas. **On Sugarloaf—Blooming time:** June–August. **Locations:** Wet areas along Mount Ephraim Road; likely along other damp roadsides and the Yellow Trail. **Similar species:** Wild yellow flax or Virginia yellow flax *(L. virginianum)* is a plant of drier habitats, which has been reported on Sugarloaf, although I have not seen it here. Its flowering branchlets are not angled or ridged but round in cross section. St. John's-worts *(Hypericum* spp.) have 5-petaled yellow flowers and similar leaves, but their leaves are all opposite.

Maple Family

Aceraceae

Trees of the maple genus (one of only two genera in the maple family) are important woodland trees, primarily of North America, Europe, and Asia. They are often cultivated for shade and ornament, prized for their spectacular autumn foliage, and used for timber and as the source of maple syrup. The maple genus is represented by three species on Sugarloaf. The red maple *(Acer rubrum)* is common on and around the mountain and is included in this illustrated guide to wildflowers because of its early crimson spring flowers. *See* Botanical Key and Guide to Trees, Shrubs, and Woody Vines for brief descriptions of other species. **Family characteristics:** 2 genera and 112 species worldwide. **Flowers:** Regular, 5-parted or 4-parted (sometimes lacking petals). **Fruit:** In maple genus, a twin pair of winged samaras. **Leaves:** Opposite; simple or compound. **Growth habits:** Trees and shrubs. **Occurrence on Sugarloaf:** Red maple is common mountainwide. A few sugar maples *(A. saccharum),* the species yielding sap for maple syrup, are planted at West View and near the base of the mountain. Box-elder or ash-leaved maple *(A. negundo)* is a common tree of moist soils around the mountain base.

Tree

Red Maple

Acer rubrum L.
Maple Family (Aceraceae)

One of the first arboreal signs of spring in the mid-Atlantic region, including Sugarloaf country, is the crimson glow in the red maple treetops. This tree's tiny but profuse red flowers, which appear weeks before its leaves, are offset by the pale gray bark characteristic of the species. The tree continues its crimson show when its red samaras follow on the heels of the flowers, and then it dazzles onlookers again in autumn with multicolored foliage displays. Red maple is the state tree of Rhode Island. **Flowers:** Before the leaves in early spring. Small, usually red, sometimes yellow-green flowers with 5 tiny petals and slightly shorter sepals; borne along the branchlets in dense lateral clusters. Usually unisexual but may be perfect. **Fruit:** Twin winged samaras, usually ⅔–1" long, on thin stalk. Pale pink to bright red (sometimes yellow) wings connected at an inverted V-shaped angle. **Leaves:** Opposite, simple, deciduous; 2–6" long, with leaf width equal to or a little greater than length; 3–5 broad lobes with shallow sinuses between them. Margin coarsely toothed. Dark green above, paler and often glaucous below. Petiole 2–4"

Red Maple

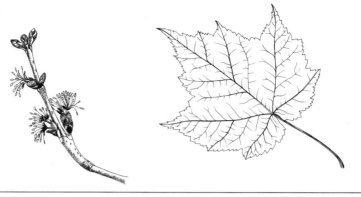

long, sometimes red. Leaves turn red, yellow, and orange in autumn. Trees may turn a uniform hue, or the leaves may show all three colors on the same blade. **Height and growth habits:** A medium-sized tree with a rounded crown. **Bark and twigs:** Bark smooth and pale gray on young trees. Darkening and breaking into large plates with age. Winter twigs reddish or orange with clusters of round red buds. No unpleasant odor when twig is broken (*see* "Similar species"). **Habitat and range:** Newfoundland to southeastern Manitoba; south to Florida and Texas. **On Sugarloaf—Blooming time:** Earliest spring. **Fruiting time:** Soon after the early spring flowers. **Locations:** Very common mountainwide; look for the tree in bloom in spring and when its leaves turn brilliant colors in autumn. **Similar species:** Could be confused with silver maple *(A. saccharinum)*, which has more deeply and narrowly sinused leaves; early spring flowers with no petals that are more often yellow-green or yellow-orange than red; flaky, almost shaggy bark on mature trees; and twigs that have a rank odor when crushed. Silver maple is very common along the Potomac and Monocacy Rivers but not on Sugarloaf.

Wood-Sorrel Family

Oxalidaceae

The bulbs, leaves, and seeds of native wood-sorrel family members are eaten by mourning doves and bobwhites; some songbirds eat the seeds. Three wildflowers of the wood-sorrel family grow on Sugarloaf. Violet wood-sorrel *(Oxalis violacea)* is a spring favorite of Tina's and mine. **Family characteristics:** 7–8 genera and 900 species worldwide. Cosmopolitan. **Economic importance:** Little economic importance, but the tuberous roots and leaves of some species are used as cooked vegetables and salad greens. **Flowers:** Perfect, regular, and 5-parted. **Fruit:** Usually a capsule, rarely a berry. **Leaves:**

Alternate, palmately or pinnately compound, often with a sour taste. **Growth habits:** Mostly herbaceous. **Occurrence on Sugarloaf:** Yellow wood-sorrel *(O. stricta)* is common in open woods and mowed areas. Creeping wood-sorrel *(O. corniculata)* is found in mowed areas, but it is not as common as yellow wood-sorrel and is mentioned only under yellow wood-sorrel's "Similar species" section. Violet wood-sorrel grows primarily on the western/southwestern side of the mountain.

Violet Wood-Sorrel

Oxalis violacea L.
Wood-Sorrel Family (Oxalidaceae)

A charming spring wildflower of the eastern United States, violet wood-sorrel is uncommon on Sugarloaf. **Flowers:** 5 purplish-pink petals, often with a white blush at the center of the flower. Flowers ½" or more across, growing in small clusters (or solitary) from a long stalk. **Leaves:** Compound basal leaves only, each with 3 sessile, inversely heart-shaped leaflets that are

Violet Wood-Sorrel

creased down the middle. Leaves ¾–1½" across, borne on stalks of varying lengths. Leaflets usually bear brown or purplish splotches. **Height and growth habits:** 4–8"; the flowers are taller than the cloverlike leaves. **Habitat and range:** Dry to moist upland woods and prairies; Massachusetts to North Dakota; south to Florida and Texas. **On Sugarloaf—Blooming time:** April–July. **Locations:** White Trail and other mountain trails, Monocacy Natural Resources Management Area. **Similar species:** Other wood-sorrels (*Oxalis* spp.) on Sugarloaf have yellow flowers.

Yellow Wood-Sorrel (Common or Upright Wood-Sorrel)

Oxalis stricta L.
Wood-Sorrel Family (Oxalidaceae)

An extremely common, nearly cosmopolitan weed. In recent years botanists have lumped another *Oxalis* species—*O. europaea*—with this one. **Flowers:** Yellow, 5-petaled; flowers ¼–½" across, in small clusters on long stalks. **Leaves:** Alternate (but may appear opposite), compound. Each leaf has 3 inversely heart-shaped sessile leaflets that are creased or folded along the midrib and that are sour to the taste. Leaves ¾–1½" across, usually long-stalked (stalk length varies). **Height:** 6–15". **Range:** Nearly cosmopolitan, probably native to North America. **On Sugarloaf—Blooming time:** Spring– fall. **Locations:** Extremely common, especially in open mowed areas, mountainwide. **Similar species:** Creeping wood-sorrel *(O. corniculata)* is so similar it is not treated individually in this book. Creeping wood-sorrel is, well, creeping, with trailing, rooting stems. Its leaves may have a purplish cast.

Geranium Family

Geraniaceae

This is the family of the familiar garden and potted geraniums, which are not in the *Geranium* genus but represent a large group of hybrids arising from a South African genus, *Pelargonium*. Plants of the *Pelargonium* genus are also cultivated for their aromatic oils (used in perfumes). Sugarloaf's wild geraniums are in the *Geranium* genus. Many members of the *Geranium* genus go by the name "cranesbill" because the fruit is shaped like that bird's beak. In addition to the species described and illustrated here, three other smaller-flowered plants of the *Geranium* genus might be found on Sugarloaf. Carolina cranesbill *(G. carolinianum)* has flowers ¼–½" across and palmately lobed leaves. Its mature sepals come to a small bristle-tipped point (awned). Small-flowered cranesbill *(G. pusillum)* is a weaker stemmed plant, sometimes partially prostrate, with almost round, deeply cut leaves. Its sepals may be slightly pubescent but are "awnless." Dove's-foot cranesbill *(G. molle)* is similar to small-flowered cranesbill but has less deeply lobed leaves and a longer-beaked fruit. It has awnless but pubescent sepals. **Family characteristics:** The cosmopolitan family has 11 genera and 700 species worldwide. **Flowers** are mostly perfect and regular (although in the *Pelargonium* genus they may be slightly irregular), 5-parted. Fruit is a schizocarp, often with a central "beak." **Leaves** are alternate, opposite, or whorled (in the *Geranium* genus stem leaves are opposite/whorled). **Growth habits:** Mainly herbaceous or small shrubs.

Wild Geranium (Spotted or Wild Cranesbill)

Geranium maculatum L.
Geranium Family (Geraniaceae)

A midspring wildflower with showy flowers. **Flowers:** Lavender-pink, with 5 petals that are broadly rounded or squarish at the apex. Flowers ¾–1¾"

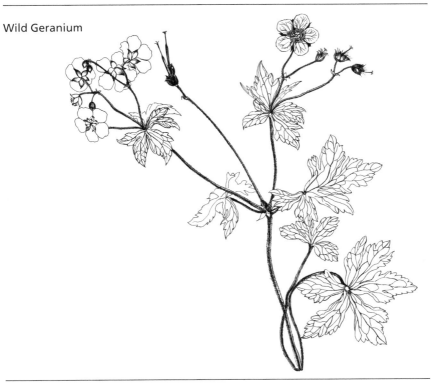

Wild Geranium

across in small terminal clusters. **Leaves:** Opposite or whorled, deeply divided into 3–7 toothed, palmately arranged lobes. Lower leaves (including basal) long-stalked, uppers short-stalked or sessile; 2–6" across. **Height:** 6"–2'. **Habitat and range:** Open woods, meadows, roadsides; Maine to Georgia, west to Manitoba, Nebraska, and Oklahoma. **Herbal lore:** According to Foster and Duke, authors of Peterson Field Guides' *Field Guide to Medicinal Plants: Eastern and Central North America,* the tannin-rich root is "highly astringent" and "styptic" and was "once used to stop bleeding, diarrhea, dysentery, relieve piles, gum diseases, kidney and stomach ailments." "Externally," they say, it was "used as a folk cancer remedy." **On Sugarloaf— Blooming time:** April–June. **Locations:** Red Trail and Orange Trail, although small populations are being crowded by garlic-mustard *(Alliaria petiolata)*; may be found along other trails and roadsides. **Similar species:** Other cranesbills *(Geranium* spp.) have smaller flowers.

Touch-Me-Not or Impatiens Family

Balsaminaceae

Only two species of this family grow on Sugarloaf and in Maryland. **Family characteristics:** This family of only 4 genera and 500 to 600 species is best known for the genus *Impatiens* and its many cultivated varieties of garden flowers. Sugarloaf's native wildflowers belong to the *Impatiens* genus. The family is characterized by irregular **flowers,** which often have a petal-like sepal modified into a spur at the back of the flower, and watery translucent stems.

Spotted or Orange Jewelweed (or Touch-Me-Not)

Impatiens capensis Meerb.
(Yellow or Pale Jewelweed or Touch-Me-Not)
(Impatiens pallida Nutt.)
Touch-Me-Not or Impatiens Family (Balsaminaceae)

A favorite fall rite of children is popping the ripe seedpods of the jewelweeds or touch-me-nots. Held lightly between thumb and forefinger, they will burst open, creating a surprising and delightful tactile sensation. The name "jewelweed" may refer to the jewel-like flowers or seeds or perhaps to the way raindrops bead on the succulent leaves. **Flowers:** Orange, often spotted reddish-brown, on a hanging flower stalk. (*See* mention of yellow or pale jewelweed *under* "Similar species" *below.*) Approximately 1" long and irregular in shape, with 3 petals in front of a spurred saclike sepal. **Fruit:** A small green elongated capsule that explodes when ripe. **Leaves:** Alternate, simple, ovate or elliptic, 1–4" long, juicy when crushed. Rounded teeth often have

sharp points at their tips. **Height:** 2–5'. **Habitat and range:** Moist woods, streams, and springs; Newfoundland to Saskatchewan, south to the Carolinas, Alabama, and Oklahoma. **Herbal lore:** The crushed leaves are an important folk remedy for poison ivy. Also used as a poultice for insect bites, encounters with stinging nettles (the two plants grow side by side along the C&O Canal), burns, cuts, and other skin ailments. **On Sugarloaf—Blooming time for both species:** Midsummer through midautumn. **Locations for Spotted Jewelweed:** Streams and springs along the White Trail, Yellow Trail, Blue Trail, and Mount Ephraim Road. **Location for Yellow Jewelweed:** Lower part of Bear Branch (Mount Ephraim Road). **Similar species:** Less common on and around Sugarloaf and preferring less acidic soil, yellow or pale jewelweed *(Impatiens pallida)* is nearly identical in appearance except for the yellow flower color.

Ginseng Family

Araliaceae

Plants of the ginseng family include tropical and temperate trees, shrubs, and herbs. The family is best known for our native American ginseng *(Panax quinquefolius)*, now rare due to overharvesting for commercial export and herbal use. **Family characteristics:** 70 genera and 700 species worldwide. Many plants in tropical America and Indonesia and Malaysia. **Economic importance:** American ginseng and other family members are used medicinally. According to Heywood's *Flowering Plants of the World*, "The thin 'rice paper' is obtained from the pith of *Tetrapanax papyrifera*." Several ivies *(Hedera)* and other members of the family are grown as indoor houseplants and garden ornamentals. **Flowers:** Frequently borne in clusters (simple or compound umbels). Usually perfect and regular (although outermost flowers may be irregular) with 5 sepals and most often 5 petals. **Fruit:** A berry or drupe. **Leaves:** Usually palmately or pinnately compound or lobed. **Occurrence on Sugarloaf:** Wild sarsaparilla *(Aralia nudicaulus)* is very sparsely scattered throughout Sugarloaf's woodlands; dwarf ginseng *(Panax trifolius)* grows along Furnace Branch in the Monocacy Natural Resources Management Area.

Wild Sarsaparilla

Aralia nudicaulis L.
Ginseng Family (Araliaceae)

Wild sarsaparilla is a plant of the northern woods that grows in the mountains south to Georgia. Its root was used as the source of beverages and medicines by American Indians and European settlers. It is related to American ginseng *(Panax quinquefolius)*, which was once abundant throughout a similar geographic range but has been eradicated in many areas due to overcollecting and selling to foreign markets during the eighteenth and nineteenth centuries. Wild sarsaparilla is rather rare on Sugarloaf and, as with all plants here, should be left strictly alone. **Flowers:** Tiny, greenish-white, 5-petaled; usually growing in 3 small round umbels on a stalk separate from the leaf stalk. **Leaves:** The large basal leaf is usually divided into 3 groups of 5 toothed leaflets; leaf is taller than the flower stalk. Leaflets vary in size and are ovate, obovate, or elliptic with round, heart-shaped (cordate), or unequal bases. **Height:** 6–20". **Habitat and range:** Cool woodlands, southern Canada to Nebraska and Colorado; south to Georgia mountains. **Herbal lore:** American Indians used the root tea as a beverage and medicinally for many conditions. The fresh root was used as a poultice for burns and sores. Foster and Duke report in Peterson Field Guides' *Field Guide to Medicinal Plants: Eastern and*

Central North America that wild sarsaparilla "was used in 'tonic' and 'blood-purifier' patent medicines of the late 19th century." **On Sugarloaf—Blooming time:** Late April–early June. **Locations:** White Trail, Blue Trail, Mount Ephraim Road. **Similar species:** In the absence of American ginseng, none.

Dwarf Ginseng

Panax trifolius L.
Ginseng Family (Araliaceae)

American Indians used this plant medicinally, but unlike its highly prized sister plant, the larger American ginseng *(P. quinquefolius)*, dwarf ginseng has had some luck holding its own in the wild. Dwarf ginseng grows along Furnace Branch in the Monocacy Natural Resources Management Area. **Flowers:** Tiny, white or sometimes pink, 5-petaled, borne in small round umbels. **Leaves:** Whorled, usually with 3 leaves per plant, each leaf palmately divided into 3 (or 5) sessile or nearly sessile leaflets. Leaflets are finely toothed, lanceolate, oblanceolate, or elliptic, 1–3" long. **Height:** 3–8". **Habitat and range:** Moist woods, bottomland woods, and floodplains; eastern United States and Canada, south in the mountains to Georgia. **On Sugarloaf—Blooming time:** March–May. **Location:** Furnace Branch. **Similar species:** None, really. Wild sarsaparilla *(Aralia nudicaulis)* is a larger plant with umbels and leaves on separate stalks and leaflets usually 5 per leaf.

Carrot or Parsley Family

Apiaceae
(Umbelliferae)

An important culinary plant family which includes food plants such as carrot, celery, parsnip, parsley, fennel, dill, coriander, and caraway but also poison-hemlock (reputed to have killed Socrates) and other extremely toxic plants. Several spring and summer wildflowers of the carrot or parsley family grow on Sugarloaf, including Queen Anne's lace (or wild carrot), the same species as the garden carrot. Several others grow elsewhere in the region, including the late winter-blooming harbinger of spring *(Erigenia bulbosa)*, found along the Potomac River, and the infamous poison-hemlock *(Conium maculatum)* and water-hemlock *(Cicuta maculata)*. The latter two species, both highly toxic, grow in the Comus-Barnesville countryside. Tina and I once saw a single specimen of cowbane or water dropwort *(Oxypolis rigidior)* growing in a spring along Mount Ephraim Road. Water parsnip *(Sium suave)* is a wetland plant that also might be found in Sugarloaf's seeps and springs. **Family characteristics:** 300 genera and 3,000 species worldwide. Cosmopolitan; many plants in temperate zones. **Economic importance:** Food, flavorings, and medicines. **Flowers:** 5-parted, mostly perfect and regular, usually borne in compound or simple, often flat-topped, clusters called umbels. **Fruit:** A dry schizocarp (a fruit splitting at maturity into two 1-seeded closed segments). **Leaves:** Alternate, usually compound, often with a leafy sheath at the petiole base. **Growth habits:** Mostly herbaceous plants; some family members are partly woody, shrubby, or treelike. **Occurrence on Sugarloaf:** Several species common in a number of different habitats.

Sweet Cicely (Hairy or Bland Sweet Cicely)

Osmorhiza claytonii (Michx.) C. B. Clarke
Carrot or Parsley Family (Apiaceae)

A rather tall mid to late spring wildflower with downy-soft fernlike leaves and small clusters of tiny white flowers. **Flowers:** White or greenish-white, ⅛" or less across, in small umbels; 5 notched petals apparent with hand lens. **Leaves:** Alternate (or almost opposite), compound, 2 or 3 times divided. Each leaflet strongly toothed and often lobed. Softly pubescent, especially along the leaf veins, petioles, and petiolules. Leaves up to several inches (or nearly a foot) long; leaflets vary in size. Lower leaves long-stalked, uppers short-stalked to nearly sessile. **Height:** 1–3'. **Habitat and range:** Moist woods; eastern United States and Canada. **Herbal lore:** This plant and the closely related long-styled sweet cicely or aniseroot *(O. longistylis)* were used medici-

nally by American Indians, according to Foster and Duke (Peterson Field Guides' *Field Guide to Medicinal Plants: Eastern and Central North America*). Root tea was used for sore throats and coughs. The plant was poulticed on boils and cuts. **On Sugarloaf—Blooming time:** May–June. **Locations:** Bear Branch, Mount Ephraim Road; may be found along other mountain roads and trailsides. **Similar species:** Long-styled sweet cicely or aniseroot (already mentioned under **Herbal lore**) is very similar in appearance but is nearly hairless. Native to the area, it has been reported on Sugarloaf, but I have yet to identify it here. The fernlike leaves distinguish sweet cicely from honewort *(Cryptotaenia canadensis)*. Yarrow *(Achillea millefolium)* and Queen Anne's lace *(Daucus carota)* have large, showy umbels.

Queen Anne's Lace (Wild Carrot or Bird's Nest)

Daucus carota L.
Carrot or Parsley Family (Apiaceae)

One of the most common summer wildflowers of the eastern United States, Queen Anne's lace is a naturalized Old World species and the same species as the cultivated carrot. Abundant in the fields ringing Sugarloaf, this plant also is common along mountain roads and open trailsides. **Flowers:** White, in large, showy compound umbels. Each individual flower 5-parted, tiny,

the outer ones usually larger and irregular, the central flower often purple. Each flat umbel circular, 2–7" across, with leafy bracts at the base. Umbels one to several per plant. After flowering, the umbel curls inward, suggesting a bird's nest. **Leaves:** Alternate, twice pinnately compound, finely cut and feathery. Leaves vary greatly in length (from 1½–14"!) and have a mild carroty smell when crushed. Petioles are sheathed. Petioles and plant stalk covered with bristly hairs. **Height and growth habits:** 1–6'; branched or single-stalked. **Habitat and range:** Dry fields, roadsides, disturbed sites; Eurasian native now naturalized throughout much of North America.

Herbal lore: Various plant parts have been used to remedy bladder, kidney, and liver problems and to increase menstrual flow and expel worms, according to Hutchens's *Indian Herbalogy of North America*. In Peterson Field Guides' *Field Guide to Medicinal Plants: Eastern and Central North America*, Foster and Duke report: "Seeds a folk 'morning after' contraceptive. Experiments with mice indicate seed extracts may be useful in preventing implantation of fertilized egg. (Not recommended for such uses, but scientists should investigate.)" **Warning:** Could be confused with extremely poisonous members of the carrot family. **On Sugarloaf—Blooming time:** Summer–fall. **Locations:** Roadsides, trailsides, parking areas, fields. **Similar species:** Likely to be confused on Sugarloaf with yarrow *(Achillea millefolium)*, another abundant summer wildflower. Yarrow is a member of the aster or daisy family. Upon close examination the small individual "flowers" in yarrow's flower clusters are composed of several to many central yellowish, tan, or gray disk flowers, surrounded by white ray flowers. Yarrow's floral clusters are irregularly shaped, and its leaf petioles are not sheathed. (*See* yarrow text and illustration.) Poison-hemlock *(Conium maculatum)* grows in wet meadows near the mountain. Extremely toxic, this plant has smooth (not pubescent) stalks that are usually spotted with purple. It blooms in late spring and early summer. Other carrot family members found locally in the wild have dissimilar leaves although the umbels may be similar to those of Queen Anne's lace.

Honewort (Wild Chervil)

Cryptotaenia canadensis (L.) DC.
Carrot or Parsley Family (Apiaceae)

Native to the eastern United States and Canada, honewort is a common early summer wildflower on Sugarloaf. **Flowers and fruit:** Very tiny white flowers with 5 incurved petals in small irregular umbels; soon replaced by elongated, somewhat flattened beaked and erect fruit. **Leaves:** Alternate, compound, usually divided into 3 ovate-lanceolate leaflets that are sharply and sometimes doubly or triply toothed. Some leaflets may be cleft. Leaves have sheathed petioles or are nearly sessile toward the top of the plant. Overall leaf size varies from leaves of several inches long and wide toward base of the plant to an inch or less toward plant's apex. Glabrous or nearly so. Central plant stalk smooth, green, and glabrous. **Height and growth habits:** 10"–4'; branched or single-stalked. **Habitat and range:** Rich woods; eastern Canada south to Georgia and Texas; Japan. **On Sugarloaf—Blooming time:** June–August. **Locations:** West View, Mount Ephraim Road, Sugarloaf Mountain Road, some trailsides. **Similar species:** The leaves separate this plant from Queen Anne's lace *(Daucus carota)*. Leaves (but not flowers) could be con-

fused with white avens *(Geum canadense)* or short-styled snakeroot *(Sanicula canadensis).*

Short-Styled Snakeroot (Canada or Black Snakeroot)

Sanicula canadensis L.

Carrot or Parsley Family (Apiaceae)

A summer-blooming plant with tiny white or greenish-white flowers borne in small roundish bristly clusters. **Flowers:** Minute, white or greenish-white; the greenish bristly flower clusters on short individual stalks toward the apex of the plant, themselves loosely clustered and those clusters borne on longer stalks. **Fruit:** Small and roundish with hooked bristles. **Leaves:** Alternate, compound, the lower leaves usually long-stalked, several inches across, and divided into 3 leaflets; the outer 2 leaflets are so deeply cleft that the leaf appears to have 5 leaflets. Leaflets sharply, often doubly toothed. Middle leaflet also may be lobed but usually not so deeply cut as the outer 2. Upper leaves reduced in size and more obviously 3-leafleted. Uppermost leaves may be tiny. **Height:** 1–4'. **Habitat and range:** Dry or moist woods; Vermont and southern Ontario to South Dakota; south to Florida and Texas. **Herbal lore:** American Indians used the root as a heart remedy and menstrual aid. The plant was also used as an abortive agent. The leaves were poulticed for in-

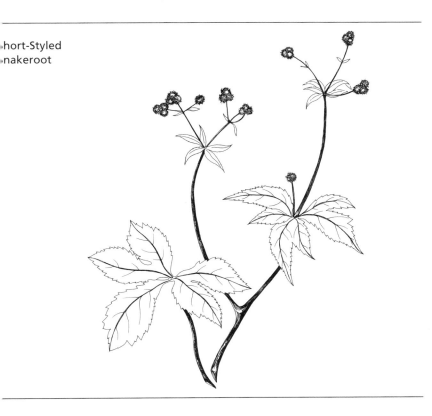

flammation and bruises (all according to Peterson Field Guides' *Field Guide to Medicinal Plants: Eastern and Central North America* by Foster and Duke). **On Sugarloaf—Blooming time:** June–August. **Locations:** Most trails and roadsides; moderately common. **Similar species:** A related species, clustered snakeroot *(S. gregaria),* is less common on the mountain. It has greenish-yellow flowers with styles (*see* Glossary) protruding beyond the flower and bristles. Two other *Sanicula* species are native to Maryland but have not been reported here. The leaves and bristly fruit of white avens *(Geum canadense)* could be mistaken for snakeroot, although the flowers are dissimilar (compare illustrations). *See also* honewort *(Cryptotaenia canadensis).* Short-styled snake-root, white avens, and honewort may all be found growing side by side on and near the mountain.

Gentian Family

Gentianaceae

Two members of this family grow on Sugarloaf; several others that are considered uncommon to very rare are indigenous to the region according to Fleming, Lobstein, and Tufty (*Finding Wildflowers in the Washington-Baltimore Area*). **Family characteristics:** This cosmopolitan family of 75 genera and 1,000 species includes herbaceous ornamentals and plants used as medicinals and as culinary flavorings. **Flowers** are perfect, usually regular, and 4- or 5-parted. **Fruit** is a capsule or, rarely, a berry. **Leaves:** Opposite or whorled, simple, entire. **Occurrence on Sugarloaf:** The two Sugarloaf species are easily overlooked: pennywort *(Obolaria virginica)* because it is diminutive and rose pink *(Sabatia angularis)* because it is uncommon.

Pennywort

Obolaria virginica L.
Gentian Family (Gentianaceae)

A small plant with a fleshy stalk and purple-green leaves. Clusters of pennywort spring from Sugarloaf's moist woodland floor during the spring. **Flowers:** White or pale lavender, ⅓–⅔" long, upright, funnel-shaped, with 4 pointed lobes; flowers grow along the upper portion of the fleshy plant stalk. Corolla lobes may be minutely toothed (visible with hand lens). Sessile or nearly so, with deeply divided 2-lobed calyx. Flowers clustered in the axils of small purple-green obovate leaves. The leaves and calyx lobes of a similar color and texture and nearly indistinguishable. **Leaves:** Opposite, simple, the upper leaves as described above, ¼–¾" long; the lower ones scalelike and tiny. **Height and growth habits:** 3–6"; single-stalked or slightly branched, overall plant outline narrowly conical, ovoid, or obovoid. (Easily overlooked because it's so small.) **Habitat and range:** Rich, moist woods; New Jersey to southern Illinois, south to Florida and Texas. **On Sugarloaf—Blooming time:** April–May. **Locations:** Yellow Trail, Mount Ephraim Road, especially near Bear Branch. **Similar species:** Could possibly be confused with squawroot *(Conopholis americana)* at a glance, but squawroot has yellowish flowers turning brown. For an illustration of pennywort, refer to *Newcomb's Wildflower Guide* or *Herbaceous Plants of Maryland*.

Rose Pink (Common Marsh-Pink)

Sabatia angularis (L.) Pursh
Gentian Family (Gentianaceae)

We have not seen this wildflower growing on Sugarloaf but have found it blooming in an adjacent overgrown field in Comus. **Flowers:** Pink, 5-petaled (petals slightly joined at the base), star-shaped, ¾–1½" across, with a greenish or yellow center. Flowers borne in loose terminal clusters. **Leaves:** Opposite, simple, ovate, entire, sessile, ½–1½" long. Plant stalk strongly angled. **Height and growth habits:** 1–3'; usually branched. **Habitat and range:** Open woods, fields, clearings; eastern United States. **On Sugarloaf—Blooming**

ime: July–September. **Similar species:** None likely in the immediate Sugar-loaf area. Several other members of the genus are found on the coastal plain. For an illustration of this plant, consult *Newcomb's Wildflower Guide* or *A Field Guide to Wildflowers of Northeastern and North-Central North America* by Peterson and McKenny.

Dogbane Family
Apocynaceae

A largely tropical family of mostly woody plants which includes rain forest trees, shrubs, and lianas. Sugarloaf's three species (two common and one uncommon and mentioned only briefly) are all herbaceous plants. Two are native, and one, periwinkle *(Vinca minor),* was introduced from Europe. **Family characteristics:** The dogbane family has 200 genera and 2,000 species worldwide. **Flowers** are perfect with (usually) 5 sepals and 5 lobes or petals united into a tube. **Leaves** are simple, opposite or whorled. Leaves and other plant parts usually emit a milky sap. Some species yield latex, which is used commercially to make rubber. The family includes important ornamentals such as frangipani *(Plumeria)* and oleanders *(Nerium).*

Periwinkle (Myrtle)
Vinca minor L.
Dogbane Family (Apocynaceae)

A garden plant that escapes from cultivation, periwinkle has trailing, often partially woody stems. Periwinkle is one of Sugarloaf's first spring flowers, growing in mats along mountain roadsides. **Flowers:** Violet or blue-violet,

---

Periwinkle

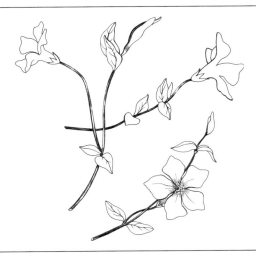

star-shaped; 5 petals are bluntly pointed at the apex, somewhat wedge-shaped and fused together to form a funnel-shaped tube at the base of the flower. Flowers are usually marked with a whitish star at the center and are about an inch (or less) across, growing on a longish stalk. **Leaves:** Opposite, simple, entire, evergreen; ovate-lanceolate or elliptic, deep green and glossy above (although new spring growth is a lighter green), paler below, on short petiole or nearly sessile; ½–2" long. **Growth habits:** A creeping ground cover; some growth (especially new) is upright, but the overall effect is of a low-growing plant. **Habitat and range:** Native to southern Europe, periwinkle has escaped cultivation in the eastern United States, where it often thrives along roads and in open woods. **On Sugarloaf—Blooming time:** March–June. **Locations:** Common along mountain roadsides and especially prevalent just below West View and near the Potomac Overlook; some trailsides, including the White Trail near the mountain base. **Similar species:** Color is similar to spring-blooming violets, but flower shape is very different.

Indian Hemp

Apocynum cannabinum L.
Dogbane Family (Apocynaceae)

Indian hemp is a widely distributed North American plant that is quite common along Sugarloaf's roadsides and open trailsides. **Flowers:** Small, white or greenish-white, 5-lobed, somewhat tubular or bell-shaped, ⅛–¼" long, in terminal clusters. **Fruit:** Long, slender paired follicles (which look like long pods), green in summer and turning brown later. After splitting open to re-

Indian Hemp

lease seeds, the fruits often hang on through the winter. **Leaves:** Opposite, simple, with entire margins and short petioles. Ovate-lanceolate or elliptic, 1–6" long. Leaves and petioles emit milky sap. **Height and growth habits:** 1–4'; erect plant with stiff stalk and ascending branches. **Habitat and range:** Fields, woodland borders, disturbed sites; eastern United States and Canada; west—in places—to the Pacific. **Herbal lore:** Plant stems were used for fiber and cordage, according to Foster and Duke (Peterson Field Guides' *Field Guide to Medicinal Plants: Eastern and Central North America*). They also report that Indian hemp's milky sap was used as a folk remedy for venereal warts, and the plant was used to treat heart ailments and as a diuretic. Compounds identified in Indian hemp have shown antitumor activity, according to Foster and Duke; but they also warn that the plant contains "toxic cardioactive (heart-affecting) glycosides." **On Sugarloaf—Blooming time:** June–August. **Locations:** Yellow Trail; Sugarloaf roadsides. **Similar species:** Spreading dogbane *(A. androsaemifolium)* has pinkish flowers that are slightly larger than Indian hemp's and have spreading or recurved lobes. It is uncommon on Sugarloaf and is not included in this guide. Milkweeds *(Asclepias* spp.), like Indian hemp, have opposite or whorled leaves that emit a milky sap. However, milkweed flowers are uniquely structured *(see* next entries).

Milkweed Family

Asclepiadaceae

Most plants of the milkweed family grow in tropical and subtropical regions. Three herbaceous genera are indigenous to Maryland: only one, the milkweed genus *(Asclepias),* is represented on and around Sugarloaf. **Family characteristics:** Worldwide the family includes 250 genera and 2,000 species. **Flowers** of the family are perfect, mostly regular, with a 5-lobed bell-shaped, funnel-shaped, or saucer-shaped corolla and usually a 5-parted crown called a corona which is attached to the flower's anthers or corolla. **Fruit:** A follicle, often produced in pairs. **Leaves:** Opposite, whorled, or sometimes alternate; simple. Many plants emit a milky juice.

Common Milkweed

Asclepias syriaca L.
Milkweed Family (Asclepiadaceae)

The milkweeds attract many species of butterfly and serve as host plants for monarch butterfly larvae. Common milkweed is abundant in fields and meadows and along roadsides throughout the Sugarloaf region. This milk-

Common Milkweed

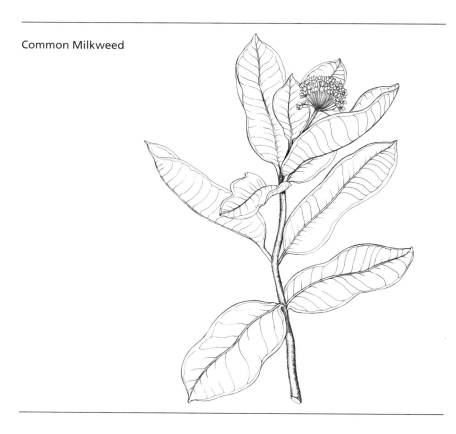

weed species and several others are occasionally found on Sugarloaf itself.
Flowers: Small, dusky pink, in large round clusters. Flower configuration
unique to milkweeds: the 5 petals are reflexed beneath a 5-parted crownlike
corona. Each flower ⅓–⅔" from tip of corona to bottom of reflexed petal.
Fruit: A favorite of children, autumn milkweed follicles split open to release
many seeds, bearing fluffy hairs that suit them for blowing or flinging
through the air. Warty-looking follicles 2–6" long. (Symbiosis between common milkweed and human children not yet scientifically proven.) **Leaves:**
Opposite, simple, with entire margins, short petiole, and prominent central
vein. Veins and petioles exude a mildly toxic milky juice. Leaves lanceolate,
ovate, elliptic, or oblanceolate, 3–12" long; grayish and felty-pubescent below. **Height:** 3–5'. **Habitat and range:** Meadows, roadsides, disturbed sites;
eastern Canada and United States, west to Manitoba and Oklahoma. **Herbal
lore:** Common milkweed is potentially toxic but was used by American Indians and early American physicians for many ailments, according to Foster
and Duke (Peterson Field Guides' *Field Guide to Medicinal Plants: Eastern
and Central North America*). American Indians made a laxative and diuretic
tea from the roots of the plant and applied the milky juice to warts and ring-

worm. Early American doctors used the plant to treat asthma and rheumatism. According to Peterson Field Guides' *A Field Guide to Edible Wild Plants of Eastern and Central North America* by Lee Peterson, both the toxicity and bitterness of common milkweed's milky juice "are dispelled upon boiling," rendering the leaves, flower buds, flowers, and young pods desirable as cooked vegetables. (However, gathering wild plants is not allowed on Sugarloaf or in most other public and private parks.) **On Sugarloaf—Blooming time:** June–August. **Fruiting time:** Fruits mature and split open during autumn. **Locations:** Sugarloaf roadsides and encircling fields; possible along open trailsides. **Similar species:** Several other local milkweeds (*Asclepias* spp.) are briefly mentioned in the next entries. Leaves of common milkweed are similar to Indian hemp *(Apocynum cannabinum)* and spreading dogbane *(Apocynum androsaemifolium)*—species that also emit milky juice from their leaves—but the milkweed flower structure is distinctive.

Other Milkweed Species
Asclepias

Several other milkweed species are indigenous to the Sugarloaf region and have been reported on and around the mountain.

Butterfly Weed (*A. tuberosa* L.) has brilliant orange flowers and mostly alternate leaves that do not emit a milky juice. As the name suggests, this wildflower attracts butterflies.

Swamp Milkweed (*A. incarnata* L.) has pink or rose-purple flowers and grows in freshwater marshes and wet meadows and around ponds. Its flowers are more brightly colored and its leaves more narrowly lanceolate than those of common milkweed.

Poke Milkweed (*A. exaltata* L.) has white flowers (which may be tinged with lavender or green) in loose, drooping clusters. Its leaves are tapered at both ends.

Four-Leaved Milkweed (*A. quadrifolia* Jacq.) bears pink, lavender, or white flowers. Its middle leaves are usually in a whorl of 4, while its upper and/or lowermost leaves are often merely paired. Fleming, Lobstein, and Tufty list several additional native species in *Finding Wildflowers in the Washington-Baltimore Area.*

Nightshade or Tomato Family
Solanaceae

A fascinating plant family that includes potatoes, tomatoes, eggplant, peppers, tobacco, and belladonna; like the carrot or parsley family, a medley of foods and poisons! **Family characteristics:** 85 genera and 2,800 species worldwide. Cosmopolitan. **Economic importance:** This family is extremely important for its food plants and also for garden ornamentals such as petunias *(Petunia)*. Several highly poisonous plants of the family, including belladonna *(Atropa belladonna)*, contain powerful alkaloids that have served as traditional medicines for centuries. Tobacco *(Nicotiana tabacum)* has long been a cash crop for southern and mid-Atlantic farmers. **Flowers:** Usually perfect and regular with 5 (rarely 4 or 6) sepals that are fused (at least at the base) and 5 petals, fused at the base or united more completely to form a tubular or trumpet-shaped corolla. Some flowers have swept-back petals. **Fruit:** A berry or capsule. **Leaves:** Simple, alternate. **Growth habits:** Herbs, shrubs, vines, and trees. **Occurrence on Sugarloaf:** Several nightshade family members grow on and around the mountain. They bloom from late spring through fall and are most common in open areas: roadsides and some trailsides, especially along the Yellow Trail; West View, East View; fields surrounding the mountain.

Horse Nettle

Solanum carolinense L.
Nightshade or Tomato Family (Solanaceae)

This plant bears sharp prickles. Common in the fields ringing Sugarloaf, horse nettle blooms from late spring through autumn. **Flowers:** White or lavender with a central column of yellow stamens; 5-lobed and star-shaped, ¾–1¼" wide; in small clusters. **Fruit:** A poisonous orange-yellow berry, ⅓–¾" across; resembles the cultivated tomato. **Leaves:** Alternate, simple, with large blunt teeth or shallow lobes. Overall outline ovate, 2–5" long. Pubescent and sharply prickly, especially along the lower veins. Petioles and plant stalk also usually prickly. **Height and growth habits:** 1–4'; erect and often branched. **Habitat and range:** Dry fields, disturbed sites; indigenous to the southeastern United States but spreading northward to Vermont, Ontario, and Minnesota and westward. **Herbal lore:** While Foster and Duke note in Peterson Field Guides' *Field Guide to Medicinal Plants: Eastern and Central North America* that horse nettle is toxic and that childhood fatalities from ingesting it have been recorded, they also report that this plant has had a colorful medicinal history: "Properly administered, berries were once used for epilepsy; diuretic, pain-killing, antispasmodic, aphrodisiac. Berries fried in grease were used as an ointment for dog's mange. American Indians gargled wilted leaf tea for sore throats; poulticed leaves for poison-ivy rash; drank tea for worms." **On Sugarloaf—Blooming time:** May–October. **Locations:** Yellow Trail; roadsides and fields on and adjacent to the mountain. **Similar species:** Jimsonweed *(Datura stramonium)*, a larger plant, has trumpet-

shaped flowers. Bittersweet nightshade *(Solanum dulcamara)*, a woody vine, has deep violet (rarely white) flowers with strongly curved back petals and leaves with 2 separate leaflets or lobes at the base. Black nightshade *(S. nigrum)* has very small (¼–½") white or pale violet flowers. The ground-cherries *(Physalis* spp.) have yellow or greenish-yellow flowers. Short descriptions of those other nightshade family species found on Sugarloaf follow.

Other Nightshade (or Tomato) Family Members

Solanaceae

Numerous other nightshade family members, native and naturalized, grow in eastern North America, and several can be found on and around Sugarloaf and have already been mentioned in the "Similar species" section of the horse nettle *(Solanum carolinense).* Like horse nettle, the following species can be found blooming from late spring or summer into the fall.

Bittersweet Nightshade (*Solanum dulcamara* L.) is a shrubby Eurasian vine that has become naturalized in open woods, thickets, and disturbed

Bittersweet Nightshade

sites throughout our area. **Flowers** are violet or blue (rarely white), 5-lobed, ½–1" across, with swept-back lobes suggesting a shooting star and yellow stamens in a narrow central column. Flowers in small nodding clusters. **Fruit:** A small oval berry, green at first, becoming bright red at maturity. **Leaves:** Alternate, simple and/or compound; 1–3" long, ovate, heart-shaped, or (often) ovate above with 2 small lateral ovate lobes or separate leaflets at the base. **Herbal lore:** Although highly toxic, both this and the following species have had widespread use as Old World medicinals. **On Sugarloaf—Locations:** West View; trails and roadsides mountainwide.

Black Nightshade (*Solanum nigrum* L.) has white or pale violet star-shaped **flowers,** ¼–½" across, with 5 swept-back lobes and yellow stamens in a central yellow beak. **Fruit** is a black berry. **Leaves** are alternate, simple, ovate or deltoid with blunt, irregular teeth or a smooth or shallowly wavy-toothed margin; ¾–3" long, may be purple-tinged below. **Height and growth habits:** 1–2½'; usually branched. **On Sugarloaf—Locations:** Trails and roadsides, especially near the mountain base.

Jimsonweed (*Datura stramonium* L.). Although I have never seen it growing on the mountain, jimsonweed is common in the fields ringing Sugarloaf and is likely near the mountain base and perhaps along some trails, especially the Yellow Trail. It is a very distinctive plant with white or pale lavender, 3–5"-long, trumpet-shaped **flowers** and **fruit** that is a spiny, ovoid, 1½–

Black Nightshade

Jimsonweed

2"-long capsule. **Leaves:** Alternate, simple, with sharp, shallow teeth or lobes; ovate or deltoid, 2–8" long. **Height:** 1–5'. **Herbal lore:** A highly toxic plant that has been used (and continues to be used) for a number of medical conditions, from vertigo to Parkinson's disease. It is a strong hallucinogen and has led to many recorded fatalities. **On Sugarloaf—Locations:** Look for it in fields and disturbed sites near the mountain base.

Ground-Cherries (*Physalis* spp.). Two native species of ground-cherry grow on Sugarloaf. They have yellow or greenish-yellow nodding, bell-shaped **flowers** with 5 shallow lobes and a darker center. Flowers ½–1½" long. **Fruit** is a berry enclosed in a lanternlike calyx. **Leaves** are alternate, simple, toothed to nearly entire. Clammy Ground-Cherry (*P. heterophylla* Nees) has a viscid-pubescent stalk, yellow or greenish-yellow flowers with a brownish or purplish center, and a yellow berry (enclosed in lanternlike calyx). **Leaves** are ovate, 2–5" long, with shallow, irregular teeth to nearly entire. Leaf bases are rounded, truncate, or cordate and often unequal. **Height:** 1–3'. **Herbal lore:** According to Foster and Duke *(Field Guide to Medicinal Plants: Eastern and Central North America),* "American Indians used tea of leaves and roots for headaches; wash for burns, scalds; in herbal compounds to induce vomiting for bad stomachaches; root and leaves poulticed for wounds. Seed of this and other *Physalis* species are considered useful for difficult urination, fevers, inflammation, various urinary disorders. Plant compounds are being researched for antitumor activity. Warning: Poten-

Ground-Cherry

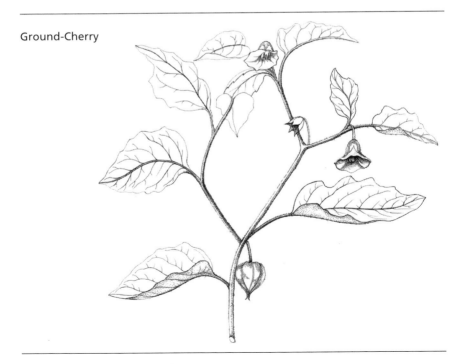

tially toxic." **On Sugarloaf—Locations:** Yellow Trail; roadsides and trailsides mountainwide, especially near the base of Sugarloaf and in surrounding fields. Virginia Ground-Cherry (*P. virginiana* Mill.) is very similar to clammy ground-cherry; this species has a pubescent or nearly glabrous stalk, but it is not viscid. **Fruit:** Berry enclosed in lanternlike calyx is orange or reddish at maturity. **Leaves** are ovate-lanceolate, tapered at both ends, and more or less shallowly toothed. **On Sugarloaf—Locations:** Same as clammy ground-cherry.

Morning Glory Family

Convolvulaceae

This family includes many plants that are garden ornamentals; one very important food crop, sweet potatoes *(Ipomoea batatas)*; and some plants that serve as medicines. **Family characteristics:** There are 50 genera and 1,500 species in this nearly cosmopolitan family of mainly twining and climbing herbaceous (and some woody) plants. The **flowers** are often large and showy with usually 5 sepals and a 5-parted funnel-shaped corolla. **Occurrence on Sugarloaf:** Several species grow on and around Sugarloaf, mainly along roadsides and in fields, hedgerows, and disturbed sites.

Vines

Morning Glories, Wild Potato Vine, and Bindweeds

Ipomoea, Calystegia, Convolvulus
Morning Glory Family (Convolvulaceae)

These plants are trailing or twining vines with large, showy funnel-shaped flowers. They bloom from summer through early fall. Several species of morning glory, potato vine, and bindweed grow on Sugarloaf, mostly along roadsides and in thickets around the mountain base.

Wild Potato Vine (Wild Sweet Potato)

Ipomoea pandurata (L.) G. Mey.

Flowers: Large, white, broadly funnel-shaped, with purple or deep pink center; 5 fused lobes form a star around the seams where they are fused; 1¾–4" long. Sepals glabrous or barely pubescent. **Leaves:** Alternate, simple, heart-shaped or slightly lobed near the base. Glabrous or nearly so, 1–4" long, on long petioles. Stem often reddish or purplish. **Growth habits:** A trailing or twining vine from a large and deep tuberlike root. **Habitat and range:**

Woods, fields, thickets, disturbed sites; Connecticut to southern Ontario, Michigan, and Kansas, south to Florida and Texas. **Herbal lore:** According to Foster and Duke (Peterson Field Guides' *Field Guide to Medicinal Plants: Eastern and Central North America*), "American Indians poulticed root for rheumatism, 'hard tumors.' Root tea used as a diuretic, laxative, and expectorant, for coughs, asthma, beginning stages of tuberculosis; 'blood purifier'; powdered plant used in tea for headaches, indigestion." **On Sugarloaf— Locations:** Mount Ephraim Road, other roadsides and trailsides. **Similar species:** Purplish blush at center of large white flowers and glabrous or nearly glabrous sepals should separate this plant from the following morning glories and bindweeds.

Ivy-Leaved Morning Glory

Ipomoea hederacea Jacq.

Ivy-leaved morning glory has blue, purple, or sometimes white **flowers** that often have a white tube and are 1–2" long. Sepals are very hairy at the base. **Leaves** are deeply 3-lobed (or rarely 5-lobed or entire); trailing plant stalk pubescent with backward pointing hairs. **Habitat and range:** Fields, roadsides, and disturbed sites; introduced from tropical America. **On Sugarloaf— Locations:** Mount Ephraim Road and other roadsides and some trailsides.

Common Morning Glory

Ipomoea purpurea (L.) Roth

Flowers are blue, purple, white, or variegated, 1¾–3" long, with sepals that are pubescent, especially at the base. **Leaves** are heart-shaped (rarely lobed). **Habitat and range:** Field borders, roadsides, disturbed sites; introduced from tropical America. **On Sugarloaf—Locations:** Roadsides and some trailsides.

Hedge Bindweed

Calystegia sepium (L.) R. Br.
(Convolvulus sepium)

Hedge bindweed has white (sometimes pink) **flowers** that are similar in shape to the preceding species and 1½–3" long. **Leaves** are triangular in outline with (usually) a pair of square lobes at the base. **Habitat and range:** Thickets, fields, roadsides, disturbed sites; native to temperate America and Eurasia (our plants are both native and introduced). **Herbal lore:** The root has been used as a purgative and for jaundice and gall bladder problems. **On Sugarloaf—Locations:** Very common in fields and thickets around the base of Sugarloaf.

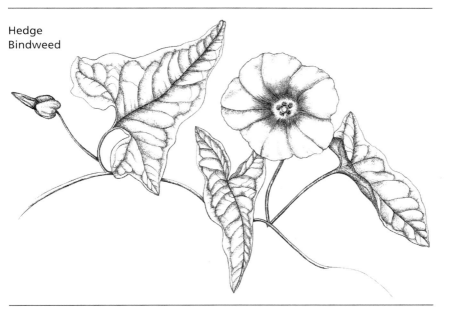

Hedge Bindweed

Field Bindweed

Convolvulus arvensis L.

Flowers white or pink, smaller than all of the preceding morning glory family species, about ¾–1" long. **Leaves** narrowly triangular, usually with 2 small pointed lobes at the base that give the leaf an arrow shape. (However, leaf-shape variable). **Habitat and range:** Fields, roadsides, disturbed sites; native of Europe, now widely naturalized in the United States and southern Canada. **On Sugarloaf—Locations:** Roadsides, some trailsides.

Phlox Family

Polemoniaceae

This family is best known for garden ornamentals. Several members of the phlox family grow in our region, but none is common on Sugarloaf. **Family characteristics:** 18 genera and 300 species worldwide. A wide-ranging family in tropical and temperate zones with a large concentration in western North America. **Economic importance:** Many species cultivated as garden flowers. **Flowers:** Usually perfect and regular with 5 fused sepals and 5 petals often fused into a tubular base and flared at the apex. According to botanist Cris Fleming, spirally twisted flower buds are another characteristic of this family. **Fruit:** A capsule. **Leaves:** Variable: opposite or alternate, simple or compound. **Growth habits:** Mainly herbs, some shrubs, small trees, and lianas. **Occurrence on Sugarloaf:** Wild blue phlox *(Phlox divaricata)* grows along Furnace Branch in the Monocacy Natural Resources Management Area. This is a common wildflower along the nearby Potomac. *See* next entry, wild blue phlox, "Similar species" section, for brief descriptions of other local species.

Wild Blue Phlox

Phlox divaricata L.
Phlox Family (Polemoniaceae)

These tall wildflowers form a spring display that nearly rivals that of the native Virginia bluebells. Wild blue phlox blooms in spring along Sugarloaf-area rivers and streams, including Furnace Branch. **Flowers:** Violet or blue, ¾–2" across, 5-lobed with lobes united to form a narrow tube at the back. Lobes bluntly rounded at the tip and often shallowly notched. In showy terminal clusters. **Leaves:** Opposite, simple, sessile, entire, ovate-lanceolate to oblong, 1–3" long. **Height:** 8–20". **Habitat and range:** Moist woods, bottomland woods, floodplains; eastern United States and southeastern Canada. **On Sugarloaf—Blooming time:** Wild blue phlox blooms from April to June. **Locations:** Furnace Branch, Monocacy Natural Resources Management Area. **Similar species:** Two other phlox species were identified on Sugarloaf in a 1987 Stronghold plant survey conducted by Richard Wiegand. Wild sweet William *(P. maculata)* has purple or pink (rarely white) flowers and blooms in late spring and summer. This plant is 1–3' tall and grows in wet

Wild Blue Phlox

meadows, seeps, and on stream banks. The familiar garden phlox *(P. paniculata)* blooms later still (from July through October). It is a very tall plant (2–6') with deep pink flowers in the wild (other colors in cultivation). It grows along Mount Ephraim Road. An additional species, moss phlox or moss pink *(P. subulata)*, is a creeping species of open rocky habitats that is common throughout the Washington area. It has rose-pink to white flowers and small linear or awl-shaped leaves. Consult Brown and Brown's *Herbaceous Plants of Maryland* for descriptions and illustrations of other species found in the state.

Borage or Forget-Me-Not Family

Boraginaceae

This is the family of the medieval medicinal and culinary garden herb called borage *(Borago officinalis)*, the poetic forget-me-nots *(Myosotis)*, and one of Maryland's best-loved spring wildflowers, Virginia bluebells or mertensia *(Mertensia virginica)*. The Monocacy, Potomac, and other nearby rivers are lined with Virginia bluebells in spring. In the first chapter of his book *Watching Nature: A Mid-Atlantic Natural History*, author and naturalist Mark S. Garland writes, "The spring wildflower displays along Piedmont floodplains are one of the continent's greatest floral shows." Virginia bluebells star in this show. A few Virginia bluebells grow along Bear Branch and nearby Bennett Creek but not in the profusion that they do in larger floodplains. At least three other family members grow on or near Sugarloaf: Virginia stickseed or beggar's lice *(Hackelia virginiana)*, which is rare on the mountain, and two other species common in surrounding fields, viper's bugloss *(Echium vulgare)* and corn gromwell *(Lithospermum arvense)*. Tina and I have not seen the latter two on Sugarloaf so we mention them here only in passing. Many other family members are indigenous to Maryland. **Family characteristics:** 100 genera and 2,000 species worldwide. Found in temperate and subtropical regions with many species in the Mediterranean and western North America. **Economic importance:** Ornamentals, dye plants, and herbals. **Flowers:** Regular, often perfect. Usually 5-parted with petal-like lobes often arising from a more or less bell- or trumpet-shaped tube. Flowers often borne in one-sided uncurling clusters. In many species (such as *Mertensia virginica*) the flowers are pink in bud and blue when open. **Fruit:** Usually 1–4 (often 4) nutlets. **Leaves:** Mostly alternate (lower leaves may be opposite in some species), simple, entire. **Growth habits:** Herbs, shrubs, trees, and vines. In our native flora all plants are herbaceous. **Occurrence on Sugarloaf:** Virginia bluebells along Bear Branch; a few Virginia stickseed plants along woodland trails.

Virginia Bluebells (Mertensia, Virginia Cowslip)

Mertensia virginica (L.) Pers. ex Link
Borage or Forget-Me-Not Family (Boraginaceae)

One of the most striking native wildflowers of the eastern United States, Virginia bluebells line stretches of rivers and streams in abundant clusters throughout the Washington-Baltimore area. **Flowers:** A gorgeous sky blue (buds and young flowers are pink or lavender). Nodding, 5-parted, and trumpet-shaped, about 1" long, in clusters. **Leaves:** Alternate, simple, with entire margins, ovate or elliptic, 2–7" long. Base usually either tapered or rounded and sessile (or nearly so). **Height:** 1–2'. **Habitat and range:** Wooded floodplains, bottomland woods, alluvial soils; New York to Alabama, west to Wisconsin, Iowa, and eastern Kansas. **On Sugarloaf—Blooming time:** April– early May. **Locations:** Bear Branch (lower section); Bennett Creek near Mount Ephraim Road bridge. **Similar species:** None on or near Sugarloaf.

Virginia Stickseed (Beggar's Lice)

Hackelia virginiana (L.) I. M. Johnst.
Borage or Forget-Me-Not Family (Boraginaceae)

A plant of eastern North American upland woods, Virginia stickseed is very uncommon on Sugarloaf. Only a handful of Virginia stickseed (also called beggar's lice) plants grow along the Blue Trail. **Flowers:** Tiny, white, with 5 roundish lobes. Flowers ⅛" or less across, in one-sided clusters (racemes). **Fruit:** Small, prickly, and roundish, attaching to animal fur and clothing; contains nutlets. **Leaves:** Alternate, simple, entire, elliptic-lanceolate, tapered at both ends. Upper leaves sessile, lower ones petioled. Blades fuzzy-rough above, finely pubescent below, 1–5" long or longer. Large basal leaves usually absent when plant is in flower. Plant stalk pubescent. **Height and growth habits:** 1–4'; branched. **Habitat and range:** Upland woods; southern Quebec to North Dakota, south to Georgia and Texas. **On Sugarloaf—Blooming time:** July–September. **Location:** Blue Trail. **Similar species:** Not likely to be confused with any other Sugarloaf wildflowers.

Vervain Family
Verbenaceae

This family includes many important ornamentals, medicinals, and the tree that gives us teak. One member of the vervain family is common on Sugarloaf: white vervain *(Verbena urticifolia).* **Family characteristics:** 100 genera and 2,600 species worldwide. Mainly tropical and subtropical. **Economic importance:** Teak comes from the Southeast Asian tree *Tectona grandis.* Chaste-tree *(Vitex agnus-castus)* is an ornamental shrub often planted in the Washington area. It's called chaste-tree because its leaves and flowers were believed to "cool the heat of lust." Lantana *(Lantana camara)* is another popular ornamental. Many other family members are valued for their essential oils, as herbal medicines, teas, fruits, and gums, according to Heywood *(Flowering Plants of the World).* **Flowers:** Mostly perfect, often slightly irregular. Sepals and petals usually 4 or 5; fused at the base. Flowers often small and borne in spikes, heads, or cymes. **Fruit:** A drupe, nutlet, or capsule. **Leaves:** Usually opposite or whorled, simple. **Growth habits:** Herbs, shrubs, lianas, trees. **Occurrence on Sugarloaf:** White vervain is quite common here, especially along area roadsides. Two other species, rarely seen, are mentioned in the "Similar species" section of the white vervain description (next entry).

White Vervain
Verbena urticifolia L.
Vervain Family (Verbenaceae)

White vervain is a tall summer–fall wildflower of the eastern United States and Canada. One of three vervain species found on Sugarloaf, this is the only common one. The others are briefly mentioned here under "Similar species."

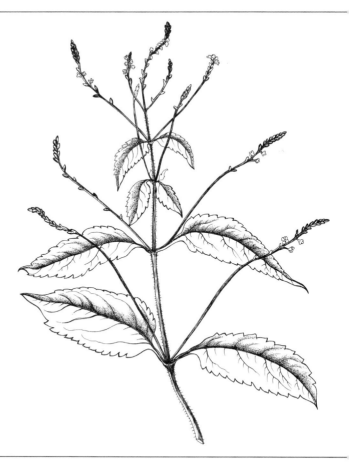

Flowers: Tiny, white, 5-lobed, in slender, often branching spikes. Individual flowers ¹⁄₁₆-¼" across, with only a few in bloom at a time. Spikes up to several inches long, green overall, with a few white flowers. **Leaves:** Opposite, simple, toothed (sometimes doubly so), ovate to lanceolate, with petioles to nearly sessile toward the top of the plant, 2–6" long. **Height:** 2–5'. **Habitat and range:** Fields, meadows, thickets, moist open woods, and disturbed sites; eastern Canada to North Dakota, south to Florida and Texas. **On Sugarloaf—Blooming time:** June–October. **Locations:** Mount Ephraim Road, Comus Road, other mountain roadsides and trailsides. **Similar species:** Blue vervain *(V. hastata)* bears violet-blue flowers. Narrow-leaved vervain *(V. simplex)* has purple or lavender flowers and narrow leaves tapered at the base. Both species were reported as scarce on Sugarloaf in a 1987 Stronghold plant survey by botanist Richard Wiegand. They bloom from early summer through early autumn.

Mint Family

Lamiaceae
(Labiatae)

An extremely important family for humanity with numerous culinary herbs including mints, oregano, marjoram, thyme, sage, and basil. Many members of this large family grow on Sugarloaf. **Family characteristics:** 200 genera and 3,200 species worldwide. Cosmopolitan. **Economic importance:** In addition to the culinary herbs, largely of Mediterranean origin, Heywood's *Flowering Plants of the World* notes many other uses of mint family members. The *Coleus* genus gives rise to popular house and garden plants. Patchouli is derived from a species of *Pogostemon,* and many other family plants yield essential oils used as fragrances. One family member, *Ocimum sanctum,* is sacred to Hindus, according to Heywood, and is frequently grown near temples. Perilla, a problematic invasive on Sugarloaf, is prized for perilla oil in India, where it is used in printing inks and paints. It is also used medicinally in Asia. Mint family members are perhaps best loved as refreshing beverages and beverage garnishes: hot and cold teas, a sprig of mint in a glass of lemonade or a mint julep. **Flowers:** Usually perfect, usually irregular, corolla typically 2-lipped and 5-lobed but may be 4-lobed as in our native Virginia bugleweed *(Lycopus virginicus).* **Fruit:** Usually 4 nutlets (sometimes fewer); rarely a drupe. **Leaves:** Opposite or whorled, usually simple. Stems often four-sided (or square). **Growth habits:** Herbs, sometimes shrubs, rarely trees or vines (in our native flora all are herbs or low shrubs). **Occurrence on Sugarloaf:** Mint family members grow in all Sugarloaf habitats, blooming from very early spring through fall, with most plants flowering during the summer.

Horse-Balm (Richweed or Stoneroot)

Collinsonia canadensis L.
Mint Family (Lamiaceae)

A summer to early fall wildflower with strongly lemon-scented flowers and large ovate leaves. **Flowers:** Yellow or pale gold, irregular, with an elongated, fringed lower lip and lemony fragrance. Stamens dramatically protruding. Each flower ½–1" long, borne in (usually) branching terminal clusters. **Leaves:** Opposite, simple, ovate, toothed; base rounded, tapered, or nearly cordate, apex pointed. Upper leaves short-petioled to nearly sessile; lower leaves long-petioled. Leaf blades 2–10" long and rather broad. **Height and growth habits:** 2–5', branching toward the top. **Habitat and range:** Moist, rich woods; Quebec to Wisconsin; south to Florida and Arkansas. **Herbal** lore: A widely used herbal that has served as a poultice for burns, sprains, and wounds, a diuretic, and a gargle for hoarseness. In its latter capacity, Hutchens reports, it's been called "a clergyman's friend" (*Indian Herbalogy of North America*). Foster and Duke (Peterson Field Guides' *Field Guide to*

Horse-Balm

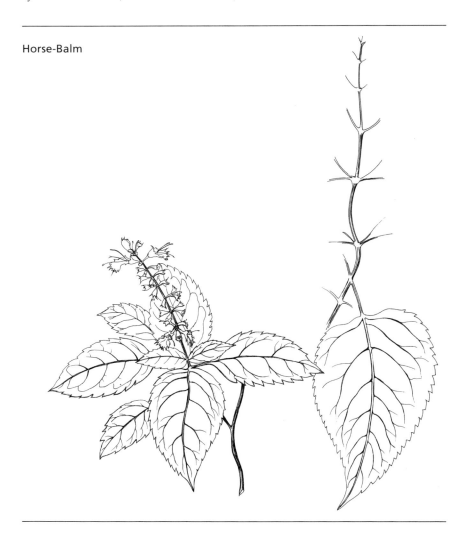

Medicinal Plants: Eastern and Central North America) warn that even small doses of the fresh leaves may cause vomiting. **On Sugarloaf—Blooming time:** July–September. **Locations:** Mount Ephraim Road, Sugarloaf Mountain Road, White Trail, and Yellow Trail. **Similar species:** None really. Fringed, lemon-scented flowers distinguish it from other mints; broadly ovate, opposite leaves differ from those of the yellow-fringed orchid (*Platanthera ciliaris*).

Bee-Balm (Oswego-Tea)

Monarda didyma L.
Mint Family (Lamiaceae)

A favorite plant of gardeners and the hummingbirds every gardener hopes to attract. Bee-balm's scarlet flowers appear along the banks of Bear Branch in midsummer. **Flowers:** Brilliant red, tubular, with 2 widely divergent lips. Long stamens protrude beneath the upper lip. Individual flowers are each slightly more than an inch long, surrounded by purplish or reddish bracts and borne in a showy round cluster. **Leaves:** Opposite, simple, toothed, ovate-lanceolate or deltoid-ovate, 2–6" long. **Height:** 2–5'. **Habitat and range:** Moist woods and thickets, stream banks; Maine to Michigan, south along the mountains to Georgia (some authorities suggest the New England plant populations are garden escapes). **Herbal lore:** According to Foster and Duke (Peterson Field Guides' *Field Guide to Medicinal Plants: Eastern and Central North America*), "American Indians used leaf tea for colic, gas, colds, fevers, stomachaches, nosebleeds, insomnia, heart trouble, measles,

Bee-Balm

and to induce sweating. Poultice used for headaches. Historically, physicians used leaf to expel worms and gas." **On Sugarloaf—Blooming time:** July–September. **Locations:** Lower stretches of Bear Branch. **Similar species:** Most apt to be confused with cardinal flower *(Lobelia cardinalis),* which also has scarlet flowers and grows along Bear Branch. Cardinal flower has alternate leaves, and its flower clusters are long and upright (not round). Another *Monarda* species, wild bergamot *(M. fistulosa),* has been identified in the past on Sugarloaf, although I have yet to see it here. Its summer flowers are lavender or pink.

Virginia Bugleweed (Virginia Water Horehound)

Lycopus virginicus L.
Mint Family (Lamiaceae)

Virginia bugleweed has minute flowers clustered in the leaf axils and (frequently) purple-tinged leaves. A rather common plant of Sugarloaf's moist, rich soils. **Flowers:** Tiny, white, slightly irregular, 4-lobed (the upper lobe often notched), in dense roundish clusters in the leaf axils. (The clustered greenish nutlets that follow the flowers are as showy.) **Leaves:** Opposite, simple, lanceolate, narrowly ovate, or elliptic, toothed until just below the middle and then strongly tapered to a sessile or barely petiolate, narrowly wedge-shaped base. Usually purple-tinged but sometimes simply dark green; 1–5" long. **Height:** 6–24". **Habitat and range:** Moist to wet soil; eastern United States. **Herbal lore:** Foster and Duke (Peterson Field Guides' *Field Guide to Medicinal Plants: Eastern and Central North America*) report: "Tra-

Virginia Bugleweed

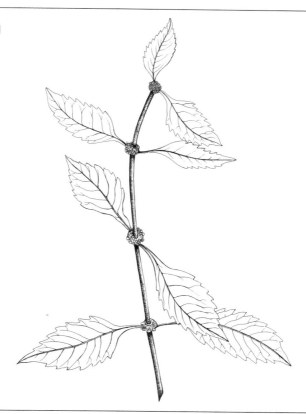

ditionally, used as a mild sedative, astringent; especially for heart diseases, chronic lung ailments, coughs, fast pulse, thyroid disease, diabetes. Science has confirmed the potential value of this plant in treating hyperthyroidism." **On Sugarloaf—Blooming time:** July–October. **Locations:** Rich, moist soil mountainwide, including Blue Trail, Yellow Trail, and White Trail. **Similar species:** The tapered, wedge-shaped leaf base of this plant distinguishes it from other common opposite-leaved plants blooming in late summer and fall on the mountain. Two other species of *Lycopus* may be encountered here. The leaves of cut-leaved water horehound *(L. americanus)* are more deeply toothed than those of Virginia bugleweed, and the lower leaves are usually lobed, giving the leaf an oaklike appearance. An uncommon *Lycopus* species was reported on or near the mountain in a 1987 Stronghold plant survey conducted by botanist Richard Wiegand. Stalked water horehound *(L. rubellus)* has leaves tapering to a well-defined petiole and white flowers that may be purple-spotted. This plant was once on the watch list of *Rare, Threatened, and Endangered Plants of Maryland.* In recent years the plant has been downgraded to S4 status, meaning there are currently enough plants in the state to sustain its existence in Maryland.

American Germander (Wood Sage)

Teucrium canadense L.
Mint Family (Lamiaceae)

A rather tall mint family member with unusual flowers. **Flowers:** Pink-purple, irregular, ⅓–¾" long. Although the flower looks like the blooms of other mint family members, on close inspection most of its upper lip is missing, and the arching stamens protrude from the upper part of the corolla base. Flowers borne in a tall, terminal, spikelike raceme. **Leaves:** Opposite, simple, toothed. Ovate, lance-ovate, or oblong, 1¾–5" long, on short petioles (or nearly sessile). **Height and growth habits:** 1–4'; usually unbranched. **Habitat and range:** Moist or wet soil in a variety of habitats; most of the United States and Canada. **Herbal lore:** According to Foster and Duke, American germander or wood sage has been used medicinally as a tea for inducing menstruation, urination, and perspiration and as a treatment for lung problems, piles, and worms. They also note that it has been applied externally as an antiseptic and used as a gargle. **On Sugarloaf—Blooming time:** June–September. **Locations:** Moist and wet areas on and around the mountain, including along Mount Ephraim Road. **Similar species:** Use the spikelike raceme with its flowers missing most of their upper lips and the usually unbranched growth habit to separate this species from other mint family members.

Showy Skullcap

Scutellaria serrata Andrews
Mint Family (Lamiaceae)

This plant has been put on the watch list by the Maryland Department of Natural Resources, which means that it has been identified as a candidate for potential rare, threatened, or endangered status. On a June day I noticed a beautiful specimen of showy skullcap in bloom on the mountain during a botany field trip. The following day I returned to the spot to describe it for this book, but the flower was gone. If this plant was picked by a human visitor, that person further compromised an imperiled Sugarloaf plant species. **Flowers:** Showy violet or blue-violet irregular flowers, which are erect and 2-lipped, with a hooded upper lip; ¾–1¼" tall, with the upper lip usually slightly darker than the lower one. Flowers grow in a (usually simple) terminal raceme. (A few single flowers may be found in the uppermost leaf axils.) **Leaves:** Opposite, simple, ovate-elliptic with toothed margin, tapered base, and pointed apex; 1–4" long, glabrous or minutely pubescent. Petiole up to or exceeding ½", may appear more pubescent than the leaf blade. **Height and growth habits:** 10"–2', rather upright and usually unbranched. Plant stalk square. **Habitat and range:** Piedmont and mountain woodlands, Pennsylva-

nia and Ohio to North Carolina and Tennessee. **On Sugarloaf—Blooming time:** Late May–June. **Locations:** Trails and roadsides. If you are lucky enough to come upon this uncommon and elegant member of the mint family, please do not disturb! **Similar species:** Of the other skullcap species found on Sugarloaf: hyssop skullcap *(S. integrifolia)* has untoothed leaf margins, mad-dog skullcap *(S. lateriflora)* bears one-sided racemes from the leaf axils, and hairy skullcap *(S. elliptica)* has smaller flowers, sometimes in branching terminal clusters. Hairy skullcap leaves are more pubescent than showy skullcap's, with more rounded teeth and apex.

Hyssop Skullcap

Scutellaria integrifolia L.
Mint Family (Lamiaceae)

Most skullcaps of northeastern North America have toothed leaves. This is Sugarloaf's only skullcap with entire (untoothed) leaves. A few of hyssop skullcap's lower leaves may be toothed, but these usually fall early. **Flowers:** Violet-blue, often with white or whitish markings; irregular, 2-lipped, with the upper lip arching above the lower one in a hooded fashion and the lower lip horizontally flared and more or less 2-lobed. Lips emerge from a funnel-shaped base. Flowers ¾–1¼" long, erect or semierect, in terminal clusters (racemes). **Leaves:** Opposite, simple, entire (although a few lower leaves may

be toothed). Narrowly lance-elliptic, lanceolate, or oblanceolate, with a bluntly pointed apex and tapered base. Sessile or short-petioled (although when lower toothed leaves are present, these may have longer petioles); ⅔–2⅓" long. There are often extra pairs of smaller leaves in the axils of the main leaves. **Height:** 1–2½'. **Habitat and range:** Fields, open woods; Massachusetts to Florida, west to Ohio, Tennessee, and Texas. **On Sugarloaf—Blooming time:** May–July. **Locations:** Trails and roadsides, including Yellow Trail and the road up the mountain. **Similar species:** The entire leaves separate this species from other skullcaps.

Other skullcaps (*Scutellaria* spp.) of Sugarloaf

Mint Family (Lamiaceae)

Several other skullcaps (*Scutellaria* spp.) are indigenous to Maryland and the two that follow grow on Sugarloaf.

Mad-Dog Skullcap (*S. lateriflora* L.). The plant name reflects the herbal history of this species. It was used to treat rabies. **Flowers:** Blue, pink, violet,

Mad-Dog Skullcap

or white, less than ½" long, in one-sided racemes springing from the leaf axils. **Leaves:** Opposite, simple, lance-ovate, toothed, 1–5" long, petioled. **Height:** 6"–3'. **Habitat and range:** Moist woods, wet meadows, riverbanks, and bottomlands; much of the United States and Canada. **On Sugarloaf—Blooming time:** June–September. **Locations:** Moist areas along Mount Ephraim Road; also likely in wet areas near the Yellow Trail. **Similar species:** Use the one-sided axillary racemes to separate mad-dog skullcap from similar species.

Hairy Skullcap (*S. elliptica* Muhl. ex Spreng.). As the name implies, this plant tends to be hairy. **Flowers:** The lips are violet-blue, and the flower tube is often a paler hue. A few specimens on Sugarloaf are nearly white with only a faint lavender blush on the lower lip. Flowers ½–¾" long, borne in branched or simple terminal racemes and from the uppermost leaf axils. **Leaves:** Opposite, simple, elliptic-ovate, with rounded teeth, 1–3" long, petioled. **Height:** 1–3'. **Habitat and range:** Dry upland woods, fields, and thickets; eastern United States. **On Sugarloaf—Blooming time:** May–June. **Locations:** Dry stretches of mountain roadsides (including the road up the mountain) and trailsides. **Similar species:** Showy skullcap (*S. serrata*) is glabrous or barely pubescent, with slightly larger flowers. Mad-dog skullcap (*S. lateriflora*) has one-sided axillary racemes with smaller flowers. It grows in wet, rather than dry, areas. Hyssop skullcap (*S. integrifolia*) has mostly entire leaves.

American Pennyroyal

Hedeoma pulegioides (L.) Pers.
Mint Family (Lamiaceae)

You are more likely to notice American pennyroyal through your nose rather than your eyes. This inconspicuous plant gives off a strong aroma when its leaves are crushed. Oil of pennyroyal is a traditional insect repellent. According to Foster and Duke (Peterson Field Guides' *Field Guide to Medicinal Plants: Eastern and Central North America*), it can be lethal if ingested. Common along many Sugarloaf trails, American pennyroyal often grows underfoot. **Flowers:** Tiny blue, irregular, 2-lipped (upper lip notched, lower lip 3-lobed) corollas are ephemeral; the more persistent tubular green calyx has 3 teeth above and 2 long, narrow, curved teeth below. Flowers in tufts in leaf axils. **Leaves:** Small, opposite, simple; lanceolate, elliptic, ovate, or obovate. Entire or with a few blunt teeth, short-petioled or nearly sessile, ¼–1¼" long; often with extra pairs of smaller leaves in the axils. Plant stalk downy. **Height and growth habits:** 4–18"; usually branched. **Habitat and range:** Upland woods, clearings; New Brunswick and Quebec west to Wisconsin and Nebraska, south to Georgia and Arkansas. **Herbal lore:** Leaf tea traditionally used to treat colds, coughs, fevers, and kidney and liver problems, among other conditions, according to Foster and Duke, but see warning above. **On**

American Pennyroyal

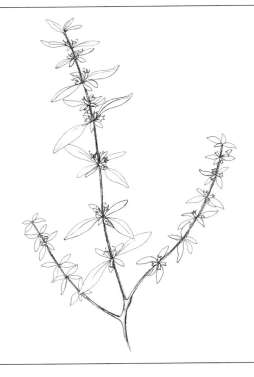

Sugarloaf—Blooming time: July–September. **Locations:** White Trail, Blue Trail; common mountainwide. **Similar species:** Once you know the scent, you will not confuse American pennyroyal with any other herbaceous plant in Sugarloaf's flora. The small leaves and flowers distinguish it from most other local members of the mint family.

Dittany

Cunila origanoides (L.) Britton
Mint Family (Lamiaceae)

Before setting out this September morning—a day on which I planned to write my description of dittany —I was flipping through a two-year-old field diary when my eyes fell on these words: "The dittany is so lovely, with lavender flowers, oregano-scented leaves, and a wiry Mediterranean stalk. I have a great affinity for this plant—and for the sun shining down on me this morning." Two years later, nearly to the day, I say ditto to those observations about dittany—and the day on Sugarloaf. **Flowers:** Small, lavender, in axillary and terminal tufts. Each flower irregular, 5-lobed, the lobes extending from a tube (but may appear 4-lobed as the 2-lobed upper lip is so shallowly lobed). Darker purple spotting usually visible with a hand lens; 2 stamens

Dittany

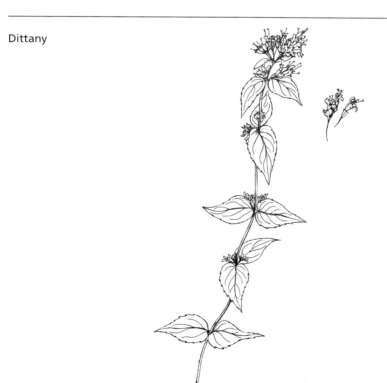

very visibly protruding. Each flower ⅛–⅓" long. (Dittany flowers can be white, but known Sugarloaf specimens are all lavender.) **Leaves:** Opposite, simple, ovate, toothed, glabrous or nearly so. Sessile or short-petioled, ½–2½" long. Oregano-scented. **Height and growth habits:** 8–36", branched. Plant stalk wiry-stiff and woody (at least at the base). **Habitat and range:** Dry woods; southern New York and Pennsylvania to Illinois and Missouri, south to the Carolinas and Oklahoma. **Herbal lore:** In Peterson Field Guides' *Field Guide to Medicinal Plants: Eastern and Central North America,* Foster and Duke report, "Leaf tea a folk remedy for colds, fevers, headaches, snakebites; thought to induce perspiration and menstruation." **On Sugarloaf—Blooming time:** August–October. **Locations:** White Trail, mountain roadsides; moderately common mountainwide. **Similar species:** The wiry stalk, branched growth habit, and oregano-scented leaves distinguish dittany from other native mint family members.

Gill-over-the-Ground (Ground Ivy)

Glechoma hederacea L.
Mint Family (Lamiaceae)

A Eurasian native, now widely naturalized in eastern North America and an abundant invasive in regional bottomlands. Gill-over-the-ground has heart-shaped, kidney-shaped, or round leaves that have a spicy odor when crushed. **Flowers:** Violet-blue, irregular, with larger, lobed lower lip that is

Gill-over-the-Ground

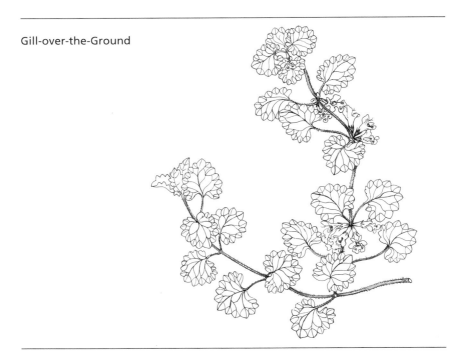

often spotted purple; ⅓–½" long. Calyx toothed and tubular. **Leaves:** Opposite, simple, heart-shaped (cordate), kidney-shaped (reniform), or rounded (rotund) with blunt or rounded teeth (crenate). (The leaves of this plant provide an excellent opportunity for botanical vocabulary building!) Leaves ½– 2" wide, on (often) pubescent petioles. Pungent when crushed. **Height and growth habits:** Several inches to over 1'; sprawling, often forming mats. **Habitat and range:** Roadsides, lawns, disturbed sites; Eurasian native, widely naturalized. **Herbal lore:** In *A Modern Herbal,* first published in 1931, Grieve wrote: "From early days, Ground Ivy [gill-over-the-ground] has been endowed with singular curative virtues, and is one of them most popular remedies for coughs and nervous headaches. It has even been extolled before all other vegetable medicines for the cure of consumption." **On Sugarloaf—Blooming time:** Spring–early summer. **Locations:** Lawns at base of mountain; roadsides and trailsides. Very common. **Similar species:** Purple dead-nettle *(Lamium purpureum)* is an upright plant with purplish-pink flowers. Henbit *(Lamium amplexicaule)*—which is scarce on Sugarloaf— also has purplish-pink flowers and upper leaves clasping the stalk.

Purple Dead-Nettle (Red Dead-Nettle)

Lamium purpureum L.
Mint Family (Lamiaceae)

A Eurasian native that has become naturalized in many parts of North America. Common in Sugarloaf area fields and in mowed areas along roadsides. **Flowers:** Small, purplish-pink, irregular, 2-lipped, typical mint-family flowers growing in small clusters (or sometimes singly) in the upper leaf axils. **Leaves:** Opposite, simple. Heart-shaped, triangular, or ovate, downy soft.

Purple Dead-Nettle

Upper leaves crowded on stem, usually angling downward, often purplish, on very short petioles. Lower leaves on longer petioles. Bluntly toothed, ¼–1" long. Plant stalk rather stout, square, may be tinged red or purple. **Height and growth habits:** 4–12", upright or lightly prostrate at base. **Habitat and range:** Fields, gardens, and waste places; Eurasian native, widely naturalized in North America. **On Sugarloaf—Blooming time:** Early spring through fall. **Locations:** Mountainwide, especially at base and along roadsides. **Similar species:** May be confused with other mint family members. Henbit *(L. amplexicaule)* has kidney-shaped, scallop-toothed leaves, and its upper leaves clasp the stem. Gill-over-the-ground *(Glechoma hederacea)* is a creeping plant with violet-blue flowers.

Henbit

Lamium amplexicaule L.
Mint Family (Lamiaceae)

Very similar to the preceding species—purple dead-nettle *(L. purpureum)*—henbit is abundant in the farm fields ringing Sugarloaf and occasionally pops up beside a mountain trail or road. Henbit **flowers** are a deep purplish-pink, and its bluntly toothed upper **leaves** clasp the plant stalk and are not as crowded on the stalk as the leaves of purple dead-nettle. Not nearly as common on Sugarloaf Mountain as purple dead-nettle.

Heal-All (Self-Heal, Prunella, Heart of the Earth, Blue Curls)

Prunella vulgaris L.
Mint Family (Lamiaceae)

A rather scraggly member of the mint family, heal-all has long been held in high esteem by European and Asian herbalists. When the plant was brought to North America, it readily naturalized and is now common in many habitats. Thus a prized medicine of two continents has become a third continent's weed. On Sugarloaf heal-all is found along roads and parking areas and next to trails through open woods. **Flowers:** Dark or light blue-purple, irregular, with a hooded upper lip and a lower lip which is usually fringed; ¼–½" long. Flowers borne in dense barrel-shaped terminal heads, usually with more sepals showing than flowers. Sepals are stiff, fringed, and flattened with bristly looking hairs. **Leaves:** Opposite, simple, lanceolate, ovate, or elliptic, with entire margins or irregular, shallow teeth; ½–2½" long. Petiole usually short on upper leaves, often longer on lower ones. Leaves are glabrous or lightly pubescent and often feel slightly rough on top. Plant stalk squarish. **Height and growth habits:** 2–18", upright or sprawling. **Habitat and range:** Fields, lawns, waste places, and roadsides; Eurasian native, naturalized throughout much of North America. **Herbal lore:** British, European,

Heal-All

and Chinese herbalists have found many uses for this plant, and modern research supports their faith in it. It has been used externally to treat wounds, as a gargle for throat infections, and in China as a cooling plant for the liver and an aid to circulation. Foster and Duke note in Peterson Field Guides' *Field Guide to Medicinal Plants: Eastern and Central North America:* "Research suggests the plant possesses antibiotic, hypotensive, and antimutagenic qualities. Contains the antitumor and diuretic compound ursolic acid." **On Sugarloaf—Blooming time:** June–October. **Locations:** West View, East View, roadsides and trailsides mountainwide. **Similar species:** Often growing near, and blooming at the same time as, wild basil *(Satureja vulgaris).* Wild basil flowers are purplish-pink, and they grow in round or elliptically shaped heads that have a fuzzy appearance. Wild basil leaves are softly pubescent to the touch, and the plant stalk is very pubescent.

Wild Basil (Field Basil)

Satureja vulgaris (L.) Fritsch.
Mint Family (Lamiaceae)

A summer–fall blooming plant with distinctive fuzzy-looking flower heads.
Flowers: Purplish-pink, irregular, 2-lipped, the lower lip 3-lobed. Flowers

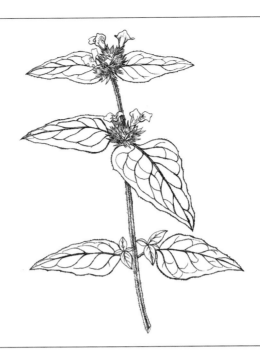

¼–½" long, growing in elliptical or round bristly-fuzzy heads toward the top of the plant. **Leaves:** Opposite, simple, ovate, 1–2" long. Margins smooth or with a few shallow, irregular teeth. Leaves soft-pubescent to the touch, nearly sessile to long-petioled. Plant stalk square and pubescent. **Height and growth habits:** 6"–2½'; upright or slightly sprawling. **Habitat and range:** Woodlands, roadsides; much of the United States and Canada, also widespread in Europe. **On Sugarloaf—Blooming time:** June–October. **Locations:** West View; along roads and trails mountainwide. **Similar species:** The summer-blooming mints can be tricky to identify. The elliptical or round fuzzy flower head and purplish-pink flowers should distinguish wild basil from heal-all *(Prunella vulgaris)* and Sugarloaf's other mint family members.

Catnip (Catmint, Catnep)

Nepeta cataria L.
Mint Family (Lamiaceae)

Best known as a feline intoxicant, catnip is a Eurasian native that has been used as a folk remedy for various medical conditions. **Flowers:** Irregular, 2-lipped, with a toothed lower lip; white or pale lavender with purple or pink spots. Each flower small, ⅛–½", in downy-soft, gray-green, elongate terminal heads. **Leaves:** Opposite, simple, heart-shaped, toothed, ½–3½" long.

Very soft and downy, gray-green, with petioles. Aromatic, but some (non-feline) inhalers may find the scent unpleasant. **Height and growth habits:** 1–4'; usually much-branched; dramatically square-stemmed, downy gray-green overall. **Habitat and range:** Disturbed sites; widely naturalized Eurasian. **Herbal lore:** Anyone with a family cat is familiar with the feline fascination for catnip. Catnip's flowers and leaves have been steeped (by humans) as tea to treat colds, fevers, chicken pox, headaches, problem menses, and colic. According to Grieve (*A Modern Herbal,* first published in 1931), "Catnep tea is a valuable drink in every case of fever, because of its action in inducing sleep and producing perspiration without increasing the heat of the system. It is good in restlessness, colic, insanity and nervousness, and is used as a mild nervine for children, one of its chief uses being . . . the treatment of children's ailments." **On Sugarloaf—Blooming time:** Early summer–early fall. **Locations:** Roadsides and open areas along Yellow Trail; moderately common. **Similar species:** The combined characteristics of height (this species is taller than most other Sugarloaf mint family members), pale flower color, and overall gray-green downiness separate catnip from our other mints.

Motherwort

Leonurus cardiaca L.
Mint Family (Lamiaceae)

Motherwort's herbal history is rich and complex. As its name implies, this plant has been used medicinally as an herbal childbirth aid. Its Latin species epithet, *cardiaca,* refers to its use as a remedy for heart ailments. **Flowers:** Irregular, 2-lipped, pink or purplish and white, with a fuzzy upper lip and spiny calyx. Clusters of stalkless flowers encircle the stout, ridged, square plant stalk in the upper leaf axils. **Leaves:** Opposite, with upper leaves small and mostly 3-toothed or 3-lobed. Much larger lower leaves palmately 3–5 lobed (similar to maple leaves). Upper leaves may be less than an inch long, lower ones up to several inches. Most leaves petioled, the lower with long petioles. **Height:** 2–5'. **Habitat and range:** Open woods, roadsides, fields, disturbed sites; an Asian native, cultivated as a home medicinal and now widely spread in the United States and Canada. **Herbal lore:** Motherwort is a time-honored treatment for many medical conditions associated with child-birth, menstruation, and menopause as well as heart palpitations, stom-achaches, insomnia, fevers, and neuralgia. According to Foster and Duke in Peterson Field Guides' *Field Guide to Medicinal Plants: Eastern and Central North America,* "Scientists have found extracts to be antispasmodic, hypo-tensive, and sedative. Experimentally, leonurine, a leaf constituent, is a uter-

ine tonic." **On Sugarloaf—Blooming time:** May–August. **Locations:** West View; Sugarloaf trails and roadsides. **Similar species:** Use the 3–5 lobed leaves to separate this species from other mint family members.

Perilla (Beefsteak Plant)

Perilla frutescens (L.) Britton
Mint Family (Lamiaceae)

Perilla has long been employed in Asia as food and medicine, but it can be toxic to humans and cattle in large doses and has been used as a fish poison. This Asian native is becoming increasingly common along Sugarloaf's trails and roadsides and may be crowding out native plants. **Flowers:** Tiny, irregular, purplish-pink, in long, spiky racemes, both terminal and from the leaf axils. The calyx is prominent, and the dried calyx persists through fall and winter. **Leaves:** Opposite, simple; broadly ovate to ovate-oblong, strongly toothed and markedly veined. Petioles quite long and often purplish (as is the young leaf blade). Leaves 1" to several inches long, exuding a strong, exotic scent when crushed. Plant stalk square, usually purplish or burgundy. **Height:** 6"–4'. **Habitat and range:** Roadsides, waste places. Native to India, widely escaped throughout the eastern United States. **Herbal lore:** Used in Asian medicine for abdominal disorders, fevers, coughs, and other medical conditions. Also a flavoring in Oriental foods. (*See* warning in introduction to plant.) **On Sugarloaf—Blooming time:** August–October. **Locations:** A very common trailside and roadside plant. **Similar species:** Use these characteristics to distinguish perilla from other mints on Sugarloaf: tiny flowers in long, spiky racemes; purplish stalk; large leaves with strong, unusual scent. Perilla grows in colonies and blooms late.

Perilla

Other Mint Family Members

Lamiaceae

The following members of the mint family grow on or near Sugarloaf Mountain and are encountered infrequently along roadsides and trails.

Lyre-Leaved Sage (*Salvia lyrata* L.). The basal leaves of this plant are lyre-shaped and grow in a rosette. **Flowers:** Violet or blue, irregular, about an inch long; 2-lipped flowers have a 2-lobed lower lip which is larger than the upper lip. Flowers borne in whorled layers in a spikelike raceme. **Leaves:** Stem leaves opposite, simple; entire, wavy-toothed, or lobed; sessile or nearly so. Few stem leaves per plant. Basal leaves usually deeply pinnately lobed or toothed and long-stalked (leaf shape suggesting a lyre). Plant stalk fuzzy. **Height:** 1–3'. **Habitat and range:** Woods, fields, meadows, thickets; eastern and central United States and southeastern Canada. **Herbal lore:** According to Foster and Duke (Peterson Field Guides' *Field Guide to Medicinal Plants: Eastern and Central North America*), "American Indians used root in salve for sores. Whole plant tea used for colds, coughs, nervous debility; with honey for asthma; mildly laxative and diaphoretic. Folk remedy for cancer

Lyre-Leaved
Sage

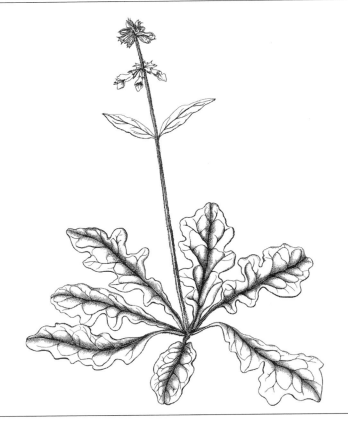

and warts." On Sugarloaf—Blooming time: April–June. Locations: Mount Ephraim Road; possible along other roads and trailsides. Similar species: Use the basal leaf rosettes to help distinguish this plant from other mint family members.

Bugle (Bugleweed, Ajuga) (*Ajuga reptans* L.). A Eurasian native which has escaped from cultivation and now thrives in grassy areas, gardens, and roadsides. Bugle forms mats along the ground as it spreads from leafy runners. **Flowers:** Purple or blue, irregular, with a small upper lip and larger 3-lobed lower lip (middle lobe of lower lip is larger than side lobes and is often lobed itself). Flowers borne in whorled clusters in a leafy spike. **Leaves:** Opposite, simple, ovate, oblong, or obovate; often wine-red, purplish, or copper-tinted, with wavy-toothed or bluntly toothed margins. Lowest leaves on petioles, upper stem leaves usually sessile or nearly so. **Height and growth habits:** 3–12"; leafy runners hug the ground, and flowering stalks are more or less erect. On Sugarloaf—Blooming time: April–July. Locations: Yellow Trail, Mount Ephraim Road. Uncommon on Sugarloaf. Similar species: Use leaf color and growth habit to help distinguish this plant from other mint family members.

Mint Genus Members (*Mentha* spp.). Three members of the mint genus may be found on Sugarloaf, but they are all uncommon on the mountain. Wild Mint (*M. arvensis* L.) has lilac or white flowers growing in small clusters in the leaf axils and ovate or oblong leaves with a strong mint smell. It is a native species. The following two were introduced. Peppermint (*M. x piperita* L.) bears purplish or pink flowers in dense terminal spikes, which may be interrupted. Leaves strongly peppermint-scented, the larger ones petioled. Spearmint (*M. spicata* L.) also bears purplish or pink flowers in spikes—sometimes interrupted. Its leaves are sessile or nearly so and smell like, well, spearmint!

Olive Family

Oleaceae

This family gives us olives, jasmine, lilacs, forsythia, and our own native fringe-tree. **Family characteristics:** 30 genera and 600 species worldwide. Nearly cosmopolitan. **Economic importance:** The olive tree (*Olea europaea*) is widely grown for fruit and oil, ash species (*Fraxinus* spp.) yield timber, and many other family members are grown for ornament and perfume. **Flowers:** Regular, perfect or unisexual, usually with 4 sepals and 4 petals (petals and sepals often united). **Fruit:** A drupe, capsule, berry, or samara. **Leaves:** Usually opposite; simple or pinnately compound. **Growth habits:** Mostly trees and shrubs. **Occurrence on Sugarloaf:** The fringe-tree (*Chionanthus virgini-*

cus) grows in several places on the mountain. White ash *(Fraxinus americana)* is a fairly common Sugarloaf woodland tree, which is described in the Botanical Key and Guide to Trees, Shrubs, and Woody Vines. Two nonnative shrubs, common privet *(Ligustrum vulgare)* and forsythia *(Forsythia viridissima)*, are also briefly described in the Botanical Key and Guide to Trees, Shrubs, and Woody Vines.

Tree or Shrub

Fringe-Tree

Chionanthus virginicus L.
Olive Family (Oleaceae)

A small tree or shrub that puts forth fragrant cloudlike flower clusters in spring. **Flowers:** Drooping airy clusters of white 4-petaled flowers. Individual flowers "fringe"-like, with slender delicate petals ½–1¼" long. **Fruit:** Dark, blue-black or purple, ovoid or ellipsoid drupe, ½–¾" long. **Leaves:** Opposite, simple, deciduous, 3–8" long. Ovate, obovate, or oblong-elliptic with entire margin. Gradually or abruptly pointed apex; rounded toward base but finally narrowly wedge-shaped. Petiole ½–1" long. **Growth habits:**

Fringe-Tree

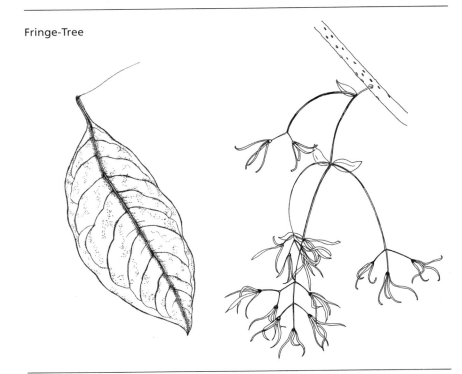

A small tree or shrub. **Bark and twigs:** Bark reddish-brown, broken into thin scales. Twigs rather stout, pubescent or not, with scaly winter buds and true end bud. **Habitat and range:** Woods, streamsides; New Jersey west to eastern Oklahoma and Texas, south to Florida. **Herbal lore:** According to *Indian Herbalogy of North America* by Hutchens, fringe-tree bark tincture has been used to treat liver and abdominal disorders and as a treatment for malaria and other medical conditions. **Wildlife lore:** Deer, quail, wild turkey, and songbirds eat fringe-tree drupes. **On Sugarloaf—Blooming time:** May–early June. **Locations:** Streams and springs along Mount Ephraim Road and the Yellow Trail; near the Red Trail; possible along other trails and roadsides but not common here. **Similar species:** None on Sugarloaf. There is one other fringe-tree species in the world, the Asian fringe-tree *(C. retusus).* It is sometimes grown in Washington-Baltimore area home gardens. Our native fringe-tree is a popular garden ornamental.

Snapdragon or Figwort Family

Scrophulariaceae

The snapdragon or figwort family is known for its ornamental flowering plants, including the colorful familiar garden snapdragon *(Antirrhinum majus).* Another popular garden plant in this family, foxglove *(Digitalis purpurea),* is the source of the important cardiac drug that bears its Latin genus name. About a dozen herbaceous wildflowers belonging to the snapdragon family are found on Sugarloaf. Most of them are native and bloom during summer and early fall, but among the introduced, spring-blooming species is the diminutive bird's-eye speedwell *(Veronica persica),* one of the mountain's earliest wildflowers. Sugarloaf's summer- and autumn-blooming members of the family include turtlehead *(Chelone glabra),* the principal host plant for the locally rare Baltimore checkerspot butterfly. A single tree species represents this family on the mountain, the widely naturalized Asian paulownia *(Paulownia tomentosa),* which produces fragrant lavender flowers in May and June. **Family characteristics:** 190 genera and 4,000 species worldwide. A cosmopolitan family. **Economic importance:** Cardiac glycosides from *Digitalis;* many ornamentals. **Flowers:** Corolla irregular or nearly regular, usually with fused petals. Often 2-lipped. Petals 4 or 5. Sepals 4 or 5 (usually fused at the base). Stamens usually 4 but sometimes 2 or 5. Pistil 1 (2-parted). **Fruit:** Usually a capsule. **Leaves:** Opposite or alternate; entire, toothed, or lobed (may be deeply so). **Growth habits:** Mostly herbs or shrubs; some trees and vines. **Occurrence on Sugarloaf:** Several common and uncommon wildflower species with showy flowers; one flowering tree.

Moth Mullein

Verbascum blattaria L.
Snapdragon or Figwort Family (Scrophulariaceae)

A common summer wildflower introduced from Eurasia and naturalized in many parts of eastern North America, moth mullein grows along the road up Sugarloaf and in area fields and disturbed sites. **Flowers:** Pale yellow or white, 5-lobed, stalked, with a purplish blush at the center and stamen filaments covered with feathery-looking purple hairs; flowers ⅔–1" across, growing in a tall unbranched, elongated flower cluster (raceme). **Leaves:** Alternate, simple, with blunt, shallow teeth (or sometimes nearly entire). Leaf shape varies from lanceolate to triangular or ovate. Stem leaves are sessile and more or less clasping; basal rosette may appear petioled. Leaves small near raceme (to less than an inch), up to several inches long at base. Leaves glabrous, but upper plant stalk is pubescent. **Height and growth habits:** 1–4'; upright or arching with one main stalk or branched. **Habitat and range:** Fields, roadsides, disturbed sites; Eurasian native, widely naturalized. **On Sugarloaf—Blooming time:** June–September. **Locations:** Sugarloaf roadsides, West View, East View. **Similar species:** Common mullein *(V. thapsus)* has large woolly leaves and brighter yellow flowers.

Moth Mullein

Common Mullein

Verbascum thapsus L.

Snapdragon or Figwort Family (Scrophulariaceae)

An imposing plant with yellow flowers in a tall, erect spike and woolly gray-green leaves. Common mullein is an Old World plant with a distinguished herbal history. **Flowers:** Yellow, with 5 lobes that are slightly irregular in size; flowers ¾–1" across, although they are soon closed and may appear smaller. Growing in club-shaped spikes several inches to over a foot tall. **Leaves:** Alternate, simple, with smooth or slightly toothed margins. Elliptic-obovate, 5–14" long, gray-green, with the texture of flannel. Upper leaves sessile, lower leaves sometimes petioled. Stem leaves taper to the base and are attached to the plant stalk beneath the leaf (the botanical term for such a downward extended attachment is "decurrent"). Common mullein is a biennial. During its first year it forms a large basal rosette of woolly leaves; the

Common Mullein

flowering plant stalk arises the second year. **Height and growth habits:** 2–6';
an upright plant, usually bearing a single tall flower stalk. **Habitat and range:**
Fields, roadsides, disturbed sites; a European native, now widely naturalized
in temperate North America. **Herbal lore:** An Old World cure for earache,
mullein flowers have been steeped in olive oil, and the oil then dribbled into
the afflicted ear. In Peterson Field Guides' *Field Guide to Medicinal Plants:
Eastern and Central North America,* Foster and Duke report on a number of
health conditions that have been treated with mullein. The leaves, they say,
are "high in mucilage" and therefore "soothing to inflamed mucous membranes." The plant has been used as a remedy for many bronchial conditions,
and the leaves have been poulticed on tumors, ulcers, and piles. "Asian Indians used the stalk for cramps, fevers and migraine," according to Foster and
Duke. In her book *Wildflower Folklore,* Laura C. Martin notes a very different use for mullein plant stalks: Roman soldiers dipped them in tallow and
burned them as torches. She also claims that Roman women employed the
plant's yellow dye for hair color. **On Sugarloaf—Blooming time:** June–September. **Locations:** Yellow Trail, roadsides. **Similar species:** Clasping-leaved
mullein *(V. phlomoides),* a less commonly naturalized European species,
grows in some fields adjacent to Sugarloaf. Its leaves are rounded, cordate, or
truncate at the base, and they clasp the plant stalk. They are not decurrent or
only mildly so.

Foxglove Beardtongue (White Beardtongue)

Penstemon digitalis Nutt. ex Sims
Snapdragon or Figwort Family (Scrophulariaceae)

Many beardtongue species (*Penstemon* spp.) grow in eastern North America,
and several are native to Maryland. Foxglove beardtongue is the only one
we've encountered on Sugarloaf. **Flowers:** Irregular, white to pale lavender,
tubular and flared with a 2-lobed upper lip and 3-lobed, often purple-
striped lower lip. Flowers ¾–1¼" long in ascending terminal clusters (panicles). **Leaves:** Stem leaves opposite, simple; oblong, lanceolate, or triangular,
usually toothed, sessile, 1–4" long. Leaf base rounded or heart-shaped (cordate). There may be a basal rosette of larger petioled leaves that are elliptic
or oblanceolate. **Height:** 1–4'. **Habitat and range:** Open woods, fields
and prairies, roadsides; eastern United States and Canada. **On Sugarloaf—
Blooming time:** May–July. **Locations:** Yellow Trail, mountain roads; likely
elsewhere but not common on the mountain. **Similar species:** Could be confused with monkey flowers (*Mimulus* spp.), which have yellow blushes at the
center of their flowers, or turtlehead *(Chelone glabra),* which is later blooming and bears white flowers with downward arching upper lips in dense
spikes.

Downy False-Foxglove

Aureolaria virginica (L.) Pennell
(Gerardia virginica)
Snapdragon or Figwort Family (Scrophulariaceae)

Downy false-foxglove is a summer-blooming plant of eastern North America that grows along Sugarloaf's trails and roadsides. **Flowers:** Sun-yellow, funnel-shaped, flaring to 5 shallow, rounded lobes; 1–2" long, borne terminally and from the uppermost leaf axils. **Leaves:** Opposite, simple (although lower leaves may be deeply lobed), with short petioles to sessile or nearly so. Upper leaves ovate-lanceolate, usually entire. Lower leaves often with blunt teeth or deeply cut lobes. Leaves are downy-pubescent to the touch and variable in length (from less than an inch to several inches long). Plant stalk also downy. **Height and growth habits:** 2–4'; branched or unbranched. **Habitat and range:** Dry woods and borders of dry woods; Massachusetts to Ontario and Michigan; south to Florida and Alabama. **On Sugarloaf—Blooming time:** June–August. **Locations:** White Trail, Mount Ephraim Road, other trails and roadsides. **Similar species:** A later-blooming species, fern-leaved

Downy
False-Foxglove

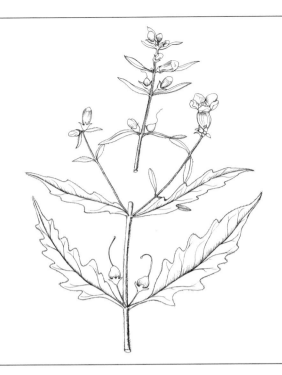

false-foxglove *(A. pedicularia)*, is rare on the mountain. This species is similar to downy false-foxglove, but it blooms during the fall and has a viscid-pubescent plant stalk and finely cut fernlike leaves. Two additional false-foxglove species are indigenous to Maryland (*see* Brown and Brown's *Herbaceous Plants of Maryland* for illustrations and descriptions).

Turtlehead (White Turtlehead, Balmony)

Chelone glabra L.
Snapdragon or Figwort Family (Scrophulariaceae)

Turtlehead serves as the principal host plant for the Baltimore checkerspot butterfly *(Euphydryas phaeton)*, Maryland's official state insect (*see* "Wildlife lore" *below*). This plant has also enjoyed a rich herbal history. Turtlehead arises from Sugarloaf's springs and seeps along Mount Ephraim Road and the Yellow Trail. **Flowers:** White or pale pink, irregular, 2-lipped (the upper lip arching downward and strongly suggesting a turtle's head). Flowers about 1" long, in dense spikes. **Leaves:** Opposite, simple, lanceolate, toothed. Sessile or nearly so, 2½–6" long. **Height and growth habits:** 1–3'; unbranched or branched toward the top. **Habitat and range:** Wet woods and meadows, marshes, seeps, and stream banks; Newfoundland to Minnesota, south to Georgia and Alabama. **Herbal lore:** Turtlehead leaves have been used in ointments for piles, ulcers, herpes, and inflamed breasts, according to Foster and Duke in Peterson Field Guides' *Field Guide to Medicinal Plants: Eastern and Central North America*. Hutchens reports in *Indian Herbalogy of North America*: "Balmony [turtlehead] is a bitter tonic and among the best medicine there is for improving appetite. When the stomach action is weak, balmony has a stimulating influence." She also writes that the plant "is regarded by some physicians as having no superior in expelling worms," adding, "When worms are present, we have found they are more prone to treatment each month at full moon." Worm sufferers beware: do not try to harvest this or any other plant on Sugarloaf, even when the moon is full!

Wildlife lore: The Baltimore checkerspot (sometimes called simply "the Baltimore") is one of our most beautiful butterflies, its orange, black, and white pattern suggesting the crest of Lord Baltimore. However, as development has meant the disappearance of the moist habitats required by the Baltimore checkerspot's only local host plant, the turtlehead, the butterfly has become locally rare to uncommon. Deer have also wreaked havoc on turtlehead populations. During 2002 the Baltimore checkerspot was officially listed as a threatened species in Maryland. Butterfly conservationist Pat Durkin (cofounder of the Washington Area Butterfly Club) explains the life cycle of the Baltimore checkerspot and how it is tied to the turtlehead: "The butterfly has only one brood each year, which flies for only three weeks from mid-June to early July. The females lay their eggs at this time on the turtlehead leaves. The caterpillars hatch a few days later and spin communal webs on the plant,

Turtlehead

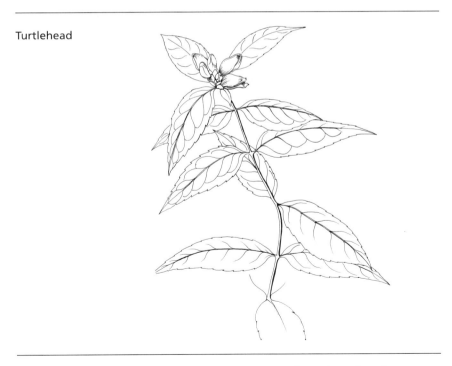

usually embracing several leaves. When they consume those leaves, they move onto others. They eat, grow, and shed skins three times before frost. Shorter days and colder nights stimulate them to descend the plant, roll themselves into some duff beneath it, and convert the water in their bodies to an organic antifreeze so they don't freeze. Right about now [she wrote on March 25] they are becoming active again, returning to the turtlehead for two more instars before turning into chrysalids later in the spring. They emerge in June to start the cycle all over again." **On Sugarloaf—Blooming time:** August–October. **Locations:** Wet areas on lower parts of the mountain: most common along Mount Ephraim Road. **Similar species:** Foxglove beardtongue *(Penstemon digitalis)* blooms earlier in the summer in dry habitats, and its upper lip is 2-lobed and opening upward or outward (rather than arching downward). Red turtlehead *(Chelone obliqua)* is a very rare, threatened plant of Maryland's coastal plain (not found on Sugarloaf). It has deep pink flowers.

Butter-and-Eggs

Linaria vulgaris Mill.
Snapdragon or Figwort Family (Scrophulariaceae)

Flowers are butter yellow and egg-yolk orange and bear a strong resemblance to the cultivated snapdragon (which is in the same family). **Flowers:** Irregular, in a crowded upright raceme; flowers yellow with a darker blush

Butter-and-Eggs

on the upper part of the lower lip. The 2-lipped flowers are 2-lobed above and 3-lobed below and bear a slender spur at the back. About an inch (plus or minus) long. **Leaves:** Alternate (but may be nearly opposite), simple, small, and linear with entire margins. Sessile or tapered to a petiole-like base, ½–2" long. **Height:** 6"–3'. **Habitat and range:** Dry fields, roadsides; a European native now widely naturalized in temperate North America. **Herbal lore:** In Peterson Field Guides' *Field Guide to Medicinal Plants: Eastern and Central North America,* Foster and Duke report: "In folk medicine, leaf tea used as a laxative, strong diuretic; for dropsy, jaundice, enteritis with drowsiness, skin diseases, piles. Ointment made from flowers used for piles, skin eruptions. A 'tea' made in milk has been used as an insecticide." **On Sugarloaf—Blooming time:** June–October. **Locations:** Mount Ephraim Road; other mountain roadsides and possible along open sections of trail. **Similar species:** None on Sugarloaf.

Square-Stemmed Monkey-Flower
Mimulus ringens L.
Snapdragon or Figwort Family (Scrophulariaceae)

Use your imagination to see a monkey's face in this flower. **Flowers:** Irregular, pinkish, violet or blue-violet (rarely white) with a yellow blush at the center; 2-lipped with a 2-lobed upper lip and broader 3-lobed lower lip. Calyx narrow, tubular, with 5 vertical ribs, each rib ending in a sharp, thin tooth. Flower stalk longer than the calyx. Flowers about an inch long (give or take), including the calyx and ⅔–1⅓" wide. Borne from the upper leaf axils. **Leaves:** Opposite, simple, toothed; lanceolate, oblong, or oblanceolate, usually tapered to the base (sometimes rounded at the base), sessile. Lower leaves 1½–4" long, upper leaves much smaller. Plant stalk more or less squared and slightly ridged. **Height:** 1–3'. **Habitat and range:** Wet meadows and woods, freshwater marshes, river and stream banks, edges of ponds; Nova Scotia and Quebec to Saskatchewan, south to Georgia, Louisiana, and Oklahoma. **On Sugarloaf—Blooming time:** June–September (this species and the one mentioned under "Similar species"). **Locations:** Yellow Trail (near spring on eastern side of the mountain); look for both species of monkey-flower in damp soils around the mountain base. **Similar species:** Winged monkey-flower *(M. alatus)* has been reported on the mountain, although we have yet to see it here. Distinguish winged monkey-flower, which is less common on Sugarloaf, by its petioled leaf and flower stalk shorter than the calyx. Winged monkey-flower usually has thin "wings" along the ridges of the plant stalk.

Maryland Figwort (Carpenter's Square)

Scrophularia marilandica L.
Snapdragon or Figwort Family (Scrophulariaceae)

Maryland figwort has reddish-brown or greenish irregular **flowers** in large, branched terminal clusters. Individual flowers are ¼–⅔" long, 2-lipped, with an erect 2-lobed upper lip and the middle lobe of the lower lip bent downward. In addition to the 4 developed stamens, 1 showy purple or brown sterile stamen is borne under the upper lip of the flower. **Leaves** are opposite, simple, ovate or broadly lanceolate, coarsely toothed, long-petioled; leaf blade 3–10" long. **Height:** 3–8'. **Habitat and range:** Open woods; Quebec to Minnesota, south to South Carolina and Louisiana. **On Sugarloaf—Blooming time:** June–August. **Location:** Blue Trail along the northern ridge of the mountain. Rare on Sugarloaf. **Similar species:** None likely on Sugarloaf. A similar species, hare figwort *(S. lanceolata),* is also native to Maryland. It bears a greenish-yellow sterile stamen, and its flowers are glossy on the outside, while Maryland figwort's are dull.

Common Speedwell

Veronica officinalis L.
Snapdragon or Figwort Family (Scrophulariaceae)

A trailing plant with upright clusters of small flowers. **Flowers:** White or pale lavender with darker lavender stripes, ¼" or less across, 4-lobed; the lowest of the 4 lobes narrower than the upper 3. Growing in upright clusters (racemes) from the upper leaf axils. **Leaves:** Opposite, simple, regularly toothed, short-stalked or sessile. Elliptic, ovate, or obovate, usually narrowing to the base, ½–2" long, softly pubescent. **Height and growth habits:** 4–

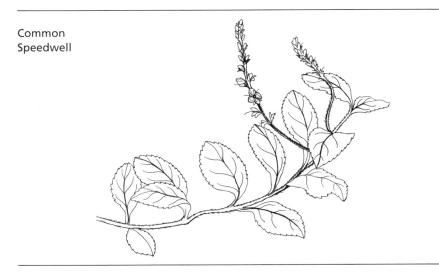

Common
Speedwell

10", trailing along the ground and culminating in one or more usually up-right flower clusters. **Habitat and range:** Fields, woods; a European native now widely established here. **Herbal lore:** Traditional European herbal. Root or leaf tea had many uses as a diuretic, expectorant, and tonic. **On Sugar-loaf—Blooming time:** May–July. **Locations:** Yellow Trail; mountain base and roadsides; quite common on and around Sugarloaf. **Similar species:** Bird's-eye speedwell *(V. persica)* has blue and white flowers growing on long stalks. Bird's-eye speedwell flowers are produced singly, rather than in clusters, although there are often several flowers per plant. Thyme-leaved speedwell *(V. serpyllifolia)* has tiny leaves that are entire or only slightly toothed.

Bird's-Eye Speedwell

Veronica persica Poir.
Snapdragon or Figwort Family (Scrophulariaceae)

A small and delicate sprawling plant. Native to Asia, it has become natural-ized in lawns, gardens, and waste places across North America. **Flowers:** Blue and white, more or less striped, irregular, with 4 lobes of unequal size (the

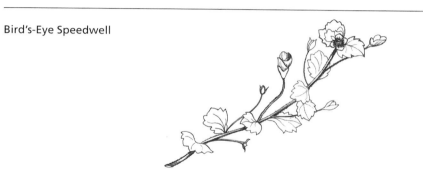

Bird's-Eye Speedwell

lower one narrowest); ¼" or less across on long stalks, growing singly (but usually several per plant) from the leaf axils. **Leaves:** Simple, lower leaves op-posite, but upper ones may sometimes be alternate. Small, ovate or elliptic, ¼–3/4" long with blunt teeth. Short-stalked to nearly sessile. Plant stalk prostrate and hairy. **On Sugarloaf—Blooming time:** Late winter through summer. **Locations:** Mountain base in mowed areas; Bear Branch. **Similar species:** Thyme-leaved speedwell *(V. serpyllifolia)* has leaves that are entire or only slightly toothed. Common speedwell *(V. officinalis)* bears small clusters of white or pale lavender flowers with darker lavender stripes. Several other *Veronica* species, some of them introduced from Europe and Asia, are found in Maryland. Consult Brown and Brown's *Herbaceous Plants of Maryland* or *Newcomb's Wildflower Guide* if you find a *Veronica* species which doesn't fit the descriptions given in this book.

Thyme-Leaved Speedwell
Veronica serpyllifolia L.
Snapdragon or Figwort Family (Scrophulariaceae)

Thyme-leaved speedwell, introduced from Europe and now widely natural-ized, can be found in grassy areas on and near Sugarloaf. It differs from the preceding speedwell *(Veronica)* species in the following ways: the small **leaves** are entire or only slightly toothed. The blue and white **flowers** are borne in elongated terminal clusters (racemes). **On Sugarloaf—Blooming time:** Spring–summer. **Similar species:** The blue and white flowers of bird's-eye speedwell *(V. persica)* are borne singly (although there are usually several per plant), from the leaf axils, and common speedwell *(V. officinalis)* bears white and lavender flowers. Both bird's-eye and common speedwell have regularly toothed leaves.

Tree

Paulownia (Royal Paulownia, Empress Tree, or Princess Tree)
Paulownia tomentosa (Thunb.) Siebold & Zucc. ex Steud.
Snapdragon or Figwort Family (Scrophulariaceae)

An Asian ornamental that was brought to this country during the 1800s, paulownia has escaped from garden cultivation and become widely natural-ized in the eastern and midwestern United States. The tree is named for Anna Paulowna, a nineteenth-century princess of the Netherlands. Very few paulownia trees are growing on Sugarloaf, but the tree thrives along nearby stretches of the Potomac. It is a quick-growing but short-lived tree. **Flow-ers:** Tall candelabra-like clusters of fuzzy tan flower buds unfurl to fragrant lavender flowers in May. Each erect flower cluster up to 12" tall with 20 or more flowers per cluster. Irregular flowers unevenly 5-lobed, bell-shaped, downy, yellow and white inside, with velvety tan sepals. Flowers 1½–2¾" long, appearing just before the leaves. (Paulownia is a late leafer.) **Fruit:** Up-right clusters of woody, ovoid, nutlike 1–2" capsules. Each capsule has a sharp beak at the apex. Capsules split in half to release winged seeds. **Leaves:** Simple, opposite, deciduous. Large, heart-shaped (cordate), downy all over. Margin entire (but young trees often bear leaves with 2 shallow lobes near the base); 4–10" long, or longer. Petiole 2½–8" long, densely pubescent. **Growth habits:** Tree with stout spreading branches forming a rounded crown. **Bark and twigs:** Bark light brown or gray; may be slightly furrowed. Twigs stout, reddish-brown with rounded leaf scars. (Pith chambered or hollow.) In winter mature trees usually have clusters of both this year's fruit and next year's flower buds. **Habitat and range:** Naturalized in woods, fields, vacant lots, along rivers, roads, and railroad tracks throughout our area and

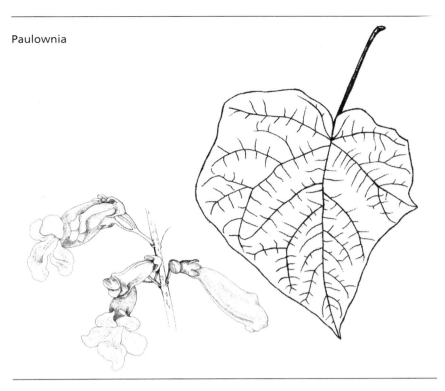

much of the eastern United States. Native of China, cultivated in Japan and Europe for several centuries. **Herbal lore:** According to Foster and Duke (Peterson Field Guides' *Field Guide to Medicinal Plants: Eastern and Central North America*), "In China, a wash of the leaves and capsules was used in daily applications to promote the growth of hair and prevent graying. Leaf tea was used as a foot bath for swollen feet. Inner-bark tincture (soaked in 2 parts whisky) given for fevers and delirium. Leaves or ground bark were fried in vinegar, poulticed on bruises. Flowers were mixed with other herbs to treat liver ailments. In Japan the leaf juice is used to treat warts. Warning: Contains potentially toxic compounds." **On Sugarloaf—Blooming time:** May–June. **Locations:** Roadsides (including the road up the mountain); some trailsides but not common. **Similar species:** None likely on the mountain proper, but leaves could be confused with catalpa (*Catalpa* spp.) leaves. Two native American catalpas and an Asian species are widely cultivated in the Washington-Baltimore area, and the American species are prone to escape from cultivation (rarely the Asian tree does too). The American catalpas bear white flowers; the Asian produces yellow ones. Catalpa fruit is a long, slender beanlike capsule. In the absence of flowers or fruit, examine the leaves (catalpas are often whorled) and the inside of the twigs. Catalpa twigs have solid piths.

Broomrape Family

Orobanchaceae

Plants of the broomrape family typically lack chlorophyll and exist by feeding parasitically from the roots of other plants. **Family characteristics:** 17 genera and 150 species worldwide. **Flowers:** Irregular, perfect (except in *Epifagus* genus), calyx 2–5 lobed, corolla 4–5 lobed. **Fruit:** A capsule. **Leaves:** Alternate, scalelike, whitish, brownish, or yellowish. **Growth habits:** Root-parasitic herbs. **Occurrence on Sugarloaf:** Squawroot *(Conopholis americana)* is quite common, especially along Mount Ephraim Road near Bear Branch. One-flowered cancer-root or ghost-pipe *(Orobanche uniflora)* is uncommon on the mountain. A third species, not treated in this guide, is likely here, but we have not seen it: beechdrops *(Epifagus virginiana)* blooms from August to October beneath beech trees.

Squawroot

Conopholis americana (L.f.) Wallr.
Broomrape Family (Orobanchaceae)

A strange-looking fleshy parasitic plant growing in clusters above tree roots. Each plant resembles an elongate pine cone and is yellowish overall, turning brown. **Flowers:** Creamy yellow, irregular and tubular, ⅛–½" long, growing up and down the stout fleshy plant stalk, each flower horizontal or curving downward above a brownish scale. **Height and growth habits:** 2–8"; upright or leaning, with very stout yellowish stalk. **Habitat and range:** Rich woods (parasitic on tree roots); Nova Scotia to Wisconsin, south to Florida and Alabama. **On Sugarloaf—Blooming time:** Spring–early summer. **Locations:** Woods near Mount Ephraim Road; Yellow Trail, Blue Trail; moderately com-

Squawroot

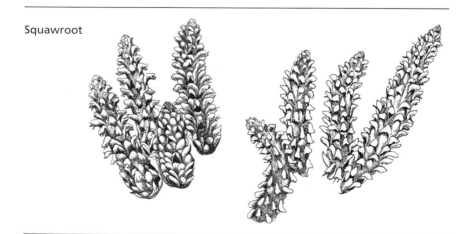

mon mountainwide but often camouflaged on forest floor. **Similar species:** The very stout plant stalk distinguishes this plant from similar species.

One-Flowered Cancer-Root (Ghost-Pipe, One-Flowered Broomrape)

Orobanche uniflora L.
Broomrape Family (Orobanchaceae)

A parasitic plant lacking chlorophyll. **Flowers:** Creamy white or pale lavender, 5-lobed, ¾–1" long, funnel-shaped, and widely flared. One to several single flowers; each flower on an individual 2–10" creamy white glandular-pubescent stalk. No apparent leaves. **Habitat and range:** Moist woods and

One-Flowered
Cancer-Root

stream banks; United States and Canada. **On Sugarloaf—Blooming time:** April–June. **Locations:** Blue Trail and other trails, Mount Ephraim Road. **Similar species:** The only Sugarloaf wildflower with which cancer-root is apt to be confused is the Indian pipe *(Monotropa uniflora),* which has a stiff waxy flower and thick (but not stout) scaly stalk.

Bignonia or Trumpet-Creeper Family

Bignoniaceae

This family of trees, shrubs, and woody vines (rarely herbs) is represented on Sugarloaf by a climbing vine with showy orange-red flowers: the trumpet creeper *(Campsis radicans).* Mainly a tropical family, with many important ornamental and timber species, the family includes two trees indigenous to the southern and central United States: the northern catalpa *(Catalpa speciosa)* and the southern catalpa *(C. bignonioides).* Both have been widely planted in the East, where they have become naturalized in many places, including in our region. (However, neither has been identified on Sugarloaf.) **Family characteristics:** Woody plants of this family of 100 or more genera and 800 species usually have 5 sepals and 5-lobed (frequently showy bell- or funnel-shaped) **flowers.** The **fruit** is a capsule, often elongated. **Leaves** are usually opposite; simple or compound.

Woody Vine

Trumpet Creeper

Campsis radicans (L.) Seem. ex Bureau
Bignonia or Trumpet-Creeper Family (Bignoniaceae)

A trailing or (more often) climbing woody vine of the eastern and central United States; moderately common in thickets and hedgerows on and around Sugarloaf. **Flowers:** Brilliant orange-red trumpet-shaped flowers, culminating in 5 shallow, spreading lobes; 2–3" long in showy terminal clus-

Trumpet Creeper

ters. **Leaves:** Opposite, odd-pinnately compound, with 5–13 sharply toothed, ovate-lanceolate leaflets. **Habitat and range:** Woods, hedgerows, thickets, and roadsides; eastern and central United States. As Brown and Brown point out in *Woody Plants of Maryland,* trumpet creeper is "very plentiful in old tobacco fields in Southern part of Maryland." **On Sugarloaf—Blooming time:** June–September. **Locations:** Mostly along roadsides (mountainwide); some trailsides. **Similar species:** When in flower not likely to be confused with any other plant in our native flora.

Bellflower or Bluebell Family

Campanulaceae
[Including plants sometimes placed in a separate family—the Lobelia Family (Lobeliaceae)]

This family, containing many plants that are valued garden ornamentals, is well represented on Sugarloaf. **Family characteristics:** 70 genera and 2,000 species worldwide in temperate, tropical, and subtropical zones. **Economic importance:** Ornamentals, some medicinals. **Flowers:** Usually 5-parted with petals or lobes united and often extending from a bell-shaped or tubular base. Many members of the family have blue flowers, although our most spectacular native family member—the cardinal flower *(Lobelia cardinalis)*—has scarlet flowers. Regular or irregular. Usually borne in clusters. **Fruit:** A capsule or berry. **Leaves:** Alternate (rarely opposite), usually simple. **Growth habits:** Mostly herbs; some shrubs and trees. **Occurrence on Sugarloaf:** Several species in a variety of habitats. An important Sugarloaf wildflower family.

Venus's Looking-Glass

Triodanis perfoliata (L.) Nieuwl.
(Specularia perfoliata)
Bellflower or Bluebell Family (Campanulaceae)

A late spring to early summer wildflower, widely distributed in North America and extending southward into the Tropics. Venus's looking-glass is common along Sugarloaf's roadsides. **Flowers:** Violet, violet-blue, or violet-pink 5-lobed flowers grow from the upper leaf axils; ½–¾" across, stalkless or nearly so. **Leaves:** Alternate, simple, heart-shaped (cordate), ovate or round (rotund); sessile with cordate, clasping base; ¼–1¼" long, usually shallowly toothed. **Height:** 5–30". **Habitat and range:** Fields, rock outcrops, disturbed sites; Maine and British Columbia, south to Tropics. **On Sugarloaf—Blooming time:** May–July. **Locations:** Sugarloaf roadsides; also may be found along

Venus's
Looking-Glass

trails. **Similar species:** Combination of leaf shape and arrangement and flowers separate Venus's looking-glass from other Sugarloaf wildflowers.

Cardinal Flower

Lobelia cardinalis L.
Bellflower or Bluebell Family (Campanulaceae)

The cardinal flower, as vividly scarlet as the native bird, is one of the most striking wildflowers in the eastern North American flora. Cardinal flowers thrive in the seeps and on the stream banks along Mount Ephraim Road. A drive or stroll down this scenic road during late summer or early fall is apt to yield sight of these brilliantly hued flowers in bloom. **Flowers:** Scarlet, irregular, 2-lipped, with a 2-lobed upper lip, a 3-lobed lower one, and a tubular base. Sexual parts protrude in a beaklike fashion. Flowers 1–2" long and wide in upright clusters (racemes); 5 sepals are thin (almost hairlike). **Leaves:** Alternate, simple, lanceolate to oblong or narrowly ovate, tapered to apex and base, pubescent or glabrous. Toothed, often irregularly so (sometimes dentate). Short-petioled to sessile, 2–7" long. **Height and growth habits:** 1–5'; usually unbranched. **Habitat and range:** Stream and river banks, seeps, springs, marshes, pond edges, and wet meadows; New Brunswick to Minnesota, south to the Gulf of Mexico. **Herbal lore:** American Indians used the roots and leaves of this plant for a number of conditions, including syphilis, typhoid, fevers, headaches, and rheumatism. In Peterson Field Guides' *Field Guide to Medicinal Plants: Eastern and Central North America,* Foster and Duke report that cardinal flower's root tea was considered both a worm expellant and a love potion! The plant is potentially toxic. Please remember that all plants on Sugarloaf and most other eastern North American natural areas are protected and must not be disturbed. **On Sugarloaf—Blooming time:** July–September. **Locations:** Mount Ephraim Road, Comus Road, Yellow Trail. **Similar species:** Bee-balm or Oswego-tea *(Monarda didyma)* grows along the lower stretches of Bear Branch. Its scarlet flowers are borne in dense roundish terminal heads, and its leaves are opposite. Other local *Lobelia* species are blue or bluish-white.

Cardinal Flower

Indian Tobacco

Lobelia inflata L.
Bellflower or Bluebell Family (Campanulaceae)

Indian tobacco has a long history of herbal use among American Indians. The plant has toxic properties (*see* "Herbal lore" *below*). Indian tobacco is one of Sugarloaf's most common summer wildflowers. **Flowers:** Pale blue, lavender, or (rarely) white, with a cream or yellow blush at the center; irregular, with 3 pointed lower lobes and 2 narrower upper lobes. Flowers small (¼–⅓" long) in upright terminal clusters (racemes) and/or growing from the upper leaf axils. As the corolla withers, the calyx swells to a round or ovoid shape (thus the Latin *inflata*). **Leaves:** Alternate, simple, with (some-

Indian
Tobacco

times white-tipped) teeth. Ovate, oblong, or obovate, sessile or nearly so, usually hairy below; ½–2½" long. **Height and growth habits:** 6–30"; often branching. **Habitat and range:** Dry open woods, fields; southeastern Canada to Minnesota, south to Georgia and Mississippi. **Herbal lore:** American Indians smoked the leaves to remedy sore throats, asthma, and other bronchial conditions. Indian tobacco was used to treat fevers and whooping cough, as a sedative, and to induce sweating and vomiting, according to Foster and Duke. In Peterson Field Guides' *Field Guide to Medicinal Plants: Eastern and Central North America,* they report, "Lobeline, one of 14 alkaloids in the plant, is used in commercial 'quit smoking' lozenges and chewing gums— said to appease physical need for nicotine without addictive effects." They caution that the plant is considered toxic "due to its strong emetic, expectorant, and sedative effects," adding, "This plant has rightly or wrongly been implicated in deaths from improper use as a home remedy." **On Sugarloaf— Blooming time:** July–November. **Locations:** Mountain trails and roadsides; common along the road up the mountain. **Similar species:** At a glance it resembles some of the summer mints, all of which have opposite leaves. Spiked lobelia *(L. spicata)* is rare on the mountain. It is a taller plant with a long, leafless flower cluster. Its leaves are only slightly toothed or smooth-margined, and some form a basal rosette. Spiked lobelia blooms along Mount Ephraim Road earlier in the summer. Great blue lobelia *(L. siphilitica)* is a much bigger plant with larger deep blue flowers.

Great Blue Lobelia (Great Lobelia)

Lobelia siphilitica L.
Bellflower or Bluebell Family (Campanulaceae)

American Indians used the root of great blue lobelia to treat syphilis, giving rise to its Latin name, *Lobelia siphilitica.* Like its sister plant the cardinal flower *(L. cardinalis),* great blue lobelia is a Sugarloaf wildflower of uncommon beauty. **Flowers:** Deep sapphire or violet, irregular, 2-lipped, the upper lip 2-lobed, the lower lip 3-lobed. Lips are joined to form a tube, which is striped white on its lower side. Flowers ¾–1" long, in a dense upright raceme. **Leaves:** Alternate, simple, lanceolate-elliptic, oblong, or oblanceolate, shallowly and irregularly toothed, sessile, 2–5" long. **Height:** 1–3'. **Habitat and range:** Swamps, stream banks, wet ground; Maine to Manitoba and Colorado, south to North Carolina and Texas. **Herbal lore:** As well as employing the root as a syphilis treatment, American Indians used the leaves of this plant to treat a number of internal ailments, including coughs, croup, worms, and nosebleeds. The leaves were also used as poultices for persistent sores. **On Sugarloaf—Blooming time:** August–October. **Locations:** Wet areas along Mount Ephraim Road; possible along moist stretches of Yellow,

Great Blue Lobelia

Blue, and White Trails. **Similar species:** Other blue lobelias on Sugarloaf have paler flowers. The flowers of this plant are deeply hued.

Spiked Lobelia (Pale-Spike Lobelia)

Lobelia spicata Lam.
Bellflower or Bluebell Family (Campanulaceae)

Spiked lobelia resembles a summer-blooming orchid at first glance. Our rarest lobelia on Sugarloaf, a few specimens of this tall but delicate wildflower grow along Mount Ephraim Road. **Flowers:** Pale lavender, pale blue, or creamy white with the lower lip 3-lobed and the upper lip smaller and 2-lobed. Lobes extend from a small tube. Flowers each ¼–⅓" long and wide, borne in a spikelike raceme. **Leaves:** Alternate, simple, and in a basal rosette.

Stem leaves few, with shallow, irregular white-tipped teeth or margins nearly entire; lanceolate or obovate, sessile or short-stalked, ¾–3" long. Basal leaves larger, usually obovate or ovate, paler and downy below. **Height and growth habits:** 1–3', usually single-stalked. **Habitat and range:** Variable habitat; eastern Canada to Minnesota, south to Georgia and Arkansas. **On Sugarloaf— Blooming time:** June–July. **Location:** Mount Ephraim Road. **Similar species:** Indian tobacco *(L. inflata)* is usually a smaller plant with a branched growth habit. Its calyx becomes much more inflated as the flower fades (only slight inflating in spiked lobelia). Indian tobacco is far more common on Sugarloaf. Great blue lobelia *(L. siphilitica)* has larger, deeper blue flowers and grows in wet areas. A casual look at spiked lobelia could suggest an orchid, such as downy rattlesnake-plantain *(Goodyera pubescens)*. Compare leaves.

Madder Family

Rubiaceae

This family is best known for coffee, quinine, and gardenias. Several wildflowers belonging to the madder family grow on Sugarloaf. **Family characteristics:** 450 genera and 6,500 species worldwide. Cosmopolitan but mostly tropical and subtropical. **Economic importance:** In addition to coffee *(Coffea)*, quinine *(Cinchona)*, and gardenia *(Gardenia)*, madder family genera include other medicinals, dye plants, and ornamentals. **Flowers:** Perfect, mostly regular, usually with 4 or 5 sepals and 4 or 5 petals. **Fruit:** A capsule or berry. **Leaves:** Opposite or whorled, simple, usually entire. **Growth habits:** Trees, shrubs, and herbs. **Occurrence on Sugarloaf:** Long-leaved houstonia—or long-leaved summer bluets—*(Houstonia longifolia)* is one of Sugarloaf's most prevalent summer wildflowers. The other species described and illustrated in the next entries are also fairly common on the mountain. Cleavers and wild licorice are in the bedstraw genus *(Galium)*. Several other members of the genus grow on or around the mountain or are indigenous to this area. Consult Brown and Brown's *Herbaceous Plants of Maryland* for a more thorough treatment of the *Galium* genus. A shrub called buttonbush *(Cephalanthus occidentalis)* is briefly described in the Botanical Key and Guide to Trees, Shrubs, and Woody Vines.

Cleavers

Galium aparine L.
Madder Family (Rubiaceae)

Cleavers is a member of the bedstraw genus, which is characterized by small, usually 4-lobed (sometimes 3-lobed) flowers, squared (4-angled) stems, and

whorled leaves. Cleavers and the following species, wild licorice *(G. circaezans)*, are the two most common bedstraws on Sugarloaf. **Flowers:** Tiny white or greenish-white 4-lobed flowers in small terminal and axillary clusters. Each flower about ⅛" across. **Leaves:** In whorls of (usually) 6–8; linear or narrowly oblanceolate, sessile, and bristle-tipped. Stiff, rough hairs along the leaf margins, lower leaf blades, and plant stalk give the plant a prickly-sticky feeling. Leaves are sessile and vary in length from an inch or less to several inches. **Height and growth habits:** 10" to several feet, usually sprawling but often with upper third or so of plant upright. **Habitat and range:** Moist woods, thickets, and disturbed sites; most of temperate North America—circumpolar. **Herbal lore:** Cleavers has a solid herbal history as a diuretic, blood purifier, and folk remedy for cancer. **On Sugarloaf—Blooming time:** May–August. **Locations:** Mountain roadsides and trailsides; quite common on and around Sugarloaf. **Similar species:** Size of leaf whorls (6–8 leaves per whorl) and overall clingy-bristliness of plant separate cleavers from other bedstraws on the mountain.

Wild Licorice

Galium circaezans Michx.

Madder Family (Rubiaceae)

Wild licorice has tiny greenish **flowers**. Its **leaves** are in whorls of 4 and are wider than those of other *Galium* species. Another common Sugarloaf bedstraw. **Habitat and range:** Dry woods; eastern United States. **On Sugarloaf—Blooming time:** Late spring–early summer. **Locations:** Mountainwide.

Partridgeberry (Twinberry, Squawvine)

Mitchella repens L.

Madder Family (Rubiaceae)

A delicate woodland plant with small mid to late spring flowers, evergreen foliage, and red berries that persist through the winter. **Flowers:** White or pale pink, ½" long, usually in terminal pairs, with 4 (rarely 3, 5, or 6) flared

Partridgeberry

lobes that arise from a tube and are fuzzy on the upper surfaces. **Leaves:** Opposite, simple, round-ovate with blunt apex and entire margin; ¼–1" long. Dark evergreen with pale green or white central veins. **Fruit:** Small scarlet berries that are edible but tasteless. The two ovaries of the paired flowers ripen into a single "twin" berry. **Growth habits:** A trailing plant forming evergreen mats on the forest floor. **Habitat and range:** Woodlands; southeastern Canada to Florida and Texas. **Herbal lore:** An important herbal plant used by American Indian women for ease of childbirth. Partridgeberry has also been used internally as an antidote for difficult menstruation and externally as a remedy for sore nipples. **On Sugarloaf—Blooming time:** May–June. **Locations:** Blue Trail, Bear Branch, Mount Ephraim Road. **Similar species:** None on Sugarloaf.

Long-Leaved Houstonia (Long-Leaved Summer Bluets)

Houstonia longifolia Gaertn.
(Hedyotis longifolia)
Madder Family (Rubiaceae)

Long-leaved houstonia (or long-leaved summer bluets) blooms through the heat of the summer with springlike freshness and grace. This is a common Sugarloaf trailside wildflower. **Flowers:** White or pale lilac, ¼" long, funnel-shaped with 4 spreading lobes; in small terminal clusters. **Leaves:** Opposite, simple, sessile, with smooth margins. Oblong-lanceolate to nearly linear, ½–1½" long. Basal rosette of leaves may or may not be present at blooming

Long-Leaved
Houstonia

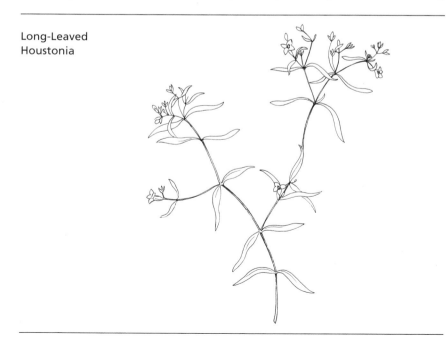

time. **Height and growth habits:** 4–10"; usually branched near the top. **Habitat and range:** Dry, rocky woods and rocky outcrops; southeastern Canada to South Carolina and Arkansas. **On Sugarloaf—Blooming time:** June–September. **Locations:** Trailsides and roadsides mountainwide. **Similar species:** Bluets *(Houstonia caerulea)* have slightly larger pale blue flowers and bloom in the spring. Other *Houstonia* species are found in Maryland but have not been reported on Sugarloaf.

Bluets (Quaker-Ladies)

Houstonia caerulea L.
(Hedyotis caerulea)
Madder Family (Rubiaceae)

A delicate flower of eastern North America, bluets grow in meadows, fields, lawns, and open woods. Bluets are common in the Washington-Baltimore area, but we haven't seen them growing on Sugarloaf. However, they have been reported on the mountain. Bluets' spring **flowers** are 4-lobed and pale blue, often with a yellow center. From ⅓" to ½" wide, they are slightly larger than long-leaved houstonia *(H. longifolia)* flowers. **Leaves** are opposite, simple, entire; up to ½" long at the base of the plant, where they often form a rosette. Smaller pairs of leaves higher on the plant stalk. **Blooming time:** April–September.

Honeysuckle Family

Caprifoliaceae

Members of the honeysuckle family produce fruit that is highly prized by wildlife. On and around Sugarloaf Mountain, birds and mammals feast on the fruit of the common elderberry *(Sambucus canadensis)*, Japanese honeysuckle *(Lonicera japonica)*, and viburnum species *(Viburnum)*. Local members of this family also provide twig and foliage browse for white-tailed deer. **Family characteristics:** 15 genera and 400 species throughout the world but mostly in temperate and boreal zones. **Economic importance:** Many ornamentals; elderberries *(Sambucus)* used in wine making. **Flowers:** Perfect, corolla usually 5-parted, regular or irregular. **Fruit:** Berry, drupe, or capsule. **Leaves:** Opposite, usually simple (pinnately compound in *Sambucus*). **Growth habits:** Shrubs and small trees, woody vines. **Occurrence on Sugarloaf:** Viburnums are fairly common, especially along mountain roads. Common elder grows mainly at and near the mountain base. Japanese honeysuckle is an invasive vine which can be found almost anywhere but is most abundant in hedgerows, fields, disturbed sites, and open woods.

Japanese Honeysuckle

Lonicera japonica Thunb.
Honeysuckle Family (Caprifoliaceae)

"One of the worst plant pests yet introduced in Maryland" is how Brown and Brown describe this vigorous trailing, climbing, twining vine in their book *Woody Plants of Maryland*. Indeed, this Asian native, planted as an ornamental and for erosion control, has truly outworn its welcome everywhere in eastern North America where it has invaded field and woodland, crowding out and killing native plants. Japanese honeysuckle has made major inroads in Sugarloaf country, smothering hedgerows and invading wooded habitats, especially at lower elevations. However, its flowers contribute mightily to the romance of June. Their fragrance is somewhere between orange blossom and gardenia, and they appear during firefly season. On a moonlit night nearing the summer solstice, the spell is hypnotic. Which is not to forgive or forget the destructive power of this plant. **Flowers:** White (turning yellow with age), irregular, with a long, narrow, curved lower lip and wider, lobed upper lip. Lips emerge from a long, narrow tube. Stamens and pistil prominent. Flowers 1¼–2" long, very fragrant, growing from the leaf axils,

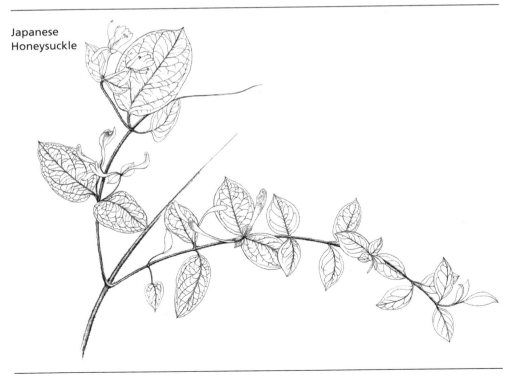

Japanese
Honeysuckle

often in pairs. **Fruit:** A small black berry. **Leaves:** Simple, opposite, ovate or oblong, mostly entire (on young spring growth the leaves are often toothed or lobed), short-stalked or nearly sessile. Leaves 1–3" long. **On Sugarloaf— Blooming time:** Late spring–early summer and then again some years lightly blooming in the fall. **Fruiting time:** Late summer–fall. **Locations:** Unfortunately ubiquitous. **Similar species:** Tartarian honeysuckle *(L. tatarica)*, which is not treated individually in this guide, is a Eurasian shrub which has also escaped from cultivation and established itself in the fields and hedgerows ringing Sugarloaf. Its pink or white flowers appear in April and May, and its fused pairs of red berries mature around the time the Japanese honeysuckle is in full bloom.

Shrub

Common Elderberry (Elder)

Sambucus canadensis L.
Honeysuckle Family (Caprifoliaceae)

Common elderberry is used for wine and jelly making and has long been an important herbal. According to the Peterson Field Guides' *Trees and Shrubs,*

Common Elderberry

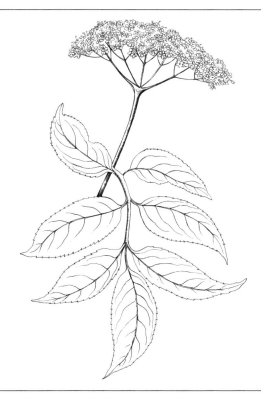

"Ripe fruits are eaten by 43 species of birds, including pheasant, mourning dove, and wild turkey." **Flowers:** Tiny (⅛–¼" across), usually 5-petaled, white or pale creamy yellow, in large flat-topped clusters (called cymes). **Fruit:** A purple-black berrylike drupe, edible when ripe. (However, bark, leaves, and unripe fruit contain toxins.) **Leaves:** Opposite, pinnately compound with 5-ll (usually 7) ovate, obovate, lanceolate, or elliptic leaflets. Leaflets toothed, 1½–4" long. Overall leaf several inches long. **Height and growth habits:** A 3–12' shrub. **Habitat and range:** Moist woods, fields, thickets, and roadsides; Nova Scotia and Quebec west to Manitoba, south to Mexico and the West Indies. **Herbal lore:** All parts of the elderberry have been used in herbal medicine, internally (including as a laxative and diuretic) and as a poultice for pain and swelling. *See* warning about toxicity *above*. **On Sugarloaf—Blooming time:** May–July. **Locations:** Moist areas of Sugarloaf, mostly around the mountain base. **Similar species:** When not in flower, could be confused with young ash trees (*Fraxinus* spp.). The red-berried elder *(S. racemosa)* bears flowers and red fruits in an elongated, rather than flat-topped, cluster. Not indigenous to Sugarloaf, red-berried elder can be found in the Maryland mountains farther west.

Shrub

Maple-Leaved Viburnum (Dockmackie)
Viburnum acerifolium L.
Honeysuckle Family (Caprifoliaceae)

Aptly named: but for its shrubby growth habit, this viburnum could easily be mistaken for a red maple. **Flowers:** Tiny, creamy white, with 5 lobes that are rounded, squared, or bluntly pointed at the apex. Individual flowers ¼" or less across in roundish, flat-topped clusters (cymes) 1–4" wide. **Leaves:**

Maple-Leaved
Viburnum

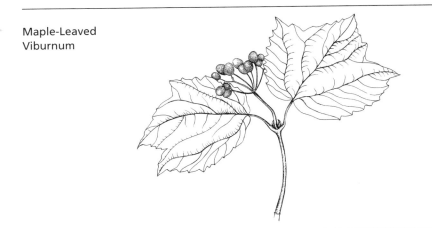

Opposite, simple, maplelike, usually 3-lobed, with toothed margin. Leaf blade is palmately veined, 2–6" long, downy-pubescent below, on ⅓–1" petiole. **Fruit:** A blue-black single-stoned drupe, ellipsoid to nearly round, ¼–⅓" long. Drupes borne in showy clusters. **Height and growth habits:** A 3–10' shrub. **Habitat and range:** Moist or dry woods; Quebec and New Brunswick to Minnesota, south to Florida and Louisiana. **On Sugarloaf—Blooming time:** April–June. **Locations:** Mount Ephraim Road; other Sugarloaf roadsides and trailsides. **Similar species:** The leaf closely resembles the leaf of the red maple *(Acer rubrum),* a tree that is common on the mountain. Use the shrubby growth habit, flowers, fruit, and pubescent leaves to distinguish maple-leaved viburnum from red maple. The other viburnums (*Viburnum* spp.) commonly found on Sugarloaf have unlobed leaves.

Shrubs or Small Trees

Other Viburnums (including arrowwoods)

Viburnum

Honeysuckle Family (Caprifoliaceae)

Ten or so other viburnums are native to the northeastern United States, and several additional species have become naturalized. A few grow on and around Sugarloaf. This can be a confusing genus for nonbotanists. Viburnums support a wide range of wildlife species. According to Brown and Brown's *Woody Plants of Maryland,* "The fruits are eaten by wild turkey, ruffed grouse, ring-necked pheasant and several species of thrushes and other large songbirds. Squirrels and rabbits eat the fruits or use the bark and twigs are important browse for deer."

Black-Haw (*Viburnum prunifolium* L.). **Flowers:** Small, white, fragrant, 5-lobed flowers in branched, flat-topped cluster (cyme). **Fruit:** Blue-black berrylike drupe. **Leaves:** Opposite, simple, ovate, oblong, elliptic, or obovate, with fine, sharp teeth. Glabrous to slightly scurfy-pubescent, on short petiole; 1–3" long. (Leaves resemble those of black cherry—*Prunus sero-*

Black-Haw

tina—but cherry's are alternate.) **Growth habits:** Large shrub or small tree. **Habitat and range:** Woods, thickets, roadsides; eastern and central United States. **Herbal lore:** According to Foster and Duke (Peterson Field Guides' *Field Guide to Medicinal Plants: Eastern and Central North America*), "Root- or stem-bark tea used by American Indians, then adopted by Europeans for painful menses, to prevent miscarriage, relieve spasms after childbirth. Considered uterine tonic, sedative, antispasmodic, and nervine. Also used for asthma. Research has confirmed uterine-sedative properties. Warning: Berries [which are actually drupes] may produce nausea and other discomforting symptoms." **On Sugarloaf—Blooming time:** April–May. **Locations:** Mount Ephraim Road and other Sugarloaf roadsides; possible along trails. **Similar species:** Use unlobed leaves with fine, sharp teeth to separate from other Sugarloaf viburnums.

Arrowwood (including Southern Arrowwood and Northern Arrowwood) (*V. dentatum* L.). Once considered two separate species, southern arrowwood *(V. dentatum)* and northern arrowwood *(V. recognitum)* have been "lumped" (joined under one botanical name) by some botanists. Arrowwood is a shrubby species of Mount Ephraim Road's springs and seepage swamps. The **leaves** are unlobed, strongly pinnately veined, and each

Arrowwood

lateral vein ends in a single coarse tooth. Margins bear 4–22 pairs of teeth. Petioles are ¼–1¼" long. Shrub 3–10' tall.

Downy Arrowwood (*V. rafinesquianum* Schult.) varies from the preceding species in minor ways. Its petiole is shorter than that of *V. dentatum* (usually ¼" or less, at least on leaves near flower clusters), and its **leaves** have only 4–10 pairs of teeth. The height of this shrub rarely surpasses 5'. I have never positively identified this plant on the mountain; it is listed in a 1987 Stronghold plant survey. Look for it in rocky, dry areas of the mountain.

See Brown and Brown's *Woody Plants of Maryland* for descriptions of additional indigenous viburnums.

Aster or Daisy Family

Asteraceae
(Compositae)

One of the largest and most recently evolved flowering plant families, the aster or daisy family is represented in the flora of every continent but Antarctica. Many familiar plants belong to this family, including sunflowers, daisies, marigolds, chrysanthemums, dandelions, lettuce, endive, chicory, and artichokes. Maryland's state flower—the black-eyed Susan *(Rudbeckia hirta)*—is a member of the aster family. **Family characteristics:** 1,100 genera and 20,000 species. Members of the family are common or abundant in wide-ranging habitats worldwide but are not common in tropical rain forests. **Economic importance:** Plants are sources of food, herbal medicine—purple coneflower *(Echinaceae purpurea)* is a family member—and garden ornamentals. **Flowers:** The flowers of the aster family are extremely complex. They are basically of two types, with enormous variation within the types, and what you see is not what you think you're seeing. A single daisy, for instance, is actually a multiflowered head containing many tiny disk or tubular flowers in the center, surrounded by many ray flowers, each ray appearing to be a single petal. Flower heads may contain both disk and ray flowers (daisy, black-eyed Susan, sunflower), just ray flowers (dandelion), or only disk flowers (thistles, burdock). Sometimes the flower heads are so tiny and tightly clustered that it's difficult to tell the disk flowers from the ray flowers (goldenrods contain both, but their disks and rays are minute). The disk or tubular flowers are usually regular and 5-lobed (this is often clear with the naked eye or a hand lens). The ray flowers are irregular. The leafy structures below the flower heads—what appear to be sepals—are actually modified leaves called involucral bracts or phyllaries. The calyx (all sepals together) may be modified into a pappus in this family. According to the definition in Brown and Brown's *Herbaceous Plants of Maryland,* the pappus of the aster family "is never green and leaflike [as in most plants]; it may be lacking, or modified into a ring of thin scales, barbed awns, or numerous, long bristles which may be barbed, plumose (branched), or smooth." **Fruit:** A dry fruit called an achene which may have pappus "hairs" and may be spread by wind or barbs that attach to passing animals (included humans). **Leaves:** Alternate or opposite, simple or compound. **Occurrence on Sugarloaf:** Several dozen species representing this family are found on Sugarloaf. One of our earliest wildflowers, the European herbal called coltsfoot *(Tussilago farfara)*, is a member of this family, but most aster family members bloom during summer and fall. Asters *(Aster),* goldenrods *(Sol-*

idago), and other family members are Sugarloaf's most common fall-blooming plants.

Golden Ragwort (Heart-Leaved Groundsel, Squaw-Weed)

Senecio aureus L.
Aster or Daisy Family (Asteraceae)

A spring woodland wildflower which looks as if it belongs in a late summer meadow with its golden blooms. **Flower heads:** Yellow rays surrounding golden disks in a typical daisy configuration; ½–1¼" across with only a few rays (about 7–12), in terminal clusters. **Leaves:** Two types. The basal leaves are simple, ovate or heart-shaped (cordate), with a deeply cordate base and roundish apex. Margins are tightly toothed with blunt teeth. Leaf blades 1–5" long, on long petioles. Stem leaves alternate, sparse, deeply pinnately lobed, and sessile or short-stalked. Central plant stalk may be sparsely hairy and sometimes purplish. **Height:** 1–3'. **Habitat and range:** Moist woods, swamps, wet fields; eastern Canada to Minnesota, south to Georgia and Arkansas. **Herbal lore:** Foster and Duke report in Peterson Field Guides' *Field Guide to Medicinal Plants: Eastern and Central North America* that golden ragwort was used by American Indians and settlers to treat menstrual irregularities, childbirth complications, lung problems, and dysentery. They also note that it may contain toxic alkaloids. **On Sugarloaf—Blooming time:** Late April–June. **Locations:** Mountain road; some trailsides. **Similar species:** *see* next entry, balsam ragwort *(S. pauperculus).* I have seen a few specimens of round-leaved ragwort *(S. obovatus)* growing in the Monocacy Natural Resources Management Area. Very similar to golden ragwort, it has basal leaves that are tapered (rather than cordate) at the base.

Golden Ragwort

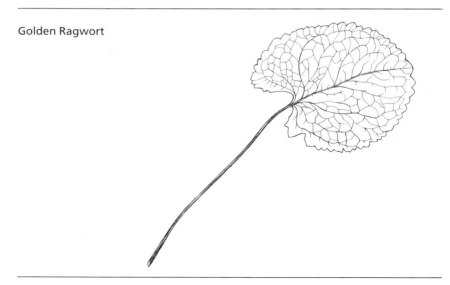

Round-Leaved
Ragwort

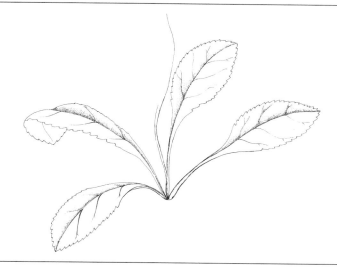

Balsam Ragwort

Senecio pauperculus Michx.
Aster or Daisy Family (Asteraceae)

This plant appears on the *Rare, Threatened, and Endangered Plants of Maryland* list as a watch list species, a designation meaning that it is not currently considered rare but could become rare in the future. **Flower heads and stem**

Balsam Ragwort

leaves are similar to those of the preceding entry, golden ragwort *(S. aureus)*. However, this plant blooms slightly later (May–July), and its basal leaves are narrowly elliptic-oblanceolate and tapered to the base. Compare illustrations. **Habitat and range:** Fields, meadows, prairies, beaches, and cliffs; Canada and northern United States (south to Georgia mountains in the East, Oregon in the West). **On Sugarloaf—Locations:** Mount Ephraim Road; road up the mountain; possible along open trailsides; fields and meadows ringing Sugarloaf.

Ox-Eye Daisy

Leucanthemum vulgare Lam.
(Chrysanthemum leucanthemum)
Aster or Daisy Family (Asteraceae)

"He loves me, he loves me not" are the words most often associated with this summer wildflower. A naturalized Eurasian species, ox-eye daisy blooms in fields and along roadsides across North America. Ox-eye daisies are abundant in the Sugarloaf region. **Flower heads:** Large, usually solitary heads (1–2½" across) at the terminus of a single stalk. Ray flowers white; disks a sunny

Ox-Eye Daisy

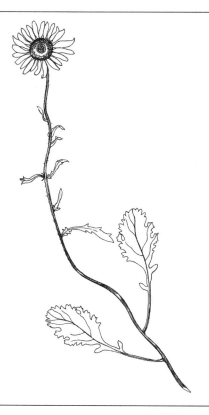

yellow. **Leaves:** Narrow alternate, simple leaves grow along the solitary stalk. Often small and linear toward the top, lower leaves are irregularly toothed and lobed (more dramatically so toward the base of the plant). Size variable. **Height:** 8"–3'. **Habitat and range:** Fields, meadows, roadsides; Eurasian native, now naturalized throughout most of temperate North America. **On Sugarloaf—Blooming time:** Late spring–summer. **Locations:** Roadsides, open trailsides; fields surrounding Sugarloaf. **Similar species:** Mayweed *(Anthemis cotula)* has finely dissected fernlike leaves with a disagreeable odor. A naturalized European species that is uncommon on Sugarloaf, mayweed is not described individually in this book.

Black-Eyed Susan

Rudbeckia hirta L.
Aster or Daisy Family (Asteraceae)

The black-eyed Susan is Maryland's state flower and one of our most beautiful summer wildflowers. **Flower heads:** Rays (8–21) are a strong, sunny golden-yellow surrounding a chocolate cone of disk flowers. Flower heads 1½–4" across, borne singly on a long, bristly stalk. **Leaves:** Alternate, simple, soft, and very bristly-hairy, with smooth margins or an occasional stray tooth. Lanceolate to oblong, upper leaves sessile, lower ones sometimes peti-

Black-Eyed
Susan

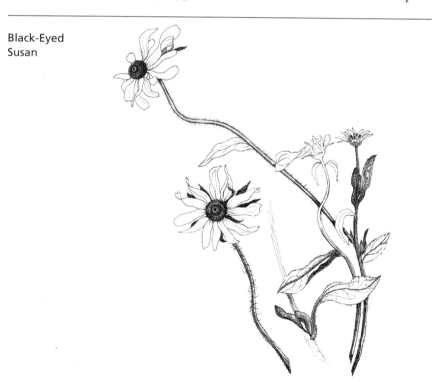

oled, 1½–6½" long. **Height and growth habits:** 1–3'. Usually single-stalked, but some plants growing along the roadsides develop multiple stalks after they have been mowed. **Habitat and range:** Meadows, roadsides, clearings; most of the United States, southern Canada, and into Mexico. **Herbal lore:** According to Foster and Duke (Peterson Field Guides' *Field Guide to Medicinal Plants: Eastern and Central North America*), American Indians used root tea to treat colds and expel worms and externally as a wash for swelling, body sores, and snakebite. They report that the root juice was used for earaches. They also warn that some people's skin is sensitive to the touch of the plant. **On Sugarloaf—Blooming time:** June–October. **Locations:** Clearings and roadsides mountainwide; abundant in local meadows. **Similar species:** Three-lobed (or thin-leaved) coneflower *(R. triloba)* has been reported on Sugarloaf. It has a branched growth habit (black-eyed Susan may be branching after it has been mowed), and its lowest leaves are usually 3-lobed.

Green-Headed Coneflower (Tall or Cut-Leaved Coneflower)

Rudbeckia laciniata L.
Aster or Daisy Family (Asteraceae)

A tall wildflower (3–10') with greenish-yellow central disk flowers and 6–16 drooping lemon-yellow rays. **Flower head** 1½–4" wide. The lower **leaves** are large, alternate, and deeply pinnately divided (appearing somewhat fernlike), with irregularly toothed, pointed lobes. Upper leaves merely 3-lobed, 2-lobed, or simple. Green-headed coneflower grows in moist habitats from Quebec to Florida, west to Montana and Arizona. It has been used medicinally by American Indians, internally (root tea for indigestion) and externally (flowers as a burn poultice). "Cooked spring greens were eaten for 'good health,'" according to Foster and Duke (Peterson Field Guides' *Field Guide to Medicinal Plants: Eastern and Central North America*). **On Sugarloaf—Blooming time:** July–September. **Locations:** Mount Ephraim Road; possible along other roadsides and trails. **Similar species:** Use the fernlike divided leaves to separate this species from similar aster family members.

Wingstem

Verbesina alternifolia (L.) Britton ex Kearney
(Actinomeris alternifolia)
Aster or Daisy Family (Asteraceae)

Wingstem is a tall (3–8') summer-to-fall-blooming aster or daisy family member with drooping yellow ray **flowers** similar to the preceding species, green-headed coneflower *(Rudbeckia laciniata)*. Wingstem's disk flowers are often described as moplike. Its **leaves** are alternate, simple, lanceolate or lance-elliptic, toothed or nearly entire, several inches long, and usually ta-

Wingstem

pered to the base. They are often slightly rough to the touch. The most distinctive feature of this plant is the vertically winged plant stalk. Wingstem grows in moist woods, fields, thickets, ditches, and bottomlands from New York and southern Ontario to Florida, Louisiana, and Nebraska. **On Sugarloaf—Blooming time:** July–October. **Locations:** Mount Ephraim Road; possible along other roadsides and trailsides. **Similar species:** Winged plant stalk separates wingstem from all other similar species with the exception of crownbeard *(V. occidentalis)*. Crownbeard is similar to wingstem but has opposite leaves. It has been reported on Sugarloaf.

Other Aster or Daisy Family Members with Showy Heads of Both Ray and Disk Flowers

Asteraceae

Tickseed Sunflower (*Bidens polylepis* S. F. Blake) bears very showy golden-yellow **flower heads** that are 1½–2½" across. **Leaves** are opposite, pinnately compound. Tina and I have not seen this wildflower on Sugarloaf, but it is a striking part of the late summer and autumn landscape in the surrounding countryside. For descriptions of *Bidens* spp. common on Sugarloaf, *see* Beggar-Ticks (Sticktight) (*Bidens frondosa* L.) and Spanish Needles (*Bidens bipinnata* L.).

Helianthus Sunflower Species *(Helianthus).* Several species of sunflower grow in the Sugarloaf area. None is common on the mountain itself, but here

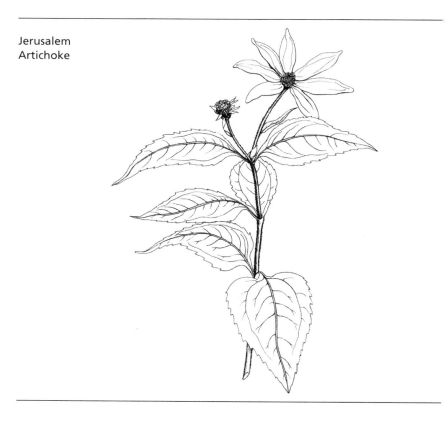

Jerusalem
Artichoke

is a list of species you might find blooming near the mountain during summer and fall: Jerusalem Artichoke (*H. tuberosus* L.), Thin-Leaved Sunflower
(*H. decapetalus* L.), Woodland Sunflower (*H. divaricatus* L.), Pale-Leaved
Sunflower (*H. strumosus* L.), Giant Sunflower (*H. giganteus* L.). All species
bear showy **flower heads** with yellow ray and disk flowers. **Leaves** are opposite and simple.

Common Fleabane (Philadelphia Fleabane, Philadelphia Daisy)

Erigeron philadelphicus L.
Aster or Daisy Family (Asteraceae)

Growing in many parts of North America, common fleabane blooms in
spring but resembles the later fall-blooming asters. One of three frequently
observed fleabane species on Sugarloaf, this one is the first to bloom. **Flower
heads:** White or pale pink ray flowers around a yellow center of disk flowers;
100–150 or more rays are thin and flexible. Flower heads are ½–1" across and

borne in small clusters or singly at plant terminus. **Leaves:** Alternate, simple, with sparse, often irregular pointed or rounded teeth or entire margins. Leaves and plant stalk downy-hairy. Leaf bases are sessile and usually clasping. **Height and growth habits:** 6"–3', usually single-stalked until flower heads divide at top (although mown specimens along roadsides may be branched). **Habitat and range:** Open woods, fields, roadsides; widespread in North America. **Herbal lore:** Plant was a folk remedy for many conditions, including diarrhea, painful urination, diabetes, hemorrhaging, fevers, and coughs. **On Sugarloaf—Blooming time:** April–June. **Locations:** Very common, especially along mountain roadsides. **Similar species:** Daisy fleabane *(E. annuus)* is also common on the mountain; it has leaves that are tapered to the base but not clasping. It blooms slightly later than common fleabane, although their blooming times overlap. Lesser daisy fleabane *(E. strigosus)* also blooms a little later. It has leaves with few to no teeth and hairs hugging the plant stalk (rather than spreading). Robin's plantain *(E. pulchellus)* is rare on Sugarloaf and has a larger flower head. Local asters *(Aster* spp.) bloom in late summer and early fall.

Daisy Fleabane

Erigeron annuus (L.) Pers.
Aster or Daisy Family (Asteraceae)

Very similar to common fleabane, this plant also lines Sugarloaf's roadsides, along with the following species. It blooms slightly later (beginning in late May) and differs from the preceding species in the following ways: it has only 40–100 (or slightly more) ray **flowers** per blossoming head (for those who have time to count), and its stem **leaves** taper to a sessile base but do not clasp the stem. *See also* next entry, lesser daisy fleabane. **Habitat and range:** Disturbed sites; much of the United States and Canada. **On Sugarloaf—Blooming time:** May–autumn. **Locations:** Common mountainwide, especially along roadsides.

Daisy
Fleabane

Lesser Daisy Fleabane

Erigeron strigosus Muhl. ex Willd.
Aster or Daisy Family (Asteraceae)

This plant is not quite as common as the two preceding species, but it also grows along Sugarloaf roadsides, from late spring through autumn. Very similar to daisy fleabane *(E. annuus)*, its **leaves** are untoothed or only slightly toothed, and the hairs along the plant stalk are appressed (lying flat to the stem). **Habitat and range:** Disturbed sites; much of the United States and southern Canada.

Asters

Asters L.
Aster or Daisy Family (Asteraceae)

As the violets are to spring in northeastern North America and on Sugarloaf, the asters are to autumn. Springing forth from the rocks in all their white and lavender profusion, they defy identification. This is an extremely tough genus to figure out. Minute differences in involucral bracts (or phyllaries—the sepal-like leafy bracts below the flower heads) are the dubious means of separating two common species. Within each species there is tremendous variation in the size and shape of leaves. Hybridization may confuse the picture even more. Frequent mowing along the roadsides, which interferes with the natural growth habits of these plants, makes aster identification all the more baffling. Asters are organized here according to flower color with as much helpful information as we can give. If you find yourself with a plant that shows characteristics of one species and another, I'm afraid all we can say is, "Join the club."

Like other members of the aster or daisy family, asters bear unusual flowers that are among the most highly evolved in the plant world. The "flowers" are actually flower heads made up of disk flowers (tiny tubular, 5-lobed, perfect flowers that collectively form the center of the flower head and are yellow, brown, or reddish) and ray flowers (which are white, lavender, purple, or blue and look like petals but are actually individual pistillate flowers). *See* the aster or daisy family description for more information.

Flower Color White (or Palest Lavender)

Aster with Stalked Leaves; Lowest Leaves Heart-Shaped

White Wood Aster (*Aster divaricatus* L.). This is Sugarloaf's most common aster and blessedly the easiest to identify. **Flower heads:** White, in rather flat-topped or rounded terminal clusters. Individual flower heads slightly ragged in appearance with several irregularly spaced white rays and yellow, brown, or purplish central disks; flower head ¾–1" across. **Leaves:** Alternate, simple, toothed, heart-shaped (cordate) or ovate, on petioles, the lower leaves often larger and more heart-shaped than upper ones. Upper leaves have shorter petioles, and upper leaf blades may be untoothed. Leaves 1–4" long. **Height:** 1–3'. **Habitat and range:** Woodlands, southeastern Canada to northern Georgia mountains. **On Sugarloaf—Blooming time:** Late summer through fall. **Locations:** West View; most trails and roadsides. **Similar species:** No other white aster common on Sugarloaf has large stalked, heart-shaped leaves, but this plant could be confused with similar species growing elsewhere in Maryland.

White
Wood Aster

Asters with Mostly Sessile Leaves

Calico Aster (Starved Aster) [*Aster lateriflorus* (L.) Britton]. The calico aster has many small flower heads on lateral branches, each with a pink, purple, or gold center of tiny disk flowers. **Flower heads:** ¼–½" wide, each with 9–15 white or slightly purplish ray flowers and variously colored disk flowers. Flower heads usually clustered along lateral branches. **Leaves:** Alternate, simple, lanceolate, sessile, with a few sharp teeth. **Height and growth habits:** 1–4'; very long and spreading side branchlets. **Habitat and range:** Woods, fields, thickets; Nova Scotia and Ontario south to Florida and Texas. **On Sugarloaf—Blooming time:** Late summer–fall. **Locations:** Yellow Trail, Mount Ephraim Road. **Similar species:** The combination of lateral branches, tiny ray flowers, and variously colored disk flowers helps separate this plant from similar asters. The following two species have slightly larger flower heads.

Heath Aster (*Aster pilosus* Willd.). An aster with small white flower heads growing on a stiff, branched stalk. **Flower heads:** ½–3/4" across, white rays with yellow or brown central disks. Flower heads grow along stiff side stalks. The phyllaries (leafy bracts below flower head) are pointed and usually re-

flexed (curved backward). **Leaves:** Alternate, simple, sessile or nearly so (except for lower leaves), narrowly lanceolate or linear. Pubescent, with entire or slightly toothed margins. (Lowest leaves, which often fall early, usually have petioles.) From ⅓" to 4" long. **Height and growth habits:** 1–5'; stalk stiff, often hairy, and much branched, with flower heads along side branchlets. **Habitat and range:** Open, usually dry habitats; Nova Scotia south to northern Florida, west to Minnesota and Louisiana. **On Sugarloaf—Blooming time:** Late summer–fall. **Locations:** West View, Yellow Trail, roadsides. **Similar species:** Flower heads are larger than those of calico aster *(A. lateriflorus)*. Similar to following species, which has less reflexed phyllaries.

    Bushy Aster *(Aster dumosus* L.). Very difficult to distinguish from preceding species. Although bushy aster **flower heads** may be lavender or blue, all the specimens we've found on Sugarloaf are white. To differentiate this species from heath aster *(A. pilosus),* look for phyllaries (leafy bracts below flower head) that do not curve dramatically outward and backward, although they might be slightly reflexed. Consult a technical botany manual for additional distinguishing characteristics. **Habitat and range:** Dry or moist, often sandy soil. Most common on the coastal plain. Maine to Florida, west to Michigan and Louisiana. **On Sugarloaf—Locations:** Yellow Trail, Mount Ephraim Road.

Panicled Aster (Tall White Aster) (*Aster lanceolatus* Willd.). *(Aster simplex)*. A tall aster with flower heads slightly larger than the three preceding species and borne in loose terminal clusters rather than along spreading side branchlets. **Flower heads:** Rays usually white (may be pale violet, but Sugarloaf specimens we're familiar with are white), numerous (20–40), with yellow disks turning brown. Flower heads ¾–1" across in mostly terminal clusters. **Leaves:** Simple, alternate, untoothed or with a few teeth. Narrowly lanceolate and tapered to a sessile or slightly clasping base. May have a very

Panicled
Aster

short petiole. Glabrous, 2–8" long. **Height and growth habits:** Tall, 3–6', rather narrowly upright for an aster. **Habitat and range:** Moist meadows, ponds, and streamsides; southeastern Canada to North Carolina, west to North Dakota and Texas. **On Sugarloaf—Blooming time:** Late summer through fall. **Locations:** Wet places along Mount Ephraim Road; Yellow Trail. **Similar species:** The combination of height, habitat, and narrowly lanceolate leaves helps distinguish this aster from all white asters previously described. Flower heads are larger and ray flowers more numerous than in following species.

Flat-Topped Aster (*Aster umbellatus* Mill.). Rare on Sugarloaf, the flat-topped aster grows in a few seeps and wet ditches along Mount Ephraim Road. Although somewhat similar to the preceding species and sharing a similar habitat, the flat-topped aster can be readily distinguished from the panicled aster by the following characteristics: **flower heads** are smaller (½–3/4" across), rays are fewer (7–15), and flowers are borne in flat-topped clusters. **Habitat and range:** Wet woodlands and clearings; southeastern Canada south to northern Georgia, west to Minnesota and Kentucky. **On Sugarloaf—Blooming time:** Late summer through fall. **Location:** Mount Ephraim Road.

Flower Color Lavender, Purple, or Blue

Flower Heads ½" Across or Slightly Wider

Heart-Leaved Aster (Blue Wood Aster) (*Aster cordifolius* L.). A common aster with numerous small lavender or pale blue flower heads and heart-shaped (cordate), sharply toothed leaves. **Flower heads:** Lavender or pale blue rays, with yellow disks turning pink early; ½–⅝" across in many-headed clusters. **Leaves:** Alternate, simple, lower leaves petioled, 2–4" long, cordate, and sharply toothed. Petioles usually slender but may be slightly winged (although they do not have the wide, dramatically clasping wings of the following species' petioles). Upper leaves smaller, ovate-elliptic or lance-shaped with fewer or no teeth; short-petioled to nearly sessile. **Height and growth habits:** 1–4'; usually branched. **Habitat and range:** Woodlands and clearings; Nova Scotia to Minnesota; south to northern Georgia and Missouri. **On Sugarloaf—Blooming time:** Late summer through fall. **Locations:** Yellow Trail, Mount Ephraim Road, quite common on and near Sugarloaf. **Similar species:** The following species all have slightly larger flower heads. The wavy-leaved aster *(A. undulatus)* is most similar, but its leaves have only slightly toothed or wavy margins, and the petioles on lower leaves are wide and clasping.

Wavy-Leaved Aster (*Aster undulatus* L.). Almost as common as the preceding species, this aster is most easily distinguished by its lower leaves with winged and clasping petioles. **Flower heads:** Rays lavender or pale violet-blue, with yellow disks usually turning brown;. ¾–1" across, in mostly terminal clusters. **Leaves:** Alternate, simple, with wavy-edged, smooth, or slightly toothed margins. Lower leaves 1–4½" long, ovate, cordate, or lanceolate, with petioles that are dramatically winged and clasp the stem. Upper leaves are smaller and may be sessile and somewhat clasping. **Height:** 6"–4'. **Habitat and range:** Dry woods and clearings; Maine to Indiana, south to Tennessee and Louisiana. **On Sugarloaf—Blooming time:** Late summer through fall. **Locations:** Sugarloaf Mountain Road, Mount Ephraim Road; not quite as common on and near Sugarloaf as preceding species. **Similar species:** The heart-leaved aster (*A. cordifolius*) has sharply toothed leaves.

Purple-Stemmed Aster (Bristly Aster) (*Aster puniceus* L.). A tall aster growing in wet soil. **Flower heads:** Lavender, 1–1½" across, in clusters at and toward the top of plant. **Leaves:** Simple, alternate, lanceolate, sessile or nearly so with clasping base. Shallowly toothed or with a nearly smooth margin. Often rough to the touch above, glabrous below or with a few hairs along the midrib; 1½–6" long. **Height and growth habits:** Tall, 2–7', spreading or not. The stalk is usually reddish or purplish and hairy (but may also be smooth and green). **Habitat and range:** Wet soil in swamps, seeps, springs, and other moist environs; Newfoundland to Saskatchewan, south in mountains to Georgia and Alabama, west to Nebraska. **On Sugarloaf—Blooming time:** Late summer through fall. **Locations:** Bear Branch; may also be present in other wet places. **Similar species:** *see* following species.

Crooked-Stemmed Aster (*Aster prenanthoides* Muhl. ex Willd.). This aster shares a similar habitat with the preceding species and has been reported on Sugarloaf although we have never found it growing here. It is usually not as tall as the purple-stemmed aster (1–3½') and has a zigzag stem and leaves with deeply clasping bases. **Habitat and range:** Stream banks, wet places; eastern United States.

Late Purple Aster (*Aster patens* Aiton). This aster has deep violet flower heads and smooth-margined, clasping leaves that nearly encircle the stem. **Habitat and range:** Dry open woods and rocky outcroppings; eastern United States. **On Sugarloaf—Locations:** We have yet to find this aster on Sugarloaf, but it grows in the area and might be found along the Blue Trail and the higher sections of the Yellow Trail.

Toothed White-Topped Aster (Stiff Aster)

Seriocarpus asteroides (L.) B.S.P.
(Aster paternus)
Aster or Daisy Family (Asteraceae)

As if the aster genus wasn't confusing enough all on its own, here is a similar plant of a different genus. Closely resembling *Aster* species, this wildflower blooms a little earlier in the summer. A prominent contemporary botanist has reclassified this plant, placing it in the *Aster* genus. Just one of the many complications that makes botany so interesting! **Flower heads:** White or pink rays around central disk flowers. Rays few (4–8, usually 5); flower heads about ½" across, borne in flat-topped clusters. **Leaves:** Alternate, simple, sessile above, long-petioled below, sometimes with a leaf rosette at the base of the plant. Leaves with shallow teeth or nearly entire (especially toward the top of the stalk). Ovate-lanceolate or elliptic above, becoming obovate toward the plant base. Lower leaves 2–4" long, uppers much smaller. **Height:** 6–24". **Habitat and range:** Dry woods, fields, thickets; eastern United States. **On Sugarloaf—Blooming time:** June–September. **Locations:** White Trail; uncommon on the mountain. **Similar species:** Early blooming time and presence of very few ray flowers (usually 5) separate this plant from Sugarloaf *Aster* species.

Beggar-Ticks (Sticktight)

Bidens frondosa L.
Aster or Daisy Family (Asteraceae)

Both common names of this plant refer to the ability of the barbed achene (the dry fruit) to "stick tight" to animal fur or clothing, hitching a ride to a new propagation site. **Flower heads:** Orange-yellow central disk flowers in narrow, erect heads with or without a few surrounding yellow ray flowers. Flowering heads surrounded by 5–10 narrow leafy bracts. Bracts have spiny-looking hairs along margins. **Leaves:** Opposite, pinnately compound, with 3–5 leaflets per leaf. Leaflets lanceolate (rarely ovate), sharply toothed. Leaves (especially lower ones) up to several inches long, with petioles. **Height:** 8"–4'. **Habitat and range:** Moist fields, meadows, roadsides, disturbed sites; much of the United States and southern Canada. **Herbal lore:** This is one of several *Bidens* species that has been used medicinally in the Old and New Worlds. According to Hutchens (*Indian Herbalogy of North America*), members of the *Bidens* genus have been valued as emmenagogues (agents stimulating menstruation), expectorants, antispasmodics, and diaphoretics (agents inducing perspiration). **On Sugarloaf—Blooming time:** August–October. **Locations:** Yellow Trail, Mount Ephraim Road, and Sugarloaf Mountain Road; may be found along other roadsides and trailsides.

Similar species: Another very similar species, tall beggar-ticks or sticktight *(B. vulgata)*, has been reported here. It has 10–20 leafy bracts beneath each yellow flowering head. The nodding bur-marigold *(B. cernua)*, also reported here, has simple, lanceolate leaves and showy flowers with bright gold rays (rays occasionally absent).

Spanish Needles

Bidens bipinnata L.
Aster or Daisy Family (Asteraceae)

This plant is named for its barbed, linear achenes, which are far more no-ticeable than the rather inconspicuous flower heads. **Flower heads:** Small,

yellow, with either dark yellow disk flowers only or also with a few paler yellow rays. Each head ¼–¾" long on short to long stalk. Heads borne terminally and from the leaf axils. **Fruit:** Straight, slender, needlelike achenes, each bearing 2 to 4 terminal barbs (called awns). As achenes mature they change from green to brown and diverge in a three-dimensional star-shaped pattern (suggesting a fireworks explosion). **Leaves:** Opposite; pinnately, bipinnately, or tripinnately compound, fernlike, with toothed and lobed leaflets. Leaf length variable (overall leaf up to several inches long). **Height and growth habits:** 1–3'; usually branched; plant stalk squared. **Habitat and range:** Dry to moist fields, roadsides, disturbed sites; Massachusetts to Florida, west to Nebraska, California, and Mexico, also east Asia. **Herbal lore:** "Cherokees used leaf tea as a worm expellent. Leaves were chewed for sore throats. Plant juice once used for eardrops and as a styptic," according to Foster and Duke (Peterson Field Guides' *Field Guide to Medicinal Plants: Eastern and Central North America*), who warn that the plant may be an irritant. **On Sugarloaf— Blooming and fruiting time:** Late summer through fall. **Locations:** Roadsides (including Mount Ephraim Road and Comus Road); also possible along trails. **Similar species:** The fernlike leaves separate this species from other members of the genus found on Sugarloaf.

Quickweed (Galinsoga)

Galinsoga quadriradiata Ruiz & Pav.
(Galinsoga ciliata)
Aster or Daisy Family (Asteraceae)

A common garden weed, this plant is a tropical American native that has become widely naturalized. **Flower heads:** Small, ¼" across, with central golden disks and (usually) 5 triple-lobed white rays. Heads growing in sparse terminal clusters. **Leaves:** Opposite, simple, ovate or ovate-lanceolate, toothed, pubescent, 1–3" long. The upper leaves on short petioles to nearly sessile, the lower ones on longer petioles. Plant stalk hairy. **Height and growth habits:** 6–18"; usually branching. **Habitat and range:** Gardens, grassy areas, and disturbed sites; native of Central and South America, now cosmopolitan. **On Sugarloaf—Blooming time:** June–November. **Locations:** Common along the mountain road and in grassy areas; may also be found in open areas along trails. **Similar species:** Smooth galinsoga *(C. parviflora)* is very similar but glabrous or with appressed hairs. It has been reported on the mountain, but we have yet to see it here.

Quickweed

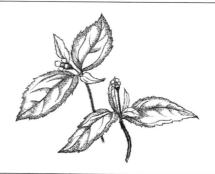

Yarrow

Achillea millefolium L.
Aster or Daisy Family (Asteraceae)

A common summer wildflower that is often confused with Queen Anne's lace. Yarrow has finely divided, strongly aromatic leaves. This plant has been a popular medicinal herbal throughout the northern climes where it grows. **Flower heads:** Flat or convex clusters of small white or whitish flower heads. Each tiny head composed of several to many tan, yellow, or gray central disk flowers surrounded by 5 (give or take) white ray flowers. Each ray has 3 rounded or pointed teeth at the apex. Overall cluster 1–4" across, irregular in shape, suggesting a fried-egg outline (as compared to the more uniformly

rounded Queen Anne's lace umbel). Rarely, yarrow flower clusters are pink. **Leaves:** Alternate, pinnately compound, delicate, feathery, and strongly scented when crushed. Each leaf 1" to several inches long. Leaves and plant stalk softly hairy. **Height and growth habits:** 1–4'; branched or unbranched. **Habitat and range:** Fields, roadsides, disturbed areas; Europe and North America (may be native and/or introduced). **Herbal lore:** Foster and Duke report in Peterson Field Guides' *Field Guide to Medicinal Plants: Eastern and Central North America* that more than 100 biologically active compounds have been identified in yarrow. It has long been employed externally as a styptic poultice and internally as a treatment for colds, flu, and gastric problems in both the New World and the Old World. Foster and Duke warn that it could cause dermatitis and may be toxic in large doses taken over long periods of time. **On Sugarloaf—Blooming time:** Late spring–fall. **Locations:** Roadsides and parking areas; trailsides in open areas. **Similar species:** Queen Anne's lace *(Daucus carota)* has more uniformly round flower clusters and sheathed petioles. Several highly poisonous members of the carrot family (Apiaceae) could be confused with yarrow.

Horseweed

Conyza canadensis (L.) Cronquist
(Erigeron canadensis)
Aster or Daisy Family (Asteraceae)

This tall plant is widely distributed in North America. Horseweed is quite prevalent along the lower stretches of Mount Ephraim Road near Bear Branch and Bennett Creek. **Flower heads:** Small (⅛–¼" tall), in large, branched clusters springing from the upper leaf axils. Each small flower head greenish with many upright whitish rays that do not spread. When heads go to seed they resemble diminutive dandelion seed heads. **Leaves:** Alternate, simple; linear, elliptic, or oblanceolate. Upper leaves often entire, lower ones usually toothed (sometimes with just a few shallow, irregular teeth). Leaves pubescent with long, bristly hairs below and along the margins, 1–5" long. (Basal leaves may be larger but often have died back by flowering time.) Plant stalk bristly-hairy. **Height and growth habits:** 1–7'; erect main stalk usually unbranched, flower clusters branched. **Habitat and range:** Dry fields, roadsides, disturbed sites; southern Canada through the United States to tropical America. **On Sugarloaf—Blooming time:** July–November. **Locations:** Mount Ephraim Road and other roadsides; trails, including the Yellow Trail. **Similar species:** Separate from pilewort *(Erechtites hieracifolia)* and other similar aster family members by entire upper leaves.

Goldenrods (and Silverrod)

Solidago
Aster or Daisy Family (Asteraceae)

Goldenrods appear in field and woodland during mid to late summer, seeming to spell the season's end. Their golden plumed flower clusters are a familiar sight in Sugarloaf country well into autumn. Goldenrods are not the common cause of late summer allergies, although they are often falsely blamed for the misery wrought by the less visually conspicuous but simultaneously blooming ragweeds. Several species of goldenrod (and the intriguing silverrod) grow on and around Sugarloaf, and Brown and Brown describe more than thirty in *Herbaceous Plants of Maryland*. Their descriptions are preceded by this warning: "This is a large, difficult genus because the plants of a species may vary greatly; many species are closely similar, and numerous hybrids occur." The next entries describe a few goldenrod species you are likely to encounter on the mountain. For those intrepid souls determined to plumb the taxonomic depths of this genus, good luck! Please consult Brown and Brown or another comprehensive botanical guide if you find a plant that doesn't match our illustrations and descriptions. We are indebted to Cristol Fleming (co-author of *Finding Wildflowers in the Washington-*

Baltimore Area) for the botanical key she created to identify local goldenrod species. Aspects of her key are incorporated in the descriptions that follow.

Goldenrods (*Solidago* species) with elongated, one-sided terminal flower clusters (one-sided racemes) and leaves gradually lengthening to longest, lowermost leaves

Canada Goldenrod (Tall or Common Goldenrod)
Solidago canadensis L.
Aster or Daisy Family (Asteraceae)

Canada goldenrod is a tall plant with one-sided flower clusters (one-sided racemes). This is one of Sugarloaf's most common goldenrods. **Flower heads:** Golden-yellow, in feathery terminal clusters. Each small flower head (⅛" long or less) has 7–17 yellow rays and 2–8 tiny disks. **Leaves:** Alternate, simple, sharply toothed (although uppermost leaves may have few to no

Canada
Goldenrod

teeth). Lanceolate, elliptic, or lance-linear, sessile, tapered at both ends, usually with 3 main longitudinal veins (excluding uppermost leaves). Leaves 2" or less at top of stalk, gradually lengthening to lowermost leaves, which are often 5" or more in length. Glabrous or minutely pubescent above, pubescent below, especially along the veins. Plant stalk downy, at least above the middle. **Height and growth habits:** 1–6'; often branching toward the top, with arching flower clusters. **Habitat and range:** Fields, meadows, thickets, roadsides, open woods; most of the United States and southern Canada. **Herbal lore:** According to Peterson Field Guides' *Field Guide to Medicinal Plants: Eastern and Central North America* by Foster and Duke, "American Indians used root for burns; flower tea for fevers, snakebites; crushed flowers chewed for sore throats. Contains quercetin, a compound reportedly useful in treating hemorrhagic nephritis. Seeds eaten as survival food." They warn that some people are allergic to this plant (although most allergies attributed to goldenrods are caused by ragweed). **On Sugarloaf—Blooming time:** Summer–fall. **Locations:** Yellow Trail, Mount Ephraim Road; quite common mountainwide. **Similar species:** Rough-stemmed goldenrod (*S. rugosa*) has leaves with net veins. Late goldenrod (*S. gigantea*) has a smooth, glaucous (not downy) plant stalk. Other common Sugarloaf goldenrods with one-sided terminal flower clusters have lowest leaves much larger than upper and not gradually lengthening as in this species.

Late Goldenrod (Smooth Goldenrod)
Solidago gigantea Aiton
Aster or Daisy Family (Asteraceae)

Late goldenrod very closely resembles Canada goldenrod. This plant's most distinctive difference is its smooth (not downy) plant stalk, which is often covered with a whitish bloom (glaucous). **Locations:** Mountain clearings; common in fields surrounding Sugarloaf.

Rough-Stemmed Goldenrod
Solidago rugosa Mill.
Aster or Daisy Family (Asteraceae)

Like the two preceding species, rough-stemmed goldenrod bears **flower heads** in terminal, one-sided racemes. This goldenrod has 6–11 ray flowers per flower head. As the name implies, the plant stalk is rough to the touch. Distinguish this goldenrod from Canada and late goldenrod by its **leaves**, which are net-veined and are also rough. (Canada and late goldenrod mature stem leaves usually have 3 longitudinal veins.) **Blooming time:** Late summer–fall. **Locations:** Mount Ephraim Road; common mountainwide.

Rough-Stemmed
Goldenrod

Goldenrods (*Solidago* species) with elongated, one-sided terminal flower clusters (one-sided racemes) and lower stem and basal leaves much larger than upper ones

Early Goldenrod

Solidago juncea Aiton
Aster or Daisy Family (Asteraceae)

A goldenrod known to flower as early as June, this is Sugarloaf's first blooming goldenrod. **Flower heads:** Golden-yellow, in feathery one-sided terminal clusters; 6–12 ray flowers per head. **Leaves:** Alternate, simple (often with small leaves in leaf axils). Upper and middle stem leaves entire or barely toothed along upper half of blades, lanceolate-elliptic, tapered to base, slightly fragrant, usually sessile. Lower leaves sharply toothed, much larger than upper leaves, becoming petioled. Oblanceolate, lanceolate, or elliptic basal leaves on long, often winged petioles. Upper leaves may be an inch or less in length, while lowermost leaves may be 10" to 1'. **Height:** 1½–6'. **Habitat and range:** Open woods, fields, clearings, roadsides; eastern Canada and the United States west to Mississippi and Missouri and south, in the mountains, to Georgia and Alabama. **On Sugarloaf—Blooming time:** June–September. **Locations:** Mount Ephraim Road and other mountain roadsides; possible along cleared sections of trail. **Similar species:** Gray goldenrod

(*S. nemoralis*) has grayish leaves, as the name implies. Elm-leaved goldenrod (*S. ulmifolia*) has stem leaves with sharp teeth. Neither species is common on Sugarloaf.

Gray Goldenrod

Solidago nemoralis Aiton
Aster or Daisy Family (Asteraceae)

Gray goldenrod has one-sided terminal flower clusters with 5–9 rays per **flower head.** It is a small plant (only ½–3' tall), with a grayish, finely pubescent plant stalk and gray-green pubescent **leaves. On Sugarloaf—Locations:** Roadsides, trailside clearings, surrounding fields (uncommon on Sugarloaf).

Gray Goldenrod

Elm-Leaved Goldenrod

Solidago ulmifolia Muhl. ex Willd.
Aster or Daisy Family (Asteraceae)

I have yet to see this goldenrod growing on Sugarloaf, but it was identified here in a Stronghold plant survey during the 1980s. Elm-leaved goldenrod has only 1–6 rays per **flower head** (and 2–7 disk flowers). Its one-sided terminal flower clusters arch outward, and the plant's outline suggests an American elm or a vase. Its **leaves** are thin and coarsely toothed. The much larger basal leaves may be absent by flowering time. **On Sugarloaf—Locations:** Wherever you happen to find it!

Goldenrod (and silverrod) (*Solidago* species) with narrow upright terminal flower clusters and sometimes a few flower clusters in the uppermost leaf axils. Flower clusters not one-sided.

Silverrod

Solidago bicolor L.
Aster or Daisy Family (Asteraceae)

Our only white goldenrod, this is a late summer and fall plant of delicate beauty. **Flower heads:** Small rays are creamy white, 7–9 per flower head; tiny disks are yellow. Each flower head ¼–⅓" long. Flower heads in upright ter-

Silverrod

minal clusters and springing from the uppermost leaf axils. **Leaves:** Alternate, simple. Upper leaves lanceolate or elliptic; lower leaves oblanceolate or obovate. Upper leaves untoothed, sessile; lower leaves toothed and often tapered to a petiole. Uppermost leaves may be less than an inch long; lower ones up to several inches. **Height and growth habits:** 6–30"; usually upright; single-stalked or branched. **Habitat and range:** Dry woods, rocky outcrops, roadsides; Nova Scotia and Quebec to Wisconsin; south to Georgia and Louisiana. **On Sugarloaf—Blooming time:** Late summer–fall. **Locations:** West View, Mount Ephraim Road; quite common here. **Similar species:** Other goldenrods (*Solidago* spp.) have yellow rays, but note that silverrod disks are yellow and the white rays may wither early. Hairy goldenrod *(S. hispida)*, occasionally found growing here, is very similar to silverrod but has yellow ray flowers.

Goldenrods (*Solidago* species) with flower clusters in the leaf axils

Blue-Stemmed Goldenrod (Wreath Goldenrod)

Solidago caesia L.
Aster or Daisy Family (Asteraceae)

Blue-stemmed goldenrod is one of the easiest indigenous goldenrods to identify as long as you don't expect its stem to be blue. In fact, its graceful,

often arching stalk may be green, purple, or blue, but it can usually be counted on to have a purplish bloom. **Flowers:** Yellow, in small tufts in the leaf axils. Each with few (2–6) ray flowers and 3–7 tiny central disk flowers. **Leaves:** Alternate, narrowly lanceolate, sharply toothed. Sessile or with a very short petiole. **Height and growth habits:** 1–3', often arching. **Habitat and range:** Woods, thickets; Nova Scotia and Wisconsin south to Florida and Texas. **On Sugarloaf—Blooming time:** August–November. **Locations:** Green Trail near the stone steps, White Trail, mountain road, Sugarloaf Mountain Road. **Similar species:** Use the combination of flowers growing primarily in the leaf axils and narrow, lanceolate leaves to identify this species. Other goldenrods on and around Sugarloaf may have a few flower clusters in the uppermost leaf axils, but their primary clusters are terminal. Zigzag goldenrod *(S. flexicaulis),* native to Maryland's mountains and piedmont, also has flower clusters in the leaf axils, but its leaves are much broader and ovate, and its plant stalk is grooved or angled. We have not seen it growing on Sugarloaf.

Goldenrods (*Solidago* species) with flat-topped terminal clusters

Lance-Leaved Goldenrod (Grass-Leaved Goldenrod)

Solidago graminifolia (L.) Salisb.
(Euthamia graminifolia)
Aster or Daisy Family (Asteraceae)

The lance-leaved goldenrod is Sugarloaf's only goldenrod with flat-topped terminal clusters of flowering heads. Some botanists, including Stanwyn G. Shetler of the Smithsonian Institution, consign the flat-topped goldenrods to a separate genus *(Euthamia)*. **Flower heads:** 12–25 golden rays and about 5–10 tiny disks are borne in dense roundish, flat-topped terminal clusters. **Leaves:** Alternate, simple, lanceolate, entire, with usually 3 (sometimes 5–7) main parallel veins. **Height and growth habits:** 1–4'; branched toward the top. **Habitat and range:** Dry or moist fields, meadows, and clearings; fresh-

Lance-Leaved
Goldenrod

water marshes; Newfoundland and Quebec west to British Columbia, south to North Carolina, Missouri, and New Mexico. **On Sugarloaf—Blooming time:** July–October. **Locations:** Yellow Trail; Sugarloaf area springs, seeps, fields, meadows, and clearings. **Similar species:** Use the combination of flat-topped flower clusters and entire leaves to distinguish this goldenrod from others on Sugarloaf. Another species with flat-topped flower clusters, the slender-leaved goldenrod *(S. tenuifolia)*, grows farther east on Maryland's coastal plain.

Plantain-Leaved Pussytoes

Antennaria plantaginifolia (L.) Richardson
Aster or Daisy Family (Asteraceae)

An aptly named plant, the whitish flowers do indeed resemble "pussy toes," and the basal leaves look remarkably like plantain leaves. There are several pussytoes species in Maryland. They are difficult to distinguish from one another, but this is the only one common on Sugarloaf. **Flower heads:** White or pale pink, fuzzy, in several small terminal clusters or "toes." Each "toe" is a group of tiny disk flowers and is ¼–3/4" tall. **Leaves:** Basal leaves often remain from previous year and are a darkened green, truly resembling plantain leaves. New basal leaves are fresh spring green, obovate or elliptic, with 3 or more prominent parallel veins. Margins untoothed except for a small

Plantain-Leaved
Pussytoes

point at the apex. Basal leaves are 1–4" long. Stem leaves are alternate, sessile, and lance-shaped, shorter and narrower than the basal ones. The plant stalk is appropriately woolly. **Height and growth habits:** Pussytoes first blooms when only a few inches high, then grows to reach a foot or more. Upright or nodding. **Habitat and range:** Open woods, fields, roadsides; southeastern Canada to Montana, Texas, and Georgia. **Herbal lore:** According to Foster and Duke (Peterson Field Guides' *Field Guide to Medicinal Plants: Eastern and Central North America*), this plant was boiled in milk and used to treat dysentery and diarrhea. The leaves were poulticed for sprains, bruises, and snakebite. **On Sugarloaf—Blooming time:** April–June. **Locations:** Mountain road, Mount Ephraim Road; common mountainwide. **Similar species:** Field pussytoes (*A. neglecta*) is a local native which grows in a few Sugarloaf locations and is only mentioned here. Its basal leaves have only one prominent main vein running the length of the blade.

New York Ironweed

Vernonia noveboracensis (L.) Michx.
Aster or Daisy Family (Asteraceae)

New York ironweed's purple flowers are a dramatic sign of late summer and early autumn in the eastern United States and in the fields of Sugarloaf country. Lifelong Sugarloaf environmental activist Minny Pohlmann says this

New York
Ironweed

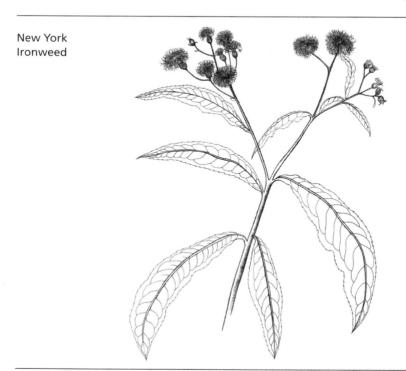

was her husband Ken's favorite flower. **Flower heads:** Deep purple or deep pink-purple in loose flat-topped or concave clusters. Flowers all disk type, each individual one with 5 pointed lobes; flowers borne 30–55 per ½"–1" head. Overall cluster 2 to several inches across. Threadlike tips on pointed bracts at base of flower heads. **Leaves:** Alternate (or sometimes nearly opposite), simple, with fine, sharp teeth or nearly entire. Narrowly lanceolate, usually tapered to the sessile or nearly sessile base; 3–10" long. **Height:** 3–10'. **Habitat and range:** Wet meadows, fields and woods, stream and river banks, freshwater marshes; Massachusetts to Florida, west to Pennsylvania, West Virginia, and Alabama. **On Sugarloaf—Blooming time:** August–October. **Locations:** Yellow Trail, wet fields and streamsides, springs of mountain roadsides and surrounding countryside. **Similar species:** Joe-Pye-weeds (*Eupatorium* spp.) have paler purplish-pink flower heads and opposite or whorled leaves. Mistflower *(Eupatorium coelestinum)* has paler violet or violet-blue flower heads, opposite leaves, and is a shorter plant. Broad-leaved ironweed *(V. glauca)* is uncommon in the Washington-Baltimore area, and we have never seen it on Sugarloaf. As its name suggests, it has a broader leaf.

Mistflower (Wild Ageratum)

Eupatorium coelestinum L.
Aster or Daisy Family (Asteraceae)

Mistflower contributes welcome color to the late summer and autumn landscape in the eastern United States. The bright blue-violet flowers of the mist-

Mistflower

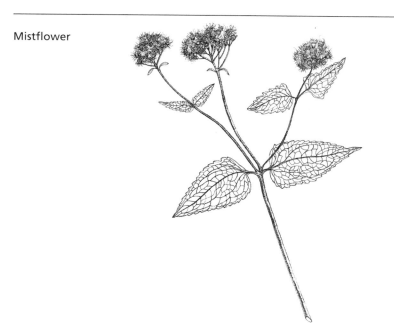

flower brighten Sugarloaf's roadsides (and some trailsides). **Flowers:** Violet or blue-violet. Tiny disk flowers are borne in button-shaped heads that are then grouped in larger flat or roundish terminal clusters. **Leaves:** Simple, opposite; cordate, triangular, or ovate with blunt or pointed teeth and short petioles (upper leaves may be nearly sessile); 1–5" long. **Height:** 6"–3'. Plant stalk may be reddish or purplish. **Habitat and range:** Woods, clearings, fields, and stream banks; New York to Illinois; south to Florida and Texas (and the West Indies). **On Sugarloaf—Blooming time:** July–October. **Locations:** Common along mountain roadsides; less common along trails. **Similar species:** Asters (*Aster* spp.) bear disk and ray flowers.

Hollow Joe-Pye-Weed

Eupatorium fistulosum Barratt

Sweet Joe-Pye-Weed

E. purpureum L.
Aster or Daisy Family (Ateraceae)

Joe-Pye-weeds served as important medicinals for American Indians and early settlers (*see* "Herbal lore" *below*). Two species of Joe-Pye-weed are

Hollow
Joe-Pye-Weed

found on Sugarloaf. Hollow Joe-Pye-weed *(E. fistulosum)* is the more common species; sweet Joe-Pye-weed *(E. purpureum)* is less common. Because
the plants are so similar, they are treated together here, with an emphasis on
the more common species. *See* "Similar species" for distinguishing characteristics. **Flower heads:** Tiny purplish-pink disk flowers in heads of 5–7 (4–
7 in *E. purpureum*); the heads form large, domed terminal clusters that are
very striking, even from afar, due in part to the plants' considerable height.
Leaves: Opposite, simple, in whorls (*E. fistulosum* usually in whorls of 4–7;
E. purpureum: 2–5, but most often 3 or 4). Lanceolate, ovate, or elliptic,
toothed, 3–8" long, on short petioles. **Height:** Extremely tall: 3–10'. **Habitat
and range:** Moist woods (often bottomlands), thickets, marshes (*E. fistulosum* favors the slightly wetter habitats); eastern United States. **Herbal lore:**
Joe-Pye-weed species have been used herbally and homeopathically to treat
urinary tract and gall bladder problems, rheumatism, and a number of other
medical conditions. In their Peterson Field Guides' *Field Guide to Medicinal
Plants: Eastern and Central North America,* Foster and Duke say the plants'
common name is "derived from 'Joe Pye,' a nineteenth-century Caucasian
'Indian theme promoter' who used the root to induce sweating in typhus
fever." **On Sugarloaf—Blooming time:** July–October. **Locations:** Lower elevations, especially along Yellow Trail, Mount Ephraim Road, and Sugarloaf
Mountain Road. **Similar species:** Hollow Joe-Pye-weed *(E. fistulosum)* has a
purplish glaucous plant stalk that is hollow or tubed in cross section (but
please do not break the plant to look for this feature). Sweet Joe-Pye-weed
(E. purpureum) has a solid plant stalk that is also glaucous but usually purple
only at the leaf nodes. Sweet Joe-Pye-weed leaves exude a vanilla scent when
crushed. A third species, which is common farther north and grows in
higher elevations to the west and southwest, is spotted Joe-Pye-weed *(E.
maculatum)*. It has a more flat-topped (less domed) flower cluster and a
purple or purple-spotted stalk that is rarely glaucous. According to botanist
Cris Fleming, spotted Joe-Pye-weed may no longer grow in Maryland.

Round-Leaved Thoroughwort (Round-Leaved Boneset)

Eupatorium rotundifolium L.
(Eupatorium pubescens)
Aster or Daisy Family (Asteraceae)

This plant and the plants mentioned here under "Similar species" are tricky
to tell apart. Like other fall-blooming members of this family (goldenrods
and asters quickly come to mind), defying identification by humans seems
to be an evolutionary imperative! **Flower heads:** Dull white, in loose, broad,
rather flat-topped terminal clusters. Each flower is actually a head of 5–7
perfect, narrow disk (or tubular) flowers. Several to many heads then form

the broader terminal cluster. **Leaves:** Opposite, simple, ovate, broadly lance-olate, or nearly round, with 8–25 teeth along each margin (16–50 teeth per leaf blade). Leaves sessile or nearly so and finely hairy; ¾–4½" long. (Note: uppermost leaves sometimes alternate.) **Height:** 1–4'. **Habitat and range:** Woods, dry fields, clearings: Maine to Florida, west to Ohio, Oklahoma, and Texas. **On Sugarloaf—Blooming time:** Late summer through fall for this species and those mentioned under "Similar species." **Locations:** Mountain-wide (with round-leaved thoroughwort more common than the two species detailed below. White snakeroot is the most abundant white *Eupatorium* species on Sugarloaf). **Similar species:** The following two species are so sim-ilar that they will not be described separately: (1) White thoroughwort or white boneset *(E. album)* has narrower lanceolate leaves that are usually downy-pubescent. This species is more common on the coastal plain but has been reported on Sugarloaf in the past. (2) Upland boneset *(E. sessilifolium)* has narrow, lanceolate, but nearly glabrous leaves. All species mentioned here so far have sessile or nearly sessile leaves, distinguishing them from white snakeroot *(E. rugosum),* which has leaves with petioles. Common boneset *(E. perfoliatum)* has at least some perfoliate leaves (leaves that ap-pear to be pierced by the plant stalk).

Boneset (Thoroughwort)

Eupatorium perfoliatum L.
Aster or Daisy Family (Asteraceae)

Boneset was an herbal medicine staple for American Indians and early Eu-ropean settlers. *See* "Herbal lore" *below* to learn about this plant's herbal history and its ongoing interest for researchers. Thanks to a quirky leaf char-acteristic, boneset can be told readily from other local white-flowering members of the *Eupatorium* genus. **Flower heads:** Small chalky white disk flowers (10–25 per head) form fuzzy flat-topped or multileveled terminal and upper axillary clusters up to several inches across. **Leaves:** Opposite, simple; lanceolate, toothed, sessile, with at least some of the leaf bases so per-fectly fused that the plant stalk appears to pierce through one double leaf. When leaves are fused, the term is "connate"; when appearing to be pierced by the stem, "perfoliate." One botanical manual describes boneset's leaves as "connate-perfoliate." Plant stalk hairy. **Height:** 2–5'. **Habitat and range:** Moist or wet woods, meadows, and thickets; much of the eastern United States and Canada. **Herbal lore:** According to Foster and Duke (Peterson Field Guides' *Field Guide to Medicinal Plants: Eastern and Central North America*), boneset was a "common home remedy of nineteenth-century America, extensively employed by American Indians and early settlers. Widely used, reportedly with success, during flu epidemics in nineteenth

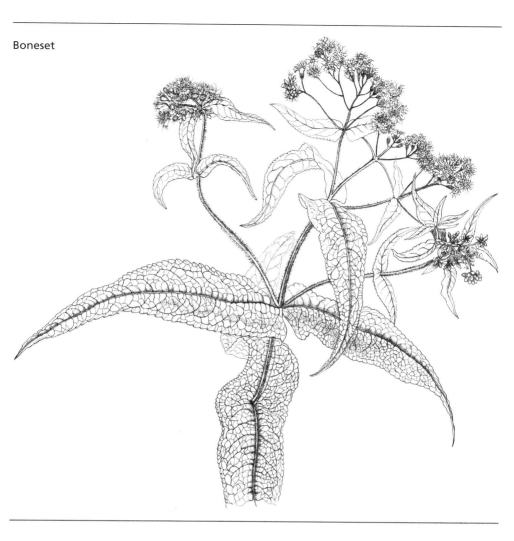

and early twentieth century. Leaf tea once used to induce sweating in fevers, flu, and colds; also used for malaria, rheumatism, muscular pains, spasms, pneumonia, pleurisy, gout, etc. Leaves poulticed onto tumors. West German research suggests nonspecific immune system–stimulating properties, perhaps vindicating historical use in flu epidemics." However, Foster and Duke add the warning: "Emetic and laxative in large doses. May contain controversial and potentially liver-harming pyrrolizidine alkaloids." The herb is extremely bitter to the taste and therefore disliked by children, according to Hutchens, who reports in her book *Indian Herbalogy of North America*, "In these cases a thick syrup of Boneset, ginger and anise is used . . . for coughs." **On Sugarloaf—Blooming time:** July–October. **Locations:** Wet areas along Mount Ephraim Road and the Yellow Trail; other low, wet areas surrounding

Sugarloaf. **Similar species:** Use the connate-perfoliate leaves (*see* "Leaves") to distinguish this species from other white-flowering *Eupatorium* locals (and add to your botanical vocabulary!).

White Snakeroot

Eupatorium rugosum Houttuyn.
Aster or Daisy Family (Asteraceae)

This plant has a rich but ignominious history (*see* "Herbal lore" *below*). One of several members of the *Eupatorium* genus found on Sugarloaf, white snakeroot blooms from late summer through midautumn. **Flower heads:** A brilliant white, in branched, flat-topped or rounded clusters of tiny disk flowers. **Leaves:** Opposite, simple, ovate or heart-shaped, 2–7" long, toothed, on slender petioles, ¾" or more in length. **Height:** 2–5'. **Habitat and range:** Upland woods, thickets, and clearings, Nova Scotia to Saskatchewan, south to Georgia and Texas. **Herbal lore:** American Indians used white snakeroot as a poultice for snakebite. Root tea was used for fevers, diarrhea, painful urination, and other conditions. The plant should be considered toxic. "Milk sickness" may result when milk of cows who have grazed white snakeroot is consumed. Brown and Brown note in *Herbaceous Plants of Maryland* that this was the cause of death for Abraham Lincoln's mother, according to legend. **On Sugarloaf—Blooming time:** August–October. **Locations:** Yellow Trail, West View, mountain road, Mount Ephraim Road. **Similar species:**

White Snakeroot

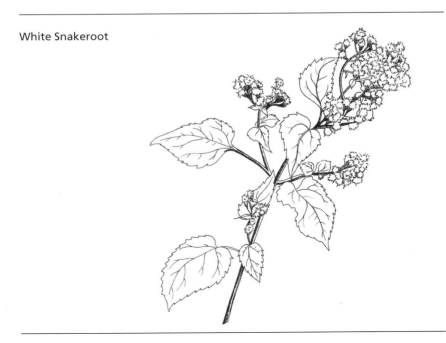

Long-stalked, ovate or heart-shaped leaves distinguish this plant from bone-set *(E. perfoliatum)* and other white-flowered members of the genus.

Common Burdock

Arctium minus Bernh.
Aster or Daisy Family (Asteraceae)

A common field and roadside weed, burdock is most easily recognized by its fruiting "burs," which stick to clothing and animal fur during the fall and winter. **Flower heads:** Bristly, round, with small cluster of purplish-pink (rarely white) disk flowers borne at the center. Bristly bracts have inward hooks. Flowering head ½–1" wide, sessile or short-stalked, in terminal and axillary clusters. **Fruit:** Familiar burbears tiny achenes at the center. **Leaves:**

Common
Burdock

Alternate, simple, the lower leaves huge (rhubarblike) and hollow-petioled. Lower leaves up to 2' or more; upper leaves 1" to several inches. Leaf blades more or less ovate, often with heart-shaped (cordate) base. Margins entire, shallowly toothed, or wavy-toothed. Most leaves petioled, the lower ones very long-petioled. **Height and growth habits:** 2–4'; usually branched. **Habitat and range:** Fields, roadsides, disturbed sites; Eurasian native widely naturalized in the United States and southern Canada. **Herbal lore:** The roots, seeds, and leaves of this species and a similar Old World plant, great burdock *(A. lappa)*, have been traditionally valued medicinally for a wide range of internal and external symptoms. **On Sugarloaf—Blooming time:** Summer–early fall. **Locations:** Sugarloaf Mountain Road, Mount Ephraim Road, and other mountain roadsides; West View; Yellow Trail; possible along other trails. **Similar species:** Great burdock has larger flower heads (1–1½") on longer stalks and lowest leaves with solid (not hollow) petioles. It has not been reported on Sugarloaf. Another Eurasian species *(A. tomentosum)*, also unlikely on Sugarloaf, has burs with weakly bristled bracts. Both species, while not apt to be seen here, are sparingly naturalized in Maryland, according to Brown and Brown's *Herbaceous Plants of Maryland*. Common cocklebur (or clotbur) *(Xanthium strumarium)* has a more elongate (cylindric or ovoid) bur with very strongly hooked prickles and leaves that are often lobed (sometimes shaped like maple leaves).

Common Cocklebur (or Clotbur)

Xanthium strumarium L.
Aster or Daisy Family (Asteraceae)

This cosmopolitan weed makes itself known in autumn when the hooked prickles of its egg-shaped burs attach to clothing and animal fur. An abundant weed of Sugarloaf farm fields, common cocklebur grows along the Yellow Trail. Small staminate **flowers** are borne in short racemes; small pistillate **flowers** are borne in a cylindric or ovoid yellowish, brownish, or greenish bur that is covered with hooked prickles. These burs hitchhike on passing wildlife when achenes mature in the fall. **Leaves** are alternate, simple, coarsely toothed, and often shallowly lobed (like a maple leaf), on long petioles.

Pale Indian Plantain

Arnoglossum atriplicifolium (L.) H. Rob.
(Cacalia atriplicifolia)
Aster or Daisy Family (Asteraceae)

American Indians valued this plant as an externally applied medicinal *(see "Herbal lore" below)*. Rare on Sugarloaf, a few specimens of pale Indian plantain grow along Mount Ephraim Road in moist fields not far from the confluence of Bear Branch and Bennett Creek. Pale Indian plantain has small erect, tubular creamy white **flower heads** growing in flat clusters. Individual disk flowers 5-lobed, with 5 or more per small head and numerous heads per flat cluster. Main stem **leaves** are alternate, simple, fan-shaped, with triangular teeth or shallow lobes; 1–6" long and wide, on long petioles. Upper leaves may be small, narrow, and untoothed or barely so. Pale green and glaucous beneath. Pale Indian plantain is 3–6' tall and has a rounded or slightly grooved very glaucous stalk. **Habitat and range:** Dry or moist woods, fields, meadows; eastern United States. **Herbal lore:** According to Foster and Duke (Peterson Field Guides' *Field Guide to Medicinal Plants: Eastern and Central North America*), "American Indians used the leaves as a poultice for cancers, cuts, and bruises, and to draw out blood or poisonous material." **On Sugarloaf—Blooming time:** July–September.

Spotted Knapweed
Centaurea maculosa Lam.
Aster or Daisy Family (Asteraceae)

In some parts of western Maryland and elsewhere in the eastern United States, this plant has become a problematic invasive. A few specimens of

Spotted Knapweed

spotted knapweed, a European species, can be found growing in grassy areas of the Yellow Trail. **Flower heads:** Lavender or lavender and white thistlelike flower heads are ¾–1¼" across. Some of the involucral bracts beneath the flowers are black-tipped. **Leaves:** Alternate, mostly compound, but some may be simple, especially toward the top of the plant. Simple leaves linear; compound are pinnately divided into linear leaflets. Upper leaves may be only ½" long, lower ones up to 6" or longer. **Height:** 1–4'. **On Sugarloaf— Blooming time:** June–August. **Locations:** Yellow Trail, Mount Ephraim Road, fields near the mountain. **Similar species:** Bachelor's button or corn-flower *(C. cyanus)* usually has flowers that are a brilliant blue, although some may be purple or white. A naturalized native of the Mediterranean region, it springs up in the fields ringing Sugarloaf during spring and summer, although we have never seen it on the mountain. Bachelor's buttons some-times grow in such profusion that a "cornflower"-blue wash is visible from the mountain summit. Local botanist Kerrie Kyde brought this to my atten-tion, and I am grateful to her for it. Thistles *(Carduus* and *Cirsium* species) have spiny-tipped leaves.

Canada Thistle

Cirsium arvense (L.) Scop.
Aster or Daisy Family (Asteraceae)

One of many species of thistle found in North America, Canada thistle is a Eurasian native with pink or pale purple **flower heads** 1" or less high and alternate, moderately to deeply lobed spiny **leaves.** It has become a prob-lematic invasive in pastures and fields of Maryland and elsewhere in the northern United States and Canada. **On and around Sugarloaf—Blooming time:** June–August. **Locations:** Mount Ephraim Road, Sugarloaf Mountain Road, fields; possible along trails.

Other Thistles

Bull Thistle

Cirsium vulgare (Savi) Ten.
Aster or Daisy Family (Asteraceae)

A tall naturalized Eurasian thistle with purple flower heads 1½–2½" high. **Flower heads** include prickly green bracts. Alternate **leaves** deeply dissected with spine-tipped lobes and teeth. Plant stalk bears prickly vertical "wings." **On and around Sugarloaf—Blooming time:** June–September. **Locations:** Mount Ephraim Road, Sugarloaf Mountain Road, and other roadsides; Yel-low Trail; fields.

Field Thistle

Cirsium discolor (Muhl. ex Willd.) Spreng.
Aster or Daisy Family (Asteraceae)

Not as common on and around Sugarloaf as the two preceding species, field thistle is native to the eastern United States and Canada. Field thistle has purple **flower heads** 1½–2" high. Its plant stalk is furrowed but does not bear bristly vertical wings (as bull thistle's does). **On and around Sugarloaf— Blooming time:** July–October. **Locations:** Sugarloaf Mountain Road, other area roadsides, trailsides, fields.

Nodding Thistle (Musk Thistle)

Carduus nutans L.
Aster or Daisy Family (Asteraceae)

A Eurasian native, this thistle has nodding reddish-purple **flower heads** with reflexed purplish bracts below. The plant stalk has vertical wings similar to bull thistle's. **On and around Sugarloaf—Blooming time:** June–September. **Locations:** Sugarloaf Mountain Road, other area roadsides; trailsides and fields.

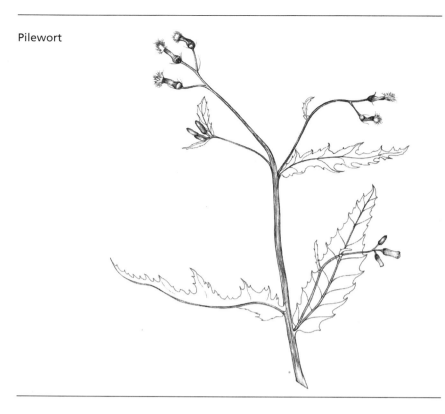

Pilewort (Fireweed, Sneezeweed)

Erechtites hieracifolia (L.) Raf.
Aster or Daisy Family (Asteraceae)

Pilewort is likely to go unnoticed until going to seed in late summer or early fall, when its silky dandelion-like pappus bristles burst forth. A common Sugarloaf plant. **Flower heads:** Whitish disk flowers only, their tops just barely visible at the apex of a green involucre composed of linear leafy bracts that are fused in a tubular envelope which is ½–1" long and swollen at the base. Flower heads usually borne in loose terminal and upper axillary clusters. **Leaves:** Alternate, simple (or sometimes lobed), usually sharply and irregularly toothed. Variable in shape (oblanceolate to lanceolate or elliptic) and size (2–8"). Short-petioled, nearly sessile or clasping at the base. Glabrous or pubescent. The plant stalk is ribbed or grooved and gives off a strong, rather unpleasant smell when broken or bruised. **Height:** 1–9'. **Habitat and range:** Habitat variable; common in disturbed sites, especially where fire or logging opens the forest floor (on Sugarloaf, mostly along cleared trailsides); eastern United States and Canada. **Herbal lore:** In Peterson Field Guides' *Field Guide to Medicinal Plants: Eastern and Central North America,*

Foster and Duke write about pilewort: "Tea or tincture of whole plant formerly used as an astringent and tonic in mucous-tissue ailments of lungs, bowels, stomach; also used externally for muscular rheumatism, sciatica. Used in diarrhea, cystitis, dropsy, etc." On its present-day use, they observe only, "Neglected by scientific investigators." **Blooming time:** July–October. **Locations:** Yellow Trail (common on eastern side of the mountain), Green Trail, other trails and roadsides mountainwide. **Similar species:** Could be confused with other aster family members.

Sweet Everlasting (Rabbit Tobacco, Catfoot, or Cudweed)

Gnaphalium obtusifolium L.
Aster or Daisy Family (Asteraceae)

The fuzzy white and yellowish flower heads are similar to pussytoes *(Antennaria)*, which bloom on Sugarloaf during the spring, but this wildflower blossoms during late summer and fall. The dried plant is very fragrant. **Flower heads:** Tiny bell-shaped flower heads with overlapping bracts are white and often yellow or brownish at the tip. About ¼" long in terminal and upper axillary clusters. **Leaves:** Alternate, simple, sessile, linear-lanceolate, with smooth or wavy margins, ½–4" long. Densely white-woolly below, glabrous or pubescent above. Plant stalk white-woolly. **Height:** 1–2½'. **Habitat and range:** Fields, roadsides, disturbed sites; eastern United States to Nebraska and Texas. **Herbal lore:** A reputed aphrodisiac! Also employed in the past to treat wide-ranging medical conditions, including pneumonia, sore throat, asthma, flu, bowel disorders, rheumatism, and tumors. Foster and Duke call the plant a "mild nerve sedative, diuretic and antispasmodic" in

Sweet Everlasting

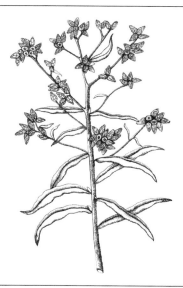

their Peterson Field Guides' *Field Guide to Medicinal Plants: Eastern and Central North America.* **On Sugarloaf—Blooming time:** August–November. **Locations:** Mountain roadsides, Yellow Trail and other open sections of trail. **Similar species:** Plantain-leaved pussytoes *(Antennaria plantaginifolia)* and other local pussytoes species bloom in the spring. Pearly everlasting *(Anaphalis margaritacea)* is another similar species, but it is rare in the Washington-Baltimore area and has not been reported on Sugarloaf. Like sweet everlasting, it blooms during summer and fall.

Common Dandelion

Taraxacum officinale Weber ex F. H. Wigg.
Aster or Daisy Family (Asteraceae)

Imagine a wildflower of daffodil-gold that appeared in your yard with no prompting and continued to blossom despite your neglect. Imagine that when it went to seed, it provided your children hours of free and natural entertainment. Add a nutritional component. This plant would be so rich in vitamins A and C that instant salads and cooked wild greens would be at your fingertips. It would be a source of a delicious coffee and even wine. Make it a medicine too, its leaves, roots, and flower heads all useful for com-

Common
Dandelion

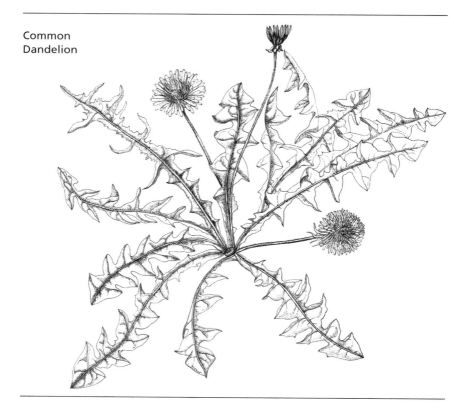

mon ailments. It would be a sort of miracle plant, would it not? Then why are we poisoning our streams to get rid of it? **Flower heads:** Sun-yellow, ¾–2" across; heads composed of ray flowers only. Head borne on a hollow stalk that emits a milky juice when broken. When flower head goes to seed, the pappus hairs attached to the dry achenes form a fuzzy round ball. The fruiting dandelion is a delight to children, who love to puff up their mouths and blow, dispersing the airborne seed and foiling their parents' quests for perfect lawns. **Leaves:** All leaves in a basal rosette, each several inches long, lanceolate or oblanceolate, and deeply (usually irregularly) toothed and lobed or divided. Short petiole often slightly winged. **Height:** 2–18". **Habitat and range:** Lawns, fields, disturbed sites; a Eurasian native which has become a cosmopolitan weed in temperate zones. **Herbal lore:** All parts of the dandelion plant are edible and medicinal. See Peterson Field Guides' *A Field Guide to Edible Wild Plants of Eastern and Central North America* (Lee Peterson) and *Field Guide to Medicinal Plants: Eastern and Central North America* (Foster and Duke) for creative uses of the lowly dandelion. Dandelion greens rival spinach in nutritional value, and the root has been esteemed by Old World herbalists for centuries. **On Sugarloaf—Blooming time:** Late winter through late fall. **Locations:** Mowed areas on and around the mountain; roadsides, some trailsides. **Similar species:** In early spring coltsfoot *(Tussilago farfara),* which is abundant along Mount Ephraim Road, could be confused with dandelion. Coltsfoot has reddish scales on its stalk, and its leaf (appearing after the flower head) resembles the outline of a colt's foot. Other aster family members with flower heads composed of yellow rays are not likely to be confused with dandelion.

Coltsfoot

Tussilago farfara L.
Aster or Daisy Family (Asteraceae)

The common name of this plant refers to the shape of the leaves, which appear after the flowers bloom. One of Sugarloaf's earliest spring wildflowers, coltsfoot is abundant along Mount Ephraim Road. **Flower heads:** Much like a small dandelion. Yellow, with numerous ray flowers and slightly darker yellow central disk flowers; ¾–1" or more across. When the plant goes to seed, the fluffy white pappus bristles are also dandelion-like. The flower stalk is thick, covered with reddish-tinged scales, and bears a single flower head. **Leaves:** Basal, roughly heart-shaped, and suggesting a colt's foot, with toothed, often shallowly lobed margins and long petioles. Leaves are 2–7" across. Appearing after the flowers have been in bloom awhile or have gone to seed. **Habitat and range:** Damp, disturbed soil; a naturalized Eurasian native. **Herbal lore:** An important cough remedy in Europe, both the leaves

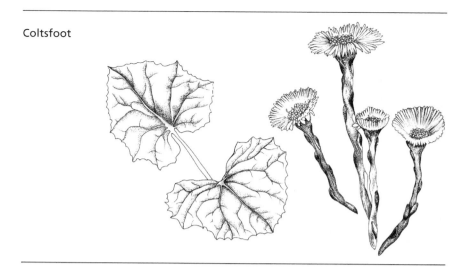

and flowers have long been used to treat a wide range of bronchial conditions. In *A Modern Herbal* Grieve wrote, "In Paris, the Coltsfoot flowers used to be painted as a sign on the doorpost of an apothecarie's shop." According to Foster and Duke, writing in Peterson Field Guides' *Field Guide to Medicinal Plants: Eastern and Central North America,* "Research suggests leaf mucilage soothes inflamed mucous membranes, and leaves have spasmolytic activity. Warning: Contains traces of liver-affecting pyrrolizidine alkaloids; potentially **toxic** in large doses." **On Sugarloaf—Blooming time:** March–early May. **Locations:** Mount Ephraim Road, Yellow Trail, Sugarloaf Mountain Road. **Similar species:** Could be confused with common dandelion. Compare leaves.

Rattlesnake Weed

Hieracium venosum L.
Aster or Daisy Family (Asteraceae)

One of many native and naturalized members of the *Hieracium* genus found in North America and one of several growing on Sugarloaf, rattlesnake weed is also one of the easiest to identify—a happy combination rarely occurring in the botanical world! **Flower heads:** Bright yellow, usually several per plant, borne at the top of the plant stalk in a loose cluster. Heads ½–1" across with 15–40 ray flowers (no disks), each ray toothed at the apex. **Leaves:** Mostly basal only, although there may be a few small leaves on the plant stalk. Basal leaves are very distinctive, with purple veins and purplish lower (and sometimes upper) surfaces. Ovate-elliptic, obovate-elliptic, or oblanceolate, they are 1–7" long, usually with long, soft hairs. Borne in a basal rosette on short purplish petioles. **Height and growth habits:** 1–2½',

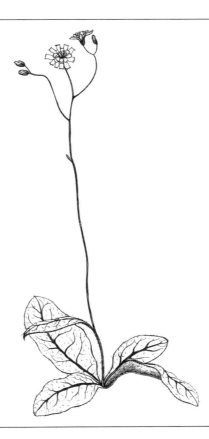

with thin, usually glabrous branched plant stalk that is upright or leaning. **Habitat and range:** Mostly dry open woods; New York to Michigan, south to Georgia and Alabama. **Herbal lore:** One of many folk remedies for snakebite. A tea was also brewed for diarrhea, coughs, and hemorrhaging. **On Sugarloaf—Blooming time:** April–June. **Locations:** Most trails and roadsides; very common along mountain road and Mount Ephraim Road. **Similar species:** The purple-veined basal leaves separate this species from others.

Field Hawkweed (King Devil)

Hieracium caespitosum Dumort.
(Hieracium pratense)
Aster or Daisy Family (Asteraceae)

A common naturalized field and roadside wildflower of late spring and summer in the eastern United States and southeastern Canada. Field hawkweed or king devil is abundant in the fields ringing Sugarloaf. It also grows along mountain roadsides and in trailside clearings. **Flower heads:** Yellow, in terminal clusters, each flower head ⅓–1" across (ray flowers only). Petal-like

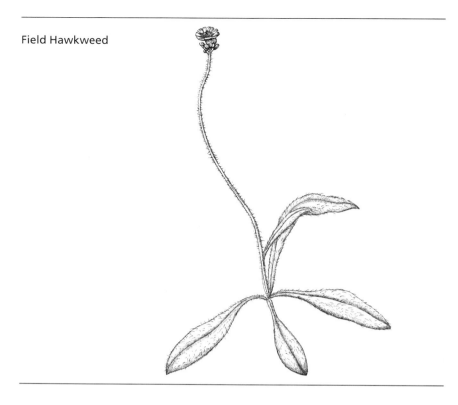

rays are fringed at the apex. **Leaves:** Basal only, in rosettes; very pubescent, entire or obscurely toothed, oblanceolate or elliptic, 2–7" long. Leafless plant stalk bristly-pubescent. **Height:** 1–3'. **Habitat and range:** Fields, clearings, roadsides, and disturbed sites; European native naturalized in eastern United States and Canada. **On Sugarloaf—Blooming time:** Late spring through summer. **Locations:** Mount Ephraim Road, Yellow Trail; more common in surrounding fields than on the mountain. **Similar species:** Rattlesnake weed (*H. venosum*) has purple-veined leaves. Other hawkweeds (*Hieracium* spp.) growing on and near Sugarloaf have at least some stem leaves.

Other Hawkweed Species

Hieracium

Several other hawkweed (*Hieracium*) species grow on Sugarloaf. The following species are all native.

Panicled Hawkweed (*H. paniculatum* L.) bears **flower heads** that are about ½" across on slender, widely branching stalks. **Leaves** are alternate, simple, and barely toothed; glabrous but for a few long hairs on their lower surfaces. **On Sugarloaf—Blooming time:** July–September. **Location:** Blue Trail.

Hairy Hawkweed (*H. gronovii* L.) is a pubescent species with **flower heads**

borne in upright, rather narrow clusters. **Leaves** are alternate, entire or nearly so, and concentrated on the lower part of the plant stalk. Basal leaves usually present. **On Sugarloaf—Blooming time:** July–September. **Locations:** Sugarloaf roadsides; possible along trails.

Rough Hawkweed (*H. scabrum* Michx.) Somewhat similar to the preceding species, rough hawkweed's basal **leaves** are usually absent or dead and drying by flowering time. Alternate stem leaves are glandular-pubescent. **On Sugarloaf—Blooming time:** June–September. **Location:** Sugarloaf Mountain Road.

Chicory

Cichorium intybus L.
Aster or Daisy Family (Asteraceae)

The root of this plant has long been dried and ground to be used as a coffee substitute. The flower heads are a beautiful sky blue. On a bright summer day the fields surrounding Sugarloaf Mountain mirror the heavens: chicory reflects the sky's blue and the white umbels of Queen Anne's lace resemble

Chicory

clouds. **Flower heads:** Blue (rarely white or pink) ray flowers. Each petal-like ray is ½–1" long, squared and fringed at the tip. Flower heads more or less cup-shaped, growing from the upper axils of the branched plant stalk. **Leaves:** Alternate, simple, and also in a basal rosette. Size and shape of leaf blade highly variable. Upper leaves are small, sessile, lanceolate, and frequently entire. Lower leaves increasingly large. Lowest leaves petioled, toothed, and lobed (much like a dandelion leaf). Uppermost leaves 1" or less, lowest up to several inches long. **Height and growth habits:** 1–4'; branched. **Habitat and range:** Fields, roadsides, disturbed sites; a European native, now cosmopolitan. **Herbal lore:** In addition to its use as a coffee substitute, chicory enjoys an ongoing herbal history. According to Foster and Duke (Peterson Field Guides' *Field Guide to Medicinal Plants: Eastern and Central North America*), the plant has been used to treat jaundice, fever, and skin problems and as a diuretic and laxative. They add: "Experimentally, root extracts are antibacterial. In experiments, animals given chicory root extracts exhibit a slower and weaker heart rate (pulse). It has been suggested that the plant should be researched for use in heart irregularities. Root extracts in alcohol solutions have proven anti-inflammatory effects in experiments." **On Sugarloaf—Blooming time:** May–October. **Locations:** Very common in local fields and along mountain roadsides and open sections of trail. **Similar species:** Tall blue lettuce *(Lactuca biennis)* has smaller flower heads and is not as common on and around Sugarloaf.

Sow-Thistle

Sonchus
Aster or Daisy Family (Asteraceae)

Two species of sow-thistle are common on Sugarloaf: spiny-leaved sow-thistle [*S. asper* (L.) Hill] and common sow-thistle (*S. oleraceus* L.). Both species are European and have become widely naturalized. These are tall plants (1–8') with pale yellow dandelion-like **flower heads.** The heads, which are loosely clustered at the top of the plant stalk and in the upper leaf axils, are composed of all ray flowers, enveloped in a green involucre, which is ⅓–1" long. Flower heads ½–1¼" wide. The main plant stalk is angled and glabrous or nearly so. **Leaves:** Alternate, simple or lobed, ovate-lanceolate to obovate-oblanceolate. Lobing is more common in common sow-thistle and is more pronounced on the lower portion of the stalk. Both species have margins with spiny teeth and sessile, clasping bases. Spiny-leaved sow-thistle has toothed earlike or heart-shaped leaf bases, which are strongly recurved. Common sow-thistle has leaf blades with pointed lobes at the base, which clasp the stalk but are not as dramatically recurved. **On Sugarloaf—Blooming time:** Midsummer through fall. **Locations:** Both species common along mountain area roadsides; likely along trails, especially the Yellow Trail. **Similar species:** Could be confused with other aster family members, particularly wild lettuces (*Lactuca* spp.).

Tall Blue Lettuce

Lactuca biennis (Moench) Fernald
Aster or Daisy Family (Asteraceae)

Flower heads: Numerous small sky-blue or lavender-blue flower heads (rarely white or yellow) in large, branched clusters. Heads ½" or less across, composed of ray flowers only. Base of flower head, the involucre, cylindrical. **Leaves:** Alternate, extremely variable, from merely toothed to deeply, pinnately lobed. Upper leaves may be narrowly lanceolate and sessile; lower often divided into several wedge-shaped lobes, on winged petioles. Size variable. **Height:** 3–15'. **Habitat and range:** Moist woods, fields, thickets, disturbed sites; widespread in the United States and Canada. **Herbal lore:** According to Peterson Field Guides' *Field Guide to Medicinal Plants: Eastern and Central North America* by Foster and Duke, "American Indians used

Tall Blue Lettuce

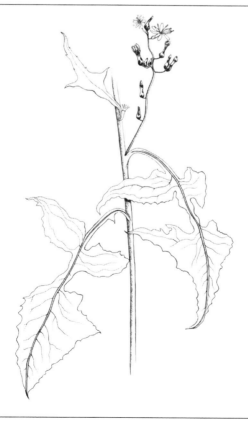

root tea for diarrhea, heart and lung ailments; for bleeding, nausea, pains. Milky stem juice used for skin eruptions. Leaves applied to stings; tea sedative; nerve tonic, diuretic. Warning: May cause dermatitis or internal poisoning." **On Sugarloaf—Blooming time:** August–October. **Locations:** Mount Ephraim Road; possible along other roadsides and trails (likely along the Yellow Trail). **Similar species:** Blue flower heads separate this plant from other *Lactuca* species common on Sugarloaf, although Florida lettuce *(L. floridana),* a closely related species with blue flower heads, is found in the Washington-Baltimore area *(see* Brown and Brown's *Herbaceous Plants of Maryland).* Chicory *(Cichorium intybus)* has larger flower heads and is far more abundant in our area.

Prickly Lettuce

Lactuca serriola L.
(Lactuca scariola)
Aster or Daisy Family (Asteraceae)

Prickly lettuce is a European native, now naturalized throughout much of the United States. It could be confused with the sow-thistles (*Sonchus* spp.), previously described. Distinguish this plant from the sow-thistles by the bristles along the main vein beneath the leaf blade and the prickles usually borne toward the base of the plant stalk. **Leaves** are variously lobed or un-lobed, with prickly-toothed margins. Prickly lettuce **flower heads** are yellow, and they are slightly smaller than those of the sow-thistles (about ¼" wide). **Height:** 2–5'. **On Sugarloaf—Blooming time:** June–October. **Locations:** White Trail (possible along other trails); roadsides mountainwide.

Wild Lettuce

Lactuca canadensis L.
Aster or Daisy Family (Asteraceae)

This lettuce species has small **flower heads** with pale yellow or reddish-yellow ray flowers. Heads are about ¼" wide. Distinguish wild lettuce from prickly lettuce (closely related preceding species) by its **leaves,** which are deeply lobed to entire but do not have spiny-toothed margins. (Margins may be toothed, but teeth don't end in spines.) **On Sugarloaf—Locations:** Mount Ephraim Road; possible along other roads and trails.

Lion's-Foot (Gall-of-the-Earth)

Prenanthes serpentaria Pursh
Aster or Daisy Family (Asteraceae)

This late summer to fall wildflower has dangling bell-shaped flower heads, which superficially suggest a lily rather than an aster family member. Its leaves are unusual: frequently unlobed on the upper stalk but variously lobed toward the plant base. **Flower heads:** Creamy white, pinkish, or greenish rays in nodding, slightly flared, bell-shaped heads. Flower heads ½–1½" long, in small clusters, growing along the upper quarter or half of the plant stalk. **Leaves:** Alternate, simple and compound, extremely variable. Upper leaves usually simple or slightly lobed; lanceolate, ovate, or elliptic, sparsely toothed to nearly entire, ½–4" long, on short petioles to nearly sessile. Lower leaves lobed or compound, more deeply cut toward the plant base. The lowest leaves are irregularly divided into several palmately arranged lobes or leaflets. Lowest leaves up to several inches across, on long petioles. **Height:** 1–4½'. **Habitat and range:** Open woods, dry fields and meadows, roadsides; Massachusetts to northern Florida, west to Kentucky, Tennessee, and Mississippi. **On Sugarloaf—Blooming time:** August–October. **Locations:** Mount Ephraim Road, other roadsides and trailsides. **Similar species:** White lettuce *(P. alba)* is rarely found on Sugarloaf and is not treated individually in this guide. White lettuce has a purplish stalk with a white bloom (glaucous). The lion's-foot stalk is red-brown (or purplish) but doesn't have a white bloom. The pappus hairs inside the flower heads of white lettuce are dark red-brown, whereas lion's-foot pappus hairs are pale brown or creamy.

Lion's-Foot

Common Ragweed

Ambrosia artemisiifolia L.
Aster or Daisy Family (Asteraceae)

Ragweed is the inconspicuous plant that causes the majority of late summer and early fall allergies in the northeastern United States, a dubious distinction often falsely attributed to the showier goldenrods (*Solidago* spp.). **Flower heads:** Greenish; small nodding staminate flower heads (bearing allergy-producing pollen) are borne in narrow upright racemes, with the pistillate flower heads clustered below. **Leaves:** Alternate above, often opposite lower down the plant stalk; compound. Leaves are deeply dissected in fernlike fashion, 1½–5" long, the lower leaves with petioles; upper leaves sometimes sessile or nearly so (and a few upper leaves may be very small and entire); pubescent or glabrous. **Height and growth habits:** 1–6'; usually branching. **Habitat and range:** Waste places; a common North American weed. **Herbal lore:** Despite its allergenic properties, common ragweed has been medicinally employed. According to Peterson Field Guides' *Field Guide to Medicinal Plants: Eastern and Central North America* by Foster and Duke, "American Indians rubbed leaves on insect bites, infected toes, minor skin

Common
Ragweed

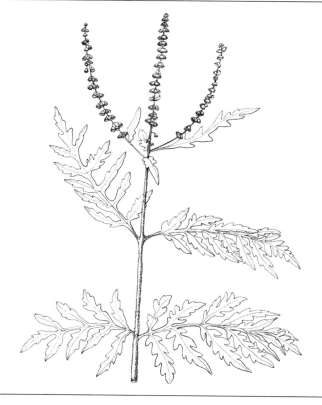

eruptions, and hives. Tea used for fevers, nausea, mucous discharges, intestinal cramping; very astringent, emetic. Root tea used for menstrual problems and stroke." **Blooming time:** Midsummer through early fall. **Locations:** Mount Ephraim Road, Sugarloaf Mountain Road, Yellow Trail, other trails and roadsides. **Similar species:** Great ragweed *(A. trifida)* has similar flowers, but its leaves are very different *(see* next entry). Mugwort *(Artemisia vulgaris),* a Eurasian native which is rare on Sugarloaf, has similar leaves that are all alternately arranged, very aromatic, and densely white-woolly below. (Common ragweed leaves are slightly aromatic, and they may be paler and woolly-pubescent below, but they are not as dramatically whitened as those of mugwort.)

Great Ragweed (Giant Ragweed)

Ambrosia trifida L.
Aster or Daisy Family (Asteraceae)

This plant has **flower heads** similar to the preceding species, but it is commonly a much taller plant (3–15'), and its **leaves** are opposite, toothed, and mostly palmately 3-lobed. Some leaves unlobed (ovate-elliptic), 2-lobed, or up to 5-lobed. An occasional plant has leaves that are all unlobed. Leaves are very large (up to several inches long and wide), lower leaves long-petioled.

Great Ragweed

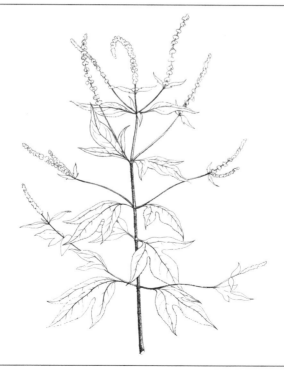

The upper part of the plant (at least) is coarsely pubescent. Great ragweed also causes the allergies commonly called "hay fever"; *see* preceding entry, common ragweed *(A. artemisiifolia).* **Herbal lore:** According to Foster and Duke (Peterson Field Guides' *Field Guide to Medicinal Plants: Eastern and Central North America),* great (or giant) ragweed has a significant herbal history. "Leaf tea," they write, "formerly used for prolapsed uterus, leukorrhea, fevers, diarrhea, dysentery, nosebleeds; gargled for mouth sores. American Indians used the crushed leaves on insect bites. The root was chewed to allay fear at night. The pollen of both this and Common Ragweed are harvested commercially, then manufactured into pharmaceutical preparations for the treatment of ragweed allergies." **On Sugarloaf—Blooming time:** Midsummer to early fall. **Locations:** Mount Ephraim Road, Sugarloaf Mountain Road, other roadsides and trails.

Mugwort

Artemisia vulgaris L.
Aster or Daisy Family (Asteraceae)

An aromatic Eurasian native, mugwort belongs to a genus that is renowned for its fragrant and medicinal plants. **Flower heads:** Tiny, green, purplish-brown, and yellow, in erect or nodding terminal clusters. **Leaves:** Alternate, compound and fernlike, with a strong resemblance to leaves of common ragweed *(Ambrosia artemisiifolia).* Leaves are green above and densely white-woolly beneath. Fragrant when torn. **Height:** 2–4'. **Habitat and range:** Fields, roadsides, waste places; widely naturalized in the United States and Canada. **Herbal lore:** An important herbal in the Old and New Worlds, mugwort has been used to treat colds, bronchitis, kidney and menstrual problems, and a wide range of other medical conditions. According to Foster and Duke, mugwort's dried leaves have been used as a "'burning stick' (moxa), famous in Chinese medicine, to stimulate acupuncture points, treat rheumatism." **On Sugarloaf—Blooming time:** July–September. **Locations:** Mount Ephraim Road; not common on Sugarloaf. **Similar species:** Common ragweed *(Ambrosia artemisiifolia),* which is far more prevalent on Sugarloaf, has leaves that may be slightly paler and woolly-pubescent beneath, but they are not as densely white-woolly or as aromatic. Common ragweed leaves are often alternate above and opposite lower down on the plant stalk.

MONOCOTYLEDONS

Arrowhead or Water-Plantain Family
Alismataceae

Family characteristics: This family usually favors wetland habitats where many plants of its 12 genera and 75 species serve as food for wildlife. The **flowers** are 3-parted. **Occurrence on Sugarloaf:** We have identified a single plant of this family, broad-leaved arrowhead *(Sagittaria latifolia)*, growing on Sugarloaf, in springs along Mount Ephraim Road. In addition, small water-plantain *(Alisma subcordatum)* was identified at the mountain by botanist Richard Wiegand in his 1987 Stronghold plant survey. Many other species in the arrowhead family are native to Maryland wetlands.

Broad-Leaved Arrowhead (Common Arrowhead, Wapato, Duck-Potato)
Sagittaria latifolia Willd.
Arrowhead or Water-Plantain Family (Alismataceae)

An aquatic plant with edible tubers that can be prepared like potatoes. (However, plant collecting on Sugarloaf is forbidden, and no wild plants should be collected without knowledge of toxic look-alikes. Even this edible plant can cause contact dermatitis, according to Foster and Duke in Peterson Field Guides' *Field Guide to Medicinal Plants: Eastern and Central North America*.) **Flowers:** White, ½–1" across, with 3 broadly ovate petals. Flowers are borne

Broad-Leaved
Arrowhead

in whorls on an upright stalk. **Leaves:** Simple basal leaves only. Blades 3–15" long, mostly arrow-shaped but varying from narrow to wide, on long petioles. **Habitat and range:** Swamps, ponds, and streams in Canada and the United States south to the Tropics. **Herbal lore:** This plant was used medicinally by American Indians for a wide range of medical conditions. It was taken internally and used as an external poultice. **Wildlife lore:** The tubers and seeds are an important food for waterfowl. **On Sugarloaf—Blooming time:** June–October. **Locations:** Seeps and springs along Mount Ephraim Road. **Similar species:** A number of *Sagittaria* species are found in Maryland waters, but this is the only one you're likely to encounter on Sugarloaf. The arrow-shaped leaves and 3-petaled flowers distinguish broad-leaved arrowhead from other plants in our mountain flora.

Arum Family

Araceae

Among members of the arum family native to the Washington-Baltimore region are the uncommon green dragon *(Arisaema dracontium)* and a number of aquatic plants including arrow arum *(Peltandra virginica)*. The arum family is represented by two species on Sugarloaf: skunk cabbage *(Symplocarpus foetidus)*, the earliest native spring wildflower on the mountain, and Jack-in-the-pulpit *(Arisaema triphyllum)*. **Family characteristics:** 110 genera and 1,800 species worldwide. Most members of the arum family are tropical, with a few in temperate zones, including several genera indigenous to the United States. **Economic importance:** Taro *(Colocasia esculenta)*, an Asian native, is one of many important food plants of the arum family. A number are grown as ornamental plants and for cut flowers; the calla lily *(Zantedeschia)* is the best known here. **Flowers:** The small true flowers are usually produced as part of a projection called a spadix (the "Jack" of Jack-in-the-pulpit), which is overhung by a leafy, often colorful bract known as a spathe (Jack's "pulpit"). Many species emit fetid odors to attract carrion flies as pollinators. Some have evolved ingenious methods of trapping the pollinators, which slide down the spathe to pollinate the true flowers of the spadix. **Fruit:** Usually a berry (occasionally dry or leathery); sometimes a multiple fruit. **Leaves:** Variable; many genera have sheathing petioles. **Growth habits:** Mostly herbaceous; according to Heywood's *Flowering Plants of the World,* "In the main they are herbaceous with aerial stems or underground tubers or rhizomes, but there are a few woody members. The family includes a number of climbers and epiphytes as well as a floating water plant *(Pistia)*." **Occurrence on Sugarloaf:** Skunk cabbage is a plant of

Sugarloaf's seeps, springs, and streams. Jack-in-the-pulpit grows in a number of habitats from rich upland woods to seeps and springs.

Skunk Cabbage

Symplocarpus foetidus (L.) Salisb. ex W. P. C. Barton
Arum Family (Araceae)

Skunk cabbage is one of the earliest spring blooms in northeastern North America. Although it can reach a height of six inches and is very distinctive up close, skunk cabbage is well camouflaged and can be tricky to find unless you know where to look for it along streams and in seeps and springs. The leaves, which appear as the flowers are dying back, are a brilliant spring green and impossible to miss. In our family the first rite of spring is always a "skunk hunting" expedition. **Flowers:** The fleshy hooded spathe is usually wine-red or brown and vertically speckled yellow or green, but may also be yellow or green with wine striations; 2–6" high. Inside is the round or ovoid spadix bearing the tiny true flowers. **Leaves:** A vibrant yellow-green, springing up along streams when the rest of the forest floor is still wintry. Prominently veined, with smooth or wavy margins, they are tightly coiled at first and then unfurl to a height of 1–3'. Leaves exude a skunky odor when crushed. **Habitat and range:** Swamps, streams, seeps, and springs; Nova Scotia and Quebec to Minnesota and Iowa, south in the Appalachians to Georgia. **Herbal**

Skunk Cabbage

lore: Skunk cabbage has been widely employed medicinally. American Indians used the root to treat convulsions, whooping cough, toothache, and other conditions. The root was also used as a poultice for wounds. Physicians later used it for epileptic seizures and severe coughs. The leaves have also been dried and reconstituted in soups and stews. **Warning:** Contains calcium oxalate crystals. Eating the fresh leaves can burn the mouth, and the roots are considered **toxic.** Only thorough drying removes irritating and toxic properties. *See* additional warning under "Similar species." **On Sugarloaf—Blooming time:** February–April. The leaves outlast the flowers and are showy throughout the spring. **Locations:** Streams, seeps, and springs along most trails; extremely abundant along Bear Branch near Mount Ephraim Road. **Similar species:** The leaves of the poisonous false hellebore *(Veratrum viride)* are often mistaken for skunk cabbage leaves. False hellebore isn't found on Sugarloaf but does grow in surrounding woodlands, where it favors the same wet habitats as does the skunk cabbage. False hellebore bears branching clusters of 6-parted yellow-green flowers. Jack-in-the-pulpit *(Arisaema triphyllum)* is in the same family as skunk cabbage and has a spathe and spadix. But Jack-in-the-pulpit blooms later in the spring and only vaguely resembles skunk cabbage.

Jack-in-the-Pulpit (Indian Turnip)

Arisaema triphyllum (L.) Schott.
Arum Family (Araceae)

A unique and charming spring wildflower, Jack-in-the-pulpit is a favorite of children. When my son was three years old, he would peek under the hooded spathe of the Jack-in-the-pulpit to the spadix inside and intone: "Jack's home, but his puppets are gone." **Flowers:** Usually vertically striped purple-brown and green but may be largely green or brown, with a pointed hood called a spathe (the "pulpit") draped over a small, erect green or brown spadix (" Jack"); 2–5" high, on a long, ascending stalk. The tiny true flowers are grouped around the base of the spadix. **Fruit:** Bright red berries in clusters; summer and fall. **Leaves:** 3 large leaflets per leaf, with untoothed or wavy margins. Each leaflet 2–10" long, ovate or elliptic, with pointed apex and rounded, wedge-shaped, or sometimes unequal base. Usually paler green below. Sessile or short-stalked leaflets on a long ascending petiole. Basal leaves only, although the leaves are usually taller than or as tall as the flower; 1–3 (most often 2) trileafleted leaves per plant. **Height:** 6–36". **Habitat and range:** Moist, rich woods; Nova Scotia to North Dakota; south to Florida and Texas. **Herbal lore:** American Indians used the dried and aged root internally for colds and other conditions and externally as a poultice for rheumatism, abscesses, and ringworm, according to Foster and Duke (Pe-

Jack-in-the-Pulpit

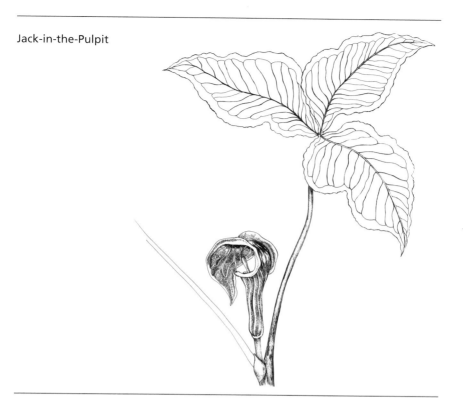

terson Field Guides' *Field Guide to Medicinal Plants: Eastern and Central North America*). From personal experience I can attest to the intensely irritating nature of the fresh plant. As a child I tasted one of the tempting red berries and then ran home in tears. I was reacting to the calcium oxalate crystals found in the fresh plant (as was my little brother, whose older sister had persuaded him to take a taste!). **On Sugarloaf—Blooming time:** April–June (common form); May–July (rarer form). **Locations:** Rich sections of woods along all trails and Mount Ephraim Road. A short hike up the Orange Trail from East View will take you to common Jack-in-the-pulpit sites. The rarer form is found in and around springs on the Yellow Trail and along Mount Ephraim Road. **Similar species:** Skunk cabbage *(Symplocarpus foetidus)* blooms earlier in spring and has a large, firm speckled spathe (*see* illustrations). Botanists used to split Jack-in-the-pulpit into three separate species. On Sugarloaf it is quite easy to recognize a locally rarer form of Jack-in-the-pulpit which was once identified as northern Jack-in-the-pulpit *(A. stewardsonii).* This form is later-blooming and is found growing in wet areas or springs. The lower outer portion of the spathe is deeply fluted with white ridges (the more common form is smooth or lightly fluted). The leaflets are green and shiny below (leaflets of the more common form are paler below).

Spiderwort Family

Commelinaceae

A single member of this family is common on Sugarloaf: a naturalized summer–fall wildflower called Asiatic dayflower *(Commelina communis)*. The native spiderwort *(Tradescantia virginiana)* grows on wooded slopes above the nearby Potomac River and might possibly be found growing here, as might cultivated members of the spiderwort genus that sometimes escape from gardens. **Family characteristics:** The family has 50 genera and 700 species of herbaceous plants worldwide, mainly in tropical, subtropical, and warm temperate regions. The **flowers** are usually perfect, with 3 petals and 3 sepals, and the **leaves** have parallel veins and sheathing bases.

Spiderwort

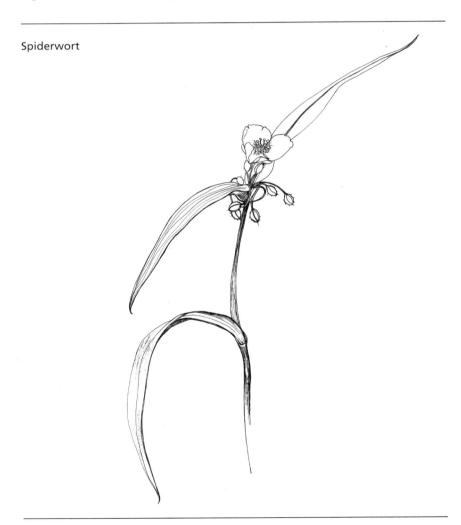

Asiatic Dayflower

Commelina communis L.
Spiderwort Family (Commelinaceae)

The Asiatic dayflower was introduced from Asia, where it is used in Chinese medicine. Considered a weed here by many, this plant has a modest beauty in bloom. The Asiatic dayflower is quite common on Sugarloaf. **Flowers:** Petals: 3—the upper 2 larger and a pale or deep, sometimes sparkly sapphire blue; the lower petal much smaller and white. Flower ½–1" across, growing singly or in a small terminal cluster. There is a folded leafy bract below the flower. **Leaves:** Alternate (although upper leaves may appear opposite), simple; lanceolate or ovate, with parallel veins (including 1 strong central vein) and entire margins. Leaves 1–3½" long, tapering to a sheathing base. **Height and growth habits:** 6–15"; upright or trailing. **Habitat and range:** Moist and/or shaded ground; disturbed sites; East Asian native, now naturalized throughout eastern United States. **Herbal lore:** In Peterson Field Guides' *Field Guide to Medicinal Plants: Eastern and Central North America,* Foster and Duke report, "In China, leaf tea gargled for sore throats; used for cooling, detoxifying, and diuretic properties in flu, acute tonsillitis, urinary infections, dysentery, and acute intestinal enteritis." **On Sugarloaf—Blooming time:** June–October. **Locations:** Trailsides, roadsides, and parking lots mountainwide. **Similar species:** None likely on the mountain. However, there are two dayflowers native to Maryland. The Virginia dayflower *(C. virginica)* has 3 blue petals. The slender dayflower *(C. erecta)* more closely resembles the Asiatic dayflower, but according to Brown and Brown's *Herbaceous Plants of Maryland,* it is found on the coastal plain (where it is rare) and in Allegany County.

Asiatic Dayflower

Lily Family

Liliaceae

Most people need little introduction to the lily family, which produces the gorgeous flowers of the *Lilium* genus as well as tulips *(Tulipa)*, hyacinths *(Hyacinthus)*, and many other popular garden plants. However, other equally well-known plants are in this family but are rarely associated with the name "lily" : onions, leeks, garlic, and asparagus, for example. The family is represented by several native species on Sugarloaf. **Family characteristics:** 280 genera and nearly 4,000 species worldwide. Cosmopolitan. **Economic importance:** Garden flowers, foods, and medicines. **Flowers:** Mostly perfect and regular, usually with 3 petals and 3 petaloid sepals, all 6 often referred to as tepals. May also have 4 or 8 tepals. Sepals not always petaloid. Flower sometimes tubular and bell-shaped. **Fruit:** A capsule or berry (or sometimes a dry indehiscent fruit). **Leaves:** Simple, usually narrow and parallel-veined (but may also be broader and net-veined). **Growth habits:** Mostly herbs from bulbs, rhizomes, corms, or tuberous roots. **Occurrence on Sugarloaf:** Several species in many habitats. In addition to the species illustrated and described in the next entries, botanist Richard Wiegand found two uncommon lily species growing at Sugarloaf in 1987: Canada lily (*Lilium canadense* L.) and Turk's-cap lily (*Lilium superbum* L.). Tina and I have yet to see either species, which may have since been eradicated by the mountain's deer, but we are looking for them. Sugarloaf lacks trilliums *(Trillium)*, which are such an important part of the lily family flora in eastern North America. The toadshade or sessile trillium (*T. sessile* L.) grows along the nearby Potomac River.

Trout-Lily (Fawn-Lily, Adder's-Tongue, Dogtooth Violet)

Erythronium americanum Ker Gawl.
Lily Family (Liliaceae)

Trout-lily is a common spring wildflower of area floodplains, bottomlands, and moist woodlands. Its mottled leaves carpet the ground in concert with spring beauty and other early flowering plants. It is not found on the mountain proper, but trout-lily lines the shores of Furnace Branch in the Monocacy Natural Resources Management Area and Bennett Creek, just north of the mountain. **Flowers:** Yellow, nodding, with 6 tepals that are reflexed when flower is mature. Flowers ¾–1½" long, borne singly on a 3–10" stalk. **Leaves:** 2 basal (or nearly basal) leaves are 2½–8" long, green with brown mottling (pattern is troutlike), ovate, lanceolate, oblanceolate, or elliptic, entire. Young sterile plants send up a single leaf, and these often grow in dense colonies. **Height:** 3–10". **Range:** Eastern United States and Canada. **On Sug-**

arloaf—**Blooming time:** March–May. **Similar species:** Use the mottled leaves to separate this species from other yellow-flowered members of the lily family. The white trout-lily *(E. albidum),* considered a rare species in Maryland, grows in a few spots along the Potomac between Sugarloaf and the District of Columbia.

Perfoliate Bellwort

Uvularia perfoliata L.
Lily Family (Liliaceae)

A nodding yellow lily with leaves pierced by the plant stalk, a growth pattern botanists refer to as perfoliate. **Flowers:** Pale yellow, bell-shaped, with or-ange granules inside, ¾–1¼" long; 6 tepals are pointed at tips. Flowers usu-ally solitary. **Leaves:** Alternate, simple, with entire margins. Very distinctly pierced by plant stalk, 1–3½" long with pointed apex and rounded base. **Height and growth habits:** 6"–2'; nodding. **Habitat and range:** Moist or dry woods, often acidic soil; eastern United States and southeastern Canada. **On Sugarloaf—Blooming time:** Late April–June. **Locations:** Yellow Trail and other trails; quite common mountainwide. **Similar species:** Sessile bellwort

(U. sessilifolia), which follows, has sessile (but not perfoliate) leaves. Smooth Solomon's seal *(Polygonatum biflorum)* has several smaller flowers per stalk.

Sessile Bellwort (Wild Oats)

Uvularia sessilifolia L.
Lily Family (Liliaceae)

Very similar to the preceding entry, perfoliate bellwort, sessile bellwort has pale yellow or straw-colored **flowers** and **leaves** that are sessile but not perfoliate (pierced by the plant stalk). Almost as common on Sugarloaf as the preceding species, sessile bellwort blooms in May and June and can be found along many trails.

Smooth Solomon's Seal

Polygonatum biflorum (Walter) Elliott
Lily Family (Liliaceae)

A beautiful spring wildflower with dangling white or yellow-green bell-shaped flowers. The plant is named for the round scars on its rootstock, according to *Newcomb's Wildflower Guide.* **Flowers:** Tubular, ½–1" long, separating into 6 short lobes, usually hanging in several pairs below the leaf axils. **Fruit:** Blue-black berry. **Leaves:** Alternate, simple, with smooth margins and parallel veins. Sessile or partly clasping, glabrous and somewhat shiny above, slightly glaucous beneath. Ovate-lanceolate or ovate-elliptic with bluntly or more sharply pointed apex and rounded to wedge-shaped

Smooth
Solomon's Seal

base (or when clasping, base may seem a bit cordate). **Height and growth habits:** 1–3', arching with flowers dangling along the plant stalk. **Habitat and range:** Moist to dry woods and roadsides; New England to Manitoba, south to Florida and northern Mexico. **Herbal lore:** An important herbal. In Peterson Field Guides' *Field Guide to Medicinal Plants: Eastern and Central North America,* Foster and Duke report that the root was widely employed internally as tea and externally as a poultice or wash by American Indians and European settlers. Conditions treated with smooth Solomon's seal included indigestion, "profuse menstruation," lung problems, coughs, insomnia, arthritis, bruises, cuts, and sores. **On Sugarloaf—Blooming time:** May–June. **Fruiting time:** Summer–fall. **Locations:** Most trails, streams, and roadsides; mountainwide but not very common. **Similar species:** Most similar are the bellworts *(Uvularia)*, but they bear only 1–3 flowers per plant. False Solomon's seal *(Smilacina racemosa)* has similar leaves and growth habit, but its leaves are larger, thicker, and more deeply veined, and its small white flowers are borne at the terminus of the plant.

False Solomon's Seal

Smilacina racemosa (L.) Desf.
Lily Family (Liliaceae)

The fruit of false Solomon's seal is as showy as the flowers. One of Sugarloaf's tallest spring wildflowers, false Solomon's seal is quite common mountainwide. **Flowers:** Tiny, creamy white, less than ¼" across in foamy looking,

False Solomon's
Seal

usually branched terminal clusters. Each flower with 6 tepals and 6 slightly longer stamens. **Fruit:** Terminal clusters of speckled red berries. **Leaves:** Alternate, simple, with entire margins and vertical veins. Ovate-lanceolate or elliptic with rounded to wedge-shaped base, on short petiole or sessile. May be finely pubescent (to touch or visible with a hand lens), but some specimens are glabrous or nearly so. Leaves pointed at apex and 3–8" long. **Height and growth habits:** 1–3'; stem arching and often somewhat zigzag. **Habitat and range:** Rich woods; Nova Scotia to British Columbia, south to Georgia and Arizona. **Herbal lore:** Widely used by American Indians and other herbalists for a variety of conditions including constipation, rheumatism, and mental instability and as a contraceptive. **On Sugarloaf—Blooming time:** May–June. **Fruiting time:** Summer–fall. **Locations:** Rich woods mountainwide; Bear Branch and Mount Ephraim Road. **Similar species:** Distinguish false Solomon's seal from smooth Solomon's seal *(Polygonatum biflorum)* and the bellworts *(Uvularia* species), which have similar leaves, by the foamy-looking clusters of small white flowers. Canada Mayflower *(Maianthemum canadense)* has flowers similar to false Solomon's seal's but is a smaller plant. Another *Smilacina* species, starry false Solomon's seal *(S. stellata)*, is rare in the Washington-Baltimore area but might possibly be found on or near Sugarloaf.

Yellow Stargrass

Hypoxis hirsuta (L.) Coville
Lily Family (Liliaceae)

[Sometimes included in Amaryllis or Daffodil Family (Amaryllidaceae)]
A lovely yellow flower blooming in the spring and summer. **Flowers:** 6 lemon-yellow tepals form a star-shaped flower, ½–1½" across. One to several flowers on a long, upright stalk. **Leaves:** Shiny, narrow, grasslike, with parallel veins and pointed apex, 3–12" long. **Height and growth habits:** 3–12"; upright. **Habitat and range:** Open woods, meadows; southeastern Canada to Georgia and Texas. **On Sugarloaf—Blooming time:** Late April–September. **Locations:** White Trail, Blue Trail, Yellow Trail, Mount Ephraim Road. **Similar species:** None on Sugarloaf.

Yellow Stargrass

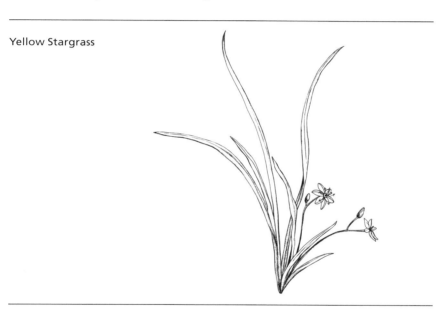

Canada Mayflower (Wild Lily-of-the-Valley)

Maianthemum canadense Desf.
Lily Family (Liliaceae)

A delicate wildflower which spreads by rhizomes, forming carpets. Abundant in the cool, moist woodlands of northeastern North America, Canada mayflower is rather uncommon on Sugarloaf. **Flowers:** Small, fragrant, creamy white, in upright terminal clusters; 4 tepals are reflexed. Each flower less than ¼" across. Flower cluster ½–2" tall. **Fruit:** Upright clusters of speckled pale red berries. **Leaves:** Alternate, simple, 1–3 per plant, sessile or

short-stalked. Deep shiny green with vertical veins and entire margins. Base heart-shaped (cordate) or rounded. Apex abruptly pointed. Leaf shape cordate or ovate. **Height and growth habits:** 2–7"; usually upright and single-stalked. **Habitat and range:** Moist woods, eastern Canada south to Maryland; in the mountains to Kentucky and Georgia. **Herbal lore:** In Peterson Field Guides' *Field Guide to Medicinal Plants: Eastern and Central North America,* Foster and Duke report on the creative historic uses of this plant: "American Indians used plant tea for headaches, and to 'keep kidneys open during pregnancy.' Also a gargle for sore throats. Root used as a good luck charm for winning games. Folk expectorant for coughs, soothing to sore throats." **On Sugarloaf—Blooming time:** Late April–June. **Fruiting time:** Summer–fall. **Locations:** Yellow Trail, Mount Ephraim Road. **Similar species:** False Solomon's seal *(Smilacina racemosa)* is a much larger plant with a greater number of leaves and 6 tepals per flower. It is more common on Sugarloaf.

Indian Cucumber Root

Medeola virginiana L.
Lily Family (Liliaceae)

Indian cucumber root is a tallish wildflower of rich, moist eastern North American woods. It forms a charming picture growing in moist areas of Sugarloaf along with cinnamon fern, royal fern, and an orchid called large whorled pogonia. The plant is showy in the fall with its purple-black berries borne above the upper leaf whorls as they blush autumn-red. **Flowers:** Greenish-yellow with 6 recurved tepals, nodding beneath the uppermost leaf whorl. Styles are long, scarlet, and reflexed. Flower ⅓–¾" across. **Fruit:** A round purple or black berry, in small terminal clusters. **Leaves:** Simple, untoothed, with parallel veins, in two-tiered whorls. The uppermost whorl

consists of 3–5 ovate-elliptic leaves that are sessile or short-stalked, 1–2" long. The lower whorl has 5–9 (rarely 11) leaves that are oblong-oblanceolate and sessile, 2–6" long, tapered at the base, and pointed at the apex. The lower leaf whorl is borne about halfway up the plant stalk. **Height and growth habits:** 1–2½'; upright with nodding flowers beneath the uppermost whorl. **Habitat and range:** Rich, moist woods; eastern Canada to Wisconsin; south to Georgia, Florida, and Louisiana. **Herbal lore:** The edible root has a cucumber flavor (but please don't sample it on Sugarloaf!). According to Foster and Duke (Peterson Field Guides' *Field Guide to Medicinal Plants: Eastern and Central North America*), "American Indians chewed root and spit it on hook to make fish bite. Leaf and berry tea administered to babies with convulsions. Root tea once used as a diuretic for dropsy." **On Sugarloaf—Blooming time:** May–June. **Locations:** Mostly the western side of the mountain in rich, moist areas near springs and streams: Blue Trail, Yellow Trail, Mount Ephraim Road. Found elsewhere in rich, moist spots. **Similar species:** None on Sugarloaf when in bloom. Before blooming, the lower leaf whorl resembles the leaves of the large whorled pogonia *(Isotria verticillata),* a rare orchid which shares the Indian cucumber root habitat on Sugarloaf. The orchid's plant stalk is thick, purplish-brown, and fleshy, while the Indian cucumber root's stalk is thinner and rather wiry, with white-woolly flecks.

Day-Lily

Hemerocallis fulva L.
Lily Family (Liliaceae)

This Eurasian native has escaped from gardens and flourishes in many part of eastern North America. Day-lily grows along Sugarloaf area roadsides. I has become a problematic invasive along some Maryland rivers. **Flowers** Large, showy orange-yellow flowers have 6 (2–5") spreading tepals, whicl join to form a short funnel at the base of the flower. Flowers borne in smal terminal clusters; each bloom lasts a single day. **Leaves:** Basal leaves only leaves are long (several inches to over 1') and linear. **Height:** 2–6'. **On Sug arloaf—Blooming time:** June–July (usually in peak bloom at the summe solstice). **Locations:** Comus and Mount Ephraim Roads; very showy displa along nearby West Harris Road.

Day-Lily

Field Garlic

Allium vineale L.
Lily Family (Liliaceae)

Field garlic is a Eurasian escape that is common in the mid-Atlantic region. It gives our fresh-mown lawns a garlicky aura, which is quite pleasant for those of us accustomed to it. Field garlic has slender, mostly hollow, upright **leaves** and bears round clusters of tiny reddish-purple, pink, white, or greenish **flowers**—or sometimes the plant produces a cluster of tiny bulblets, each tipped with a long leafy structure. **On Sugarloaf**—Look for field garlic along mountain roads and some trails and in the surrounding countryside, where it grows abundantly.

Woody Vine

Common Greenbrier (Catbrier)

Smilax rotundifolia L.
Lily Family (Liliaceae)

[Sometimes included in the separate Greenbrier Family (Smilacaceae)] Common greenbrier, a prickly climbing vine, is frequently encountered in the mid-Atlantic region and is common on Sugarloaf. **Flowers:** Small, greenish, with 6 tepals; borne in umbels of 6–25 flowers. **Fruit:** A round blue-black or black berry, about ¼" across, usually glaucous, containing 2–3 (rarely 1) seeds. **Leaves:** Alternate, simple, ovate, with a few prominent

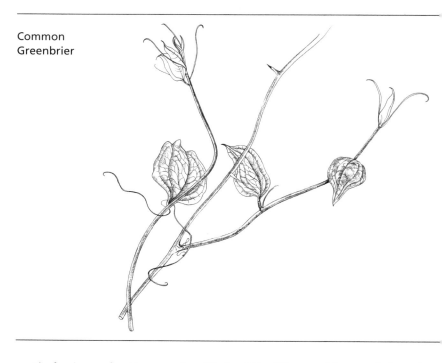

Common
Greenbrier

vertical veins and entire margins. Blades 1½–4" long, with rounded, wedge-shaped, flat across (truncate), or heart-shaped (cordate) base. **Growth habits:** A climbing woody vine that bears sharp prickles. **Habitat and range:** Open woods, thickets, and roadsides; Nova Scotia to Michigan, south to northern Florida and eastern Texas. **Herbal lore:** Young shoots, leaves, and tendrils are edible and make an excellent trail nibble in locales where harvesting is permitted (not Sugarloaf). This vine and other *Smilax* species have been used medicinally, as Foster and Duke report in Peterson Field Guides' *Field Guide to Medicinal Plants: Eastern and Central North America:* "American Indians rubbed stem prickles on skin as a counter-irritant to relieve localized pains, muscle cramps, twitching; leaf and stem tea used for rheumatism, stomach troubles. Wilted leaves poulticed on boils. Root tea taken to help expel afterbirth. We cannot confirm rumors that *Smilax* roots contain testosterone (male hormone); they may contain steroid precursors, however." **Wildlife lore:** Russell and Melvin Brown describe the importance of native *Smilax* species to local wildlife in their book *Woody Plants of Maryland:* "Tangles of greenbrier vines furnish protective cover for rabbits and other species of small wildlife; the stems and leaves are browsed by deer. The berries are eaten by a wide variety of species including wood duck, ruffed grouse, wild turkey, fish crow, black bear, opossum, raccoon, squirrel, and numerous species of song birds, especially the catbird, mocking bird, robin, and the thrushes." **On Sugarloaf—Blooming time:** April–June. **Locations:**

Mount Ephraim Road, Yellow Trail, Blue Trail, other trails and roadsides. **Similar species:** Could be confused with wild yams (*Dioscorea* spp.), but yams lack prickles. Several other woody vines in the *Smilax* genus are native to Maryland, but they are not likely to be found on Sugarloaf. However, another *Smilax* species does grow here: carrion flower *(S. herbacea)*. It lacks prickles and is a nonwoody species, but it climbs over other plants by tendrils. As its name implies, the scent of the small greenish flowers, which are borne in umbels, resembles the odor of decaying flesh. The leaves and fruit of carrion flower resemble those of common greenbrier. Because it is not common on the mountain, we mention it here only in passing.

Yam Family
Dioscoreaceae

The yam family is important for food and medicine: its largest genus, *Dioscorea*, is the source of edible yams and many modern drugs (*see* next entry). **Family characteristics:** A largely tropical family of 6 genera and 630 species, Dioscoreaceae has a few members in the temperate zone, including two species growing on Sugarloaf. Most yam family members are climbing vines. **Flowers** are small, regular, often unisexual, usually with 6 tepals. **Fruit:** A capsule or berry. **Leaves** may be opposite, whorled, or alternate; entire (or sometimes lobed or compound).

Wild Yam (Yamroot)
Dioscorea quaternata (Walter) J. F. Gmel.
Yam Family (Dioscoreaceae)

This viny plant and a second yam species noted here under "Similar species" have distinctive heart-shaped leaves. Some botanists, including Stanwyn G. Shetler of the Smithsonian Institution, lump these two species together under the name *Dioscorea villosa*. **Flowers:** Greenish or yellowish, small and rather inconspicuous, clustered on drooping stalks; male and female flowers in separate clusters and usually on separate plants. **Fruit:** A 3-winged obovoid capsule develops on those plants bearing female flowers; about 1" or more long. **Leaves:** Whorled, opposite, or alternate, simple. Lower leaves in whorls of 4–7, upper leaves opposite or alternate. All leaves heart-shaped (cordate) or ovate, with strong longitudinal veins and smooth or wavy margins. Blade 2–5" long on long petiole. **Height and growth habits:** 4–10' long; an arching or trailing vine; when plant first appears in spring, it's as a showy whorl of 4 or more leaves. **Habitat and range:** Moist open woods, thickets, roadsides; Pennsylvania to Indiana and Missouri, south to Florida and

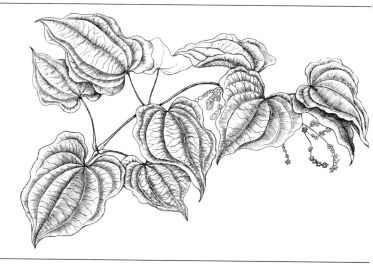

Wild Yam

Louisiana (mainly in Appalachian region). **Herbal lore:** Wild yam and other members of the yam genus are herbally significant. In Peterson Field Guides' *Field Guide to Medicinal Plants: Eastern and Central North America,* Foster and Duke write: "Of all plant genera, there is perhaps none with greater impact on modern life but whose dramatic story is as little known as *Dioscorea*. Most of the steroid hormones used in modern medicine, especially those in contraceptives, were developed from elaborately processed chemical components derived from yams." American Indians and early physicians used yam root for a number of medical conditions, and yam-derived components are used in modern medicines to "relieve asthma, arthritis, eczema, regulate metabolism and control fertility," according to Foster and Duke. The authors warn: "Fresh plant may induce vomiting and other undesirable side effects." **On Sugarloaf—Blooming time:** May–July. **Locations:** This species and a similar one are both common mountainwide. **Similar species:** Another wild yam *(D. villosa)* also grows on Sugarloaf. Very similar in appearance, this second yam species usually has lower leaves in whorls of 3 and upper leaves mostly alternate.

Iris Family

Iridaceae

This is the family of the familiar garden irises and crocuses. Several members of the *Iris* genus are indigenous to Maryland, mainly in wetlands, but are not found on Sugarloaf. One small-flowered member of the family—stout blue-eyed grass *(Sisyrinchium angustifolium)*—grows on Sugarloaf, with a second blue-eyed grass species possible. **Family characteristics:** 80 genera and 1,500 species worldwide. Cosmopolitan. **Economic importance:** Garden ornamentals include plants of the *Iris, Crocus, Gladiolus* (gladiolas), and *Freesia* genera. Saffron, a yellow culinary flavoring and dye, is obtained from the pistil of the autumn crocus *(Crocus sativus)*. **Flowers:** Perfect, regular or irregular, with 6 petaloid parts (called tepals). **Fruit:** A capsule. **Leaves:** Simple, narrow, parallel-veined. **Growth habits:** Perennial herbs growing from rhizomes, bulbs, or corms. **Occurrence on Sugarloaf:** Stout blue-eyed grass along trails, roads, grassy areas.

Stout Blue-Eyed Grass

Sisyrinchium angustifolium Mill.
Iris Family (Iridaceae)

A slender plant of grassy areas and open woods. Stout blue-eyed grass is quite common on and around Sugarloaf. **Flowers:** Blue-violet, 6-tepaled, with a yellow eye. Each tepal comes to a bristle-tipped apex. Flowers ½–¾" wide in small terminal cluster or solitary. Flower stalks encased in a flattened leafy bract called a spathe. **Leaves:** Long, slender, flattened, grasslike. In addition to the grasslike basal leaf, there is a stiff, grasslike leafy bract arising midway or higher on the winged plant stalk at the point where the flower stalks diverge. **Height:** 4–18". **Habitat and range:** Fields, meadows, lawns, damp woods; Newfoundland to Minnesota, south to Florida and Texas. **Herbal lore:** According to Foster and Duke (Peterson Field Guides' *Field*

Stout Blue-Eyed
Grass

Guide to Medicinal Plants: Eastern and Central North America), "American Indians used root tea for diarrhea (in children); plant tea for worms, stomachaches." Please remember that Sugarloaf wildflowers are not to be harvested for any reason. **On Sugarloaf—Blooming time:** May–July. **Locations:** Common along trails and roadsides but nowhere abundant. **Similar species:** Several blue-eyed grass species are native to Maryland and are described and illustrated in Brown and Brown's *Herbaceous Plants of Maryland*. Slender blue-eyed grass *(S. mucronatum)* is common in our area and might be found on Sugarloaf. Its main plant stalk is only barely winged, and its leaves are narrower and shorter. *A Field Guide to Wildflowers of Northeastern and North-Central North America* by Peterson and McKenny features illustrations of the two species side by side.

Orchid Family

Orchidaceae

The orchid family garners several superlatives: it is the largest flowering plant family in the world; it is the most highly evolved of the monocotyledons (and according to many contemporary botanists that makes it the most highly evolved plant family); and it produces some of the world's most beautiful and highly prized flowers. In addition, the orchid family produces the plant that gives us vanilla. This family has developed highly specialized, co-evolutionary relationships with its pollinators (many are bees and wasps). Orchids lack root hairs, and they depend on fungi in the soil to bring moisture to them, or in the case of epiphytes, they require 100 percent humidity. **Family characteristics:** 600 genera and 15,000 plus species worldwide. Cosmopolitan; on every continent except Antarctica and in all but the most extreme environments. Abundant in the Tropics where many species are epiphytes (" air plants" lacking roots in the soil). **Economic importance and some challenges for survival:** Vanilla flavoring is obtained from the capsules of *Vanilla planifolia*, a tropical American plant. Orchids have long been prized by collectors. According to Heywood's *Flowering Plants of the World*, "The legends surrounding the early discoveries, importations, sale, cultivation and breeding of choice orchids are among the classics of botanical and horticultural literature. The facts are no less remarkable; the privations suffered by the privately sponsored explorers, the vast losses of plants sustained on the long journeys back to Europe, the fabulous prices realized at auctions for fresh importations are well documented." Fascination with orchids, and orchid cultivation, continues to the present day. Today many orchids are in danger of extinction. The biggest threat is not orchid collection but habitat destruction. Because many orchids are rare or uncommon in their native habitats and their reproductive process is complex, they are extremely vulnerable. In Heywood's words, "The fruit (capsule) from a single fertilized flower spike may produce vast numbers of . . . seeds; figures of a million or more having been recorded from many species. In order to germinate, these minute seeds require the help of a fungus in a special symbiotic relationship; even so, it can take an inordinate amount of time for a flowering-size orchid plant to appear. The ripening of the seed in an orchid capsule usually takes from two to 18 months; the germination period is similar, but it can take a further four years for the life-cycle to be complete." **Flowers:** Usually perfect, irregular, with 3 sepals, which can be green or petaloid, and 3 petals. The lower petal is often modified into a lip, sac, or spur. The pollen is usually in a waxy mass, and it's an all or nothing situation with a pollinator. If the pollinator makes good contact with the pollen, then when the pollinator flies free, he/she takes all the pollen from that flower. In orchids with a saclike lower petal, the pollinator may become temporarily trapped, increasing the likelihood of successful pollen-gathering. **Fruit:** A capsule. **Leaves:** Alternate or (less often) opposite or whorled, or with basal leaves only; simple, with parallel veins. **Growth habits:** Perennial herbs; many tropical species are epiphytic, and some species are saprophytic. **Occurrence on Sugarloaf:** Several orchids grow on Sugarloaf, including two that are ranked as threatened species in Maryland. It is our policy not to disclose the whereabouts of rare and threatened plants. When you do encounter orchids, please enjoy their beauty at a respectful distance.

Pink Lady's Slipper (Moccasin Flower)

Cypripedium acaule Aiton
Orchid Family (Orchidaceae)

The pink lady's slipper is one of the most beautiful wildflowers in the North American flora. The large pink lower petal is shaped like a pouch, resembling a "lady's slipper" or moccasin. The pink lady's slipper loves Sugarloaf's acidic soil, while the equally lovely yellow lady's slipper *(C. calceolus)* favors the more alkaline soils of the mountains to the west. Please ensure that your children treat this irresistible wildflower with respect. **Flowers:** Irregular; lowest petal a large deep or pale pink pouch, 1–3" long, heavily veined and puckered toward a central opening. Upper 2 petals brownish-pink or greenish, narrow, pointed, and twisted; (sepals are similar in color). A green bract arises behind the flower and curves forward. One flower per plant stalk. **Leaves:** A large pair of basal leaves only; each 4–8" long, oblong or elliptic, parallel-veined, bluntly pointed, with entire margins. Leaves are finely pubescent. **Height:** 4–14". **Habitat and range:** Acidic soil in a variety of habitats; eastern Canada to Georgia and Alabama. **Herbal lore:** During the

Pink Lady's
Slipper

nineteenth century both pink and yellow lady's slippers were employed as sedatives. These rare plants should never be harvested in the wild. **On Sugarloaf—Blooming time:** Late April–May. **Locations:** Sugarloaf trails and roadsides mountainwide. **Similar species:** None on Sugarloaf.

Downy Rattlesnake-Plantain

Goodyera pubescens (Willd.) R. Br. ex W. T. Aiton
Orchid Family (Orchidaceae)

Downy rattlesnake-plantain's creamy white flowers appear in midsummer. The plant's forest-green, white-veined basal leaf rosettes are a fairly common sight along Sugarloaf's woodland trails. **Flowers:** Small, white, distinctly orchidesque flowers are borne along the upper part of a straight, pubescent stalk. **Leaves:** Very distinctive basal leaves in a low-growing rosette. Spruce green with creamy veins in a pattern suggesting rattlesnake markings, appearing long before, and lasting long after, the summer flowers. Ovate-elliptic, entire, sessile or with a short, wide petiole; 1–3" long. **Height:** 6–16". **Habitat and range:** Woods; eastern United States and Canada south to Georgia and Alabama, west to Minnesota and Arkansas. **Herbal lore:** The roots and leaves of this plant were used medicinally by American Indians and European settlers for a number of internal and external ailments. The plant is too rare to harvest today, according to Foster and Duke in Peterson Field

Downy
Rattlesnake-Plantain

Guides' *Field Guide to Medicinal Plants: Eastern and Central North America.*
On Sugarloaf—Blooming time: July–August. **Locations:** Most trails, Bear
Branch. **Similar species:** Two other rattlesnake-plantains (*Goodyera* spp.)
have been reported in Maryland in the past, but neither is likely to be found
on Sugarloaf. See text and illustrations in Brown and Brown's *Herbaceous
Plants of Maryland* for comparison. According to botanist Cris Fleming, the
historical records of these other species (*G. repens* and *G. tesselata*) may be
inaccurate, and even if they are accurate, both plants are now considered extirpated from Maryland.

Showy Orchis (Showy Orchid)

Galearis spectabilis (L.) Raf.
(Orchis spectabilis)
Orchid Family (Orchidaceae)

An uncommon spring orchid of small stature and great beauty. **Flowers:**
Several per plant stalk, strikingly bicolored (or rarely all white) with a purple,
lavender-blue, or deep rose upper lip (consisting of sepals and lateral petals)

Showy Orchis

and a white lower lip and spur. Each flower about an inch long. Approximately 3–8 flowers per plant, borne in an upright cluster. **Leaves:** 2 basal leaves per plant, obovate or elliptic, 2½–8" long, with entire margins and few parallel veins. **Height:** 3–10". **Habitat and range:** Rich, moist woods; eastern United States and Canada. **On Sugarloaf—Blooming time:** May. **Locations:** Bear Branch, Mount Ephraim Road. **Similar species:** None on Sugarloaf.

Other Orchid Family Members (Orchidaceae) of Sugarloaf

Large Whorled Pogonia
Isotria verticillata (Muhl. ex Willd.) Raf.

Large whorled pogonia is quite common in Sugarloaf's moist woods, although it is rarely seen in bloom. **Flowers:** Greenish-yellow with a 3-lobed, crested, white and purple-streaked lip and 3 very long and narrow purple-brown sepals. Sepals 1½–2½" long and spreading. Flower borne singly above a whorl of leaves. **Leaves:** Usually 5 (sometimes 6) simple, sessile, entire leaves in a single whorl on a thick, purplish, fleshy stalk. Leaves broadly obovate or oblong, 1½–5" long with vertical veins and an abruptly pointed apex. **Height:** 6–12". **Habitat and range:** Moist or dry acidic woods; eastern United States and Canada. **On Sugarloaf—Blooming time:** May–June. **Locations:** Blue Trail, Mount Ephraim Road. **Similar species:** Small whorled pogonia *(I. medeoloides)* is a globally rare and federally threatened plant that was once found in Maryland. As of 1996 there are no known populations in the state. It is 3–6" tall and has shorter sepals than its larger cousin. Indian cucumber root *(Medeola virginiana)* has a leaf whorl similar to that of the pogonias and shares the large whorled pogonia's habitat in Sugarloaf's moist woods. However, in bloom Indian cucumber root has two layers of leaf

whorls with the 6-tepaled flowers dangling beneath the upper whorl. When only leaves are present, distinguish the two species by the plant stalk: Indian cucumber root's is thin and wiry, whorled pogonia's thick and fleshy.

Yellow-Fringed Orchid (Yellow-Fringed Orchis)

Platanthera ciliaris (L.) Lindl.
(Habenaria ciliaris)

A very rare orchid, this elegant wildflower is officially listed as a threatened species in Maryland. If you should encounter it, please protect the plant and its fragile habitat by maintaining a respectful distance! Only one small population has been discovered on Sugarloaf, and these plants are on record with the Maryland Department of Natural Resources, which actively tracks threatened and endangered plant and animal species within the state. **Flowers:** A unique pale tangerine, with a hooded upper lip, dramatically fringed lower lip, and a long spur at the back (up to 1" long). Flowers borne in a dense upright spike. **Leaves:** Alternate, simple, sessile, and somewhat clasping, with parallel veins. Lower leaves oblong-lanceolate, up to several inches long; the upper leaves may be more linear and are shorter. **Height:** 1–2'. **Habitat and range:** Moist woods, bogs, swamps, seeps; Massachusetts to Wisconsin, south to Florida and Texas. **On Sugarloaf—Blooming time:** July–August. **Locations:** Locations not given in order to protect these threatened plants and their habitats. **Similar species:** None on Sugarloaf. The crested yellow orchid *(P. cristata)*, found elsewhere in Maryland and also a threatened species in the state, has a shorter spur at the back of its flower.

Large Purple-Fringed Orchid

Platanthera grandiflora (Bigel.) Lindl.
(Habenaria fimbriata)
(Habenaria psycodes var. *grandiflora)*

Large purple-fringed orchid holds an S2 ranking in Maryland, which means it is imperiled in the state due to its rarity; S2-ranked plant populations are actively tracked by the Wildlife and Heritage Division of the Maryland Department of Natural Resources. During a 1987 plant survey, botanist Richard Wiegand located a few specimens of this threatened plant on Stronghold property. Early summer **flowers** are purple or magenta (rarely white), fragrant, about 1" long with a 3-parted, deeply fringed lower lip and a spur at the back. Borne in very dense racemes that are 2–2½" thick. **Leaves** are alternate, simple, entire; lanceolate, oblanceolate, or ovate (upper leaves smaller and narrower than lower ones). **Height:** 1–4'. **Habitat and range:** Wet woods, seeps, and meadows; northeastern North America.

Green Wood Orchid

Platanthera clavellata (Michx.) Luer
(Habenaria clavellata)

The green wood orchid blooms in summer and has greenish-white flowers with a long, curved spur at the back of the bloom which is often somewhat swollen at the tip. **Flowers** are borne on a 6–18" stalk which usually has one well-developed **leaf** near the base and then scant smaller ones in an alternate pattern. Flowers often twisted or askew on the stalk. **Habitat and range:** Moist, acidic woods and seeps; eastern North America. **On Sugarloaf— Locations:** Moist areas near the mountain base.

Puttyroot (Adam-and-Eve)

Aplectrum hyemale (Muhl. ex Willd.) Torr.

During late summer puttyroot or Adam-and-Eve puts out a single large, elliptic basal **leaf,** which is crimped like a handheld fan (plicate). The leaf lasts through the winter but dies back before the flowers appear. Puttyroot's small **flowers** are yellow-green and plum-brown with a small, whitish, purple-spotted lip. They are borne in a long, loose, upright raceme. Puttyroot is 10–16" tall. It is rare on Sugarloaf. **Habitat and range:** Woods; eastern and central United States and Canada. **On Sugarloaf—Blooming time:** April–June. **Locations:** Yellow Trail, Monocacy Natural Resources Management Area.

Cranefly Orchid

Tipularia discolor (Pursh) Nutt.

A summer-blooming orchid of delicate beauty. Its single basal leaf is produced in the fall and dies back before the flowers appear. **Flowers:** Translucent purplish, purplish-brown, or green in a slender, loose raceme. Lateral petals and sepals similar: small, narrow, winglike, and graceful. Lip purplish or pink, 3-lobed with a long spur at the back. Flowers ½–1" long (including spur). **Leaf:** Single basal leaf, 2–5" long, ovate-elliptic, petioled, shallowly folded like a fan (plicate), and purplish beneath. Leaf can be seen from fall through spring. **Height:** 8–16". **Habitat and range:** Moist, rich woods; eastern United States. **On Sugarloaf—Blooming time:** July–August. **Locations:** Yellow Trail and likely along other trails; Monocacy Natural Resources Management Area.

Cranefly Orchid

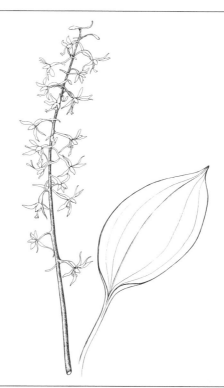

Coralroots

Corallorhiza

Two species of coralroot are found on Sugarloaf. These plants have fleshy purplish, brownish, greenish, or yellowish stalks and no green leaves. They are saprophytic (living off decayed or decaying organic matter) or root-parasitic. Spotted Coralroot [*C. maculata* (Raf.) Raf.] blooms in summer and is rare on Sugarloaf. It has ½–¾" **flowers** that are yellowish, purple, or purple-brown with a white 3-lobed lower lip that is spotted reddish-purple; 10–35 flowers borne on an 8–20" stalk. Autumn Coralroot (Small or Late Coralroot) [*C. odontorhiza* (Willd.) Nutt.] blooms from late summer through fall and is a little more common on the mountain. Its **flowers** are slightly smaller (about ¼" long), brownish-purple or brown with a purple-spotted unlobed white lip (although unlobed, the lip may have a notched or wavy-toothed margin); 3–20 flowers borne on a 4–12" stalk. **On Sugarloaf—Locations:** Yellow Trail, Mount Ephraim Road, Monocacy Natural Resources Management Area.

Large Twayblade (Lily-Leaved Twayblade)
Liparis liliifolia (L.) Rich. ex Lindl.

Large twayblade blooms in late spring and summer. Its mauve **flowers** are about ½" long with a broad, obovate lip, threadlike lateral petals, and narrow greenish sepals; 5–40 flowers borne in an upright raceme on a 4–12" plant stalk. A single pair of glossy basal **leaves**: ovate or ovate-elliptic, entire, ascending, 2–6" long. **On Sugarloaf—Locations:** This orchid has been reported at Sugarloaf, but we have not seen it growing on or near the mountain.

Nodding Ladies'-Tresses
Spiranthes cernua (L.) Rich.

This plant blooms in late summer and fall in moist woods, meadows, and swamps. **Flowers** are white or whitish (often yellowish-green toward the center), fragrant, horizontal or slightly nodding, borne densely in a spike (or spikelike raceme). Narrow **leaves** are in a basal rosette, with a few much smaller stem leaves possible. Height 4–24". **On Sugarloaf—Locations:** Wet woods and fields near the mountain base. **Similar species:** Several other ladies'-tresses species are found in Maryland. Consult Brown and Brown's *Herbaceous Plants of Maryland* for those and other additional orchid species indigenous to the state.

Botanical Key and Guide to Trees, Shrubs, and Woody Vines

Brief illustrated descriptions of Sugarloaf's woody plants are presented here, organized according to defining characteristics. Evergreen trees with needle-like or scalelike foliage are followed by broad-leaved trees and shrubs. Trees and shrubs are organized according to leaf arrangement: simple or compound; alternate, opposite, or whorled. In order to determine whether a leaf is simple or compound, look for the axillary buds on the branchlet. A bud appears at the base of the leaf petiole but not at the point where a single leaflet attaches to the larger leaf stalk. Descriptions of common woody vines follow the section on trees and shrubs. Many trees, shrubs, and vines with showy flowers are treated in greater depth in the Guide to Flowering Plants and are included here to simplify identification in the field.

Axillary bud
simple leaf

Axillary bud
compound
leaf

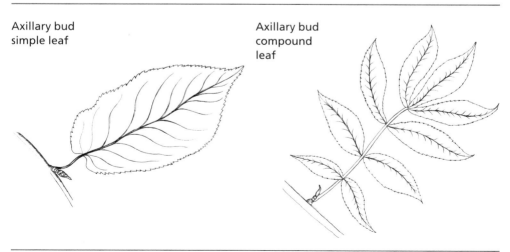

Key to Woody Plants of Sugarloaf Mountain

Evergreen Trees with Needlelike or Scalelike Foliage. Pp. 334–37
Broad-Leaved Trees, Shrubs, and Vines
  Trees with Opposite Simple Leaves. Pp. 338–39
  Shrubs with Opposite Simple Leaves. Pp. 339–42
  Trees with Opposite Compound Leaves. Pp. 342–43
  Shrubs with Opposite Compound Leaves. Pp. 343–44
  Trees with Alternate Simple Leaves. Pp. 344–60
  Shrubs with Alternate Simple Leaves. Pp. 360–63
  Trees with Alternate Compound Leaves. Pp. 363–67
  Shrubs with Alternate Compound Leaves. Pp. 367–69
  Woody Vines. Pp. 369–72

EVERGREEN TREES WITH NEEDLELIKE OR SCALELIKE FOLIAGE

Conifers (Gymnosperms) (Gymnospermae)

Pine Family (Pinaceae)

Pine Genus *(Pinus)*

Table Mountain Pine (*Pinus pungens* Lamb.). The table mountain pine is indigenous only from Pennsylvania and New Jersey to northern Georgia, growing mostly in the Appalachian Mountains, often on exposed rocky outcrops. These are the wind-sculpted, crooked, broad-branching, oriental-looking pines that grow on the summit of the mountain and on a few other high rocky outcrops on Sugarloaf. **Leaves and fruit:** Needles in bundles of 2s (rarely 3s). Cones armed with stiff, sharp spines (5–6 mm. or about

Table Mountain Pine

¼ in. long). **Similar species:** Scrub or Virginia pine *(P. virginiana)* has cones with shorter spines (1–3 mm. or ⅛ in. or less in length).

Scrub Pine (Virginia Pine) (*Pinus virginiana* Mill.). Scrub pine bears needles in bundles of 2s and cones with spines 1–3 mm. (⅛ in. or less) long. Common mountainwide.

Scrub Pine

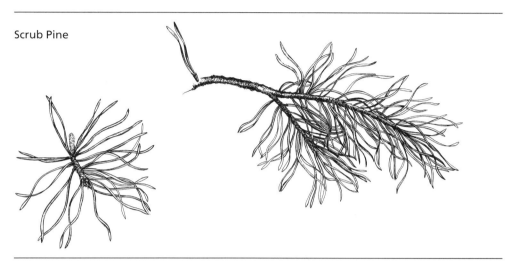

Pitch Pine (*Pinus rigida* Mill.). Pitch pine bears needles in bundles of 3s and has reddish-brown or orange-brown bark dividing into large scales that are separated by fissures on older trees. Fairly common on Sugarloaf.

Pitch Pine

Eastern White Pine (*Pinus strobus* L.). A tall tree with soft, flexible blue-green needles in bundles of 5s and long, narrow cones. Several white pines

Eastern White Pine

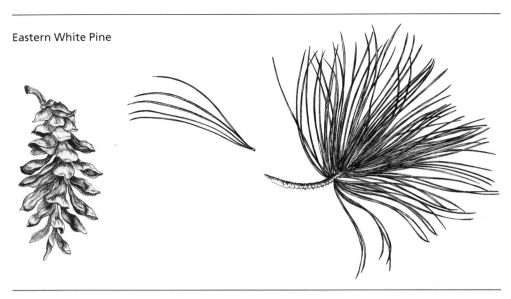

grow along the lower part of the road up the mountain, and others are
sprinkled here and there throughout Sugarloaf's woodlands.

Spruce Genus *(Picea)*

Norway Spruce [*Picea abies* (L.) H. Karst.] and Oriental Spruce [*P. orientalis* (L.) Link]. Mature Norway spruces, native to Europe, have pendulous,
usually glabrous branchlets with 4-sided, sharply pointed ⅓–1" evergreen
needles and pendulous 4–7" cones. A few mature specimens of Norway
spruce have been planted in and near what is now the Strong Memorial
Garden (*see* map in Introduction). Some oriental spruces have also been
planted in the same location and are very similar in appearance. On close
inspection the oriental spruce has shorter needles, smaller cones, and
(visible with a hand lens) minutely pubescent branchlets. Some of those
cultivated spruces have self-seeded. Several other ornamental conifers have
been planted near the Strong Mansion and in groomed areas of the Stronghold property.

Hemlock Genus *(Tsuga)*

Eastern Hemlock [*Tsuga canadensis* (L.) Carriere]. This delicately foliaged
tree of eastern North America and Sugarloaf's moist ravines and roadsides
has been hard-hit by an Asian insect invader called the woolly adelgid
(Adelges tsugae). Many of Sugarloaf's eastern hemlocks, an important food
source for mammals and birds, are dying. **Leaves and fruit:** Evergreen
needles are flat, ⅓–¾" long, rounded or slightly grooved at the apex, with
2 pale parallel bands below. Cones small (½–1" long), ovoid, pendulous.

Eastern Hemlock

Cypress Family *(Cupressaceae)*

Juniper Genus *(Juniperus)*

Eastern Red-Cedar (*Juniperus virginiana* L.). A pioneering species of eastern North American fields and clearings, eastern red-cedar is a small to medium-sized tree with both needlelike and scalelike foliage and small, round, bluish, berrylike cones. Eastern red-cedar is common on and around Sugarloaf Mountain.

Eastern Red-Cedar
scalelike foliage

BROAD-LEAVED TREES, SHRUBS, AND WOODY VINES (ANGIOSPERMAE)

Trees with Opposite Simple Leaves

I. Leaves lobed

Maple Family (Aceraceae)

Maple Genus *(Acer)*

Three species of maple are found on Sugarloaf, with a fourth species—the Silver Maple (*A. saccharinum* L.)—growing in moist lowlands nearby. The Red Maple (*A. rubrum* L.) is common all over the mountain. It has lobed, toothed leaves and early red flowers and fruit. *See* p. 157 for an illustrated description. The Sugar Maple (*A. saccharum* Marshall), with lobed but more sparingly toothed margins, is planted around the West View parking lot. There are several mature trees growing near the mountain base along

Sugar Maple

the road toward Dickerson. The sugar maple is the tree that is tapped for maple syrup. Both red and sugar maples yield vibrant autumn color. The Box-Elder or Ash-Leaved Maple (*A. negundo* L.) has opposite compound leaves. *See* p. 342. Several other *Acer* species are indigenous to eastern North America.

II. Leaves unlobed

a. Leaves heart-shaped (cordate)

Snapdragon or Figwort Family (Scrophulariaceae)

Paulownia [*Paulownia tomentosa* (Thunb.) Siebold & Zucc. ex Steud.]. A few specimens of the Asian paulownia are found on the mountain. *See* p. 224 for an illustrated description of this lavender-flowered tree with heart-shaped leaves.

b. Leaves ovate, elliptic, or oblong-elliptic

Dogwood Family (Cornaceae)

Dogwood Genus *(Cornus)*

See p. 150 for an illustrated description of our native Flowering Dogwood (*C. florida* L.), which bears tiny spring flowers surrounded by 4 showy white or pink bracts. Several other dogwood species are native to Maryland, and at least two of them might be encountered off the beaten path on Sugarloaf. The Silky Dogwood (*C. amomum* Mill.) is a shrubby wetland species, and the Alternate-Leaved Dogwood or Pagoda Dogwood (*C. alternifolia* L. f.) occurs very sparsely on Sugarloaf's northern slopes, far from the trail network.

Olive Family (Oleaceae)

Fringe-Tree (*Chionanthus virginicus* L.). The fragrant, airy clusters of fringe-tree flowers are described on p. 212 along with a general description of this small tree or large shrub.

Shrubs with Opposite Simple Leaves

I. Leaves lobed

Honeysuckle Family (Caprifoliaceae)

Viburnum Genus *(Viburnum)*

Maple-Leaved Viburnum (Dockmackie) (*Viburnum acerifolium* L.). *See* p. 242 for an illustrated description of this common Sugarloaf shrub with maplelike, usually 3-lobed leaves. Other members of the viburnum genus growing on Sugarloaf have unlobed leaves.

II. Leaves unlobed

Honeysuckle Family (Caprifoliaceae)

Viburnum Genus *(Viburnum)*

Viburnum (*Viburnum* spp.). *See* p. 243 for descriptions of several Sugar-loaf viburnum species with opposite, simple, toothed, unlobed leaves. Most are shrubby. One, the Black-Haw (*V. prunifolium* L.), may reach small-tree stature.

Honeysuckle Genus *(Lonicera)*

The Japanese Honeysuckle (*Lonicera japonica* Thunb.) is an invasive Asian vine, which is included in the woody vine section (p. 371) and in an illustrated description (p. 240). *See* the "Similar species" section of the Japanese honeysuckle illustrated description for a brief description of the Tartarian Honeysuckle (*L. tatarica* L.), a cultivated shrub which has established itself in some of the hedgerows and fields near the base of the mountain.

Staff-Tree Family (Celastraceae)

Euonymous Genus *(Euonymous)*

Three species of euonymous grow on Sugarloaf; all are shrubs with opposite, simple, finely toothed leaves. Winged Euonymous [*Euonymous alatus* (Thunb.) Siebold] is an Asian native which has been planted—and possibly escaped from cultivation—along the road down the mountain. It is the most likely of the mountain's three species to be noticed because of its location and two prominent characteristics: dramatically corky-winged branches and flaming red fall foliage. Our two native species—neither of

Winged Euonymous

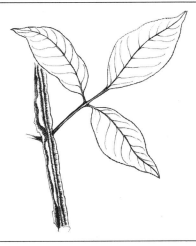

which is common near Sugarloaf's trails—are especially showy when in fruit. Wahoo or Burning Bush (*E. atropurpureus* Jacq.) is an erect shrub bearing clusters of small purple flowers in early summer followed by colorful summer–fall fruits that are purplish, smooth, deeply 4-lobed capsules above seeds enclosed in bright red fleshy seed coverings called arils. Strawberry Bush (*E. americanus* L.) is usually more of a straggling shrub (although it may also be erect) with 4-angled dark green twigs, greenish spring flowers, and a rough, warty, crimson or pink, 3–5 lobed capsule above scarlet seed coverings.

Hydrangea Family (Hydrangeaceae)

Wild Hydrangea (*Hydrangea arborescens* L.). Wild hydrangea bears flat-topped or slightly rounded clusters of creamy flowers in late spring and early summer. *See* p. 111 for an illustrated description.

Olive Family (Oleaceae)

Common Privet (*Ligustrum vulgare* L.). A common cultivated shrub with opposite, entire, 1–2" long leaves and small, white, clustered late spring to early summer flowers that are tubular with 4 flared lobes. A European native, escaped from cultivation and growing on Sugarloaf near cultivated areas and roadsides.

St. John's-Wort Family (Hypericaceae)

St. John's-Wort and St. Andrew's-Cross Genus (Hypericum)

At least one shrubby St. John's-wort species grows on Sugarloaf: Bushy St. John's-Wort (*Hypericum densiflorum* Pursh). *See* p. 77 for a brief description of this shrub and another native shrubby St. John's-wort that is common in the region. St. Andrew's-Cross [*H. hypericoides* (L.) Crantz] is a low-growing plant with a curious 4-petaled flower that looks like an off-kilter cross or butterfly. The plant appears to be herbaceous, but its stems are woody. *See* p. 77 for an illustrated description.

Other shrubs with opposite, simple, unlobed leaves you may see at Sugarloaf include the native wetland plant Buttonbush (*Cephalanthus occidentalis* L.), with flowers and fruit borne in long-stalked, globose heads and opposite or whorled leaves. Several species of cultivated shrubs grow in residential areas on and near the mountain, including Forsythia (*Forsythia viridissima* Lindl.), Garden Mock Orange (*Philadelphus coronarius* L.), and Snowberry [*Symphoricarpos albus* (L.) S. F. Blake].

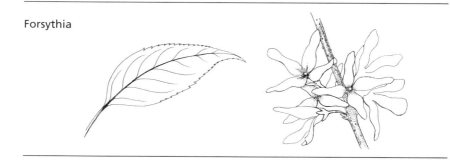

Forsythia

Trees with Opposite Compound Leaves

Leaves pinnately compound

Maple Family (Aceraceae)

Box-Elder (Ash-Leaved Maple) (*Acer negundo* L.). The Sugarloaf area's only native maple with compound leaves, box-elder is a tree of moist and alluvial soils (soils deposited by water). It grows mainly at and near the base of the mountain and along West Harris Road. Box-elder has pinnately compound leaves with 3–5 (sometimes 7) toothed, lobed, or entire-margined leaflets. The tree's flowers and fruit (twin winged samaras) are borne in drooping clusters. Box-elder twigs are often green or olive-toned. A small to medium-sized tree with finely ridged bark. Distinguish this tree from the next entry by the samaras. Box-elder's are borne in joined pairs as part of a large cluster.

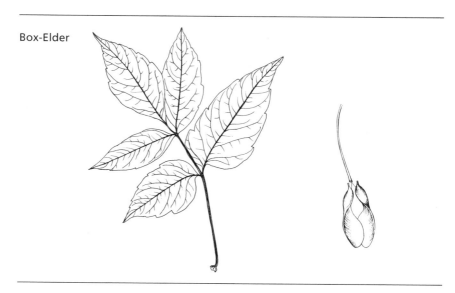

Box-Elder

Olive Family (Oleaceae)

White Ash (*Fraxinus americana* L.). A statuesque tree with dark, dramatically grooved, almost braided-looking bark. White ash is a fairly common tree of Sugarloaf's woods and surrounding countryside. The tree has pinnately compound leaves with 5–9 (usually 7) toothed, wavy, or entire-margined leaflets. Flowers are borne in reddish-purple clusters before the leaves in spring; fruit (winged samaras) borne in dangling clusters. White ash samaras, while clustered, are not joined in pairs as are the preceding species'. White ash has dramatic fall foliage that ranges from a peachy gold to almost purple.

White Ash

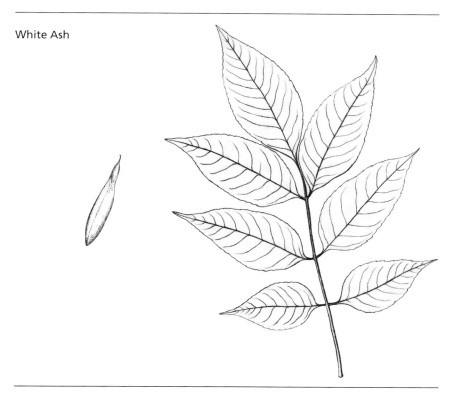

Shrubs with Opposite Compound Leaves

I. Leaves pinnately compound

Honeysuckle Family (Caprifoliaceae)

Common Elderberry (Elder) (*Sambucus canadensis* L.). Common elderberry bears flat-topped creamy flower clusters in late spring and early summer followed by purple-black berrylike drupes. *See* p. 241 for an illustrated description.

II. Leaves trifoliate

Bladdernut Family (Staphyleaceae)

American Bladdernut (*Staphylea trifolia* L.). American bladdernut grows in damp woods. Common along the Potomac, it likely grows near Bennett Creek and/or Furnace Branch. This shrub or small tree bears leaves with 3 leaflets, and it produces a curious swollen papery fruit (a capsule) containing round seeds.

Trees with Alternate Simple Leaves

I. Leaves lobed

Magnolia Family (Magnoliaceae)

Tulip-Tree (Tulip Poplar, Yellow Poplar) (*Liriodendron tulipifera* L.). *See* p. 34 for an illustrated description of this common Sugarloaf woodland tree, the first to leaf out in spring. Tulip-tree's leaves are usually 4-lobed and vaguely resemble the simple-leafed maples'.

Sycamore

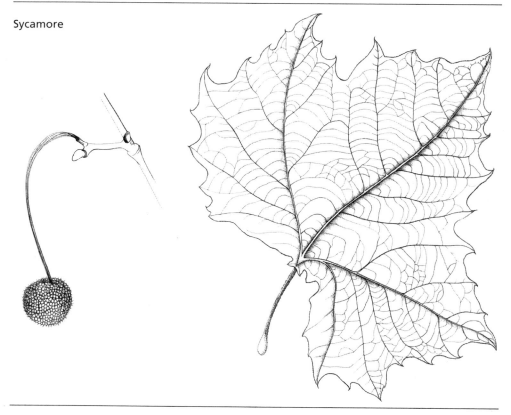

Plane-Tree Family (Platanaceae)

Sycamore (Buttonwood) (*Platanus occidentalis* L.). A large spreading tree of Sugarloaf country's moist soils and nearby Potomac bottomlands with gray and cinnamon outer bark peeling away to reveal whitish inner bark. Magnificent sycamores line regional waterways and are also sometimes found in upland woods. Look for sycamores beyond the Willow Pond on Comus Road and near the Little Monocacy bridge on West Harris Road. Sycamore leaves are lobed and toothed, and the fruit is a hanging, spherical collection of tightly packed achenes, which breaks up in early spring to be dispersed by wind and water.

Beech Family (Fagaceae)

Oak Genus *(Quercus)*

Seven species of oaks grow on Sugarloaf, making them our dominant woodland trees. All species produce acorns, a critical food source for many birds and mammals. White-tailed deer, raccoons, gray squirrels, and other mammals depend upon Sugarloaf's acorn crop, and according to one source book, wild turkeys swallow acorns whole. The first two species mentioned here represent the white oak group, with bluntly lobed leaves that are not bristle-tipped and acorns produced each year. Acorns of the white oak group are more palatable to wildlife, as they were to American Indians and colonists who relied upon them for food. The remaining oaks of Sugarloaf comprise the red or black oak group, with usually pointed,

Chestnut Oak

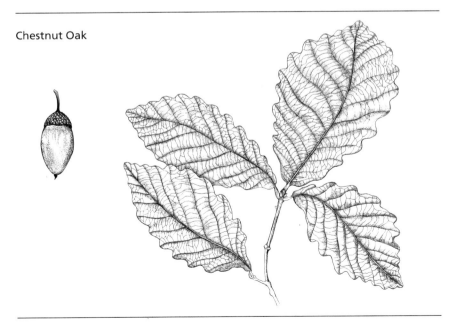

bristle-tipped lobes and acorns produced every other year. White Oak Group: Sugarloaf's most common oak species is the Chestnut Oak (*Quercus montana* Willd.), with leaves that are evenly, shallowly, and bluntly lobed (lobes could be described as large teeth). The chestnut oak is characterized by thick, ridged, and broken bark. Chestnut oak, which thrives in acidic soil and areas with rock outcrops, grows throughout Sugarloaf's woodlands and at the summit. The White Oak (*Q. alba* L.) is also common on Sugarloaf, but a little less so. White oak leaves are more deeply and less evenly lobed than those of chestnut oak. White oak bark is light gray and flaking. Red or Black Oak Group: The Red Oak (or Northern Red Oak) (*Q. rubra* L.) has leaves with pointed, bristle-tipped lobes and acorns with

Red Oak

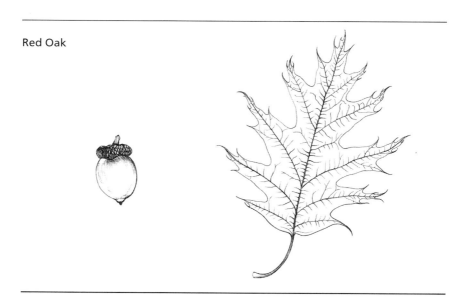

Black Oak

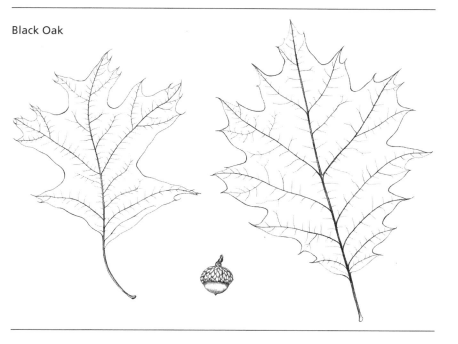

flattish, shallow caps. The bark of mature red oaks is divided vertically into smooth ridges. Our friend and botanical adviser Cris Fleming describes the pattern as "ski tracks." Red oak is a very common Sugarloaf tree, growing mountainwide. Black Oak (*Q. velutina* Lam.) bears leaves similar to those of red oak, but black oak leaves have small tufts of hairs in the lower vein axils beneath the leaf. These yellowish hairs come off when rubbed and are often described as scurfy. The black oak acorn has a deep, bowl-shaped cap that covers about half or nearly half the nut. Black oak is common on Sugarloaf, but perhaps not quite so common as red oak. The Scarlet Oak (*Q. coccinea* Munchh.) has deeply lobed leaves (cut more than halfway to the main vein) that turn a vivid scarlet in late autumn. Its acorn has a cap shaped like a child's toy top and covering one-third to one-half of the nut. Scarlet oak grows mountainwide. The Pin Oak (*Q. palustris* Munchh.) has deeply lobed leaves similar to those of scarlet oak, but its acorn is smaller and has a very shallow cap. This tree is best told from scarlet oak by growth habit: an egg-shaped or pyramidal crown with many small branches radiating out from a central trunk, the lower ones drooping. Pin oak can survive in moist, poorly drained soils and often grows in floodplains. I have not specifically identified the tree on Sugarloaf, but botanist Richard Wiegand included it in a 1987 list of Stronghold plants. It may occur naturally here, or it may be planted around the mountain's residential structures because pin oak is a popular cultivated tree. Black Jack Oak [*Q. mari-*

Pin Oak

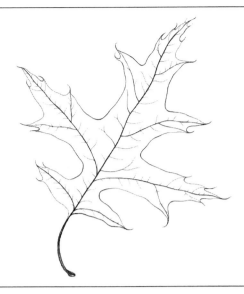

landica (L.) Munchh.] is a small, sometimes almost shrubby species, with distinctive but variable leaves. The tree's leaves are widest at the apex, suggesting a club or blackjack. Black jack leaf lobes may be rounded or bluntly pointed, but they are characteristically bristle-tipped. This tree can survive in poor, barren soils and grows near rock outcroppings on Sugarloaf. It is also found along woodland trails.

Black Jack Oak

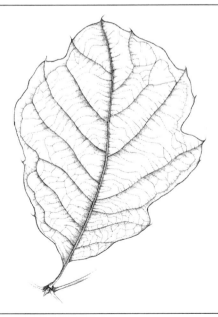

Rose Family (Rosaceae)

Hawthorn Species (*Crataegus*). Some hawthorn species have lobed leaves. These small trees of the rose family bear 5-petaled flowers (except in cultivated double-flowered species) and fruit that is a small, often brightly colored pome. Most hawthorns are armed with sharp, stiff thorns. Because this is a difficult genus for nonbotanists to separate into species, and because hawthorns do not grow wild on Sugarloaf but only in cultivation, we give only general characteristics of the genus here. For further discussion of rose family trees, *see* pp. 130–32.

II. Leaves variously lobed and unlobed

Laurel Family (Lauraceae)

Sassafras [*Sassafras albidum* (Nutt.) Nees]. Sassafras has leaves with margins that are variously lobed and unlobed but not toothed. Some are 2-lobed in a mittenlike pattern. *See* p. 39 for a description of this common Sugarloaf tree.

Sassafras

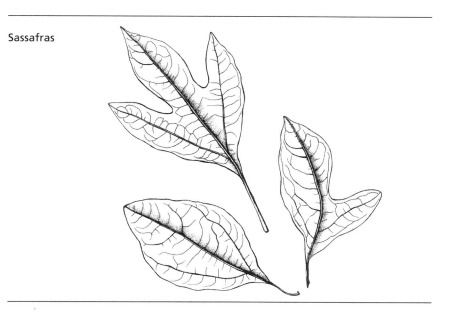

Mulberry Family (Moraceae)

Mulberry Genus *(Morus)*

The Red Mulberry (*Morus rubra* L.), a common tree of woods and hedgerows surrounding Sugarloaf Mountain, has toothed leaves that are variously lobed and unlobed, some in a mittenlike pattern (distinguish

from preceding species by toothed margins). Leaves are pubescent below and sometimes rough above. The fruit is the familiar edible purple mulberry. Another very similar species, imported from Asia, also grows here: the White Mulberry (*M. alba* L.). Distinguish the white mulberry by its glabrous leaves and fruit that is variously white, pink, purple, and black. The fruit of both species is favored by songbirds and mammals.

III. Leaves unlobed with toothed margins

a. Leaves deciduous

See Chestnut Oak (*Quercus montana*), previously described with the other oaks. This tree has leaves that could be described as either shallowly lobed or bluntly toothed.

Beech Family (Fagaceae)

American Beech (*Fagus grandifolia* Ehrh.). The American beech has smooth gray bark, 2–5½" ovate-elliptic, evenly toothed leaves, and fruit comprised of a prickly husk containing 2–3 triangular nuts. Black bear, chipmunks, and many other mammals and birds rely on beechnuts for food. Sugarloaf's beeches are most prevalent in the rich, cool, moist woods along Mount Ephraim Road and on the north and west slopes of the mountain. They are especially striking in winter with their elegant bark, persistent fluttery, straw-colored leaves, and slender, pointed reddish-brown buds.

American Beech

Chestnut Species *(Castanea)*. The once tall and massive American Chestnut [*Castanea dentata* (Marshall) Borkh.] was a dominant tree of Sugarloaf's woodlands and deciduous forests throughout eastern North America. In the early part of the twentieth century, a fungal blight, probably imported on Chinese and Japanese chestnut seedlings, swept through eastern forests, killing virtually every mature tree. Today American chestnuts on Sugarloaf and elsewhere continue to send up shoots from their healthy root systems. The shoots are able to live for a few years, sometimes surviving long enough to produce fruit. But the fungus *(Chryphonectria parasitica)* attacks the tree's bark, creating a spreading canker and cutting off the flow of nutrients. Stronghold has been conducting chestnut blight research for more than thirty years. The American chestnut has sharply toothed 5–11" leaves, showy elongated clusters of creamy white, strong-

American Chestnut

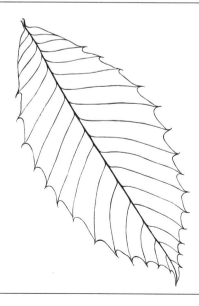

scented male flowers and 1–3 delicious edible nuts enclosed in a spiny bur. Sugarloaf's wild American chestnut saplings are scattered throughout the forests; cultivated trees are grown in research stations near the mountain base. Two chestnuts that are hybrids of one or more nonnative species flank the parking lot at the mountain base.

Elm Family (Ulmaceae)

Elm Species *(Ulmus)*. Two native elm species grow on and around Sugarloaf. The American Elm (*U. americana* L.), with its familiar vase-shaped growth habit, once lined streets and avenues throughout the United States. Many trees fell victim to Dutch elm disease, another fungal tree disease (this one of European origin and spread by the elm bark beetle), and America has been searching for a new favorite shade tree ever since. The American elm is still fairly common on and around Sugarloaf. Its leaves are 2–6" long, sharply and doubly toothed and unequal at the base. They are smooth or slightly roughened on their upper surfaces. Tiny reddish flowers are borne on pendulous stalks in early spring, followed by a flattened, long-stalked, notched samara. Samaras are widest at the middle, tapered to each end, hairy along their edges, and smooth on their flattened sides.

American Elm

American elm is able to thrive in a number of habitats on and around the mountain. Slippery Elm (*U. rubra* Muhl.) is a very similar native tree that has served as an important herbal medicine. The inner bark, with its mucilaginous coating (thus the name "slippery elm"), was made into a tea used in folk medicine for sore throats and other internal ailments and as an external treatment for wounds, burns, and ulcers. According to Steven Foster and James A. Duke (Peterson Field Guides' *Field Guide to Medicinal Plants: Eastern and Central North America*), "Science confirms tea is soothing to mucous membranes and softens hardened tissue." Slippery elm leaves are rough above (like sandpaper), its flowers are born in dense (nearly sessile and not pendulous) clusters, and the fruit is nearly circular, only slightly notched at the tip, and hairy on the sides over the seeds but not along the margins. Slippery elm grows along Sugarloaf-area streams. A third elm species, the Wych Elm or Scotch Elm (*U. glabra* Huds.), is a cultivated Eurasian species that still grows in a few places in the mountain's woodlands, probably a remnant of earlier human habitation and perhaps escaped from cultivation. This elm has very large leaves that are broadest near the abruptly pointed apex.

Hackberry (Northern Hackberry or Sugarberry) (*Celtis occidentalis* L.). Hackberry serves as the food plant for two butterfly species: the hackberry emperor and the tawny emperor. The tree has bark with warty or corky projections; ovate, toothed leaves that are slightly oblique at the base; and fruit that is a small drupe, purple or nearly black when mature. Mammals and birds feed on the fruit. Not common on or near Sugarloaf; a few trees grow near the mountain base.

Zelkovas (*Zelkova* spp.). Several Asian zelkovas have been planted near the Strong Mansion. Their leaves resemble elm leaves but are singly toothed. Zelkova bark is scaly and orange and gray.

Birch Family (Betulaceae)

Black Birch (Sweet or Cherry Birch) (*Betula lenta* L.). This tree, which goes by three different names, is common on Sugarloaf, both in the woodlands and near the summit's rocky outcroppings. The twigs have a strong wintergreen fragrance when broken. The tree was overharvested by pioneers who exploited it for wintergreen flavoring; the sap was used to make birch beer, according to *The Complete Trees of North America* by Thomas S. Elias. The seeds, buds, and twigs are food sources for mammals and birds, according to Elias. Leaves are doubly toothed. The bark is dark gray with horizontal lenticels (resembling several cherry species' bark) on young trees, growing

Black Birch

thick and irregularly furrowed with age. The tree's showy male catkins form in the fall, remaining on the tree through the winter. The conelike fruits, which ripen in fall to release their wind-borne seeds, are also rather showy. The broken-twig method is the best way to distinguish this tree from cherry species. Please do this sparingly. One broken twig with its delightful odor will satisfy both amateur botanist and a large group of children. Several White or Paper Birches (*B. papyrifera* Marshall) have been planted near residential areas on the mountain. The River Birch (*B. nigra* L.), with dramatically peeling cinnamon bark, grows along the Potomac and nearby waterways, and the Yellow Birch (*B. alleghaniensis* Britton), with gray or yellowish separating bark, grows in Maryland's higher mountains to the west.

American Hornbeam (Ironwood, Musclewood, or Blue Beech) (*Carpinus caroliniana* Walter). Look for this small tree along Sugarloaf's streams on Stronghold property and in the Monocacy Natural Resources Management Area. Leaves are doubly toothed, and the fruit is a small nut borne at the base of a leafy 3-lobed bract. The most impressive aspect of this tree is its shape and hardness. The gray-barked trunk is fluted, the wood is extremely hard to the touch (thus the name "ironwood"), and the limbs and trunk have a muscular appearance (giving rise to the name "musclewood"). I once lived on Seneca Creek where beavers would make futile attempts to fell this tree. I often pictured the poor nocturnal beaver dragging himself home at dawn with an aching jaw. Pioneers used the wood to make bowls, dishes, and tool handles, according to Elias.

American Hornbeam

Eastern Hop-Hornbeam [*Ostrya virginiana* (Mill.) K. Koch]. The leaves are very similar to the preceding species, but you can distinguish this small tree by its bark—which peels into long, thin vertical strips—and its hoplike autumn fruit. Eastern hop-hornbeam grows in Sugarloaf's upland woods.

Eastern Hop-Hornbeam

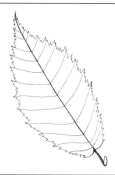

See Shrubs with Alternate Simple Leaves—pp. 361–62—for two additional birch family species growing on and near Sugarloaf.

Rose Family (Rosaceae)

Common or Downy Shadbush (Serviceberry) [*Amelanchier arborea* (F. Michx.) Fernald]. *See* pp. 130–131 for an illustrated description of this early-blooming tree with its small, edible pome.

Sweet Cherry (*Prunus avium* L.). *See* pp. 131–32 for an illustration of this early-blooming naturalized Eurasian tree.

Black Cherry (*Prunus serotina* Ehrh.). Black cherry bears elongated clusters (racemes) of small white 5-petaled flowers in spring and then small dark red or black fruits (about ¼" across). Its leaves are finely toothed with incurved teeth, and there are usually two small glandular projections on the blade near where the petiole joins the base. The lower leaf surface has a little orange pubescence near the base. According to Melvin L. Brown and Russell G. Brown's *Woody Plants of Maryland,* "Leaves, especially if wilted, are extremely poisonous if eaten by farm animals, due to cyanide type of

Black Cherry

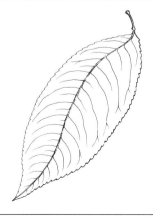

poison released. Seeds or pits are a favorite food for small rodents; the fruits are eaten by many species of songbirds." Black cherry grows in Sugarloaf woodlands and in hedgerows near the mountain base.

Other Species of Cherry, Plum, Peach, Pear, Apple, Crabapple, and Hawthorn (*Prunus, Pyrus,* and *Crataegus*). Trees of the rose family that have been cultivated for ornament and fruit over many human generations are notoriously difficult to sort out and identify. All have 5-petaled flowers (except for cultivated double-flowered forms) and fruit that is either a pome (apple, crabapple, pear, or hawthorn) or drupe (cherry, peach, plum). The very pink early-blooming small trees along roadsides are usually Peaches [*Prunus persica* (L.) Batsch], often the result of fruit tossed from a car. Peaches are grown commercially throughout Sugarloaf country, with scenic orchards visible along Peach Tree Road. Many ornamental and edible pears, plums, apples, crabapples, and hawthorns grace hedgerows and old farm fields. The white-flowering trees with egg-shaped crowns near the brick shop or administration building at the mountain base are ornamental Bradford Pears (*Pyrus calleryana* Dcne. 'Bradford'). Many other introduced species noted for their flowers or edible fruit can be found growing throughout the Sugarloaf region. Enjoy viewing (not picking) their flowers and fruit and consult a more technical botanical or horticultural manual for identification purposes.

See Shrubs with Alternate Simple Leaves *and* Shrubs with Alternate Compound Leaves for additional rose family species.

Bradford Pear

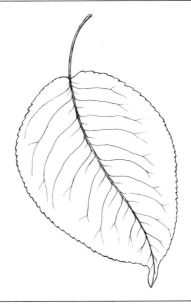

Witch-Hazel Family (Hamamelidaceae)

Common Witch-Hazel (*Hamamelis virginiana* L.). *See* p. 54 for an illustrated description of Sugarloaf's latest-blooming tree, the fall-flowering common witch-hazel. Witch-hazel flowers are yellow, and the leaves are rather wide with scallop-toothed margins. Witch-hazel is a small tree or large shrub.

Willow Family (Salicaceae)

Black Willow (*Salix nigra* Marshall). The black willow grows in Sugarloaf wetland areas such as springs and streamsides. It has toothed, lanceolate leaves and both male and female flowers borne in catkins. The bark of mature trees is dark, ridged, cracked, and sometimes flaking. According to *The Complete Trees of North America* by Elias, "Deer and rodents browse the shoots [of black willow], and sapsuckers feed on the inner bark."

Big-Toothed Aspen (Large-Toothed Aspen) (*Populus grandidentata* Michx.). Big-toothed aspen has broadly ovate leaves with large, blunt teeth on slender, sometimes flattened petioles. Male and female flowers are both borne in catkins during spring. A few specimens of this tree are found near Sugarloaf Mountain's base.

Black Willow

b. Leaves evergreen

Holly Family (Aquifoliaceae)

American Holly (*Ilex opaca* Aiton). A few American hollies grow in Sugarloaf woodlands and have been planted near residential areas on and around the mountain. The American holly has leathery leaves with spiny, outcurved teeth and fruit that is a red, round, berrylike drupe. The fruit remains on the tree through the winter where it serves as food for birds and mammals.

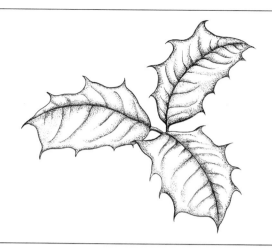

IV. Leaves entire (with unlobed, untoothed margins)

a. Leaves deciduous

i. Leaves cordate (heart-shaped)

Pea Family (Fabaceae)

Redbud (*Cercis canadensis* L.). *See* p. 141 for an illustrated description of this showy spring-flowering tree. Redbud has early purplish-pink flowers that grow along its branchlets and heart-shaped leaves. Redbud fruit is a legume.

ii. Leaves ovate, obovate, elliptic, or oblong (not cordate)

Tupelo or Black-Gum Family (Nyssaceae). [Sometimes included in the Dogwood Family (Cornaceae)]

Tupelo (Black Tupelo, Black-Gum, or Sour-Gum) (*Nyssa sylvatica* Marshall). One of Sugarloaf's most important woodland trees, the tupelo has vivid early autumn foliage that ranges in color from peach to crimson. Leaves are alternate but often crowded near the tips of branches, so may appear opposite. They are usually obovate with wedge-shaped (or sometimes rounded) bases and entire or wavy margins. Small flowers are borne in spring: male flowers in round clusters on long stalks; females on stalks with fewer per cluster. Fruit is a small ovoid or ellipsoid dark blue drupe on a slender stalk. Bark on mature trees is deeply furrowed. Tupelo flowers are an important nectar source for bees, and many birds and mammals eat the fruit.

Ebony Family (Ebenaceae)

Common Persimmon (*Diospyros virginiana* L.). Common persimmon bears oblong-ovate to ovate-elliptic leaves with entire margins. Persimmon bark is thick, dark gray, and—on mature trees—separated into small squares. Persimmon fruit, a large orange-purple berry ripening in autumn, is prized by local residents who collect it on cold days late in the season when it sweetens and loses the unpleasant texture and bitterness character-

Common
Persimmon

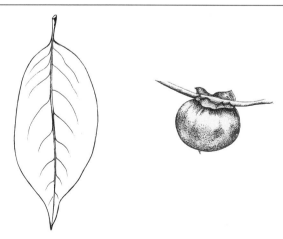

istic of the unripe fruit. The fruit is a favorite of foxes, raccoons, deer, and other mammals and birds. Indeed, a Sugarloaf country scat at the right time in autumn is almost guaranteed to be filled with persimmon seeds.

Custard-Apple Family (Annonaceae)

Pawpaw [*Asimina triloba* (L.) Dunal]. *See* p. 36 for an illustrated description of the pawpaw, a small tree of Sugarloaf's lower streamsides. The pawpaw has long leaves, purple flowers in early spring, and an edible banana-like fruit.

b. Leaves evergreen

Magnolia Family (Magnoliaceae)

Southern Magnolia (Bull-Bay Magnolia) (*Magnolia grandiflora* L.). A handful of these shiny-leaved evergreen trees with large, fragrant late spring to summer flowers have been planted around the base of Sugarloaf. A young southern magnolia near the base parking lot is the progeny of one of the historic Andrew Jackson magnolias at the White House.

Shrubs with Alternate Simple Leaves

Heath Family (Ericaceae)

Several members of the heath family are described and illustrated on pp. 95–104. These include showy flowering plants such as Mountain Laurel (*Kalmia latifolia* L.), the Pinxter Flower or Pink Azalea [*Rhododendron periclymenoides* (Michx.) Shinners], and Great Rhododendron (*R. maximum* L.). Heath family species producing edible fruit such as Blueberries (*Vaccinium* spp.) and Huckleberries *(Gaylussacia)* are also illustrated and described. Two heath family wildflowers that appear herbaceous but have woody stems are the Trailing Arbutus (*Epigaea repens* L.) and Wintergreen (*Gaultheria procumbens* L.). (*See* pp. 95–98.) Two additional heath family members that are rare to uncommon on Sugarloaf and grow far from the beaten path near Sugarloaf's springs and in seepage swamps are Maleberry [*Lyonia ligustrina* (L.) DC.] and Fetterbush [*Leucothoe racemosa* (L.) A. Gray]. Because Sugarloaf visitors are unlikely to see these last two species, we only mention them here.

Rose Family (Rosaceae)

Sugarloaf rose family shrubs with alternate simple leaves include the non-native Japanese Spiraea (*Spiraea japonica* L. f.) and native Red Chokeberry [*Aronia arbutifolia* (L.) Pers.]. *See* pp. 114–32 for descriptions of these and other rose family members. An additional rose family species with alternate simple leaves appears on botanist Richard Wiegand's 1987 list of Stronghold plant species: Ninebark [*Physocarpus opulifolius* (L.) Maxim.], a shrub with older bark shredding in long, thin strips; toothed, usually shallowly palmately lobed leaves; white or pink-tinged flowers in flat-topped clusters (corymbs); and red or purplish capsules.

Holly Family (Aquifoliaceae)

Winterberry (Black Alder) [*Ilex verticillata* (L.) A. Gray]. A deciduous holly growing near springs and streams of Sugarloaf's lower slopes, winter-berry has lanceolate, oblong, or obovate leaves with toothed margins and bright red fruit (a berrylike drupe). Another deciduous holly, Smooth Winterberry [*I. laevigata* (Pursh) A. Gray], has been identified on the mountain in the past.

Winterberry

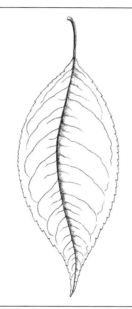

Laurel Family (Lauraceae)

Spicebush [*Lindera benzoin* (L.) Blume]. See p. 37 for an illustrated de-scription of spicebush, a shrub of Sugarloaf's moist, rich woods and streamsides. Spicebush bears yellow flowers in early spring and red drupes in late summer and fall.

Birch Family (Betulaceae)

American Hazelnut (*Corylus americana* Walter). Uncommon around Sugarloaf, hazelnut grows in moist soils near the mountain's lower slopes. Male flowers in small tight catkins are noticeable in winter; female flowers,

American Hazelnut

appearing in very early spring, are tiny and inconspicuous but noteworthy with a hand lens: pistils have short styles and two long, slender reddish-purple stigmas. Leaves, appearing later, are doubly toothed, broadly ovate, obovate, or nearly round, with round or slightly cordate bases. Fruit is an edible nut with leafy bracts attached.

Smooth Alder [*Alnus serrulata* (Aiton) Willd.]. A shrub of wet soils, including those of the seeps, springs, and streamsides along Mount Ephraim Road. Male and female flowers in separate catkins, males longer and drooping, visible through winter and opening in spring. Fruit woody and conelike, containing winged seeds. Leaves are obovate, elliptic, or ovate with fine, sharp teeth and wedge-shaped or slightly rounded (not cordate) bases.

Smooth Alder

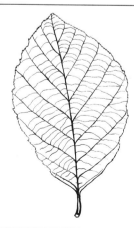

Japanese Barberry

Barberry Family (Berberidaceae)

Japanese Barberry (*Berberis thunbergii* DC.). A small spiny shrub frequently planted (often in hedges) and escaping from cultivation. Japanese barberry is found on and around Sugarloaf Mountain. It has small, entire leaves, yellow spring flowers, and round or ellipsoid red berries.

Saxifrage Family (Saxifragaceae)

[Gooseberry Family (Grossulariaceae)]

Eastern Wild Gooseberry (*Ribes rotundifolium* Michx.). This shrub bears round purplish berries and has small, toothed, palmately lobed leaves. Tina and I have not seen it at Sugarloaf, but it appears on botanist Richard Wiegand's 1987 list.

Trees with Alternate Compound Leaves

Leaves pinnately compound

Pea Family (Fabaceae)

Black Locust (*Robinia pseudoacacia* L.). See p. 142 for an illustrated description of the black locust, one of Sugarloaf country's most spectacular spring-blooming trees.

Walnut Family (Juglandaceae)

Hickory Genus *(Carya)*

Hickories (*Carya* spp.). Three species of hickory are common on Sugarloaf; several others are native to Maryland. All produce alternate, odd-pinnately compound leaves with toothed leaflets, inconspicuous spring flowers (males in hanging catkins), and nuts enclosed in a husk that splits into four sections. Hickory nuts are an important food for black bears, foxes, raccoons, squirrels, white-tailed deer, and large birds. The Mockernut Hickory [*C. tomentosa* (Poiret) Nutt.] has leaves with (usually) 7 or 9 fragrant leaflets that are pubescent below, and fruit 1½–2½" long, rounded

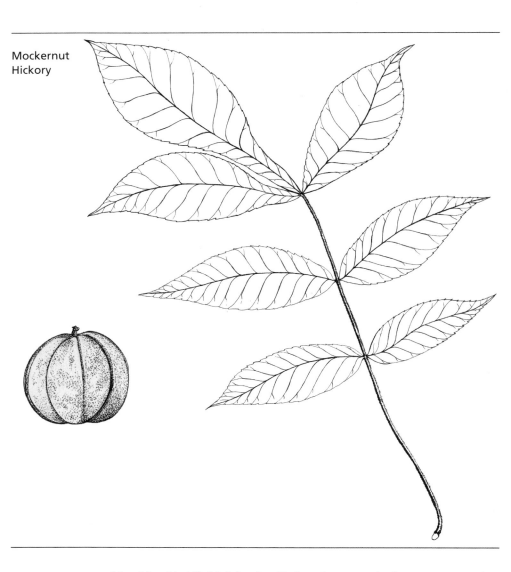

Mockernut
Hickory

or ovoid, with a ⅛–¼" thick husk splitting almost to the base to expose the nut. Bark is shallowly furrowed. The Pignut Hickory [*C. glabra* (Mill.) Sweet] differs from the mockernut in having leaves with usually 5 (rarely 7) leaflets, which are mostly glabrous. The fruit of the pignut is slightly smaller, with a thinner husk that usually splits only partway to the base. The Bitternut Hickory [*C. cordiformis* (Wangenh.) K. Koch] has leaves with 7–11 (usually 9) leaflets. It differs from mockernut hickory in having a smaller fruit, with a thinner-walled husk which splits only partway to the base and has slight wings or ridges along the lines of separation. This species has bright sulfur-yellow winter buds.

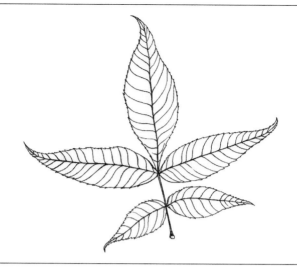

Walnut Genus *(Juglans)*

Black Walnut (*Juglans nigra* L.). Not very common on Sugarloaf Mountain itself, black walnut is very common in the surrounding countryside. The nuts are the familiar edible black walnut, popular with squirrels and other mammals as well as humans. The wood is prized for furniture-making, and the fruit husks were used to make dye in colonial times. American

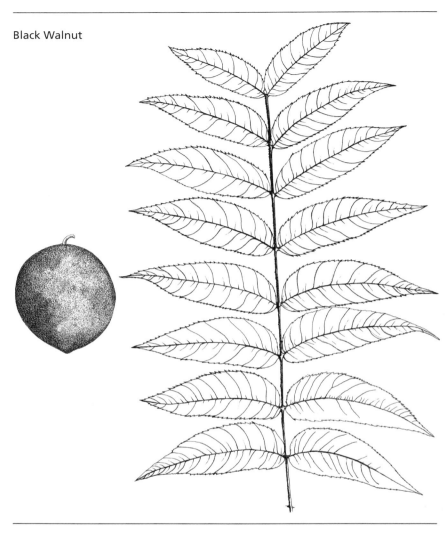

Indians used the inner bark and juice from the fruit husks medicinally, according to Foster and Duke (Peterson Field Guides' *Field Guide to Medicinal Plants: Eastern and Central North America*). Black walnut has dark furrowed bark, leaves with 15–23 sharply toothed leaflets, and a nut with a furrowed shell contained within a green limelike, fragrant husk.

Quassia Family (Simaroubaceae)

Ailanthus (Tree of Heaven) [*Ailanthus altissima* (Mill.) Swingle]. A rapidly growing Asian tree that has become widely naturalized and a threat to native plant populations. Increasingly common on and around Sugarloaf. Leaves are large with 13–25 leaflets that are entire along most of their margins with usually one or more blunt teeth near the base. Flowers midsum-

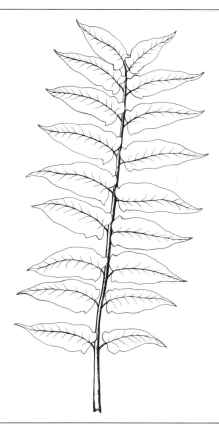

mer in large greenish clusters. Fruit a twisted, single-seeded samara persisting on the tree in large clusters after the leaves have fallen.

Shrubs with Alternate Compound Leaves

Cashew Family (Anacardiaceae)

Sumacs (*Rhus* spp.). Three shrubby sumac species grow at the edges of woodlands on and near Sugarloaf, where they serve as a winter food source for birds. According to Alexander C. Martin, Herbert S. Zim, and Arnold L. Nelson's *American Wildlife and Plants: A Guide to Wildlife Food Habits,* "Several of our most important gamebirds rely on sumac as a winter food and so do some of the songbirds which winter in the North. Sometimes, in especially severe weather, gamebirds will remain near a copse of sumacs until the supply of fruit is exhausted. In addition, rabbits and hoofed browsers feed on the bark and on the twigs and fruit of these plants." Shining Sumac (Winged or Dwarf Sumac) (*R. copallinum* L.) is a shrub or small tree abundant in Sugarloaf-area hedgerows and abandoned fields. Leaves

Shining
Sumac

Staghorn
Sumac

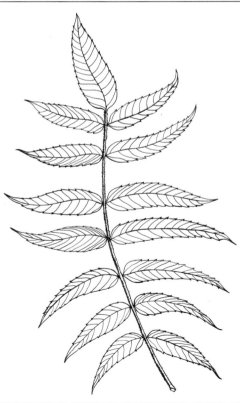

have 7–21 glossy green "shining" entire or nearly entire leaflets borne on a rachis, with wings on the rachis between leaflets. Greenish flowers in erect terminal panicles; fruit a small red pubescent drupe in terminal clusters. Smooth Sumac (*R. glabra* L.) is not as common in the Sugarloaf area; this shrub has toothed leaflets with no wings on the rachis. The twig, rachis, and petiole of this species are glabrous or nearly so and often glaucous. Staghorn Sumac (*R. typhina* L.) is a shrub or small tree with leaves lacking a winged rachis and bearing toothed leaflets. Twig, petiole, and rachis very pubescent. Fruits borne in densely pubescent clusters suggesting a stag's horns.

Rose Family (Rosaceae)

See pp. 123–28 for illustrated descriptions of rose family shrubs with alternate compound leaves. These include the Pasture Rose (*Rosa carolina* L.), Multiflora Rose (*R. multiflora* Thunb.), and several species of Blackberries, Dewberries, and Raspberries (*Rubus* spp.).

Woody Vines

Cashew Family (Anacardiaceae)

Poison Ivy [*Toxicodendron radicans* (L.) Kuntze] *(Rhus radicans)*. This is the infamous vine that causes a severe skin rash in most people after contact. Teach your children to avoid the vine with 3 leaflets per leaf. Contact with any part of the plant can cause the rash. The vine is thick and intensely hairy, and on Sugarloaf it climbs high into the trees. Leaves are alternate, trifoliate. Leaflets are entire or with a few irregular teeth or shallow lobes. They turn vivid colors in autumn. The late spring flowers are small,

Poison Ivy

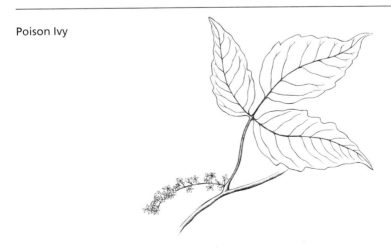

clustered, and greenish-yellow. The fruit, a small greenish white, gray, or yellowish drupe, is an important food for many bird species.

Bignonia Family (Bignoniaceae)

Trumpet Creeper [*Campsis radicans* (L.) Seem. ex Bureau]. *See* p. 228 for an illustrated description of this fairly common vine with opposite, pinnately compound leaves and brilliant red trumpet-shaped flowers.

Grape Family (Vitaceae)

Virginia Creeper [*Parthenocissus quinquefolia* (L.) Planch.]. *See* p. 154 for an illustrated description of this common vine with alternate, palmately compound leaves that turn vivid reds in autumn.

Grapes (*Vitis* spp.). Three species of wild grape grow on Sugarloaf. They bear alternate, simple, palmately veined, and usually lobed leaves (except for chicken grape, *V. vulpina*) with toothed margins. All three Sugarloaf species have leaves that are cordate at the base. Wild grape vines usually have stringy bark and tendrils for clinging to other plants or climbing surfaces. Flowers are small and 5-petaled, growing in panicles. The fruit is a berry. According to Brown and Brown's *Woody Plants of Maryland,* "Tangles of grape vines furnish cover and nesting sites for birds. The fruits are eaten by many songbirds, grouse, quail, turkey, and ring-necked pheasant. The black bear, raccoon, opossum, fox, squirrel, and skunk eat the fruits even in winter after they have dried." The most common grape species on Sugarloaf is the Pigeon or Summer Grape (*V. aestivalis* Michx.) with lobed leaves that are whitened below and covered with what Brown and Brown describe as a "light, cobwebby but persistent, reddish pubes-

Pigeon or
Summer Grape

cence." Grapes are black berries, often slightly glaucous. Chicken or Winter Grape (*V. vulpina* L.) has leaves that are unlobed or only barely so. Fruit black. Fox Grape (*V. labrusca* L.) has usually 3-lobed leaves that are covered by dense reddish hairs on their lower surfaces. The black or purple berries do not persist into winter but fall when ripe.

Moonseed Family (Menispermaceae)

Canada Moonseed (*Menispermum canadense* L.). This toxic vine is sometimes confused with wild grape, resulting in poisonings. American Indians and early physicians who understood how to work with toxic plants used Canada moonseed medicinally. Leaves are simple, alternate, palmately veined, with several shallow lobes, or nearly entire, not toothed as are grape *(Vitis)* species. The petiole is attached slightly beyond the leaf margin on the lower blade. Summer flowers are tiny, white, in clusters. Small, round black or bluish fruit resembles wild grape but is a poisonous drupe.

Canada Moonseed

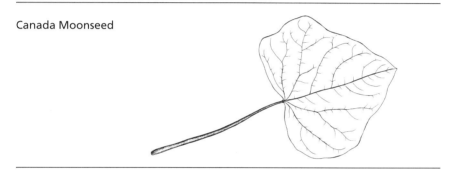

Staff-Tree Family (Celastraceae)

Bittersweets (*Celastrus* spp.). Two species of bittersweet grow in the region: the native American Bittersweet (*C. scandens* L.) and the Oriental Bittersweet (*C. orbiculatus* Thunb.), an invasive species. Bittersweet is a popular component of fall floral arrangements. The decorative fruit is small and round, with an outer orange layer splitting open to reveal a bright red aril. American bittersweet bears small greenish flowers (May–June) in terminal clusters and has finely toothed, elliptic, oblong, or ovate leaves. Oriental bittersweet has broader leaves (oblong-obovate to nearly round) with blunt teeth. Its flowers are borne in axillary clusters. Both are climbing vines.

Honeysuckle Family (Caprifoliaceae)

Japanese Honeysuckle (*Lonicera japonica* Thunb.). *See* p. 240 for an illustrated description of this fragrant but destructively invasive Asian vine.

Buttercup Family (Ranunculaceae)

Virgin's Bower (*Clematis virginiana* L.). Virgin's bower blooms in the late summer and fall. It is a climbing vine common in Sugarloaf area hedgerows and on fence lines. It grows along Sugarloaf Mountain Road. Leaves are opposite and trifoliate with coarsely toothed (or barely lobed) leaflets. The white flowers grow in profuse clusters with 4 petal-like sepals per flower (no petals). Plumelike fruits are achenes with persistent feathery styles.

Lily Family (Liliaceae)

Common Greenbrier (Catbrier) (*Smilax rotundifolia* L.). *See* p. 319 for an illustrated description of this climbing prickly vine with alternate, simple, ovate or cordate (heart-shaped) leaves.

Glossary

achene A dry, one-seeded fruit that does not split open.

aggregate fruit A compound fruit, developing from many pistils of the same flower. *See also* multiple fruit

alternate Describes a common leaf arrangement in which the leaves are alternate to, not opposite, each other on the plant stalk or branchlet.

angiosperm Belonging to the group of plants that produce seeds within ovaries. Most plants of the angiosperm group are broad-leaved. *See also* gymnosperm

anther The pollen-producing part of the stamen.

apetalous Without petals.

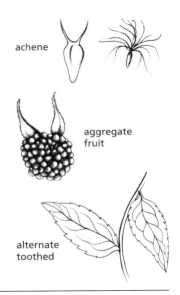

achene

aggregate fruit

alternate toothed

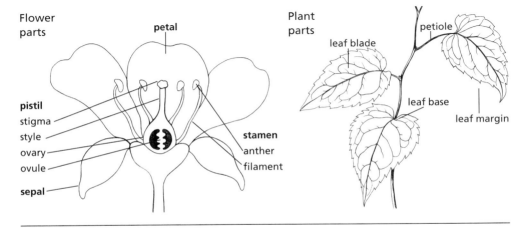

Flower parts

petal

pistil
stigma
style
ovary
ovule

sepal

stamen
anther
filament

Plant parts

leaf blade

petiole

leaf base

leaf margin

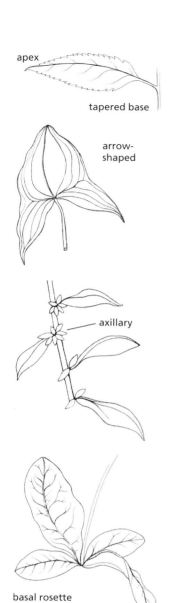

apex

tapered base

arrow-shaped

axillary

basal rosette

berry

apex The tip of a leaf blade, lobe, bud, fruit, etc. (the part farthest from the base).

arrow-shaped Shape suggests an arrowhead.

astringent Tending to contract organic tissue; styptic. Some plants, such as common witch-hazel, have astringent properties.

awn, awned An awn is a slender terminal bristle. A plant part with such a bristle is described as "awned."

axil The upper angle formed where the petiole meets the branchlet or plant stalk. (Also refers to the upper angle where two leaf veins meet.)

axillary Growing in the axil where the leaf blade or petiole joins the branchlet or plant stalk i.e., axillary bud.

banner The upper enlarged petal of a pea family (Fabaceae) flower. Also sometimes called the standard. Pea family flowers typically (but not always) consist of a banner, two side petals called wings, and two lower fused or partially fused petals forming a "keel."

basal leaf Leaf growing from the base of the plant, rather than from the upper plant stalk.

basal rosette A circular cluster of leaves growing from the base of the plant.

base The part of a leaf blade, bud, or fruit that is closest to the stem or branchlet and farthest from the apex.

bearded Bearing a tuft of hairs. Some petals or other flower parts are described as bearded.

berry A simple fruit with fleshy or pulpy ovarian material, usually containing several to many seeds. Fruit that looks like a berry but is not is described in this book as "berrylike."

bipinnately compound Refers to leaves that are twice pinnately compound.

blade The main part of a leaf (excluding the petiole).

bract A leafy plant part located below a flower or flower cluster in some species. In some cases (for instance, the flowering dogwood) the bracts are showier than the flowers themselves.

branchlet The leaf-bearing part of a branch, also referred to as a twig.

bristle-tipped Describes a lobe, tooth, or apex of a leaf that comes to a thin, sharp, threadlike point.

bud A small protuberance on a plant stalk or branchlet that contains the shoot, leaf, and/or flower in embryonic condition. An end bud or terminal bud is a bud on a woody plant at the precise end of a twig. A false end bud, which forms in the absence of a true end bud, can be told by an adjacent branchlet scar.

calyx The outer part of a flower, consisting of leafy or, rarely, petal-like parts called sepals.

capsule A dry fruit which splits open to release two or more seeds.

catkin A long, thin cluster of tiny naked (apetalous) flowers.

circumboreal Describes species occurring all the way around the North Pole, in North America, Europe, and Asia.

clasping Often refers to leaves that partly encircle and hug the plant stalk.

cleft Deeply lobed, with narrow sinuses between the lobes. Refers to leaves or petals.

common name The name or names by which a plant is known to nonbotanists. Common names—handed down through generations—often differ from region to region and are difficult to translate into other languages. Therefore, botanists use universally recognized scientific names in Latin. In this book the common name or names for the plant are followed by the Latin name in italicized type. Although common names can be confusing, they often embody folklore and poetry.

bipinnately compound

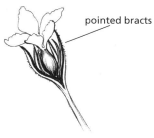
pointed bracts

bristle-tipped

bud

cleft petals

clasping

catkin

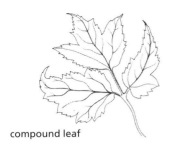
compound leaf

cone

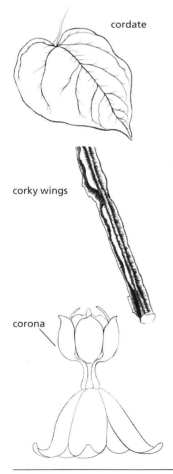
cordate

corky wings

corona

compound fruit A fruit with more than one ovary.

compound leaf A leaf that is divided into leaflets.

cone The woody, scaly structure produced by most conifers.

conifer Usually cone-producing trees of the gymnosperm group. Seeds are "naked" (not enclosed in ovaries).

cordate Heart-shaped. Often used to describe the blade or base of a leaf.

corky wings Flat woody projections on the branches of some trees and shrubs, such as the winged euonymous.

corm A short, thickened underground stem typical of some plants, such as spring beauty.

corolla All the petals of a flower, either separate or united. The corolla is often (but not always) brightly colored and showy.

corona A set of petal-like structures or appendages between the corolla and the reproductive parts of the plant. Typical of some plants, such as the milkweeds.

corymb A flat-topped or slightly rounded flower cluster with the outer flower stalks usually longer than the inner ones and the outer flowers opening first.

cosmopolitan Widely distributed around the world.

cultivation The act of growing and nurturing plants. Some plants on Sugarloaf have "escaped from cultivation," becoming viable in the wild or naturalized.

cyme A flower cluster in which the central flower opens first; if it is a complex cyme, the center flower of each branch opens first.

deciduous Describes trees and other woody plants that shed their leaves in autumn (as opposed to evergreen trees, which do not).

decoction An herbal remedy made by boiling or simmering an herb in water. Roots and twigs are often prepared this way while herbal flowers and leaves are more often infused in hot (but not boiling) water or tinctured in alcohol.

decumbent Curving or lying prostrate and then often ascending.

decurrent Describes leaves in which the blade extends downward along the petiole or along the plant stalk (as in the common mullein).

decussate Arranged oppositely (as leaves on a plant stalk) with each pair at right angles to the pair above and below.

dehiscent Splitting open at maturity to release the contents. Usually describes a dry fruit splitting open to release seeds. Opposite indehiscent.

deltoid Triangular. A fairly common leaf shape.

dioecious Having male and female flowers on separate plants.

disk flower A small tubular flower growing as part of a cluster in the center of a flower head. Disk flowers are often but not always surrounded by ray flowers, which resemble petals. Disk and ray flowers are characteristic of the aster or daisy family. The ox-eye daisy and black-eyed Susan, two familiar plants of the aster family that are common on Sugarloaf, bear flower heads with clusters of disk flowers at the center and petal-like ray flowers surrounding them. Thus what appears to be a single flower is actually a flower head containing many disk and ray flowers.

divided Cut into separate or almost separate parts. Describes leaves that are separated into individual leaflets or very deeply cut lobes.

downy Covered with fine, soft hairs.

drupe A fleshy fruit such as a cherry or peach with a single hard pit (usually containing a single seed).

ellipsoid Elliptic lengthwise and round in cross section (describes three-dimensional plant parts such as fruit).

elliptic About twice as long as broad and widest in the middle. Describes a common leaf shape.

end bud The bud at the tip of the branchlet. Also called terminal bud.

entire Smooth. Describes the margin of a leaf that is not toothed or lobed.

epiphyte A plant without roots in the soil. Epiphytes grow on other plants but not as parasites; they receive water and nutrients from the atmosphere.

erect Standing straight up.

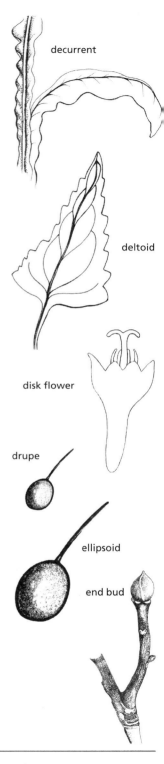

decurrent

deltoid

disk flower

drupe

ellipsoid

end bud

follicle

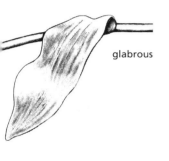

glabrous

head

evergreen Describes plants that retain their leaves throughout the year.

family Taxonomists divide plants into groups such as families, which are subdivided into genera (plural of genus) and species. Plants in this book are grouped according to family and genus.

flower The sexual reproductive part of a plant, which usually includes petals, sepals, pistil, and/or stamens.

flower head *see* head

follicle A dry, one-celled fruit developing from a simple pistil and opening along one side only.

fruit The ripened ovaries of a flowering plant, containing the seeds. Fruit may be dry or fleshy.

genus (plural genera) Plant families are divided into genera and species. Plants in this book are grouped according to family and genus.

glabrous Without hair or pubescence. Sometimes important to note for plant identification.

gland Small structure that may secrete (sometimes sticky) liquid. Some leaves have small glands on their blades or petioles, often visible only with a hand lens. When glands are present, the leaf is described as glandular.

glandular *see* gland

glaucous Chalky; covered with a white or whitish bloom. Often describes a plant stalk.

globose Spherical or close to spherical.

glossy Shiny.

growth habit The overall shape or silhouette of a plant.

gymnosperm Belonging to the group of plants that produces "naked seeds" (not enclosed in ovaries). The seeds are usually borne on woody cone scales. Conifers, with their typically needlelike or scalelike foliage, are gymnosperms. *See also* angiosperm

habit *see* growth habit

habitat The environment in which a plant (or animal) lives. Some plants prefer wetland habitats, such as a stream, pond, or swamp. Others prefer a drier woodland habitat. Soil conditions, moisture, and temperature all contribute to habitat conditions. A knowledge of wild plants must embrace an understanding of the plants' habitats.

head A flower cluster in which stalkless or short-stalked flowers are tightly clustered together. Some clover flowers are borne in heads, as are many members of the aster and mint families.

herbaceous Describes plants that do not have woody stems. Most low-growing wildflowers are herbaceous, but a few are woody.

imperfect flower A flower that contains male (stamens) or female (pistil) parts but not both. *See* perfect flower

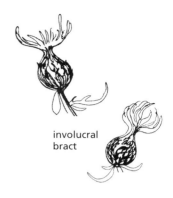

involucral bract

indehiscent Not splitting open at maturity; usually describes dry fruit. Opposite of dehiscent.

indigenous Native.

infusion An herbal remedy made by steeping an herb in hot water (compare decoction).

instar The period between molts in the larval (caterpillar) stage of a butterfly's evolution.

introduced Alien; not native. Describes a plant originally brought here from another part of the world.

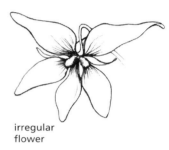

irregular flower

involucral bract In the aster or daisy family, many flower heads bear a leafy set of projections near the base that are called involucral bracts.

irregular flower An asymmetrical flower, one that lacks same-sized petals.

keel The two converging lower petals of many pea family (Fabaceae) flowers that resemble the longitudinal ridge (keel) of a ship or boat.

lanceolate Lance-shaped. A common leaf shape.

leaf The food-producing part of the plant. On broad-leaved plants leaves may be simple or compound. Leaves on conifers are typically needlelike or scale-like.

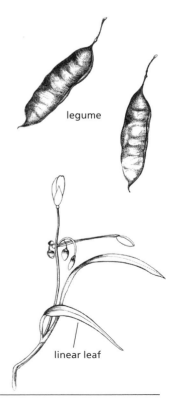

legume

leaf base *see* base

leaf blade *see* blade

leaflet A single, leaflike portion of a compound leaf.

leaf margin *see* margin

legume A pod that splits along two sides to release several seeds. Members of the pea family (Fabaceae) produce legumes.

liana A climbing woody vine.

linear Long and narrow with nearly parallel sides. Usually describes a leaf-blade shape.

linear leaf

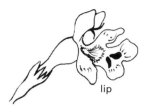

lip

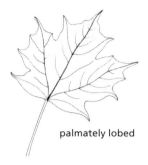

palmately lobed

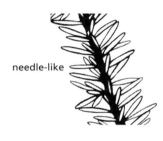

needle-like

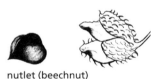

nutlet (beechnut)

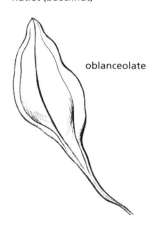

oblanceolate

lip A projection of a corolla in some flowers such as those of the mint family (Lamiaceae).

lobe A portion of a leaf blade which projects outward and is separated from other lobes by deep or shallow sinuses. Most maple and many oak leaves are lobed.

lobed Having lobes and sinuses. Describes certain leaf blades.

margin The edge of a leaf blade. May be entire (smooth or toothless), toothed, or lobed.

mucronate Topped with a short, sharp, slender point; describes the teeth or apex of certain leaf blades.

multiple fruit A compound fruit, which develops from many different flowers. *See* aggregate fruit

native Indigenous. Native plants grow naturally in the wild.

native habitat The place where a plant grows or animal lives naturally in the wild. *See* habitat

naturalized Escaped from cultivation and established as an independent population in the wild. Many Asian and European plant species have become naturalized in North America.

needlelike Describes the needle-shaped foliage of many conifers (such as pines and spruces).

nut A hard, dry, usually one-seeded fruit—such as an acorn—that does not split open.

nutlet A thick-walled achene (a dry, one-seeded fruit that does not split open) such as the fruit produced by members of the mint family (Lamicaceae). A small nut.

oblanceolate Inversely lanceolate (or lance-shaped)— broader at the top.

oblique Refers to a leaf base in which the two sides of the blade join the petiole at slightly different spots or angles. Synonymous with unequal base.

oblong About three times as long as broad with nearly parallel sides.

obovate Inversely ovate, broader at the top.

obovoid Inversely ovoid, broader at the top.

obtuse Blunt and rounded (usually describes a leaf base or apex).

ocrea A sheath or collar around the plant stalk at the leaf node; typical of most members of the smartweed or buckwheat family.

odd-pinnately compound A pinnately compound leaf with an odd number of leaflets.

opposite Describes a leaf arrangement in which the leaves are opposite each other on the plant stalk or branchlet. Also includes subopposite and whorled leaf arrangements.

orbicular Circular in outline (describes a two-dimensional plant part, usually a leaf).

ovary The part of the pistil that develops into the fruit and contains the seeds.

ovate Egg-shaped but two-dimensional. Describes a common leaf shape.

ovoid Egg-shaped (usually referring to shape of particular fruit).

ovule A plant's egg, or undeveloped female seed, contained in the ovary, which after fertilization develops into the seed.

palmate *see* palmately compound and palmate venation

palmately compound Leaflets arranged in a pattern shaped like an open hand. (Compare pinnately compound.)

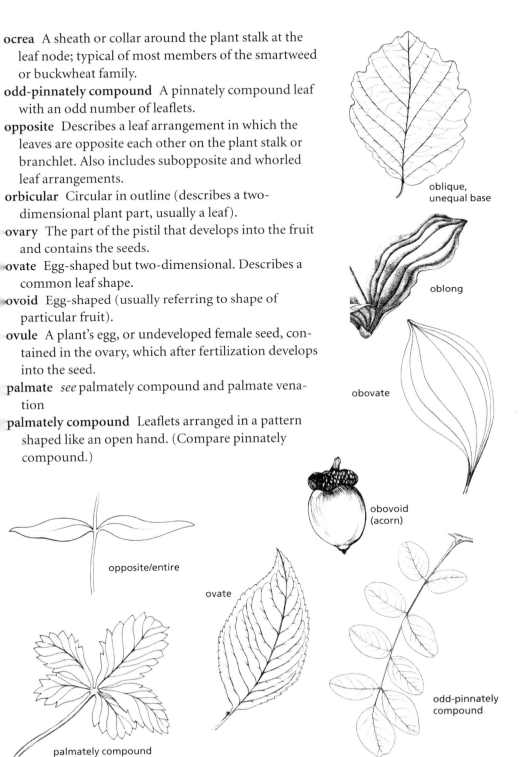

oblique, unequal base

oblong

obovate

opposite/entire

ovate

obovoid (acorn)

odd-pinnately compound

palmately compound

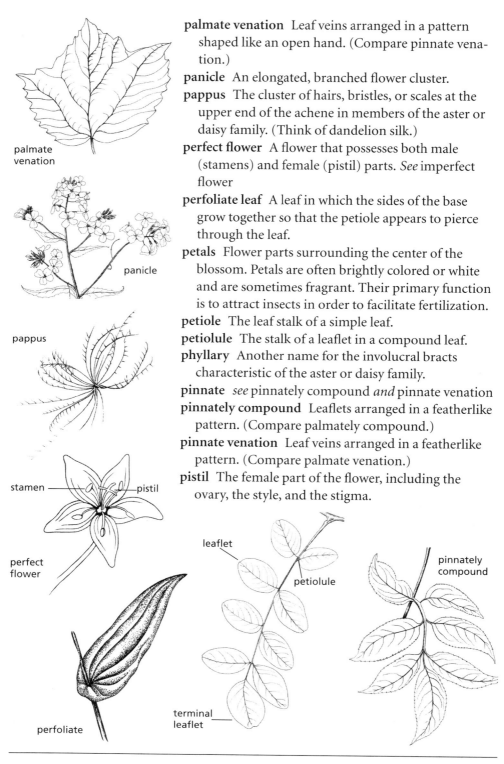

palmate venation Leaf veins arranged in a pattern shaped like an open hand. (Compare pinnate venation.)

panicle An elongated, branched flower cluster.

pappus The cluster of hairs, bristles, or scales at the upper end of the achene in members of the aster or daisy family. (Think of dandelion silk.)

perfect flower A flower that possesses both male (stamens) and female (pistil) parts. *See* imperfect flower

perfoliate leaf A leaf in which the sides of the base grow together so that the petiole appears to pierce through the leaf.

petals Flower parts surrounding the center of the blossom. Petals are often brightly colored or white and are sometimes fragrant. Their primary function is to attract insects in order to facilitate fertilization.

petiole The leaf stalk of a simple leaf.

petiolule The stalk of a leaflet in a compound leaf.

phyllary Another name for the involucral bracts characteristic of the aster or daisy family.

pinnate *see* pinnately compound *and* pinnate venation

pinnately compound Leaflets arranged in a featherlike pattern. (Compare palmately compound.)

pinnate venation Leaf veins arranged in a featherlike pattern. (Compare palmate venation.)

pistil The female part of the flower, including the ovary, the style, and the stigma.

palmate venation

panicle

pappus

stamen — pistil

perfect flower

perfoliate

leaflet

petiolule

terminal leaflet

pinnately compound

pistillate flower An imperfect flower with female parts only.

plicate Folded like a handheld fan. Describes some leaves of the orchid family.

pod A dry fruit that splits open to release seeds.

pollen Male reproductive material (usually a fine powder) produced within the anther of a flower.

pome A fleshy fruit such as an apple or pear with firm tissue (commonly called a core) surrounding several seeds. Compare drupe.

poultice External application of a fresh herb to a wound or infection.

prickle A sharp projection from the bark or epidermis of a plant.

pubescent Covered with hair. Any part of a plant may be pubescent, which is the opposite of glabrous (hairless). Pubescence may be obvious or so subtle that it's visible only with a hand lens. Plant pubescence varies from a downy fuzz to the occurrence of long, sometimes bristly hairs. Whether a plant is pubescent or not sometimes helps to distinguish it from a similar species.

raceme A more or less elongated flower cluster with stalked flowers growing from an unbranched central axis. The lowest flowers in the cluster usually open first.

rachis The term is used in this book to describe the leaflet-bearing stalk of a pinnately compound leaf.

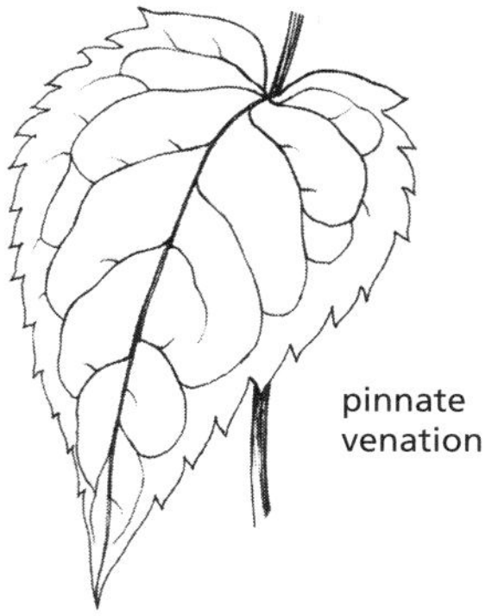

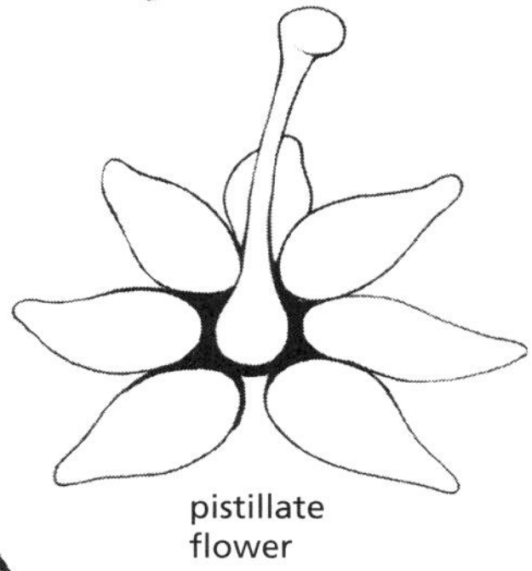

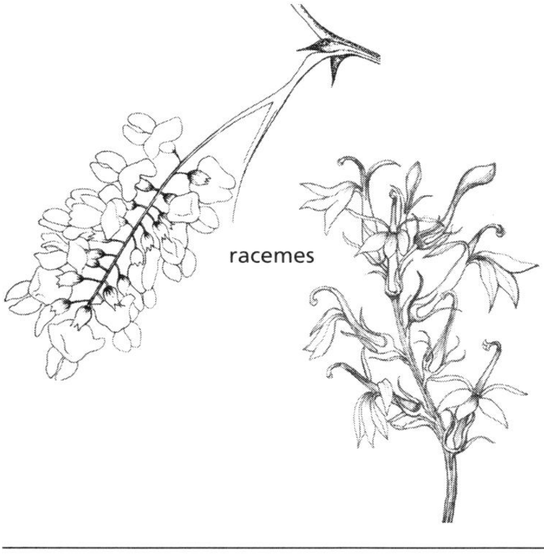

pinnate venation

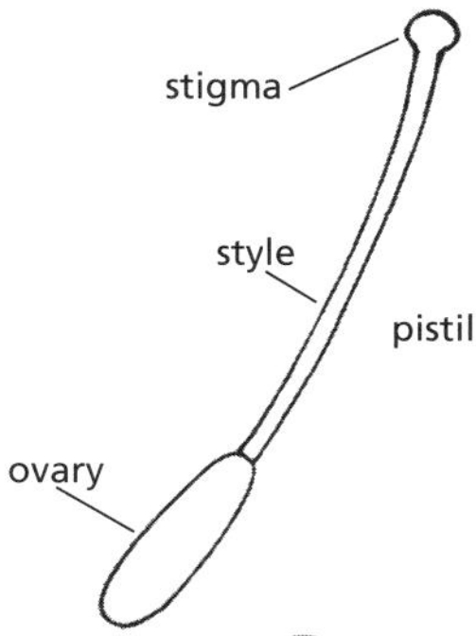

stigma

style

ovary

pistil

pistillate flower

racemes

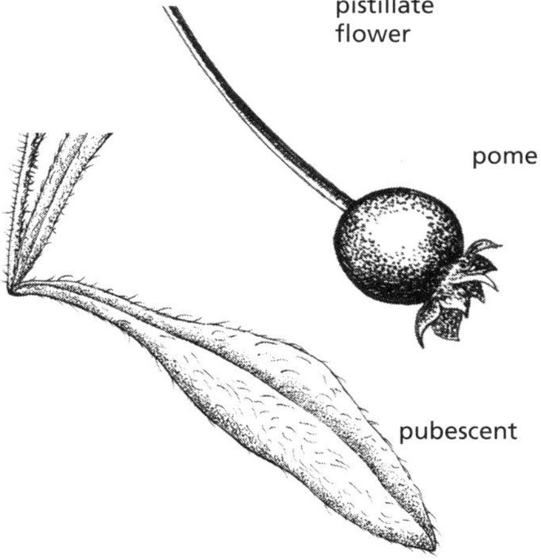

pome

pubescent

ray flowers

radiate To spread outward from a common point.

ray flower Ray flowers are the petal-like flowers of a flower head characteristic of the aster or daisy family. They are not always present in aster family members.

recumbent Leaning, resting upon the ground or other surface.

recurved Curved backward.

reflexed Bent or turned backward or downward (more dramatically than recurved).

regular flower A flower with symmetrical, same-sized petals and sepals.

reniform Kidney-shaped. Usually used to describe leaf-blade shape.

rhizome A creeping underground stem that produces roots below and shoots above. Some plants spread by means of rhizomes.

rotund Round.

samara A one-seeded, dry, flattened, winged fruit borne by some trees including elms, ashes, the tulip-tree (which bears an aggregate of samaras), and maples (which bear paired samaras).

schizocarp A fruit splitting into two closed segments at maturity. Typical of the carrot or parsley family.

scientific name Scientific names are the universally recognized names of plants in the botanical community. The scientific name of a plant family, genus, or species is in Latin. The genus and species names of a plant are given in italics after the common name in this book.

seed The fertilized, mature ovule.

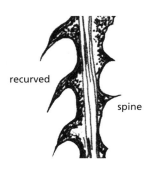

recurved

spine

reflexed

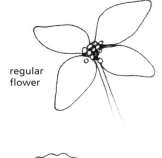

regular flower

reniform

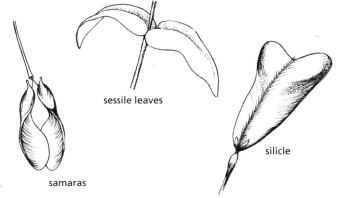

sessile leaves

silicle

samaras

sepal An individual segment of the calyx, the outer, usually leaflike layer of a flower that surrounds the corolla (or petals). Although usually leaflike, sepals may also be petal-like.

serrated (serration) Toothed (describes a leaf margin). Margins may be singly or doubly serrated.

sessile Without a petiole or flower stalk; attached directly by the base of the leaf or flower.

shrub A multitrunked woody plant that usually stands no higher than 20 feet.

silicle A dry fruit similar to a silique but shorter and usually wider. Typical of the mustard family.

silique A dry fruit characteristic of the mustard family. Usually long, narrow, and podlike.

silky Covered with fine, soft hairs.

simple fruit Fruit that contains a single ovary.

simple leaf A leaf that is not divided into leaflets.

sinus The space between the lobes of a leaf.

smooth Sometimes used in this book to describe an entire leaf margin (a margin unbroken by teeth or lobes).

spadix A spike or head bearing small flowers on a fleshy axis (as in Jack-in-the-pulpit and skunk cabbage).

spathe A large bract enclosing or partially enclosing a flower cluster (as in Jack-in-the pulpit and skunk cabbage).

species A group of similar organisms that belongs to a genus.

spike An elongated, unbranched flower cluster similar to a raceme except that the individual flowers lack flower stalks.

spine A firm, sharply pointed projection that is a modified leaf or stipule.

stamen The male part of the flower including the pollen-bearing anther.

staminate flower An imperfect flower with stamens but no pistil.

stem leaf Leaf growing along the plant stalk of an herbaceous plant. Compare basal leaf.

stigma The top of the pistil that receives pollen from the anther. *See* pistil on p. 383.

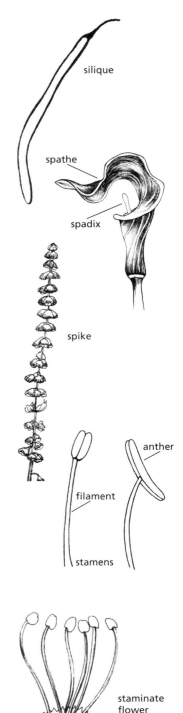

silique

spathe

spadix

spike

anther

filament

stamens

staminate flower

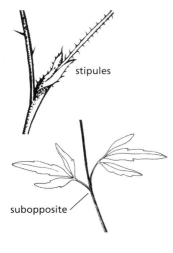

stipules

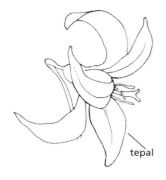

subopposite

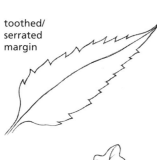

tepal

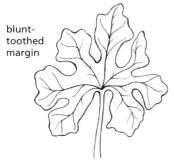

toothed/
serrated
margin

stipule A small leaflike or spiny appendage growing from where the petiole attaches to the plant stalk or branchlet. Characteristic of some plant families such as the rose family. Stipules usually grow in pairs. When they fall off, they leave stipular scars on woody plants.

style The long portion of the pistil between the stigma and the ovary.

subopposite Describes a leaf arrangement in which the leaves are nearly opposite on the plant stalk or branchlet. In botanical keys subopposite plants are grouped with opposite ones.

tepal A petal or sepal in a flower whose petals and sepals so closely resemble each other that they are nearly identical.

terminal At the top of a plant (terminal flower cluster) or the end of a compound leaf (terminal leaflet). In winter botany the bud found at the end of a branchlet is called a terminal bud or end bud.

thorn A stiff, sharply pointed woody projection which is a modified stem.

tincture An herbal medicine made by steeping the herb in alcohol (or, alternatively, glycerin).

tomentose Covered with matted woolly hairs.

toothed Describes the margin of a leaf with teeth or serrations.

tree A usually single-trunked woody plant that stands more than 20 feet high.

trifoliate Describes a compound leaf with three leaflets.

truncate Nearly straight across (or squared). Describes the base of some leaves.

blunt-
toothed
margin

trifoliate leaf

truncate
base

umbel A flat or nearly flat flower cluster with long stalks radiating from a single point along a short axis. In a simple umbel each long stalk bears a flower; in a compound umbel the longer stalks arising from a single point give rise to small flower clusters, sometimes called umbellets. Umbels are characteristic of the carrot or parsley family.

unequal base Describes a leaf base in which the two sides of the base attach to the petiole at slightly different spots or at a slightly different angle. Also called oblique.

unisexual Bearing either pistil or stamens but not both.

veins The slender vascular bundles that transport food and water through the leaf and usually are externally visible.

venation The vein pattern of a leaf. *See* palmate venation *and* pinnate venation

vine A climbing and/or trailing plant. Woody vines are grouped with trees and shrubs in this book.

viscid Sticky.

wavy-toothed Describes a leaf margin with undulating teeth.

wedge-shaped Describes the base of a leaf, petal, sepal, etc., that is shaped like the narrow end of a piece of pie.

whorled Describes a leaf arrangement in which more than two leaves are opposite each other on the plant stalk or branchlet.

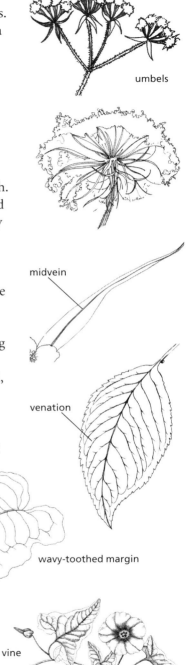

umbels

midvein

venation

wedge-shaped base

wavy-toothed margin

whorled leaves

vine

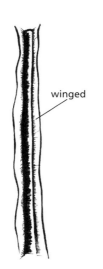

winged

wing (winged) A thin, sometimes woody projection on some seeds, plant stalks, branches, etc.

woody Describes trees, shrubs, and some vines. Woody plants contain ligneous tissue. *See* herbaceous

woolly Covered with short, soft hairs.

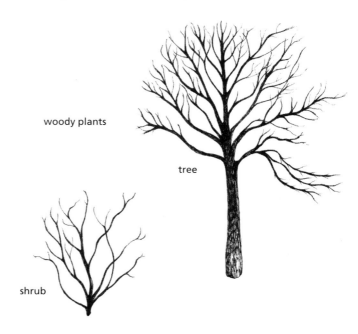

woody plants

tree

shrub

Suggested Reading
and Bibliography

Suggested Reading

When Tina Brown and I go into the field, we carry our favorite books with us. For casual wildflower walks we bring along *Newcomb's Wildflower Guide* by Lawrence Newcomb and Roger Tory Peterson and Margaret McKenny's *A Field Guide to Wildflowers*. Both books are well illustrated: Newcomb's by Gordon Morrison and Peterson and McKenny's by Peterson. Newcomb's guide has a user-friendly botanical key, the basic principles of which we have adapted for this book. However, when the key fails us (as it does occasionally), we like to have Peterson's guide, which is organized by flower color, as a backup. When we are planning a day of serious botanizing, such as the many days that went into the creation of this book, we travel less lightly, schlepping some fairly hefty tomes. We almost always carry Brown and Brown's *Herbaceous Plants of Maryland* and/or Strausbaugh and Core's *Flora of West Virginia*. We usually bring along Gleason and Cronquist's *Manual of Vascular Plants of Northeastern United States and Adjacent Canada* as well.

For tree identification I swear by *The Complete Trees of North America* by Thomas S. Elias. I have used this comprehensive, simply worded, illustrated book in the Florida Everglades, the Alaskan mountains, and everywhere else on the continent I've ever been. It has never let me down. Brown and Brown's *Woody Plants of Maryland* is comprehensive for trees and shrubs of the Sugarloaf region, and the *Flora of West Virginia* covers woody plants as well as herbaceous ones. I also like to carry my own book *City of Trees* (illustrated by my friend Polly Alexander).

When Tina and I are studying the medicinal uses of plants, the Peterson Field Guides' *Field Guide to Medicinal Plants: Eastern and Central North America* by Steven Foster and James Duke is our favorite guide to use in the field. Generally, we find the Peterson Field Guides series to be very good, including the guide to trees and shrubs and the guide to ferns.

Finding Wildflowers in the Washington-Baltimore Area by Cristol Fleming (our friend, botanical adviser, and editor), Marion Blois Lobstein, and Barbara Tufty and *Watching Nature: A Mid-Atlantic Natural History* by Mark S. Garland are excellent resources for naturalists of the Washington-Baltimore area.

Tina and I like to learn about plants as members of plant families, and our favorite book on the families is a gorgeously illustrated book called *Flowering Plant of the World* by V. H. Heywood. For simple family diagnostics, James Payne Smith Jr.'s *Vascular Plant Families* is a good, solid resource book.

For information about Sugarloaf Mountain, our companion volume, *Sugarloaf: The Mountain's History, Geology, and Natural Lore,* is available. *Maryland's Geology* by Martin F. Schmidt Jr. is a readable guide to the state's geologic past and contains simply worded descriptions of the major geologic regions of Maryland. My favorite local history book is *The Potomac* by Frederick Gutheim. Tina and I recommend *Circling Historic Landscapes: Bicycling, Canoeing, Walking, and Rail Trails near Sugarloaf Mountain, Maryland.* We also highly recommend two films available on video that were produced by Chris Haugh: *Monocacy: The Pre-History of Frederick County, Maryland* and *Sugarloaf: The Quest for Riches and Redemption in the Monocacy Valley.* Our bibliography contains many other sources that contributed to this book.

Bibliography

In lieu of notes, the sources quoted in the text are preceded here by asterisks. In most cases citations can be located by the common and/or scientific species, genus, or family names in the cited works. Consult the index of an individual source.

Baumgardt, John Philip. *How to Identify Flowering Plant Families: A Practical Guide for Horticulturists and Plant Lovers.* Portland, Oreg.: Timber Press, 1982.
*Brown, Melvin L., and Russell G. Brown. *Herbaceous Plants of Maryland.* Baltimore: Port City Press, 1984.
*———. *Woody Plants of Maryland.* Baltimore: Port City Press, 1992.
Choukas-Bradley, Melanie, and Polly Alexander. *City of Trees: The Complete Field Guide to the Trees of Washington, D.C.* Baltimore: Johns Hopkins Univ. Press, 1987.
Choukas-Bradley, Melanie, with illustrations by Tina Thieme Brown. *Sugarloaf: The Mountain's History, Geology, and Natural Lore.* Charlottesville: Univ. of Virginia Press, 2003.
Cobb, Boughton. *A Field Guide to the Ferns and Their Related Families of Northeastern and Central North America.* Peterson Field Guide Series. Boston, New York: Houghton Mifflin, 1984.
Coleman, Margaret Marshall. *Montgomery County: A Pictorial History.* Rev. ed. Norfolk/Virginia Beach: Donning Company Publishers, 1990.
Collins, Henry Hill, Jr. *Complete Field Guide to North American Wildlife, Eastern Edition.* New York: Harper & Row, 1981.

Dott, Robert H., Jr., and Roger L. Batten. *Evolution of the Earth.* New York: McGraw-Hill, 1971.

Duke, James A. *The Green Pharmacy.* New York: St. Martin's Paperbacks, 1997.

*Elias, Thomas S. *The Complete Trees of North America: Field Guide and Natural History.* New York: Van Nostrand Reinhold, 1980.

Fernald, Merritt Lyndon. *Gray's Manual of Botany.* 8th (Centennial) ed. 3d printing. Portland, Oreg.: Dioscorides Press, 1991.

Fisher, Alan. *More Country Walks near Washington.* Baltimore: Rambler Books, 1985.

*Fleming, Cristol, Marion Blois Lobstein, and Barbara Tufty. *Finding Wildflowers in the Washington-Baltimore Area.* Baltimore: Johns Hopkins Univ. Press, 1995.

*Foster, Steven, and James A. Duke. *A Field Guide to Medicinal Plants: Eastern and Central North America.* Peterson Field Guide Series. Boston: Houghton Mifflin, 1990.

*Garland, Mark S. *Watching Nature: A Mid-Atlantic Natural History.* Washington, D.C.: Smithsonian Institution Press, 1997.

Glassberg, Jeffrey. *Butterflies through Binoculars: A Field Guide to Butterflies in the Boston–New York–Washington Region.* New York and Oxford: Oxford Univ. Press, 1993.

Gleason, Henry A., and Arthur Cronquist. *Manual of Vascular Plants of Northeastern United States and Adjacent Canada.* 2d ed. Bronx, N.Y.: New York Botanical Garden, 1991.

Godfrey, Michael A. *Field Guide to the Piedmont: The Natural Habitats of America's Most Lived-In Region, from New York City to Montgomery, Alabama.* Chapel Hill: Univ. of North Carolina Press, 1997.

*Grieve, Maude. *A Modern Herbal.* 2 vols. 1931. Rept. New York: Dover, 1971.

Gutheim, Frederick. *The Potomac.* 1949; Maryland Paperback Bookshelf Edition. Baltimore: Johns Hopkins Univ. Press, , 1986.

Haller, Harry. "Mountain Beauty in Maryland: Sugar Loaf's Owner Has Provided Access to an Exciting Spectacle." Baltimore *Sunday Sun,* Sept. 12, 1937.

Hammond, Helen. "The Legacy of Stronghold: Sugarloaf's Crowning Glory." *Frederick: The Magazine for Mid-Maryland,* Oct. 1994.

Harlow, William M. *Fruit Key and Twig Key to Trees and Shrubs.* New York: Dover, 1946.

——. *Trees of the Eastern and Central United States and Canada.* New York: Dover, 1957.

*Heywood, V. H. *Flowering Plants of the World.* Updated ed. New York: Oxford Univ. Press, 1993.

Hickey, Michael, and Clive King. *100 Families of Flowering Plants.* 2d ed. Cambridge: Cambridge Univ. Press, 1988.

*Hutchens, Alma R. *Indian Herbalogy of North America.* 3d ed. Boston and London: Shambhala, 1991.

Hylton, William H., ed. *The Rodale Herb Book.* Emmaus, Pa.: Rodale Press, 1983.

Kartesz, John T., and Rosemarie Kartesz. *A Synonymized Checklist of the Vascula Flora of the United States, Canada, and Greenland*. Vol. 2. *The Biota of Nort America*. Chapel Hill: Univ. of North Carolina Press, 1980.

*Martin, Alexander C., Herbert S. Zim, and Arnold L. Nelson. *American Wildli and Plants: A Guide to Wildlife Food Habits*. 1951; rept. New York: Dover, 196

Martin, Laura C. *Wildflower Folklore*. Charlotte, N.C.: East Woods Press, Fast & McMillan Publishers, 1984.

Maryland Department of Natural Resources, Wildlife and Heritage Division *Rare, Threatened, and Endangered Plants of Maryland*. Rev. eds. Annapolis 1996, 2001. Up-to-date status of plants can be accessed on the MDNR website

McKinsey, Folger ("The Bentztown Bard"). "Natural Beauties Retained in Devel oping Sugar Loaf." *Frederick Post*, Aug. 14, 1941.

Miller, Howard, and Samuel Lamb. *Oaks of North America*. Happy Camp, Calif. Naturegraph Publishers, 1985.

Monocacy: The Pre-History of Frederick County, Maryland. A film documentary by Chris Haugh, GS Communications, Frederick, Md., 1999.

"Monocacy Natural Resources Management Area: Forest Stewardship Plan." Pre pared by Hailu Sharew, Forester. Maryland Department of Natural Resources Forest Service, 2001. Internal management plan.

Monocacy Scenic River Local Advisory Board (with technical assistance from the Maryland Department of Natural Resources). *Maryland Scenic Rivers: The Monocacy*. Annapolis: Maryland Department of Natural Resources, 1992.

Montgomery County Planning Board. *Plowing New Ground: Questions and An swers, Agricultural and Rural Open Space Preservation Program, Montgomery County, Maryland*. Rev. eds. Silver Spring, Md.: Montgomery County Planning Board, 1990, 2001.

Murie, Olaus J. *A Field Guide to Animal Tracks*. Peterson Field Guide Series. 2d ed. Boston: Houghton Mifflin, 1974.

National Geographic Society. *Field Guide to the Birds of North America*. 2d ed. 6th printing. Washington, D.C.: National Geographic Society, 1994.

Newcomb, Lawrence. *Newcomb's Wildflower Guide*. Boston: Little, Brown, 1977.

*Peterson, Lee. *A Field Guide to Edible Wild Plants of Eastern and Central North America*. Peterson Field Guide Series. Boston: Houghton Mifflin, 1978.

Peterson, Roger Tory. *A Field Guide to the Birds of Eastern and Central North America*. 4th edition. Boston: Houghton Mifflin, 1980.

*Peterson, Roger Tory, and Margaret McKenny. *A Field Guide to Wildflowers of Northeastern and North-Central North America*. Boston: Houghton Mifflin, 1968.

Petrides, George A. *A Field Guide to Trees and Shrubs*. 2d ed. Peterson Field Guide Series. Boston: Houghton Mifflin, 1972.

Press, Frank, and Raymond Siever. *Earth*. San Francisco: W. H. Freeman, 1974.

Price, Helen Urner. "Weird Mountain Beauty in New Park." Washington, D.C., *Sunday Star*, July 17, 1932.

Rothrock, Gail C., and Margaret M. Coleman, eds. *Circling Historic Landscapes: Bicycling, Canoeing, Walking, and Rail Trails near Sugarloaf Mountain, Maryland.* 2d ed. Rockville, Md.: Sugarloaf Regional Trails and the Montgomery County Historic Preservation Commission of Maryland–National Capital Park and Planning Commission, 1999.

Schmidt, Martin F., Jr. *Maryland's Geology.* Centreville, Md.: Tidewater Publishers, 1993.

Shetler, Stanwyn G., and Sylvia Stone Orli. *Annotated Checklist of the Vascular Plants of the Washington-Baltimore Area.* Part I. *Ferns, Fern Allies, Gymnosperms, and Dicotyledons.* Part II. *Monocotyledons.* Washington, D.C.: Department of Botany, National Museum of Natural History, Smithsonian Institution, 2000- 2002.

Smith, James Payne, Jr. *Vascular Plant Families.* Eureka, Calif.: Mad River Press, 1977.

Spaur, Michael L. "What's in the Name? Sugarloaf Mountain." *Frederick Post,* March 21, 1979.

Stary, Frantisek. *The Natural Guide to Medicinal Herbs and Plants.* New York: Barnes & Noble, 1996.

Strausbaugh, P. D., and Earl L. Core. *Flora of West Virginia.* 2d ed. Morgantown, W.Va.: Seneca Books, 1977.

Stronghold, Inc., Dickerson, Md. Sugarloaf Mountain newsletters, bulletins, and maps (1971–2001).

Sugarloaf: The Quest for Riches and Redemption in the Monocacy Valley. A film documentary by Chris Haugh, GS Communications, Frederick, Md., 2000.

Wiegand, Richard Harrison. "Sugarloaf Mountain, Stronghold Inc. Property, Bio-resources Survey of 1 April 1987 to 1 November 1987: Vascular Flora List." Report for Stronghold Inc., Dickerson, Md.

Wilds, Claudia. *Finding Birds in the National Capital Area.* 2d ed. Washington, D.C.: Smithsonian Institution Press, 1992.

Zomlefer, Wendy B. *Guide to Flowering Plant Families.* Chapel Hill: Univ. of North Carolina Press, 1994.

Index of Common and Scientific Names

Page numbers for detailed, usually illustrated, descriptions of plants are in italics.

Apocynaceae, 173–75
Apocynum androsaemifolium, 175,
   177; cannabinum, 21, 174–75, 177
Apple, 356
Aquifoliaceae, 357–58, 361
Aquilegia, 42; canadensis, 20, 43; vul-
   garis, 20, 42–43
Arabis, 92; laevigata, 14, 91–92
Araceae, 304–7
Araliaceae, 164–65
Aralia nudicaulis, 16, 164–65
Arbutus, Trailing, ix, x, xii, 7, 17, 95–
   96, 360
Arctium lappa, 284; minus, 27, 283–84;
   tomentosum, 284
Arisaema dracontium, 304; (A. stew-
   ardsonii), 307; triphyllum, 10, 304,
   306–7
Arnoglossum atriplicifolium, 26, 284–
   85
Aronia arbutifolia, 30, 129, 360
Arrow Arum, 304
Arrowhead, Broad-Leaved (or Com-
   mon), 13, 303–4
Arrowhead family (or Water-Plantain
   family), 303–4
Arrowwood, 243, 244; Downy, 244;
   Northern and Southern, see Arrow-
   wood
Artemisia vulgaris, 27, 301, 302
Arum family, 304–7
Aruncus dioicus, 19, 121
Asclepiadaceae, 175–77
Asclepias, 21, 175, 177; exaltata, 177;
   incarnata, 177; quadrifolia, 20, 177;
   syriaca, 175–77; tuberosa, 17, 177
Ash, 211, 242: White, 212, 343
Asimina triloba, 29, 35, 36–37, 360
Aspen, Big-Toothed (or Large-
   Toothed), 357
Aster, ix, 25, 245, 253, 255–60, 278;
   Bushy, 257–58; Calico, 256, 257;
   Crooked-Stemmed, 260; Flat-

Toppped, 259; Heart-Leaved, 259,
   260; Heath, 256–57; Paincled,
   258–59; Late Purple, 260; Purple-
   Stemmed, 260; Wavy-Leaved, 259,
   260; White Wood, 255–56; Toothed
   White-Topped, 18, 261
Aster, 25, 245, 253, 255–60, 261, 278;
   cordifolius, 259, 260; divaricatus,
   255–56; dumosus, 257–58; lanceolatus, 258–59; lateriflorus, 256, 257;
   patens, 260; (A. paternus), 261;
   pilosus, 256–57; prenanthoides, 260;
   puniceus, 260; (A. simplex), 258;
   umbellatus, 259; undulatus, 259,
   260
Asteraceae, 245–302
Aster family (or Daisy family), 245–
   302
Audubon Naturalist Society, xiv, 2
Aureolaria pedicularia, 218; virginica,
   21, 217–18
Avens: Spring, 19, 120; White, 18, 19,
   118–19, 170, 171
Axseed. See Vetch, Crown
Azalea, 95, 96, 99; Flame, 30, 100, 101;
   Pink, see Pinxter Flower

Bachelor's Buttons, 286
Balmony. See Turtlehead
Balsaminaceae, 162–63
Baltimore, Maryland, x, 34, 67, 142,
   188, 213, 225, 239, 277, 290, 298,
   304, 314
Baltimore Checkerspot Butterfly, 213,
   218, 219–20
Baltimore County, Maryland, 59
Baptisia tinctoria, 12, 137–38
Barbarea verna, 91; vulgaris, 14,
   90–91
Barberry, Japanese, 363
Barberry family, 49–50, 363
Barnesville, Maryland, 166
Basil, Wild (or Field Basil), 205–6

Bear Branch (on Sugarloaf Mountain), 6, 7, 37, 38, 39, 40, 41, 42, 48, 51, 52, 61, 62, 83, 84, 86, 87, 108, 121, 149, 163, 167, 172, 186, 187, 194, 226, 238, 260, 266, 285, 314, 327, 328

Beardtongue, 216; Foxglove (or White), 12, *216–17,* 220

Bedstraw, 235

Bee-Balm (or Oswego-Tea), 12, *193–94,* 231

Beech, American, 226, *350–51*

Beechdrops, 226

Beech family, 345–48, 350–52

Beefsteak Plant. *See* Perilla

Beggar's Lice. *See* Stickseed, Virginia

Beggar-Ticks, 28, 251, *261–62;* Tall, 262

Bellflower family (or Bluebell family), 229–35

Bellwort, 313, 314; Perfoliate, 22, *311–12;* Sessile (or Wild Oats), 22, 311, *312*

Bennett Creek, 37, 61, 62, 187, 188, 266, 285, 310, 344

Berberidaceae, 49–50, 363

Berberis thunbergii, 363

Bergamot, Wild, *194*

Betula alleghaniensis, 354; *lenta, 353–54; nigra,* 354; *papyrifera,* 354

Betulaceae, 353–55, 361–62

Bidens, 251, 261; *bipinnata,* 28, 251, *262–63; cernua,* 262; *frondosa,* 28, 251, *261–62; polylepis,* 25, *251; vulgata,* 262

Bignoniaceae, 227–29, 370

Bignonia family (or Trumpet-Creeper family), 227–29, 370

Bindweed, 18, 183; Field, *185;* Hedge, *184–85*

Birch, Black (Sweet or Cherry), x, *353–54;* River, 354; White or Paper, 354; Yellow, 354

Birch family, 353–55, 361–62

Bittercress: Hairy, 14, *88–89;* Pennsylvania, 14, 88, *89*

Bitter Dock. *See* Dock, Bitter

Bittersweet, 371; American, *371;* Oriental, *371*

Blackberry, 126, 127, 369; Common, 31, 125, *127–28*

Black Cohosh. *See* Cohosh, Black

Black-Eyed Susan, ix, 24, 245, *249–50*

Black-Gum. *See* Tupelo

Black-Gum family. *See* Tupelo family

Black-Haw, 31, *243–44,* 340

Bladder Campion. *See* Campion, Bladder

Bladdernut, American, *344*

Bladdernut family, 344

Bleeding-Heart, Eastern Wild, 53, 54

Bleeding-Heart or Fumitory family, 52–54

Bloodroot, ix, 23, 40, 42, *51–52*

Bluebell family. *See* Bellflower family

Bluebells, Virginia (Mertensia or Virginia Cowslip), 17, 187, *188*

Blueberry, xii, 95, 96, 103, 360; Common Lowbush, 104; Highbush, 104; Lowbush, 30, *103–4*

Blue-Eyed Grass, 324; Slender, 324; Stout, 22, 322, *323–24*

Bluets, 15, *239;* Long-Leaved Summer, *see* Houstonia, Long-Leaved

Boehmeria cylindrica, 28, 56, *57–58*

Boneset, 28, *280–82,* 283; Upland, 280; White, 280. *See also* Thoroughwort

Borage family (or Forget-Me-Not family), 187–89

Boraginaceae, 187–89

Botanical Key and Guide to Trees, Shrubs, and Woody Vines, 4, 40, 49, 95, 114, 131, 151, 154, 157, 212, 235, *333–72;* key to species based on leaf arrangement, *334*

Coneflower: Green-Headed, 25, *250;* Three-Lobed, 250

Conifers, 334–37

Conium maculatum, 166, 169

Conopholis americana, 10, 172, *226–27*

Convolvulaceae, 183–85

Convolvulus, 18, 183; *arvensis, 185; (C. sepium),* 184

Conyza canadensis, 26, *266*

Corallorhiza, 331–32; *maculata, 332; odontorhiza, 332*

Coralroot, 331–32; Autumn (Small or Late), *332;* Spotted, *332*

Cornaceae, 150–51, 339, 358

Cornflower, 286

Corn Gromwell, 187

Cornus, 38, 150, 151, 339; *alternifolia,* 339; *amomum,* 339; *canadensis,* 150; *florida,* 29, *150–51,* 339

Coronilla varia, 12, *136*

Corydalis: Pale or Pink, 54; Yellow, 11, 52, *53–54*

Corydalis flavula, 11, 52, *53–54; sempervirens,* 54

Corylus americana, 361–62

Cowbane, 166

Crabapple, 356

Cranefly Orchid, *331*

Cranesbill, 22, 160, 161; Carolina, 161; Dove's-Foot, 161; Small-Flowered, 161, 162

Crape-Myrtle, 144

Crataegus, 349, 356

Cress: Bulbous, *see* Cress, Spring; Cow or Field, 86; Spring, 14, *89–90. See also* Bittercress; Rockcress; Winter-Cress

Cronquist, Arthur. *See* Gleason, Henry A., and Arthur Cronquist (*Manual of Vascular Plants of Northeastern United States and Adjacent Canada*)

Crowfoot, 19; Cursed, *48;* Hooked, 17, *48*; Small-Flowered, *see* Buttercup, Kidneyleaf

Crownbeard, 251

Cruciferae. See *Brassicaceae*

Cryptotaenia canadensis, 19, 167, *169–70,* 171

Cucumber Tree, 33

Cunila origanoides, 201–2

Cuphea, Clammy, 12, *144–45*

Cuphea (C. petiolata), 144; *viscosissima,* 12, *144–45*

Cupressaceae, 337

Custard-Apple family, 35–37, 360

Cypress family, 337

Cypripedium acaule, 325–26; calceolus, 325

Daisy, Ox-Eye, 24, *248–49*

Daisy family. *See* Aster family

Dame's-Rocket (or Dame's-Violet), 14, *93–94,* 95

Dandelion, Common, 23, *290–91,* 292

Datura stramonium, 18, 178, *180–82*

Daucus carota, 18, *167–68,* 169, 265

Dayflower: Asiatic, 11, 308, *309;* Slender, 309; Virginia, 309

Day-Lily, 22, *318*

Dead-Nettle, Purple (or Red), *203–4*

Deerberry, 30, 103, *104*

Dentaria heterophylla, 15, *87–88; laciniata,* 15, *86–87,* 88

Deptford Pink. *See* Pink, Deptford

Desmodium, 12, 139; *canescens,* 140; *glabellum,* 140; *nudiflorum,* 10, *138–39; paniculatum,* 140;

Dewberry, 126, 127, 369; Common (or Northern), 31, *128;* Swamp, 31, *128–29*

Dianthus armeria, 21, *66,* 68

Dicentra, 53; *canadensis,* 54; *cucullaria,* 54; *eximia,* 54

Dickerson, Maryland, 338

Dicotyledons, 33–302

Dioscorea, 23, 321, 322; *quaternata,*
321–22; *villosa,* 321, 322

Dioscoreaceae, 321–22

Diospyros virginiana, 359–60

Dittany, *201–2*

Dock, Bitter (Broad or Broad-Leaved),
26, *73–74;* Curly, Curled, or Yellow,
74

Dockmackie. *See* Viburnum, Maple-
Leaved

Dodecatheon, 108

Dogbane, Spreading, 175, 177

Dogbane family, 173–75

Dogwood, 38, 150, 339; Alternate-
Leaved (or Pagoda), 339; Flowering, 29, *150–51,* 339; Silky, 339

Dogwood family, 150–51, 339, 358

Duchesnea indica, 19, *115–16*

Duke, James A. *See* Foster, Steven, and
James A. Duke (Peterson Field
Guide Series' *A Field Guide to Med-
icinal Plants: Eastern and Central
North America)*

Durkin, Pat, xiv, 219

Dutch Elm disease, 352

Dutchman's Breeches, 53, 54

Ebenaceae, 359–60

Ebony family, 359–60

Echium vulgare, 187

Elder, Red-Berried, 242. *See also* Elderberry, Common

Elderberry, 239; Common, 31, 239,
241–42, 343

Elias, Thomas S. *(The Complete Trees
of North America),* 353, 357

Elm, 352; American, *352;* Scotch (or
Wych), *353;* Slippery, *352–53*

Elm family, 352–53

Emperor Butterflies: Hackberry, 353;
Tawny, 353

Empress Tree. *See* Paulownia

Enchanter's Nightshade, 13, *145–46;*
Dwarf or Alpine, 146

Epifagus, 226; *virginiana,* 226

Epigaea repens, 17, *95–96,* 98, 360

Epilobium coloratum, 145

Erechtites hieracifolia, 26, 266, *288–89*

Ericaceae, 95–105, 360

Erigenia bulbosa, 166

Erigeron, 24; *annuus,* 253, *254; (E.
canadensis),* 266; *philadelphicus,*
252–53; pulchellus, 253; *strigosus,*
253, *254*

Erythronium albidum, 311; *americanum,* 22, *310–11*

Euonymus, 340; *alatus, 340–41; americanus, 341; atropurpureus, 341*

Euonymous, 340; Winged, *340–41. See
also* Strawberry Bush; Wahoo

Eupatorium, 28, 277–83; *album,* 280;
coelestinum, 28, *277–78; fistulosum,
278–79; maculatum,* 279; *perfoliatum,* 28, *280–82,* 283; *(E. pubescens),* 279; *purpureum, 278–79;
rotundifolium,* 28, *279–80; rugosum,*
28, 280, *282–83; sessilifolium,* 280

Euphorbiaceae, 152–54

Euphorbia corollata, 18, *153–54; cyparissias,* 154; *dentata,* 154; *maculata,* 154; *purpurea,* 154

Euphydryas phaeton, 218

Euthamia, 274; *(E. graminifolia),* 274

Evening Lychnis, 21, *66–67*

Evening-Primrose, Common, 14, 145,
146–48

Evening-Primrose family, 145–49

Everlasting, Sweet. *See* Sweet Everlasting

Fabaceae, 132–43, 358, 363

Fagaceae, 345–48, 350–52

Fagus grandifolia, 350–51

False-Foxglove, 218; Downy, 21, *217–
18;* Fern-Leaved, *217–18*

Fameflower, 61
Fetterbush, 360
Figwort, Hare, 222; Maryland, 12, *222*
Figwort family. *See* Snapdragon family
Flax, Ridged Yellow, 17, 21, *156;* Wild
  Yellow (or Virginia Yellow), 156
Flax family, 155–56
Fleabane, 24; Common (or Philadel-
  phia), *252–53;* Daisy, 253, *254;*
  Lesser Daisy, 253, *254. See also*
  Robin's Plantain
Fleming, Cristol (Cris), xiii, 2, 154,
  185, 266–67, 279, 327
Fleming, Cristol, Marion Blois Lob-
  stein, and Barbara Tufty *(Finding
  Wildflowers in the Washington-
  Baltimore Area),* 49, 139, 149, 172,
  266–67
Forget-Me-Not, 187
Forget-Me-Not family. *See* Borage
  family
Forsythia, 212, *341–42*
Forsythia viridissima, 212, *341–42*
Foster, Steven, and James A. Duke (Peterson Field Guide Series' *A Field
  Guide to Medicinal Plants: Eastern
  and Central North America),* 6, 35,
  36–37, 43, 44–45, 49, 50, 51–52,
  56–57, 76–77, 78, 91, 97, 98, 108,
  111, 115–16, 134, 137, 138–39, 143,
  147, 153–54, 162, 164–65, 167, 169,
  171, 175, 176, 178, 182, 184, 192,
  193, 194–95, 196, 200, 202, 205,
  207–8, 210, 216, 219, 221, 225, 231,
  233, 244, 246, 250, 262, 265, 268,
  276, 279, 280, 281, 285, 288–89,
  289–90, 291, 292, 296, 297–98,
  300–301, 302, 303, 306–7, 309, 313,
  316, 317, 320, 322, 323–24, 326–27,
  352, 366
Foxglove. *See* False-Foxglove
Fragaria virginiana, 16, *114–15*
Fraxinus, 211, 242; *americana,* 212, *343*

Fringe-Tree, 29, 211, *212–13,* 339;
  Asian, 213
Fumariaceae, 52–54
Furnace Branch (on and near Sugar-
  loaf Mountain), 7, 49, 83, 85, 89,
  97, 116, 164, 165, 186, 310, 344

Galearis spectabilis, 327–28
Galinsoga, 264; Smooth, 264
Galinsoga (G. ciliata), 264; *parviflora,*
  264; *quadriradiata,* 20, *264*
Galium, 235; *aparine,* 15, *235–36; cir-
  caezans,* 15, 236, *237*
Gall-of-the-Earth. *See* Lion's-Foot
Garland, Mark S. *(Watching Nature: A
  Mid-Atlantic Natural History),* 187
Garlic, Field, *319*
Garlic-Mustard, 13, *92–93,* 94, 162
Garrett County, Maryland, 100, 101
Gaultheria procumbens, 17, *97–98,* 360
Gaura, Biennial, 145
Gaura biennis, 145
Gaylussacia, 95, 103, 360; *baccata,* 30,
  104–5
Gentianaceae, 171–73
Gentian family, 171–73
Geraniaceae, 160–62
Geranium, 22
Geranium, 22, 160, 161, 162; *carolini-
  anum,* 161; *maculatum, 161–62;
  molle,* 161; *pusillum,* 161
Geranium family, 160–62
(Gerardia virginica), 217
Germander, American, 13, *196*
Geum canadense, 18, 19, *118–19,* 170,
  171; *vernum,* 19, *120*
Ghost-Pipe. *See* Cancer-Root, One-
  Flowered
(Gillenia trifoliata), 120
Gill-over-the-Ground (or Ground
  Ivy), *202–3,* 204
Ginseng: American, 164, 165; Dwarf,
  22, 164, *165*

Hieracium (continued)
scabrum, 295; venosum, 23, 24, 292–93, 294
Hog Peanut, 134
Holly, 361; American, 357–58. See also Winterberry
Holly family, 357–58, 361
Honesty, 14, 15, 94–95
Honewort, 19, 119, 167, 169–70, 171
Honeysuckle, 340; Japanese, 32, 239, 240–41, 340, 371; Tartarian, 241, 340
Honeysuckle family, 239–44, 339–40, 343, 371
Hop-Hornbeam, Eastern, 354–55
Hornbeam, American, 354
Horse-Balm (Richweed or Stoneroot), 191–92
Horse Nettle, 18, 178–79
Horseweed, 26, 266
Houstonia, 239; caerulea, 15, 239; longifolia, 15, 235, 238–39
Houstonia, Long-Leaved, 14, 235, 238–39
Huckleberry, xii, 95, 103, 360: Black, 30, 104–5
Hutchens, Alma R. (Indian Herbalogy of North America), 56, 169, 192, 213, 219, 261, 281
Hydrangea, Wild (or American), 31, 111–12, 341
Hydrangea arborescens, 31, 111–12, 341
Hydrangeaceae, 111–12, 341
Hydrangea family, 111–12, 341
Hypericaceae, 74–78, 341
Hypericum, 21, 74, 77, 78, 156; canadense, 77; densiflorum, 31, 77, 341; gentianoides, 77; hypericoides, 15, 77–78, 148, 149, 341; mutilum, 75–76; perforatum, 74, 75, 76; prolificum, 31, 77; punctatum, 75
Hypoxis hirsuta, 22, 315

Ilex laevigata, 361; opaca, 357–58; verticillata, 361
Impatiens, 162; capensis, 11, 162–63; pallida, 11, 162–63
Impatiens family. See Touch-Me-Not family
Indian Cucumber Root, 7, 23, 316–17, 328–29
Indian Hemp, 21, 174–75, 177
Indian Physic. See Bowman's Root
Indian Pipe, 16, 106, 107, 227
Indian Pipe family, 106–7
Indian Plantain, Pale, 26, 284–85
Indian Poke. See Hellebore, False
Indian Strawberry, 19, 115–16
Indian Tobacco, 11, 232–33, 235
Indian Turnip. See Jack-in-the-Pulpit
Indigo, Wild, 12, 137–38
Ipecac, False. See Bowman's Root
Ipomoea, 18, 183; hederacea, 184; pandurata, 183; purpurea, 184
Iridaceae, 322–24
Iris family, 322–24
Ironweed: Broad-Leaved, 277; New York, 18, 276–77
Ironwood. See Hornbeam, American
Isotria medeoloides, 328; verticillata, 12, 317, 328–29

Jack-in-the-Pulpit, 10, 304, 305, 306–7
Jeffersonia diphylla, 49
Jerusalem Artichoke, 252
Jewelweed: Spotted (or Orange), 11, 162–63; Yellow (or Pale), 11, 162–63
Jimsonweed, 18, 178, 180–82
Joe-Pye-Weed, 28, 277, 278–79; Hollow, 278–79; Spotted, 279; Sweet, 278–79
Judas-Tree. See Redbud
Juglans, 365; nigra, 365–66
Jumpseed, 13, 72

Juneberry. *See* Shadbush
Juniper, 337
Juniperus, 337; *virginiana, 337*

Kalmia latifolia, 30, 95, *98–99,* 100,
    102–3, 360
Keys. *See* Botanical Key and Guide to
    Trees, Shrubs, and Woody Vines;
    Botanical Key to Flowering Plants
King Devil. *See* Hawkweed, Field
Knapweed, Spotted, 20, *285–86*
Knotweed. *See* Smartweed, Pennsyl-
    vania
Kyde, Kerrie, xiii, 93, 286

Labiatae. See *Lamiaceae*
Lactuca, 24, 297; *biennis,* 25, 296, *297–
    98; canadensis,* 298; *floridana,* 298;
    (L. scariola), 298; *serriola, 298*
Ladies'-Tresses, Nodding, *332*
Lady's Slipper: Pink, 2, 7, *325–26;* Yel-
    low, 2, 325, 326
Lady's-Thumb, 16, 69, *70*
Lagerstroemia indica, 144
Lamiaceae, 13, 191–211
Lamium amlexicaule, 203, *204; pur-
    pureum, 203–4*
Laportea canadensis, 26, 56, 57, *59*
Lauraceae, 37–39, 349, 361
Laurel, 37. *See also* Mountain Laurel
Laurel family, 37–39, 349, 361
Leguminosae. See *Fabaceae*
Leonarus cardiaca, 207–8
Lepidium campestre, 86; *virginicum,* 86
Lespedeza cuneata, 12, *138*
Lettuce, 24, 297; Florida, 298; Prickly,
    298; Tall Blue, 25, 296, *297–98;*
    White, 299; Wild, *298*
Leucanthemum vulgare, 24, *248–49*
Leucothoe racemosa, 360
Licorice, Wild, 15, 235, 236, *237*
Ligustrum vulgare, 212, *341*
Liliaceae, 310–21, 372

Lilium, 310; *canadense,* 310; *super-
    bum,* 310
Lily: Canada, 310; Turk's-Cap, 310.
    See also Day-Lily; Trout-Lily
Lily family, 310–21, 372
Lily-of-the-Valley, Wild. *See* May-
    flower, Canada
Linaceae, 155–56
Linaria vulgaris, 11, *220–21*
Lindera benzoin, 31, *37–38,* 39, 361
Linnaeus, Carl von, 1
Linum striatum, 17, 21, *156; virgini-
    anum,* 156
Lion's-Foot (or Gall-of-the-Earth), 24,
    25, *298–99*
Liparis liliifolia, 332
Liquidambar styraciflua, 54
Liriodendron, 33; *tulipifera,* 29, 33, *34–
    35,* 344
Lithospermum arvense, 187
Little Monocacy River, 345
Lobelia, 11; Great Blue, *233–34,* 235;
    Spiked, 233, *234–35. See also* Cardi-
    nal Flower; Indian Tobacco
Lobelia, 11, 231; *cardinalis,* 194, 229,
    230–31, 233; *inflata, 232–33,* 235;
    siphilitica, 233–34, 235; *spicata,*
    233, *234–35*
Lobeliaceae, 229
Lobelia family, 229
Lobstein, Marion Blois. *See* Fleming,
    Cristol
Locust, Black, 28, 133, *142–43,* 363
Lonicera, 340; *japonica,* 32, 239, *240–
    41,* 340, 371; *tatarica,* 241, 340
Loosestrife: Fringed, 21, 108, *109–
    10;* Purple, 144; Whorled, 20,
    108–9
Loosestrife family, 143–45
Ludwigia alternifolia, 14, *148–49;
    palustris,* 15, 145, *149*
Lunaria annua, 14, 15, *94–95*
Lychnis alba. See *Silene latifolia*

Lycopus americanus, 195; rubellus, 195; virginicus, 12, 191, *194–95*
Lyonia ligustrina, 360
Lysimachia, 108; ciliata, 21, 108, *109–10; nummularia*, 108; *quadrifolia*, 20, *108–9*
Lythraceae, 143–45
Lythrum salicaria, 144

Madder family, 235–39
Magnolia: Fraser (or Mountain), 33–34; Southern (or Bull- Bay), 33, 360; Sweetbay, 34; Umbrella, 33, 37
Magnolia, 33; acuminata, 33; fraseri, 34; grandiflora, 33, 360; tripetala, 33, 37; virginiana, 34
Magnoliaceae, 33–35, 344, 360
Magnolia family, 33–35, 344, 360
Maianthemum canadense, 13, 314, *315–16*
Maleberry, 360
Mandrake. See Mayapple
Maple, 35, 338; Ash-Leaved, see Box-Elder; Red, 29, *157–58*, 243, 338; Silver, 158, 338; Sugar, 157, *338*
Maple family, 157–58, 338
Martin, Alexander C., Herbert S. Zim, and Arnold L. Nelson *(American Wildlife and Plants: A Guide to Wildlife Food Habits)*, 95, 367
Martin, Laura C. *(Wildflower Folklore)*, 216
Maryland Department of Natural Resources (Wildlife and Heritage Division), 101, 196, 329, 330
Mayapple, 23, 25, *49–50*
Mayflower, Canada (or Wild Lily-of-the-Valley), 13, 314, *315–16*
Mayflower. See Arbutus, Trailing
Mayweed, 249
McKenny, Margaret. See Peterson, Roger Tory
Meadow-Rue: Early, 46; Tall, 27, *45–46*

Medeola virginiana, 23, *316–17*, 328–29
Medicago lupulina, 134
Medick, Black, 134
Melilotus alba, 134; officinalis, 134
Menispermaceae, 371
Menispermum canadense, 371
Mentha, 211; arvensis, 211; M. x piperita, 211; spicata, 211
Mercury, Three-Seeded, 26, *152–53*
Mertensia virginica, 17, 187, *188*
Milkweed, 21, 175, 177; Common, *175–77;* Four-Leaved, 20, *177;* Poke, *177;* Swamp, *177*
Milkweed family, 175–77
Mimulus, 12, 216; alatus, 221; ringens, 221
Mint, 211, 233; Wild, *211. See also* Peppermint; Spearmint
Mint family, 13, 58, 59, 191–211
Mistflower, 28, *277–78*
Mitchella repens, 15, *237–38*
Moccasin Flower. See Lady's Slipper, Pink
Mock Orange, Garden, 111, 341
Monarda didyma, 12, *193–94*, 231; fistulosa, 194
Moneywort, 108. See also Honesty
Monkey-Flower, 12; Square-Stemmed, *216;* Winged, 216
Monocacy Natural Resources Management Area, *map, 8;* 7, 9, 41, 49, 52, 61, 62, 83, 85, 86, 87–88, 89, 92, 97, 98, 116, 159, 164, 165, 186, 246, 310, 330, 331, 332, 354
Monocacy River, 158, 186
Monocotyledons, 303–32
Monotropaceae, 106–7
Monotropa hypopithys, 106; uniflora, 16, 106, *107*, 227
Moonseed, Canada, *371*
Moonseed family, 371
Moraceae, 349–50

Morning Glory, 18, 183; Common, *184;* Ivy-Leaved, *184*

Morning Glory family, 183–85

Morus, 349; *alba,* 350; *rubra, 349–50;*

Moss-Pink. *See* Phlox, Moss

Motherwort, *207–8*

Mountain Laurel, x, xii, 7, 30, 37, 95, 96, *98–99,* 100, 102–3, 360

Mountain road (road from Sugarloaf gate to East View, West View and back down to Comus Road), 92, 95, 225, 276, 273, 282, 293

Mount Ephraim Road, 40, 45, 46, 48, 49, 52, 56, 57, 58, 59, 71, 72, 73, 76, 78, 80, 81, 83, 84, 89, 94, 96, 108–9, 112, 118, 120, 121, 122, 129, 131, 136, 138, 139, 140, 147, 148, 153, 156, 163, 165, 166, 167, 169, 172, 184, 187, 188, 190, 192, 196, 199, 211, 213, 217, 218, 220, 221, 226, 227, 230, 231, 233, 234, 238, 243, 244, 248, 250, 251, 256, 258, 259, 260, 261, 263, 266, 268, 269, 276, 279, 281, 282, 284, 286, 292, 293, 294, 298, 299, 301, 302, 303, 304, 307, 314, 315, 316, 317, 318, 321, 321, 332, 350, 362

Mugwort, 27, 301, *302*

Mulberry, 349; Red, *349–50;* White, *350*

Mulberry family, 349–50

Mullein: Clasping-Leaved, 216; Common, 17, 214, *215–16;*

Moth, 17, 18, *214*

Mustard, Field, 86. *See also* Garlic-Mustard; Mustard family

Mustard family, 1–2, 85–95

Myrtle. *See* Periwinkle

Nepeta cataria, 206–7

Nettle: False, 28, 56, *57–58;* Stinging, 27, 55, *56–57,* 58; Wood, 26, 56, 57, 58, *59. See also* Horse Nettle

Nettle family, 55–59

Newcomb, Lawrence *(Newcomb's Wildflower Guide),* 2, 5, 41, 79, 172, 173, 223, 312

New York Ironweed. *See* Ironweed, New York

Nightshade, Bittersweet, 18, 20, *179–80;* Black, 18, 179, *180, 181. See also* Enchanter's Nightshade

Nightshade family (or Tomato family), 177–83

Ninebark, *361*

Nyssaceae, 358–59

Nyssa sylvatica, 358–59

Oak, 7, 345; Black, *347;* Black Jack, *347–48;* Chestnut, x, 7, *345–46,* 350; Pin, *347, 348;* Red (or Northern Red), *346–47;* Red or Black Oak group, 346; Scarlet, *347;* White, *346;* White Oak group, 346

Obolaria virginica, 15, *172*

Oenothera biennis, 14, 145, *146–48; fruticosa,* 14, 147, *148; perennis,* 14, 78, 147, *148*

Oleaceae, 211–13, 339, 341, 343

Olive family, 211–13, 339, 341, 343

Onagraceae, 145–49

Orange-Grass or Pineweed, 77

Orchid, 10, 11; Crested Yellow, 330; Green Wood, 11, *330;* Large Purple-Fringed, 11, *330;* Yellow-Fringed, 11, 192, *329–30*

Orchidaceae, 10, 11, 324–32

Orchid family, 324–32

Orchis, Showy, 7, *327–28*

(Orchis spectabilis), 327

Orli, Sylvia Stone. *See* Shetler, Stanwyn G., and Sylvia Stone Orli *(Annotated Checklist of the Vascular Plants of the Washington-Baltimore Area)*

Orobanchaceae, 226–27

Ranunculus, 19; *abortivus*, 17, *46–47*, 120; *acris*, 47; *bulbosus, 47; hispidus*, 48; *recurvatus*, 17, *48; sceleratus*, 48
Rare, Threatened, and Endangered Plants of Maryland, 101, 195, 247
Raspberry, 126, 369; Wild Black, 127. *See also* Wineberry
Rattlesnake-Plantain, 327; Downy, 10, 235, *326–27*
Rattlesnake Weed, 23, 24, *292–93*, 294
Redbud, 28, 133, *141–42*, 358; Chinese, 141
Rhododendron, 95, 96; Great, 30, 98, 100, *102–3*, 360
Rhododendron, 95, 99, 100, 101; *calendulaceum*, 30, 100, *101; maximum*, 30, 98, 100, *102–3*, 360; *(nudiflorum)*, 99; *periclymenoides*, 30, *99–101*, 103, 360
Rhus, 367; *copallinum, 367–69; glabra, 369; (R. radicans)*, 369; *typhina, 368, 369*
Ribes rotundifolium, 363
Richweed. *See* Clearweed; Horse-Balm
Robinia pseudoacacia, 28, 134, *142–43, 363*
Robin's Plantain, 253
Rockcress, 92; Smooth, 14, *91–92*
Rosa carolina, 30, *123*, 125, 369; *multiflora*, 31, 123, *124-25*, 369; *palustris*, 123
Rosaceae, 114–32, 349, 355–56, 360–61, 369
Rose: Multiflora, 31, 123, *124–25*, 369; Pasture (Low Pasture or Carolina), 30, *123*, 125, 369; Swamp, 123
Rose family, 114–32, 349, 355–56, 360–61, 369
Rose Pink. *See* Pink, Rose
Rubiaceae, 235–39
Rubus, 126, 127, 128, 369; *alleghieniensis*, 31, 125, *127–28; flagellaris*, 31, *128; hispidus*, 31, *128–29; occi-*

dentalis, 127; p*hoenicolasius*, 31, *126–27*
Rudbeckia hirta, 24, 245, *249–50; laciniata*, 25, *250; triloba*, 250
Rue-Anemone, ix, 20, 22, 23, 25, *40–41*, 52
Rumex acetosa, 69; *acetosella*, 69; *crispus*, 74; *obtusifolius*, 26, *73–74*

Sabatia angularis, 21, *172–73*
Sage, Lyre-Leaved, *210–11*
Sagittaria, 304; *latifolia*, 13, *303–4*
St. Andrew's-Cross, 15, 74, *77–78*, 148, 149, 341
St. John's-Wort, 21, 74, 76, 78, 156, 341; Bushy or Glade, 31, 77, 341; Canadian, 77; Common, 74, 75, *76–77;* Dwarf, *75–76;* Shrubby, 31, 77; Spotted, *75. See also* Orange-Grass
St. John's-Wort family, 74–78, 341
Salicaceae, 357
Salix nigra, 357
Salvia lyrata, 210–11
Sambucus, 239; *canadensis*, 31, 239, *241–42*, 343; *racemosa*, 242
Sanguinaria canadensis, 23, 40, 42, *51–52*
Sanicula, 27, 171; *canadensis*, 119, *170–71; gregaria*, 171
Saponaria officinalis, 63
Sarsaparilla, Wild, 16, *164–65*
Sassafras, 29, 37, 38, *39*, 349
Sassafras albidum, 29, 37, 38, *39*, 349
Satureja vulgaris, 205–6
Saxifragaceae, 111, 112–14, 363
Saxifraga pensylvanica, 113; *virginiensis*, 16, 113
Saxifrage: Early, 16, *113;* Golden, 15, *113–14;* Swamp, 113
Saxifrage family, 111, 112–14, 363
Scarlet Pimpernel. *See* Pimpernel, Scarlet

Scrophulariaceae, 213–25, 339
Scrophularia lanceolata, 222; mary-
landica, 12, 222
Scutellaria, 198; elliptica, 197, 199;
integrifolia, 13, 197–98, 199; lateri-
flora, 197, 198–99; serrata, 13, 196–
97, 199
Seedbox (or Square-Pod Water-
Primrose), 14, 148–49
Self-Heal. See Heal-All
Seneca Creek, 354
Senecio aureus, 24, 246–47, 248; obo-
vatus, 24, 246; pauperculus, 24, 246,
247–48
Senna, Wild, 134
Senna marilandica, 134
Sensitive Plant, Wild (or Sensitive
Pea), 134
Seriocarpus asteroides, 18, 261
Serviceberry. See Shadbush
Shadblow. See Shadbush
Shadbush: Common (or Downy), 29,
129, 130–31, 132, 355; Smooth,
131
Shepherd's Purse, 86
Shetler, Stanwyn G., xiii, 96, 321
Shetler, Stanwyn G., and Sylvia Stone
Orli (Annotated Checklist of the Vas-
cular Plants of the Washington-
Baltimore Area), 6, 72–73, 80, 81,
82, 83
Shooting Star, 108
Silene caroliniana, 21, 68; (cucubalus),
67; latifolia, 21, 66–67; stellata, 20,
67, 68; vulgaris, 21, 67
Silverrod, 26, 266, 271–72
Simaroubaceae, 366–69
Sisyrinchium angustifolium, 22, 322,
323–24; mucronatum, 324
Sium suave, 166
Skullcap, 198; Hairy, 197, 199; Hyssop,
13, 197–98, 199; Mad-Dog, 197,
198–99; Showy, 13, 196–97, 199

Skunk Cabbage, xiii, 2, 10, 304, 305–6,
307
Smartweed, 16, 69; Long-Bristled, 16,
71; Pennsylvania, 16, 70; Water (or
Dotted), 16, 71
Smartweed or Buckwheat family, 68–
74
Smilacaceae, 319
Smilacina racemosa, 23, 313–14, 316;
stellata, 314
Smilax, 320, 321; herbacea, 321; rotun-
difolia, 32, 319–21, 372
Smithsonian Institution's National
Museum of Natural History, 6
Snakeroot, 27; Black, see Cohosh,
Black; Clustered, 171; Short-Styled
(Canada or Black), 119, 170–71;
White, 280, 282–83
Snapdragon family (or Figwort fam-
ily), 213–25, 339
Snowberry, 341
Solanaceae, 177–83
Solanum carolinense, 18, 178–79; dul-
camara, 18, 179–80; nigrum, 18,
179, 180
Solidago, 26, 245–46, 266–75; bicolor,
26, 271–72; caesia, 272–73; cana-
densis, 267–68; flexicaulis, 273;
gigantea, 268; graminifolia, 274–
75; hispida, 272; juncea, 269–79;
nemoralis, 270–71; rugosa, 268–69;
tenuifolia, 275; ulmifolia, 270, 271
Solomon's Seal: False, 7, 23, 313–14,
316; Smooth, 7, 23, 312–13, 314;
Starry False, 314
Sonchus, 24, 296; asper, 296–97; oler-
aceus, 296–97
Sorrel: Garden, 69; Sheep, 69. See also
Wood-Sorrel
Sour-Gum. See Tupelo
Sow-Thistle, 24, 296; Common, 296–
97; Spiny-Leaved, 296–97
Spanish Needles, 28, 251, 262–63

Water-Plantain, Small, 303
Water-Plantain family. *See* Arrowhead
  family
Water Purslane (or Marsh Purslane),
  15, 145, *149*
Waxweed, Blue. *See* Cuphea, Clammy
West Harris Road, 318, 342, 345
White-Cockle. *See* Evening Lychnis
White Rocks (of Sugarloaf Mountain),
  86
Wiegand, Richard, xiii, 140, 186, 190,
  195, 303, 310, 330, 347, 361, 363
Wild Oats. *See* Bellwort, Sessile
Willow, Black, *357*
Willow family, 357
Willow-Herb, Purple-Leaved, 145
Willow Pond, Sugarloaf Mountain,
  345
Windflower. *See* Rue-Anemone
Wineberry, 31, *126–27*
Wingstem, 24, *250–51*
Winterberry, *361;* Smooth, 361

Winter-Cress: Common, 14, *90–91;*
  Early, 91
Wintergreen, 17, *97–98*, 360; Striped
  or Spotted, 20, *105–6*
Witch-Hazel, Common, ix, xiii, 29,
  54–55, 357
Witch-Hazel family, 54–55, 357
Wood Sage. *See* Germander, American
Wood-Sorrel, 19; Creeping, 159, 160;
  Violet, 16, 158, *159;* Yellow, 159,
  160
Wood-Sorrel family, 158–60
Woolly Adelgid *(Adelges tsugae)*, 336

Xanthium strumarium, 27, *284*

Yam, Wild, 23, *321–22*
Yam family, 321–22
Yarrow, 19, 167, 169, *264–65*

Zelkova, 353
Zelkova, 353